To My Beautiful Jade

Happy Birthday

Love You,

Love
Lisa
Matters

Mama Carson
&
Donald
xxx
ooo

"MY JOURNEY"

Meet Colleen, also lovingly known as Mama Carson. Her life, like yours, has been full of peaks and valleys. Every blank page has allowed Colleen to grow, change, and learn to expand the person she has become. She saw herself as someone who would have moments in her life that would break her spirit, tug at her heart, and challenge her mind. Colleen overcame these moments and felt she was connecting with her inner 'hero.' In doing so, she was honest enough with herself to love herself and welcome the truth when living with wisdom.

When she trusted herself, allowed things to change and realized what she was here for, Colleen began to recover some of the deepest truths about how to live. In doing so, she stepped fully into who she was meant to be, breaking free from the confines of what was expected of her and living with courage and authenticity. Welcome to what she has discovered.

Courage of Spirit

Here's a deal about courage. We often equate courage with a grand gesture, like running into a burning building or performing an act of heroism. In other words, we associate courage with big, out-there ideas and actions. But courage also shows up in the small, in the moment decisions and actions. In those quiet, private times when we challenge ourselves to keep going, our instinct to stop or at least slow down is tempting. Real courage is that quiet little voice inside your head that says: 'Don't give up.' My spirit is the center of me, and life is full of disappointments, fears, and doubts that could and can knock me down. The thing about courage is that when you're knocked down, it makes you get right back up. Also, courage doesn't have to be dramatic, either. And it's always my decision to keep going, even when I feel tired or afraid.

There were setbacks, and some were self-imposed. The only voice being heard, the loudest one I heard, was in my head. I've learned what it means to be courageous and show up for myself every day, even if I thought I couldn't. It's not about being scared; it's about getting up, no matter how many times you fall. Even when I was tired, bruised, and lost, I still had my reason to feel fine. I wasn't weak or damaged; it was about being human. Every time I took a small step, I was showing myself how strong I was. Whether I was trying to get through another day or needing to achieve something, I kept telling myself that each small act of courage counts. The warrior in me has kept me going, and let me tell you, that warrior helps shine a light on even the darkest days.

Honesty of Heart

What you cannot give, you can't take, right? Love yourself first, then you can love others. So, I had to be vulnerable, and I had to love myself and be okay with my weaknesses and my strengths. Love for yourself isn't selfishness; it's self-improvement: how to become the best version of yourself. Self-love sometimes gets a bad press as if it were selfish or selfish to love yourself. Yet good self-esteem or ego can arise through love for yourself, from the understanding that you don't need someone else to say you are worthy of it, but that you are worthy of it, just as you are. And because, to my heart, real self-love began.

Self-love doesn't mean you feel like an angel; it means you can love yourself, your imperfections and your scars and fly anyway. If you love yourself properly and are true to yourself, then loving others healthier and more authentically is easier. Give from a place of abundance. You don't have anyone else to replace parts of yourself; you already are. And I can tell you, I didn't like this.

Wisdom of Mind

I have just a couple of remarks on wisdom. The root of wisdom is realism, life as it is, not as you wish it were, not as it appears in the fairy tales, but as it is. That meant that I had to learn not to look at the world with the rose-coloured glasses of my ideal vision and start seeing it as it was. And that requires a certain type of courage. This does not mean becoming a pessimist in any way; it is. It means recognizing that life can have its dark storms and golden suns, that I will flow with it into the deepest valleys and the highest peaks, and that I have the power and the strength to do so simply by accepting what life brings. I still had to learn this. I had to stop fighting life and start accepting its complexity.

This is the gift of realism: setbacks won't overwhelm me because I'm not fragile or too proud. Instead, they become occasions for growth because I am adaptable and hardworking. Living true to myself creates a legacy of not things accumulated but who I was. My legacy is not in fame or fortune but in what we've been led to believe. My fame is giving love. My fortune is in being loved. It is how I treated others, handled hardship, and lived honestly. That is the legacy that lives on.

Trusting the Journey

You know that little voice inside? The one that feels like it knows things even when it makes zero logical sense? That's intuition, your inner GPS, and let me tell you, it's usually spot on. It is figuring out how to trust it and go with the flow. Game-changer. When you start trusting yourself, you stop stressing over needing to know everything right now. Instead, you lean into the journey, even if you can't see the end destination. Life's constantly shifting, throwing curveballs, and nudging us to grow. And honestly? Fighting against it makes things harder. Growth comes when you let go, learn the lessons, and roll with it.

Purpose is the secret sauce that ties it all together. It's your why. It's not about having all the answers but about finding what truly sparks your fire. Once I figured out my purpose, even the challenging steps forward felt meaningful. Every stumble, every leap, it all started making sense in the bigger picture. Some stuff will fade away; some will fall into place. Find your rhythm and let life lead you. Even when the road ahead is foggy, believe you're heading where you're meant to be. At the end of the day, trust your gut. Let what's meant to stay, stay, and let what's meant to go, go. Find your rhythm, your harmony, and let yourself evolve. You don't have to have it all figured out. Just keep showing up as your beautifully imperfect self, love who you are, and embrace who you're becoming. That's the real magic of living a life that's unpretentious, purposeful, and totally yours.

"THE POWER OF WOMEN"

Colleen believes that women possess an extraordinary ability to transform lives, shape futures, and ignite revolutions. This power doesn't come from dominance or physical strength; it stems from an inner reservoir of intuition, compassion, and strength. It is a quiet but unstoppable force, driving change and inspiring generations. Colleen knows that *"women should support women"* is not new. It's a phrase splashed across social media, echoed in self-help books, and used as slogans in corporate campaigns.

As Colleen reflects on her journey, she has witnessed both ends of the spectrum: women lifting each other up with remarkable strength and, sadly, women tearing each other down in subtle, often unnoticed ways. It makes her wonder: what would the world look like if women supported each other unconditionally, free of judgment, competition, or envy? Could women create a reality where every woman thrives, knowing there's enough joy, success, and space for all women?

For centuries, society's norms have pitted women against one another. The belief that one woman's success diminishes another's opportunity runs deep, fueling unnecessary rivalry. This I do know that real progress isn't built by stepping on others; it's achieved when we rise together, celebrating each other's successes as stepping stones for collective advancement. History offers countless examples of women who understood this truth. Susan B. Anthony was arrested for voting and famously declared, *"No man is good enough to govern any woman without her consent."* Emmeline Pankhurst, a suffragette leader, rallied millions with her call, *"Deeds, not words,"* was imprisoned. Agnes MacPhail, Canada's first female MP, championed the rights of women and workers, enduring harsh criticism to pave the way for future leaders.

These trailblazers faced incredible odds but thrived by turning obstacles into opportunities. Malala Yousafzai stood for educational rights for girls despite an attempted assassination on her life, and Rosa Parks sparked a revolution by refusing to give up her seat. Their stories remind us that adversity is not an end; it's often the beginning of extraordinary transformation.

The spirit of strength isn't limited to historical figures. It shines in the lives of ordinary women: the single mother working tirelessly to secure a better future for her children, the teacher inspiring her students to dream bigger, or the female entrepreneur defying the odds to build a thriving business. Strength isn't just about surviving challenges; it's about flourishing despite them. This is why women's empowerment isn't just a movement; it's a legacy. When a young girl sees her mother pursuing her dreams, her teacher believing in her potential, or her role model breaking barriers, she also learns she can achieve greatness. Yet, modern challenges, like the rise of social media, create new hurdles.

Platforms often foster unrealistic comparisons, where curated images of "perfect lives" can breed envy. While we may double-tap in support, it's easy to fall into the trap of asking, *"Why not me?"* This mindset is a false race, an illusion that detracts from our ability to uplift one another genuinely. True support thrives not in envy but in small, meaningful acts of kindness, compliments, encouragement, and collaboration. In workplaces, competition often overshadows camaraderie. Stories of women withholding opportunities from other women or failing to support one another are too familiar. Yet, collaboration transforms these spaces into environments where everyone can succeed. Trailblazers like Marie Curie, a Scientist; Maya Angelou, a Civil Rights Activist; and Sally Ride, an Astronaut, shattered stereotypes and opened doors for others. Their achievements remind us that when one woman rises, she carries others with her.

Not all heroes wear capes, and not all warriors wield swords. The everyday heroine may not make headlines, but her impact is immeasurable. She's the grandmother sharing wisdom with her family, the nurse working overtime to care for patients, and the friend offering a shoulder to lean on. These women remind us that power isn't always loud. Sometimes, it's in the quiet strength of enduring life's trials, the gentle touch of offering comfort, or the committed determination to keep going when the odds seem impossible. Quiet strength, genuine kindness, and persistence make these unsung warriors powerful forces of transformation.

Figures like Ruth Bader Ginsburg have shown us the power of persistence. *"Women belong in all places where decisions are being made,"* she said, highlighting the ongoing journey toward equality. Her words challenge us to honour the sacrifices of those who came before us by continuing to create opportunities for others. Supporting women doesn't mean agreement on every issue.

Senator Pat Carney's courageous decision to vote against her party to preserve abortion rights in Canada exemplifies this balance. *"For personal reasons, I would not have an abortion, but that was my choice. I knew other women had their reasons to make a different one,"* she said. Her stance cost her politically but reinforced a powerful truth: support respects individuality and freedom, even amid differing beliefs.

Small, heartfelt actions often have a thoughtful impact. I recall a moment in a grocery store when I complimented a woman on her beautiful tan. She laughed, revealing it was from "aisle three," and later confided, *"You don't know how much that meant. My day started badly, but your compliment turned it around."* That simple exchange stayed with me as a reminder: admiration connects us, while envy divides us. Imagine a world where every interaction carried this energy; where women consistently chose kindness over judgment.

Motherhood, often a hotbed of criticism, is another area where support is crucial. From debates about feeding choices to the so-called "mommy wars," women frequently face scrutiny from those who should understand their struggles best. I recall a conversation about my son Chance's potty training. When another mom's response bordered on judgment, I lightheartedly replied, *"By the time he's twenty, he'll figure it out."* Humour defused the situation and reinforced my belief that confidence and acceptance disarm criticism. Motherhood is deeply personal and supporting one another without judgment creates an environment where women feel valued and not attacked.

Supporting women also requires examining our own biases. For instance, I once explained to a friend why I didn't vote for a particular female politician. My decision wasn't about gender but about alignment with values. True empowerment balances championing women with honouring diverse perspectives within the confines of positivity. Moreover, we must recognize women's sacrifices to secure freedoms we often take for granted. From education to healthcare, countless women have risked everything to advance equality. Honouring their legacy means ensuring these hard-won victories are protected and expanded.

Real support means celebrating another woman's victory, even when it highlights our struggles. It means listening without judgment, lending a hand when needed, and standing united. As Ruth Bader Ginsburg wisely said, *"Real change, enduring change, happens one step at a time."* The journey to healthy competition and welcomed connection can be challenging but worth every step. Imagine a world where every woman wakes up determined to uplift another. A heartfelt compliment in a grocery store, sharing credit at work, or being present for a friend could ripple out in ways we can't predict. Support isn't just a feel-good slogan; it's a daily practice, a choice we make repeatedly.

The women who came before us risked everything to create the opportunities we now enjoy. Their courage challenges women to choose kindness over envy, unity over division, and connection over competition. Together, we can rise and thrive, proving that there's room for all women to succeed. As Maya Angelou beautifully said:

"I've learned that people will forget what you said, people will forget what you did, but people will never forget how you made them feel."

Maya Angelou

"SHE HER ME"

welcome...

"A woman with wings symbolizes empowerment, freedom, and the relentless ability to overpower life's obstacles. Her wings are not just a symbol; they manifest her inner strength, spirit, and deep connection to her intuition, which is that guiding "inner guardian angel" that leads her with unflinching wisdom. These wings represent her fierce ability to break free from the limitations imposed by society, to rise from challenges with unmatched courage, and to accepts transformation without hesitation. They are a reflection of her creativity, sparking inspiration in others as she soars toward her dreams. This powerful image honours her uniqueness, limitless potential, and steadfast ability to lead a life of purpose, authenticity, and infinite possibilities."

Colleen C. Carson

COPYRIGHT©2024 by Colleen C. Carson

Author's Photos | Colleen Bratus & Crystal Carson
Photos | Dani Kremeniuk | Nuovo Artistic Photography

Cover Design by Author | Colleen Carson
Book Design by Author | Colleen Carson
Editor | Catherine Carrington

SHE HER ME Copyright © 2024

Printed in Canada/United States of America/Worldwide.

First Edition, 2024

ALL RIGHTS RESERVED. This book contains material protected under International and Federal Copyright Laws and Treaties.

ISBN 978-1-7753176-1-6	SHE-HER-ME	Paperback
ISBN 978-1-7753176-4-7	SHE HER ME	Audio
ISBN 978-1-7753176-3-0	SHE HER ME	Electronic
ISBN 978-1-7753176-2-3	SHE HER ME	Hardcover

DISCLAIMER:
The information contained in this book is for general informational purposes only. The author and publisher make no representations as to the accuracy or completeness of any information contained in this book and will not be liable for any errors or omissions.

The events and conversations in this book have been set down to the best of the author's ability, although some names and details have been changed to protect the privacy of individuals. For permission requests, write to the publisher through social media. Any unauthorized reprint or use of this material is prohibited.

No part of this Book may be reproduced or transmitted in any form or by any means, electronic or mechanical, including photocopying, recording, or by any information storage and retrieval system without express wrote/written permission from the author/publisher.

AUTHOR: Colleen C. Carson

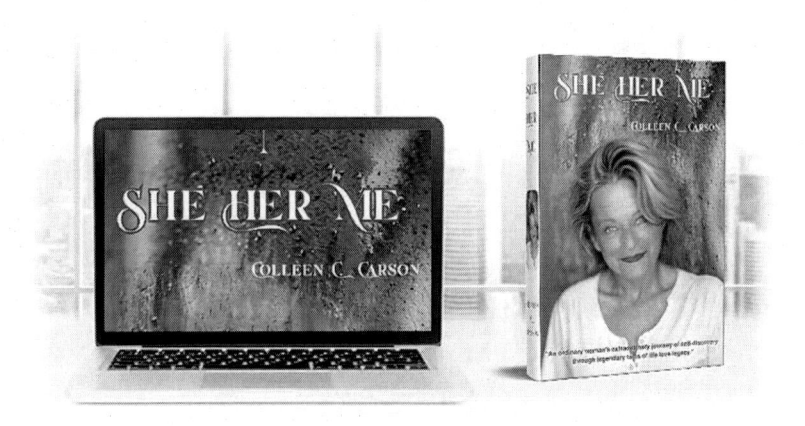

SOCIAL MEDIA:

FACEBOOK	Colleen Carson
YOUTUBE	Colleen C. Carson
INSTAGRAM	Ask Mama Carson
THREADS	Ask Mama Carson
BLUESKY	Colleen Carson
LINKEDIN	Colleen Carson
PINTEREST	Colleen Carson

"Ordinary moments through love and laughter become extraordinary memories."

Mama Carson

"Joy isn't found, it's create, start creating it for yourself."

Colleen C. Carson

"Dreams are not just for sleep; they are the opportunities life bestows upon us."

Mama Carson

"WOMANITY"

The trinity of a Woman's being is She Her Me, love life legacy. I called this the *"WOMANITY"* of the Spirit, Heart and Mind. Womanity is born from the fusion of "Woman" and "Trinity," capturing the spirit of a woman's role in shaping the humankind experience.

"To-get-her honour her journey."

"WOMANITY" isn't just a word; it's a revolution, a celebration, and a reminder of the invincible force we personify as women. It's the perfect harmony of **SHE, HER, ME,** the dreamer, the doer, and the one who boldly owns it all. SHE fuels your spirit, the part of you that dares to reach for the impossible. HER is your heart, pouring love and passion into everything you touch. And ME? ME is the anchor, the bold, unshakable core of who you truly are. Together, they're not just parts of you, they're your superpower. Womanity is life, love, and legacy in action, reminding the world that when a woman shows up fully, she doesn't just live; she leads.

SHE Spirit - Life

Colleen's *SHE Spirit* is an unstoppable force that originates confidence, courage, and conviction. When Colleen accepted her SHE Spirit, she wakened her potential, seized opportunities with passion, and lived realistically. At the heart of the **SHE** spirit are three core pillars: **S**elf, **H**onesty, and **E**nlightenment. These pillars guided her on the path to her true strength and influence.

The first pillar, Self, is all about transformation. It's not always an easy ride, but it's definitely worth it. Self begins with self-awareness, a deep understanding of your thoughts, feelings, and desires. Colleen believes it's about looking within, honouring her strengths, and acknowledging her fears. She realized it would take courage for her to face both the light and shadow within her, but doing so was the foundation of her empowerment. Self-awareness realizes that others' opinions don't define your worth but the love and respect you give yourself.

When I began to live with the power of Self, I stepped boldly into the world with intention and clarity. I stood in the truth of who I am, fully aware of my unique gifts, and I was ready to use them for a higher purpose. The journey of the Self isn't short or simple. It's ongoing, and every step is worth it. The more I welcomed who I am, flaws and all, the stronger I felt. And here's the deal: when you recognize your individuality, you inspire others to do the same. Your truth becomes contagious, and together, we create a world where everyone's voice and presence are valued.

For me, discovering my SHE Spirit felt like waking up. It was like unlocking a secret power that had always been there, but I didn't know how to tap into it. It lifted me, grounded me, and propelled me forward all at once. Suddenly, I saw myself clearly, and for the first time, I stopped apologizing for who I was.

The journey isn't always easy. Looking in the mirror means facing not only your strengths but your fears and flaws, too. But once I did that, I could breathe again. I wasn't living for anyone else's expectations; I was living for me.

When you really know yourself, you realize that your worth doesn't come from other people's approval. It's not in their compliments or criticisms. It's in the love you show yourself and the way you honour your heart, mind, and soul. That shift in mindset changes everything. When you live with purpose, you're no longer just going through the motions.

You're living your truth, and that's what matters most. It's a process, though. I'm still discovering new layers of who I am, and every step has been worth it. The more I accept myself, the more I realize the strength of being me. My power grows each time I honour my truth.

Here's what I've learned: When you accept your individuality, you give others permission to do the same. Your truth becomes contagious. It starts with you but spreads far beyond what you can see. So, I took that step. I looked inward, trusted what I found, and welcomed who I am. And you know what? That's when my life unlocked in ways I never imagined. It's bigger, brighter, and more beautiful than I ever dreamed, and it's all available to you, too, just on the other side of self-discovery.

Then there's Honesty, the second pillar. To me, Honesty is like taking a deep breath of fresh air after being stuck in a smoky room. It clears everything. But let's be real, it's not always easy. For a long time, I thought I had to soften my edges, play nice, and say what people wanted to hear. But that wasn't me. It wasn't real. The moment I decided to show up as my true Self, without the masks, without the sugarcoating, everything changed.

Living honestly doesn't mean being harsh or unkind; it means being true. It's saying the hard things with love, standing firm when the world tries to shake you. Honesty is a force. When you live with it, you free yourself and inspire others to do the same. People can feel when you're being genuine. And when you're true to yourself, it encourages others to drop their pretenses, too. That's the power of Honesty; it's not just about speaking your truth; it's about living it.

Finally, Enlightenment. For me, this one took the longest to understand. Enlightenment isn't about having all the answers but finding meaning in the questions. It's about seeing every scar, setback, and stumble as a stepping stone. The challenging moments have been my most outstanding teachers.

They've taught me strength, patience, and grace. Enlightenment is like a rainbow appearing after a storm. It's the serenity that comes when you realize even the darkest times were shaping you into someone stronger and wiser. This isn't some mystical concept; it's real and raw. Enlightenment isn't in the background; it pushes me forward. It keeps me going and pushes me to use what I've learned to lift others.

The best part is that the SHE Spirit isn't just mine. It's in every woman who has faced her storms and come out stronger. It's in every woman who has dared to be bold, to be honest, and to be openly herself. You don't have to wait for permission or the perfect moment. You have everything you need right now to step into your own SHE Spirit.

Let your truth, strength, and wisdom guide you. Let them light you up from the inside out. The world is waiting for you to show up, not as someone else or who you think you should be, but as the incredible, powerful, unstoppable woman you already are. So, are you ready? Because once you say yes to your SHE Spirit, everything changes. And trust me, you're going to love who you become.

HER Heart – Love

HER Heart is the spirit of a woman's heart is compassion, commitment, and connection that drives her forward. It is the source from which she draws the energy to nurture, heal, and uplift herself and everyone around her. When we speak of Colleen's Heart, we're not just talking about the physical organ that beats within her chest. We're talking about the core of her being, where love, passion, and resilience radiate, making self-love the foundation of everything she does.

I understand that self-love is not about perfection; it's about accepting who you are, imperfections and all. It's a commitment to growth and healing, a process that unfolds over time. Self-love isn't instant, and that's perfectly okay. In accepting my truth, I have become an advocate for others, teaching them that self-care is not selfish but essential. I feel that only when I make myself a priority I can genuinely show up for others, forming a trustworthy connection built on mutual respect and love.

At the Heart of HER Heart lies self-love. Without it, a woman is like an empty vessel, always giving from a place of lack. But when I nurture myself and filled my own cup, I become a symbol of strength and compassion, setting the standard for how others treated me. I don't seek validation from external sources because I know my worth. I understand that no matter the circumstances, I deserve to be loved. Self-love is not self-centeredness; it is the thoughtful awareness of who I am, my strengths, my weaknesses, and my inherent value in a world that often forgets to remind me of my brilliance. It is the bedrock of everything else. Let's probe deeper into the three core pillars that support **HER** Heart: **H**eroism, **E**goism, and **R**ealism.

Heroism is having the courage to love myself when everything around me tries to convince me that I'm not enough. In a world where expectations weigh heavy, and comparisons are constant, choosing to love myself despite it all is an act of bravery. I believe that self-love means showing up every day, even when the answers aren't clear, and standing firm when life throws obstacles in my path. It's about accepting who I am in all my complexities, knowing that this love will radiate outward to those around me.

Egoism, in its healthiest form, recognizes that one's needs are valid and deserve to be met. I've taught that setting boundaries is not a sign of weakness but a reflection of strength. Prioritizing my well-being is necessary to show up for others in a meaningful way. I can't pour from an empty cup. Self-care is not an indulgence; it is a necessity. By honouring my own needs, I can give others love, support, and encouragement in a healthier way.

Finally, Realism grounds me. Loving myself with realism means accepting my imperfections with kindness and celebrating my successes with humility. It's a steady confidence that arises from truly knowing myself, not through the lens of perfection, but as a genuine, evolving individual. This balance allows me to be at peace with who I am, shedding the pressures of perfection and growing into a more genuine version of myself every day.

When Heroism, Egoism, and Realism come together, they form the heartbeat of HER Heart, the essence of self-love that empowers me to care for myself, build deeper relationships, and inspire others. The more a woman supports and nurtures her true self, the more she is able to lift others up, offering them love, strength, and support. Remember to be gentle with yourself. Every step you take toward self-love moves you closer to a life of fulfillment and purpose. Love is not just an emotion; it is an experience filled with extraordinary magic. When I chose to love myself first, I unlocked my heart to a humanity of infinite love, astonishing joy, and noble promises. Are you ready to unlock your HER heart of self-love to love others in the most perfectly imperfect way?

ME Matters - Legacy

In every woman, there's this hidden force, a quiet power just waiting to wake up and take over. It's not some vague concept; it's real, an energy that pulses through every win and every challenge, shaping who we become. That's the core of **ME**, the **M**atriarch **E**volution, the journey of a woman stepping into her full self. It's about discovering your force, wisdom, and purpose. Colleen's journey shows a woman uniquely her own. Colleen's mind is where it all begins. Her power is born in her thoughts, decisions, and growth. ME Matters is all about recognizing her power and owning it. Colleen knows that life isn't just something you go through; it's something you conquer.

When living as *ME*, Colleen is not just reacting to what happens but mastering it. She is setting her own standards for success, standing strong no matter what comes her way, and using every hurdle as a steppingstone. Every bump in the road adds to her strength, and each victory builds her legacy.

ME Matters legacy originates from three cardinal pillars: *I*ntelligence, *I*ndependence, and *I*ntuition. Intelligence is my superpower, giving me the confidence to shape my journey without second-guessing myself. Independence is all about traveling my journey free from other people's expectations. And intuition? That's my inner compass, guiding me through tough times while confidently moving me forward. These traits aren't just for me; they're for everyone I have touched; everyone I have inspired to trust in their own power.

As *ME*, I've built strong relationships, showing others the power of connection. Being a Matriarch isn't just about keeping a family together; it's about leading with heart, offering wisdom, and making others feel seen and valued. *ME* fully represents that role as a leader, a nurturer, and a source of guidance. I've faced doubts, second guessed myself, compromised to fear, yet through my courage, I've come out stronger on the other side.

I've welcomed change, not as something to fear but as an opportunity to evolve. My mind and intuition have been my loyal partners, guiding ME through the rough patches. That's the real power of *ME*: looking beyond the challenging moments and seeing the growth waiting. Every experience, good or bad, has brought *ME* closer to my true self. And that's the hope I offer every woman: the strength to rise above and evolve. Where others might see failure, I see lessons. Where fear might stop someone, I find courage. That makes my journey extraordinary: the drive to face challenges, get back up after every fall, keep moving forward, and always learning. Every chapter of my life is intentional, shaped by my mind and intuition, making every moment part of my evolving legacy.

ME Matters isn't just a captivating expression; it's how I live. It's about owning my destiny, leading by example, and inspiring others to find their own strength. My legacy? It's not just for *ME*. It's for my precious daughter, Crystal, and every woman ready to rise and tap into her own extraordinary journey of self-discovery. But also acknowledging a partner that has your back and stands by you with no other excuse then love and respect.

Let me summarize the concept of **SHE HER ME** as my blueprint for life, love, and leaving a legacy that truly matters. So, what's SHE? That's my Spirit, the inner warrior that pushes me to go further, be stronger, and stand up even when the world says, "Sit down." She's not just about surviving; she's the force that makes me want to thrive. And HER? Well, that's my Heart. It's where the love flows, the courage rises, and the magic happens. She nurtures me, keeps me going, and lifts others even when life tries to bring us down. And then there's ME, my Mind. My compass. It's where I find my honesty, my lessons, my enlightenment. It's what's helped me navigate through the chaos and still come out standing, ready to learn and evolve with every step. Womanity is at the center of who I am. It's not just a fancy word; it's my power and my evolution. And every woman can tap into it to define her own journey. It's about accepting your Matriarch Evolution, owning your power, and walking through life with the understanding that you are constantly evolving and always becoming. My story isn't about perfection; it's about realism. It's about being an ordinary woman who's learned to make her life extraordinary by welcoming the truth every moment.

Heroism isn't about being flawless. It's about standing tall when life tries to knock you down and knowing that your Heart has the strength to rise again. I've welcomed egoism, recognizing that Me Matters, and that my needs, my dreams, and my desires deserve to be heard. And realism? That's simply me, keeping it honest, grounded, and practical as I face what comes my way. It's about acknowledging life's challenges and not pretending they don't exist but learning from them.

By tapping into my Spirit, my Heart, and my Mind, I've built something more significant than I could've ever imagined: a legacy filled with wisdom, courage, and the power that comes from being manifestly me. And it's not just for me. It's for every woman out there who needs to see that she, too, can evolve into her infinite self just by owning her story, her truth, and her journey.

The journey of **SHE HER ME** began with something simple: a reflection, then a book. But it evolved into more, into a powerful witness to the honesty and enlightenment that comes from being true to yourself. It proves that even the "ordinary" moments can lead to extraordinary transformations. And if I can do it, so can you. The first step is always the hardest, but it's yours to take. To create your own legacy and to live boldly and authentically? The journey starts with you and will be one unforgettable journey of self-discovery.

The question is: are you ready to step into your own Matriarch Evolution and discover the extraordinary in you? The first step is yours. Please take it. Your legacy is waiting; what are you waiting for?

"At no time allow a power title to overshadow your confidence; display appreciation but by no means diminish your worth."

Mama Carson

Chapter One: **SHE** Spirit – Life

Chapter Two: **HER** Heart – Love

Chapter Three: **ME** Matters – Legacy

"Grandpa, besides me being a girl and you being a boy, you are old, and I am young; are we important?"

"Yes, my precious. You see, I am the memories of our yesterdays, you are the dreams of our tomorrows, and together, we are the portrait of our today."

Colleen C. Carson

"Accept your uniqueness, and step boldly into your purpose, living it fully and shamelessly."

Mama Carson

"In the majestic rainbows of life, we navigate the seasons with purpose:

Spring, the dawn of innovation, where ideas bloom like vibrant flowers.

Summer, the daylight of candor, basking in the warmth of truth and authenticity.

Autumn, the dusk of solace, finding peace in the gentle surrender of letting go.

Winter, the evening of presence, a time to reflect and savour the wisdom of our journey.

Embrace each season, for within them lies the originality of a truly accomplished life of wisdom."

Mama Carson

"Fail with courage, forgive with kindness, and flourish in the light of your spirit."

Colleen C. Carson

"DEDICATION"

To my Precious Angel, Crystal Belle, my daily sunshine, who fills my every days with the beauty of wonder and the miracle of love. I wrote these memoirs so my heart may rest gently within yours, a lasting legacy of love. The heartbeat of these pages, the reason every word breathes life is because of you and Chance. May each word inspire your dreams, ignite your passions, empower your heart and remind you of your boundless potential. Together, we have journeyed through discovery, welcome our truths, and rise into the extraordinary life you were born to live where your light forever shines. In your quiet moments, open these pages for a smile, a tear of joy, and a touch of wisdom. I will always be by your side, I love you endlessly, my forever always.

&

To my dearest Donald, my sweet dawn of bliss, my lover, and the first light I see each morning. My sweet Don of joy, the one who makes every day feel like a love story. Thank you for being the incredible man who fills my heart with patience, inspiration, and the wisdom of your gentle soul. Your love is my safe haven, bringing me peace and joy beyond measure. With you, every moment is a cherished gift. Ours is a love that will never fade, a flame that burns forever, and that is eternal, forever deepening with every heartbeat. I love you more than words can say. I will always be by your side, my forever always.

"In a world constantly chasing the next trend, remember that true style lies not in what you wear, but in how genuinely you express your unique self."

Mama Carson

"THE BELLA AND SAGE STORY"

Before we begin on my journey together, let me voice a tale that I hope will inspire you. It is the story of an ordinary woman whose extraordinary journey became anything but common place. Once upon a time there was a woman called Bella who lived in a small village at the bottom of a valley, nestled between hills. Bella's imagination stretched as far as the eye could see and as high as the village tree, but her life was pinned down to the earth by obligations and fears.

Bella work hard at an occupation she didn't like, to survive. Getting out of bed felt like a battle every morning, facing the same routine that drained her of energy and passion. But deep down, Bella knew she was meant for something greater. Bella, a woman of captivating beauty and born innocence, possessed a profile defined by gentle strength. Her sparkling blue eyes held a depth that seemed to mirror the vastness of the sky on a clear day, while her flowing hair cascaded like strands of sunlight, drawing one's gaze in admiration.

Her presence educed a sense of grace and allure, leaving an impression that lingered as if each glance revealed a new layer of her gentle yet curious spirit. One day, while wandering through the woods near her home, Bella chanced upon a gentlewoman: *this Sage*. As the gentlewoman stood before her with features weathered by time yet glowing a quiet strength born of insightful wisdom and experience. Her eyes, deep and knowing, seemed to hold the secrets of ages past, while her calm demeanour displayed a serene assurance that spoke volumes without a word.

This Sage that had, in the words she spoke, all the stories and lessons of a lifetime, all the truths she'd learnt in her meditations and spiritual journey. On the face of this Sage, there were feelings of awe and respect as though one were with someone who had been given the key to the secrets of the universe itself.

Amid the greenery of a small and beautiful pond that was quiet and serene and seemed to mirror the sapphire sky overhead, like a silent mirror. Waterfalls gentled against smooth rocks on its edge, the sound acoustic to the whistling leaves around it.

Wildflowers bloom on the shore to add splashes of colour to the quiet; dragonflies dance across the water with their shimmering wings reflecting the light. This secluded oasis invites contemplation and offers a moment of calm amid the bustling rhythm of the natural world. This Sage's presence displayed a sense of tranquility that drew Bella closer. Intrigued by her peaceful demeanour, Bella approached her and asked, "Excuse me, gentlewoman. How can I become who I truly want to be?"

This Sage turned to her with a warm smile, her eyes glowing with the wisdom of countless seasons. The gentlewoman gestured for Bella to sit beside her. "Ah, my dear child," she began, her voice a gentle river of time-worn truths, "To become who you wish to be, you must first release who you have become. Each day offers a new beginning, an opportunity to cast off the doubts and fears that tether you. Yet, remember to hold close the power of the lessons you have learned along the way, for they are the very seeds from which your future self will blossom."

Bella nodded, feeling an intense significance with this Sage's words that echoed deeply within her. "I have always felt confined by the expectations of others," Bella confessed softly. This Sage nodded wisely. "No one, my child, can confine you unless you allow yourself to be confined. It is a universal challenge, dear one. Life is neither fair nor easy, it demands courage, the courage to confront fear, rather than surrendering to it and attributing your circumstances to external forces.

You possess the strength to transcend obstacles and create meaningful change where it truly matters." Listening intently, Bella's curiosity deepened, her expression revealing a touch of confusion. "I hear others suggesting what success looks like for me, but how do I know what success means to me?" she asked, her voice carrying a hint of uncertainty. This Sage's quiet smile conveyed a serene confidence born of a lifetime's understanding.

"Success, dear child," this Sage spoke, her voice carrying the weight of reflective insight, "Is not defined by the crowd's applause. It resides in the joy and satisfaction that blooms when you pursue what truly matters to you. Take the time to envision the person you aspire to be rather than conforming to others' expectations." This Sage continued, "Many voices will try to define you, but only you can distinguish the true journey within your heart and soul. Avoid wasting your precious time on blame and shame; instead, honour yourself wisely. Seek out your own summit to conquer, and with each purposeful step, master it."

Bella gazed around at the tranquil pond, reflecting the sprawling hills beyond, letting this Sage's words sink in deeply with each passing moment. "I see," Bella murmured, as a wise clarity dawned within her. "So, you are saying that it is not about where I am right now, but where I want to go. It is a decision I must make for myself, without confusion from others." Heartened by Bella's realization, this Sage nodded wisely. "Indeed, my child," she encouraged wisely. "Wisdom can be found in the counsel of those who care, as their perspectives may enlighten views you might overlook. Yet, ultimately, you possess the inherent power to define your own journey and shape your own destiny.

Explore deeply within your true self the understanding both in your strengths and limitations. Adopt each day as an opportunity for growth and learning; through this journey, you will naturally become the person you are destined to become." From that transformative day onward, Bella greeted each sunrise with a fiery determination. Armed with this Sage's thoughtful wisdom, she confronted her fears head-on, refusing to let doubt obstruct her journey.

Bella stepped through the challenging terrain of life's hills and valleys with each purposeful step, leaving a trail of positivity and inspiration in her wake. As Bella stood atop the summit of her hill, she gazed upon the village below with a heart brimming with gratitude. Shedding old self-doubts, she welcomed new beginnings and redefined success on her terms. Bella had evolved into the person she had always envisioned:

spirited, curious, inspirational, and true to herself. Through her journey, Bella realized that life's journey isn't solely about reaching her destination but about the insightful transformation and self-discovery that evolves along the way. Her conversation with this Sage was pivotal, guiding Bella toward accepting her unique and genuine self and living a life in harmony with her deepest aspirations.

(To my Readers, Bella is my Crystal, lovingly called Bella, meaning "Beautiful" by her Grandma. This Sage, (Crystal's Grandma) was full of quiet wisdom, she always had a way of speaking to Bella that carried the weight of life's lessons, gently passed down from one generation to the next. Their conversations were like whispered secrets shared and watching them together was a sight that stirred something deep within me: a touching reminder of time's passing and the lasting love that connects us all. I hope you find the same beauty in this memorable tale.)

For in this grand journey of life, dare to make your uniqueness a force for good, positively influencing the world around you. Define your aspirations clearly and let them guide your every purposeful step with depth and compassion. Remember, success is not solely measured by your destination but by the enlightened transformation you undergo along your journey. Hold fast to your summit, that ideal vision of yourself waiting to be realized. As you climb, accept the challenges and revelations that shape you into a unique person of substance and integrity. Let Bella's story remind you that life's journey is not just about reaching goals: it is about evolving into the best version of yourself: for one day you will be this Sage.

"Knowledge speaks; wisdom listen."

Mama Carson

"MY LIFE LOVE & LOSS"

In the path of life, I step each day,
Through joys and sorrows, come what may.
In whispers soft and moments bold,
Stories of love and loss unfold.

On mornings bright, with skies so blue,
I find my dreams, both old and new.
But shadows linger, dusk draws near,
And hearts, once full, may shed a tear.

For love, a flame that burns so bright,
Can warm the soul on the coldest night.
Yet love can fade like petals fall,
Leaving echoes of a whispered call.

I pursue the echoes, want for more,
But sometimes, find an empty shore.
In loss, I have learned to mend the seams,
And find the beauty in my dreams.

So, I do cherish every breath,
Welcome life, accept death.
For along my paths, I found my grace,
And upon my journey, I found my place.

Colleen C. Carson

"In the battle between hate and love, choose to be a symbol of hope; for every act of kindness creates a glow, reminding us that love always has the power to heal."

Colleen C. Carson

TABLE OF CONTENTS

- **"MY JOURNEY"** 1
  - "THE POWER OF WOMEN" 5
  - "WOMANITY" 15
  - "DEDICATION" 29
  - "THE BELLA AND SAGE STORY" 31
  - "MY LIFE LOVE & LOSS" 37
- **CHAPTER 1 – SHE SPIRIT** 43
  - "SHE GLOWS" 45
  - "SHE HER ME" 47
  - "TEARS" 48
  - "VISION BOARD" 53
  - "A CHILD GHOST" 55
  - "HER STORY" 60
  - "SILENCE LISTENS" 65
  - 'ODE TO OUR HEROES" 70
  - "THIS IS MY PARENTS" 71
  - "FOR INDEPENDENCE SAKES" 81
  - "WAS IT AUSCHWITZ" 87
  - "THE CHILD" 93
  - "MISS KITSLANO 1971" 99
  - "ALTER EGO" 103
  - "MY LIFE CHAPTERS" 109
  - "MIGHTY SWORD" 132
  - "HIGH SCHOOL FRIEND" 135
  - "LIGHTNING POWER" 139
  - "BORDER ESCAPE" 151

"BELIEVING IN YOU" 157

"MUNCHEN SPEECH" 161

"THE FREEDOM OF CHOICE" 167

"A FARE CHANCE COOKBOOK" 175

"THE AUTHOR'S JOURNEY" 181

"SHE CAN FLY" 185

"TIGER WITHIN" 189

CHAPTER 2 – HER HEART 193

"THE GENTLEMEN OF INTIMACY" 195

"FIRST DATE" 195

"MY SPANISH AFFAIR" 201

"THE SEASONS OF LOVE" 209

"BREAK OUR SILENCE" 213

"HER POWER TO RISE" 235

"LOVERS PICNIC" 239

"BEGUILED GARDEN" 243

"UNTYING THE KNOT" 247

"HELLO MS. COLLEEN" 255

"A TENDER GOODBYE" 261

"IMPERFECT PERFECT HEART" 266

"WE ARE IN LOVE" 267

"MS. PERFECTION" 273

"WHISPERS IN THE WIND" 278

"A TALE OF LOVE" 279

"THE LOVE OF FAMILY" 281

"ART OF NURTURING" 281

"PARENTAL PILLARS" 285

"BELLE & CHANCEY" 287
"I LOVE ME" 289
"MY KIDS, MY LIFE" 293
"OUR MIRACLES" 299
"FAMILY" 302
"HER SPARKLE" 303
"OUR PRECIOUS ANGEL" 309
"SILVER LINING" 317
"GRANDPARENTS" 318
"BEYOND THE ACCIDENT" 319
"WHERE DO BABIES" 329
"FARMGIRL CHELSEA" 333
"KINGDOM OF KNOWLEDGE" 341
"A MAMA'S LOVE" 344
"YOU'RE A STAR" 347
"RING MY BELL" 353
"THE MALE GENERATIONS" 357
"THE FEMALE GENERATIONS" 358
"THE COURAGE OF CHANCE" 359
"WE LOVE YOU" 365
"THE PROMISE" 377
"SUCCESS" 381
"TO CHANCE A GOODBYE" 383
"HIBITUAL HERO DOES IT AGAIN" 387
"DAUGHTERS & SONS" 393
"THE RACE" 395
"OUR LOVE" 399

CHAPTER 3 – ME MATTERS 405

- "FOLLOW YOUR PASSION" 410
- "SINGLISM OR COUPLEDOM" 415
- "THE GENERATIONS OF WOMEN" 418
- "HEAD HELD HIGH" 422
- "MY CANADA" 427
- "HEAR TO LEARN" 433
- "THE MALE EVOLUTION" 434
- "TOXIC RELATIONSHIPS" 440
- "A REFUGEE'S STORY" 447
- "FAMILY BY DESIGN" 450
- "SENSITIVE STRENGTH OF A MAN" 456
- "DEATH THE EQUALIZER" 457
- "THE SILENT GUARDIANS" 462
- "MY GOD AND ME" 465
- "BLINK OF AN EYE" 470
- "KEYS PLEASE" 472
- "PROTESTING" 476
- "MALE EGO" 477
- "SHE LOVES HER ME" 481
- "MIRROR ME PLEASE" 482
- "MY WHISPERS MY LEGACY" 487
- "PLACE AT THE TABLE" 488
- "IN LOVE WITH LOVE" 493
- "A FRIEND'S BRUNCH" 497
- "ACTIVIST AND COMMUNITY" 500
- "LIFE" 507

Unravel the Mystery...

"SHE SPIRIT"

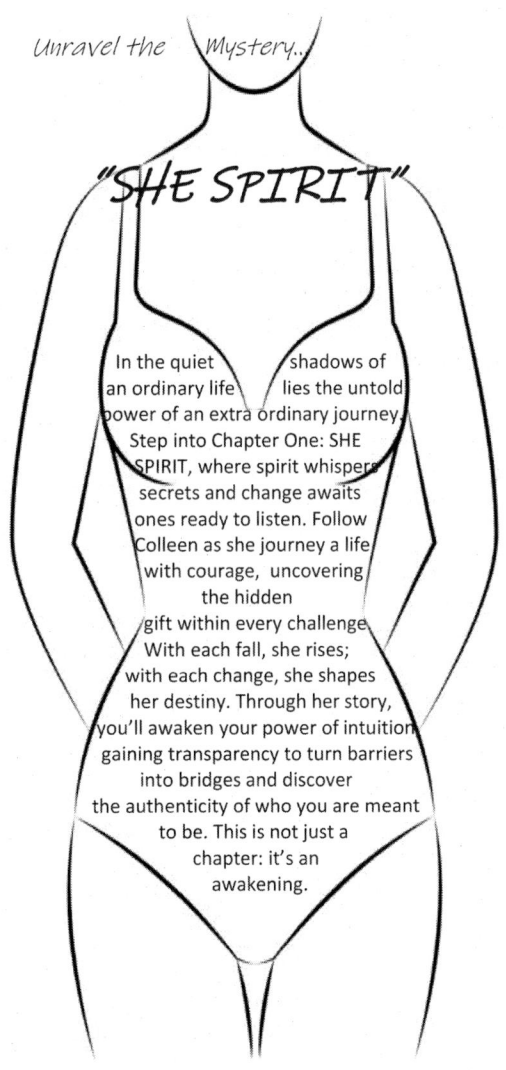

In the quiet shadows of an ordinary life lies the untold power of an extra ordinary journey. Step into Chapter One: SHE SPIRIT, where spirit whispers secrets and change awaits ones ready to listen. Follow Colleen as she journey a life with courage, uncovering the hidden gift within every challenge. With each fall, she rises; with each change, she shapes her destiny. Through her story, you'll awaken your power of intuition gaining transparency to turn barriers into bridges and discover the authenticity of who you are meant to be. This is not just a chapter: it's an awakening.

A call to unleash the quiet force within you. To embrace the confidence, power, and faith that has been waiting in the shadows of your soul.

Are you ready to uncover the mystery of your SHE Spirit?
The journey begins now. Enter...

CHAPTER ONE

"A Goddess has wisdom in her stride and power in her voice. She is unafraid to rise, unafraid to lead."

Mama Carson

"SHE GLOWS"

In her tranquil moments, she found her start,
An ordinary soul with an extraordinary heart.
She heeded the call; she dared to dream,
And into the unknown, she cast her gleam.

With each step forward, she penned her tale,
A composition of courage, she does prevail.
From beginning to end, she stood tall,
For her spirit knew no bounds, no wall.

Her story confirms her recovery,
The power of human discovery.
From impossible to possible, she rose,
In her transformation, she glows.

Her perception was her guiding light,
Each trial, each triumph, witnesses her might.
For wisdom whispered softly in her ear,
Nudging her that triumph draws near.

In guiding others, she found her promise,
She inspires love in a world seeking solace.
Her recovery began with self-discovery,
As she journeyed her, who lives in me.

Colleen C. Carson

"Without life scars, you've never danced in storms. Scars reveal our spirit; they're proof we've faced the wind, braved the rain, and risen stronger."

Mama Carson

"SHE HER ME"

"TEARS"

In the quiet depths where heartache dwells,
Tears fall like rain, the tales they tell.
No weakness found in sorrow's stream,
But courage is vast in the soul's brave dream.

When words abandon, tears arise,
Each drops a truth beneath the skies.
They speak of trials, of strength within,
Of battles fought, where hearts begin.

For in each tear, a story we find,
A tribute to the human mind.
Through pain and loss, they boldly speak,
Of spirit strong, when life feels bleak.

So let them fall, these tears so true,
They whisper loud, in shades of blue.
They mark the path where hearts unfold,
And show the worth of the stories told.

For tears are not the end, you see,
But beginnings of what can be.
They cleanse the soul, they heal the pain,
And bring us closer once again.

Cherish tears, in their tender grace,
They are not a sign of a lesser place.
But of a spirit bold and whole,
Speaking volumes from deep within the soul.

Colleen C. Carson

"Humanity's heritage is not solely built upon monuments
of stone, but upon the foundations of love left in
the hearts of generations."

Colleen C. Carson

"Your life is a story, and death your witness."

Mama Carson

"Life is your ultimate classroom, where every moment is a lesson, and every experience is an opportunity to evolve stronger and wiser."

Colleen C. Carson

"When a friend says they are too busy, it is like watching a ship sail by, leaving you standing on the shore, wondering if they will ever anchor again in the harbour of your friendship."

Mama Carson

Upon my vision board, where dreams take flight,
The SHE Spirit glows in radiant light.
A board of strength, a goddess untamed,
Her spirit whispered, her power proclaimed.

She soars with wings, intuition's grace,
Guided by stars in love's infinite space.
Her soul, a fire, a fierce, bright flame,
Journey's paths in life, not ever the same.

HER heart beats bold, a rhythm divine,
With courage and love, she draws the line.
Heroism shines in her every deed,
A legacy written of hope and need.

Egoism tempered by wisdom's glow,
Realism blossoms, her truth to show.
She nurtures her realm, her pulse its guide,
A haven of warmth where dreams reside.

ME matters stand, a legacy deep,
Roots of solve that forever keep.
A matriarch's voice, steady and true,
Self-discovering whispers of all she knew.

Mastering evolution, she charts her way,
Through storms and shadows to light of day.
Confidence blooms, her self-aware seed,
Encouragement flows, fulfilling each need.

This ordinary vision board, a mirror to see,
The extraordinary blend of SHE, HER, and ME.
A legacy is sown in spirit, heart, and mind,
A witness to passion, forever defined.

Colleen C. Carson

"A CHILD GHOST"

Colleen met Brian when he moved in next door. His backyard backed up to her parents, and let me tell you, her parents wasted no time getting involved. Five daughters, not a single one engaged or married; of course, they were all over this. And Brian? He only had eyes for Colleen. So, naturally, they invited him over for dinner, and six months later, boom, engaged.

That's when things got weird.

With the wedding about a month and a half away, Colleen started moving her stuff into Brian's house, trying to get ahead of the chaos. She was excited, but something felt off. There was an energy in the house that made Colleen feel uncomfortable. But she brushed it off as nerves. After all, she was about to get married; wasn't it normal to feel a little on edge? Brian had been renting out two rooms to young working girls, and one morning,

Colleen happened to be on the bus with one of them. Out of nowhere, the girl goes, "Brian was so loud last night. I came home, started cooking, and slamming things around. I was freaked out." Colleen froze. Stomach in knots. "That wasn't Brian," she said, barely getting the words out. "He left town two days ago." The girl just stared at her, her face going pale. A couple of days later, that same girl called Colleen, she was frantic. "Someone's in the house," she whispered. "We're too scared to go upstairs." Colleen tried to be rational. "Okay, maybe you're just freaking yourselves out," she said. But when she got there, the girls looked straight-up terrified, wide-eyed, trembling. She grabbed a broom to lighten the mood and tapped it on the ceiling. Silence. Then the knock. From upstairs. They bolted. Colleen called her Dad. He checked the place. Nothing. No one. The girls moved out after that. Probably smart.

After the wedding and honeymoon, Brian returned to work on the tugs, leaving town a lot. I tried to settle in, but the house. It had other plans. Strange noises. Objects moving. Cold drafts where there shouldn't have been any. And Boogie, our dog, would stare into empty rooms, growling at nothing. The atmosphere was thick with dread, and fear was a constant companion. Then came the night. Boogie slept in his pen at bedtime, which was part of his training. But that morning, he was barking like crazy.

In my nightie, I shuffled downstairs, half-asleep, thinking maybe it was cold, and I needed to turn the heat on. I stopped dead in the kitchen doorway. Every cupboard was wide open. Food scattered. Dishes were stacked high in the sink. Brian came down, took one look, and shrugged it off. No explanation. Nothing. Things escalated. Plants shifted. Objects flew across the hallway from the basement stairs. Then, there was the phone incident; I was talking with a friend, and suddenly, my voice started echoing back. Only, it wasn't quite my voice. It was off. Slightly delayed. As if something or someone was mimicking me.

Then, one Sunday, Brian and I came home from brunch, and every window in our house was open. Sitting on the roof, our cat, just staring down at us. Inside, everything was locked. Nothing was stolen. But Boogie, our dog, had left deep scratches on the back door like he had been trying desperately to get inside. Enough was enough. I called a medium. "Poltergeists," the woman said. "Child ghosts. They can be dangerous. Be careful." She told me to tell them to "go to the light" whenever I felt them near. And for a while? It worked. The house went still. But not for long.

When Brian and I went to a conference in Vegas, my sister and her boyfriend stayed at the house to watch Boogie. They lasted one night. Lying in bed, they heard footsteps. Heavy ones. Pounding closer. The steps stopped right at the bedroom door. Then, a knock. They locked the door and almost climbed out the window onto our roof to scream for help. But after a few agonizing minutes; silence.

They left first thing in the morning, their sense of safety shattered. Brian still refused to believe anything was wrong. Then that night, I had left her makeup bag on the kitchen table, I picked it up and headed upstairs to our bedroom. But when I reached for the doorknob, It wouldn't turn. It was like someone was holding it from the other side. Not letting me in. I dropped the bag, bolted downstairs, grabbed my coat, and ran straight to my parents' house. I couldn't ignore it anymore.

Whatever was in that house, it wasn't random. It wasn't just messing with me. It was waiting. And it only acted up when was I alone, or another woman was in the house. One night, my sister came over to stay. I ran next door to visit our Mom, my sister was getting ready in the bathroom, she always took longer than me to get ready. That's when she heard it, soft at first. A child crying. At first, she thought it was a neighbour's child. But as she listened, the sound got closer. Inside the house. She packed her stuff and left.

Then came the final straw. It was a night where the wind howled outside like a pack of wolves, making the windows rattle just enough to kick my nerves into overdrive. I was sitting wrapped in a blanket watching television in our dimly lit living room, feeling the chill creeping through the old bones of the house. Then suddenly I felt like I was being watched. Every little creak of the floorboards echoed like a shout in the heavy silence. "It's just an old house," I told myself, feeling ridiculous.

But something wasn't right. The air was thick with a tension that made my skin feel prickly, like static before a storm, and I swore I caught glimpses of movement out of the corner of my eye. Was it just my imagination? I wasn't sure. A flicker of uncertainty ran through me, sending my heart racing.

Then there was Boogie, poor boy was a bundle of energy by day, but at night? He turned into a quivering mess, staring at the hallway like someone was about to step out of the shadows. I would hear him growl, deep in his throat, a sound so low it felt like it vibrated in my chest. It was always from the same spot, an old staircase leading to the second floor, where the air felt heavier, more oppressive.

I couldn't blame him. I was spooked just standing there. As I gathered my courage and approached the stairs, a cold draft twisted around my ankles, making me shiver despite the house's heat. I paused, my teeth clenched, my heart pounding like a bass drum.

The ominous weight of the house seemed to settle on my shoulders, each step feeling like a defiance against whatever lurked at the top of the stairs. Then, without warning, the sound of laughter, childlike, giddy, broke the silence. My blood ran cold. It echoed through the dark hallways, light and innocent, yet utterly wrong. I froze, chills racing down my spine. The sound twisted in my ears; a melody wrapped in a shroud of dread.

I turned on my heels, my heart racing, but before I could escape, the frame on the wall shook violently, the picture inside rattling like it was trying to break free. I sprinted down the stairs, whatever was upstairs, it wanted me to know, I was not alone. And there it was, waiting, perhaps laughing quietly, reveling in my fear. I rushed out the front door, my heart pounding in my ears, and didn't stop until I reached her parents' house, praying I could outrun the darkness that seemed to follow me. I could feel it lurking, hovering just outside, biding its time, waiting for my next move.

We moved.

Sold the house to her other sister's boyfriend. The relief was palpable, knowing I was finally free from the haunting. Months later, my sister's boyfriend called. "Yeah," he said. "I'm selling the house." "Why?" his reply, "It's haunted." That same house?

When I was a child, I had a friend who lived in our house, Victoria. We used to walk to school together until Victoria got polio, ended up in a wheelchair, and stopped going to school. I would go visit her and we'd play board games. But life got busy with school and stuff, and several months passed. One day, I stopped by after school, only to find the house empty. Victoria had died. Her mom had moved. And that was that. Or was it?

I remember one night when I stood in our dimly lit living room, I whispered, "Victoria? Go to the light," just like the medium had told me. And then, stillness. The silence too thick. Too deep. Like the house itself was holding its breath. Then, the faintest sound. A soft laugh. And a whisper. "You're not alone." My heart slammed against my ribs. Even now, when I think back to that moment. That feeling. The silence that followed didn't feel like peace. It felt like something was waiting.

And maybe: it still is.

"Rejection is not a verdict of your worth,
but a redirection towards a path meant for you."

Mama Carson

"HER STORY"

Colleen's story? It's not some magical fairy tale, but let's be honest; it definitely has its colourful moments. She's lived a life that's more of a tasting platter than a single entrée. Honestly, who wouldn't want that kind of adventure? Her Dad used to wonder why she couldn't just settle down with one job or go to university. He worried she'd never have that stable life everyone talks about.

Colleen, though, had a different take: "Dad, who needs student loans when I can get paid to learn on the job?" She wasn't just hopping around; she was front and center, soaking in all the opportunities life threw her way.

Over the years, Colleen's worn so many hats that she could've opened a boutique called 'Hats by Me.' Some fit perfectly (like the kind of hat you wear daily), some were tight, and a few made her think, "What was I thinking?" But hey, every single one gave her a story to tell or, at the very least, a good laugh.

Take public speaking. People get freaked out by it but for Colleen? It was a chance to talk with no interruptions. Imagine a whole room of people just listening to you. It's pure bliss for a chatterbox. Her secret? Keeping them awake. And why? Because she genuinely loved connecting with people, and there's no better reward than seeing someone walk away inspired (or at least amused). Each role, each experience, taught her valuable lessons and added to her wisdom.

Then there's acting. Oh, the drama! Colleen's played queens, villains, and even Juliet, snagging a standing ovation. She was even invited to join a soap opera in LA. But, alas, her husband didn't want to move.

As for modeling? Let's just say it was an experience walking through clouds for a photo shoot and posing semi-nude (boosted her confidence). But the industry? Too pretentious. The backstabbing? Exhausting.

Fitness instructor? Oh, yeah, she did that, too. Go ahead and laugh because the thought of Colleen shouting, "Feel the burn!" is objectively hilarious. Her classes were more comedy shows than serious workouts. She had this magic knack for making people laugh so hard they forgot their thighs were on fire from squats. But she wasn't in it for the burning muscles, so she didn't stick around for long. The goal? Learn about health and fitness. The outcome? Retired from fitness with a whistle, and a lot of funny stories to tell.

Marketing? It's a nonstop dilemma, for sure. She loved it until she realized some people thought creativity meant just making logos bigger. "Bigger is not a strategy, Sir!" But hey, pitching brands? Not so different from pitching books. Little did she know, all those lessons would come in handy later on as an author.

And then there's entrepreneurship. Whoa, being your own boss sounds glamorous until you realize your boss is also you, and sometimes you can be a real jerk. Colleen launched businesses with nothing but a dream, a prayer, and a tight budget, which made a shoestring look luxurious. But image consulting became her go-to. The secret to fixing someone's fashion disaster? Confidence. Even if they swear Crocs are business casual, you smile, nod, and work your magic.

One of her favourite ventures? Being a chef. She started a catering business with pots, a $10 ad, and a truckload of hope. Twenty years later, she was still serving up everything from intimate dinners to chaotic weddings. Sure, she burned a few things along the way, but people always came back for seconds, so she must've been doing something right.

Wedding planning was like its own comedy special. Between brides, grooms, and occasionally the overbearing Mothers of the Bride, it was basically a circus with champagne. Colleen dealt with everything from flower mix-ups to last-minute seating chart redesigns. But when she saw a couple take their first dance? Pure magic. Especially when it was to "Rest Of My Life" by Bruno Mars.

Business consulting was a trip. My goal was to help people avoid my mistakes. The reality? Listening to people pitch ideas that should've stayed in their dreams, really! But fundraising? Now, that was a blast. My secret weapon? Food. If you can bake a killer cookie, you can convince anyone to open their wallet. And the Terry Fox Run? That fundraiser was my favourite.

Songwriting, though? The romanticized version is poetic lyrics flowing from my soul. The reality? Rhyming "love" with "dove" and "shove." But writing, in any form, was my happy place. Editing? That's where the tantrums came out, though. Nothing would humble me more than rereading my work at 2 a.m. and questioning my life choices.

But the roles that really shaped me? Motherhood and marriage. Being a mom was like managing a tiny, unpredictable festival: a nurse, negotiator, referee, chef, therapist, and even a coach. My children would ask the weirdest questions, like, "If fish don't have ears, how do they hear us talking about them?" There is no poker face for that one. Through it all, they taught me more about love and life than I ever could've imagined.

And marriage? Well, that was its own adventure. It taught me the art of compromise (like pretending duct tape fixes are chic or nodding when your husband insists he didn't leave his socks on the floor). My first marriage ended, and that's okay. Sometimes love evolves, and part of growing up is realizing when it's time to move on. Divorce wasn't a failure; it was a chance to find myself, and I did. I also found the love of her life. YAYYY!!!

And don't even get me started on all the courses I've taken. I could've funded a European vacation with what I spent on them. Oh, wait, I did that, too! There was even a brief stint training to be an assistant chemist. My science teacher would have been more confused than proud. "Wait, you went from chemistry to entrepreneurship?" Yep, I am living proof that life's educational opportunities can take you anywhere, especially when you have no clue where it's all headed. Oh, did I mention now Author, Playwright, and soon to be inspirational speaker, not bad for seventy-four, right?

My life has been a mosaic of bold moves, unexpected wins, and lessons learned in the heat of uncertainty. Every hat I wore, every detour I took, and every misstep shaped me into the unstoppable force I am today: fearlessly authentic, insatiably curious, and ready to tackle every new chapter with open arms and a heart full of determination.

Here's the deal: My life's opportunities are like walking along the ocean's edge. Every wave? A new horizon calling me forward. The dreams? The seagulls overhead, some I'd chase with all my heart, others I'd watch from afar. But every one of them whispered a promise that if I spread my wings, something more significant would await me. The shifting sand beneath my feet? It's just life's way of reminding me that, though things change, solid ground is always there, ready for my next step.

Like I have said many times, "My life wasn't or isn't about living my destination; it's living my journey, knowing that each step, each wave, unfolds something transformative. My powers have always been within me; they're not going anywhere.

"SILENCE LISTENS"

Oh, go with Colleen and let her take you back to when she was a little girl, crossing her legs on her living room floor. She would be staring at the elders with ears pricked open like a puppy, hearing all that the elders of the house were saying. And oh, what stories they'd tell! We were entering a time machine that transported us back in time to prohibition when Uncle Sam felt he could outwit everyone by outlawing sparkling tea. But oh no, not on their watch! They would chuckle and reminisce about how every speakeasy turned into a real-life game of hide-and-seek with the fuzz (the term for police).

Can you imagine it? They'd be grumbling like agents, never to be caught having a taste of the illicit beverage! It felt like a gangster film, except with fewer fedoras and fewer giggles. The elders' bathtub gin and cellar hooch stories made it sound like the coolest thing since sliced bread! It was as if they were reporting on the freshest gossip from the adult world, and we kids, staring with surprise, had no choice but to listen. And oh, the laughter! Others would be laughing so loudly they would almost twirl themselves out of their chairs, snapping at their knees as if trying to catch on fire laughter. So, as the ladies were whizzing by on their cigarettes and wine, fancy and strange, the guys were whizzing by on their cigars or pipes, guzzling beers or scotches, working like steam engines.

But, well, in between all this, we kids weren't just twiddling our thumbs! Ah no, we were in it, playing games and having the time of our lives. It was our mini carnival of laughter and games in the living room. And sometimes, the elders with us would end up in song and dance. So, you see, it was not just about the grown-ups having all the fun with their fancy talk and smoky treats. We kids knew how to make our magic, with laughter and merriment, into every moment. Ah, those were the days! And then, there were the times when the room would hush, and the elders' voices would turn somber, like a cloud passing over the sun. They would speak of the Great Depression, their words heavy with the weight of memories and hardships endured. It was as if the air held its breath, waiting to hear their tales of strength in the face of hardship.

But it did not stop there. Oh no, they would burrow even deeper into the shadows of history, recounting their experiences of the First and Second World Wars. The room would grow still, each word hanging like a solemn vow in the air. They had walked through the fires of war, while others had faced the darkness of concentration camps or the uncertainty of internment camps. You could see it in their eyes, the echoes of those turbulent times etched in every line and wrinkle.

And as they spoke, we children listened, our young minds trying to grasp what they had endured. It was an exercise in mourning, a reminder that there was pain and survival behind every smile, every laugh.

But even within those solemn silences, there was still hope, a spark that could not be killed. In the darkness, they had managed to go on, rebuild, and construct a better future. When we heard their stories, we felt a sense of wonder and thanksgiving for the lives they had lost. So, as the stories were told, we sat in quiet reverence, honouring the courage of those who had come before us. In their words, we children found not just history but also a timeless lesson in character, reminding us that there is always hope, even in the darkest times. Those moments in my family's history echoed with compassion and strength. It all began with my grandmother, a mere twelve years old when the world around her shattered into fragments of fear and despair.

The Nazis tore her from the warm embrace of her parents and sister, thrusting her into the cold, merciless jaws of a concentration camp. In that cruel spiral of fate, she bid farewell to her childhood innocence, never to see her parents again. But amid the darkness, a flicker of hope endured, and decades passed, each day marked by the relentless search for her sister, an inspiration of love guiding her through despair. And then, against all odds, the day of reunion dawned like a radiant sunrise after the darkest night.

I can still feel the tremble of emotion that vibrated through our family as my grandmother and her sister embraced, their tears mingling in a river of joy and relief. It was a celebration of love triumphant over hatred, of family reunited against all odds. You must remember that social media was not available to assist in my grandma's search. Now, let's turn our gaze to the elders, those wise guardians of memory and history. They spoke of valour and sacrifice with each word, painting vivid portraits of battles fought on distant shores. Their voices carried the weight of years, each syllable a witness to the human cost of conflict in war. I can see them now with tears streaming down weathered cheeks, others reaching out with trembling hands to offer comfort and solace.

But amid the sorrow, there was a spirit that defied despair. For these elders, their warlike experiences were not just chapters in history but pillars of strength upon which the foundation of freedom stood. I can hear their voices, crackling with emotion but strong with conviction, speaking of fighting for themselves and the generations to come. 'We had to,' they'd mutter, 'fought for our freedom, but also, most importantly, for our children's and future children's freedom.

From dusty textbooks to the reverberations of war stories, I followed the steps of warriors who braved oppression. Their bravery and their spirit are a light shining in the night, showing me through the shadows of ignorance and indifference. But it's not just in the great dramas of war and revolution that I find reminders of the cost of freedom. It is not only at work; it is in the mundane, too: the laughter of children in the playground but the quiet dignity of elders reading stories on a porch swing. It is simply in my ability to speak loudly with the confidence that I am entitled to speak without fear or hesitation.

And so, in this world, I carry with me the value of freedom as a precious flower in my hands. For I know it is not something to be taken for granted, but to cherish and keep untouched with all the fibres of my being. And in that holy call, I find my calling: to honour the martyrs of old by leading a life worthy of the liberty they gave their all for. Freedom is a valuable right that we must respect and answer to. It is not a freedom bestowed by statute or the authority of the law but a principle that determines our lives and societies. For us to truly appreciate and defend our freedom, we must know what it means and what we can do to protect it.

For one thing, respect for liberty means acknowledging its importance to our identities and possibilities. It's what we base our hopes and goals on. If we love our freedom, we celebrate the sacrifices of those who came before us to get it, and we celebrate their legacy by using it wisely. Responsibility, in contrast, is the obligation associated with liberty. It requires that we exercise our freedoms consciously and carefully, always aware of our impact on others. That means acknowledging the rights of others while asserting our own and creating a tension that brings peace and mutual respect into our societies.

Further, the responsibility for our freedom goes beyond our individual choice. It entails engaging in political life, debate, voting, and pushing for policies that protect our rights and liberties. As informed and engaged citizens, we are all helping to maintain and build upon the liberties we value. In addition, caring for our freedom means we must respond to obstacles and injustices that put it at risk. It involves challenging discrimination, inequality and authoritarianism, which distort freedom and equality for all. We remain alert and strong, guarding our own liberties and those of our children.

> "True liberty is not merely inherited; it is protected through our actions today, establishing a legacy where every step we take promises future generations to walk in the fullness of freedom's light."

The cornerstone of democracy is the acceptance of its principles in our daily lives and actions. By representing them, we keep freedom alive as a beacon of hope and possibility for all. By sacrificing our individual lives to defend liberty, we help create a better tomorrow. Let's stand tall and believe that we have now sworn the future to ourselves.

"ODE TO OUR HEROES"

In the past, they stood strong, brave and true,
Fighting for freedom, for me and for you.
Their voices rose up in the heat of the fight,
Showing us all how to stand for what's right.

Today, we carry their fire, their light,
In small acts of kindness, in courage, we unite.
With every step forward, we honour their ways,
Building a future where hope always stays.

Tomorrow holds promise, bright and wide,
With new heroes rising, standing side by side.
They'll dream big and bold, with hearts full of grace,
Facing the challenges that time may take place.

So, let's remember, in all that we do,
The heroes of yesterday, today, and those new.
Together we're stronger, our spirits aligned,
In a world built on kindness, with love intertwined.

In the rising of love and the conquering of hate,
That should be our fate, not a coward's debate.
With hearts joined together, we'll stand up and say,
In hero's power, in unity we'll stand on liberty day.

Colleen C. Carson

This is my Parents

Love

Just Married

Fifty Years

Looking back on my life feels like flipping through a worn-out photo album, each image tinged with the bittersweet hues of nostalgia. I like to think of myself as a bit of a cultural cocktail: Italian at heart, French in style, Irish in life, and Polish in culture. It's like a cocktail that's equal parts sweet and strong, with a twist of something ineffable. Growing up in a Canadian European household with such diverse roots wasn't just unique; it was special, though at times, overwhelming.

My Mom was elegance personified, born in Bordeaux, France. She carried herself with the kind of grace that made her seem untouchable, like a character from an old black-and-white film. Her Dad, my Irish Grandfather, brought a fiery spark to our family mix: stubborn, funny, and deeply loyal. Then there was my Dad, born in a small Italian town, radiating warmth like the sun-drenched village square.

People called him "The Godfather," not just because of his looks but because of his undeniable presence. His Mother, my Polish Grandmother, added a rich layer to our heritage. Together, they created a mosaic of influences that coloured every corner of my childhood.

I can still hear the echoes of that childhood, vibrant and alive with cultural richness. My parents wanted my sisters and me to grow up surrounded by art, music, and literature, though it often felt like they were trying to cram a whole world of culture into our tiny lives. My dad's Stradivarius violin would sing through the house, mingling with the sound of my piano practice.

He played with a passion that made the strings weep, and as a family, we sang together in the church choir and at home, our harmonies sometimes reminiscent of the Von Trapp family. Music wasn't just a pastime; it was a way of life.

Beyond the music and the art, my parents instilled lessons into our upbringing, lessons about respect, equality, and the weight of integrity. "Your word is your bond," my Dad would say, his voice steady and firm. He had this way of making you believe that anything was possible if you worked hard enough.

And that integrity was the foundation of character, something that applies to everyone, no matter who you are. My Mom, on the other hand, was softer but no less impactful. She was an avid reader, self-taught, and endlessly curious. Despite leaving school after the fourth grade, she had an intellectual depth that made me think she'd secretly earned a Ph.D. in literature and psychology. She had an incredible ability to see the power of words and understand the complexity of the human mind. Her influence deepened my appreciation for knowledge. For the longest time, I thought my Mom had a university education because she was brilliant.

She didn't share her background with us until we were adults. Her self-taught journey is proof of determination and a love for knowledge. Her hunger for learning taught me that learning isn't confined to classrooms.

It's found in the pages of books, in conversations, in simply paying attention to the world. She was my first and most enduring example of strength. I was proud of her and felt lucky to call her my Mom. My dad was pursuing a higher education in medicine, but the war changed everything for him.

My childhood was filled with laughter and dreams, and the bond we shared as a family was unbreakable. I discovered early on that my admiration for my parents came from the deep love and guidance they offered. They were the quiet influencers of my life, providing a steady presence throughout my journey.

As a child, I sometimes felt lost in a world that seemed so vast and confusing. But my parents were always there, guiding me through. "You can do anything you set your mind to, Colleen," my Dad would say, and those words became a rallying cry in my heart. I could see the faith in his eyes, making me feel like I could conquer anything.

His encouragement wasn't just words; it was the foundation of my self-discovery. Whenever he cheered me on, I felt like my potential was expanding and reaching new heights. My parent's belief in me helped me navigate moments of doubt. Armed with his wisdom, I learned that the only limits I faced were the ones I set for myself.
And my Mom? She added another layer of encouragement. With her loving touch and heartfelt support, she'd whisper, "Dream big, Colleen." Her words planted seeds of ambition in my mind, nurturing

them with her steadfast belief in me. Over the years, our relationship grew into rich conversations filled with wisdom, where every word carried the warmth of parental care.

Of course, we had our disagreements now and then, but we would agree to disagree, and our love always shone through. My parents transitioned from being mere storytellers to becoming my mentors, lighting the path ahead with their love and insights. They instilled the courage to chase my dreams, reassuring me that stumbling was part of the journey as long as I got back up again.

They had a unique approach to parenting. Instead of punishing us for every mistake, they focused on teaching us responsibility, life lessons, and the value of earning what we wanted. Their motto was simple: "Nothing worthwhile comes easy. You've got to earn it, and once you do, share it with others."

Our home had three bedrooms, but one was off-limits because it belonged to my parents. This left the five of us to share the other two rooms. My sister and I shared one and immediately drew an imaginary line down the middle, claiming our territories. I got the side with the window for the view and breeze, while she ended up with the door. It seemed fair to me.

But our parents pointed out a flaw in our plan; respecting this line when one side was the only way in or out was impossible. After days of awkward tiptoeing around, we finally admitted defeat and came up with a better arrangement. It was a lesson in teamwork, whether we liked it or not.

I organized a rugby championship in high school, and we were confident we'd win. The tournament weekend arrived, and I called a last-minute meeting at my friend's house. I promised I'd be home by 11:00 p.m., but time slipped away. When I got home at 11:30, my parents were waiting in the living room. No cell phones back then, and they were upset.

I apologized, but my Dad wouldn't let it go: "You want us to respect you, but you don't think it's necessary to respect us." That weekend, I was grounded and devastated. It was a tough lesson, but I never forgot it. Keeping my word became one of my most important values. It's a lesson that's stuck with me, etched into the core of who I am. Over the years, I've repeated those words to myself whenever I've faltered. They taught me that promises aren't just words; they're commitments. It was a harsh lesson for a teenager, but I'm grateful for it now.

My Mom's approach to discipline was different, subtle, and almost surgical. She never yelled, but her quiet firmness had a way of cutting through any argument. I remember watching her navigate a heated disagreement with my sister, her calm presence diffusing the tension. When I asked her how she managed it, she simply said, "Psychology." That one word sent me on a journey of discovery, poring over books and spending hours people-watching downtown, trying to unravel the mysteries of human behaviour.

Those afternoons outside The Bay on Granville and Georgia weren't just idle moments. They were a window into the complexity of people, the way a slumped shoulder could speak of defeat, or a hurried step could hint at hidden urgency. Years later, when a friend was studying for his master's in psychiatry, he told me he'd learned more from our conversations than his professors; I felt a quiet pride. My Mom's influence had planted those seeds, nurturing a curiosity that would shape my understanding of the world.

Yet, even as I cherish these memories, there's a heaviness to them, a sense of loss for what was and what can never be again. My parents, with all their wisdom and love, were human. They made mistakes, ones I could forgive even as they shaped me. Unlike my sisters, I saw my parents as ordinary people yet extraordinary parents, navigating their own struggles while trying to guide us through ours. That perspective made their imperfections easier to bear, but it also added melancholy to our relationship.

As I grew older and became a Mother, I drew on their lessons. In moments of doubt, I'd hear my Dad's steady voice or feel the gentle touch of my Mom's encouragement. They had given me a foundation of values, respect, responsibility, and empathy that I tried to pass on to my children. But parenting isn't about replication; it's about adaptation, and there were times when I questioned whether I was doing it right.

I realized how much their love shaped me in the quiet moments of reflection. It wasn't loud or showy but steady, like a heartbeat. They taught me to dream big but stay grounded, accept challenges, and cherish small joys. Their legacy isn't just in the lessons they imparted but in the way they lived, imperfectly, authentically, with a love that endures even in their absence.

Sometimes, when our house is quiet, I think of my Dad's violin or my Mom's quiet strength, and the ache of missing them feels almost unbearable. But that ache is a reminder of how deeply they are spun into the fabric of who I am. Their voices may have faded, but their lessons echo on, guiding me through the muddle of life.

I am my Father's daughter, my Mother's child, a cultural cocktail, a montage of influences, a reflection of their love and spirit. And while the past can never be reclaimed, its memories are a treasure chest I carry with me, a bittersweet reminder of the foundation they built and the woman I've become.

Watching my parents love each other was like watching the sweetest, most heartwarming movie, one of those timeless classics you can't help but get lost in, the kind that leaves you smiling through tears. Their love was something special, something rare, and if I close my eyes, I can almost picture them now, laughing together in heaven, probably still wrapped up in each other like they always were. I was lucky to witness it; honestly, it's a privilege I never took for granted. But let me take you back to where it all began because their story? Oh, it's a good one.

It was wartime, and my Mom, Veronique, was just your average young French girl with her head full of dreams. She wasn't the kind to sit around waiting for love to knock on her door; no, she took matters into her own hands, or maybe I should say knees. And what did she do? She climbed all 283 steps of Saint Joseph's Oratory, saying a prayer at each one, asking for a love that would last a lifetime.

If that doesn't scream determination, I don't know what does. And wouldn't you know it? A few weeks later, in walks Archie, a soldier with a grin that could melt butter, asking her out for a bite to eat on a lazy Sunday afternoon. Talk about divine intervention, right?

But here's where things take a turn. That Sunday lunch? Not exactly the romantic rendezvous she was hoping for. Archie told her his buddy and date were coming to lunch as well, And before anyone could call it a double date, things spiraled into full-blown chaos.

Archie had to go pick up his friend, Johnnie, my Dad, but at some point, he found himself locked out of Johnnie's place. Naturally, the only solution? My Mom climbed through a window like a wartime spy, only to find Johnnie waiting for them inside. Awkward doesn't even begin to cover it. Meanwhile, Archie was outside, shouting, "Johnnie, open the dang door!" Turns out Archie lived with Johnnie. Classic.

Now, about that date of Johnnie's, he left the room and came back and told them that she conveniently had to work that day, wartime duties and all. But my Mom always said she suspected Johnnie had dropped her the moment he laid eyes on Veronique. And honestly, who could blame him? My Mom had this way about her: graceful, witty, and full of life. Actually, her friends nicknamed my Mom Veronica Lake, a famous movie star in the forties.

Things only got messier from there. Somewhere along the way, Johnnie also decided he was pretty fond of Veronique. One thing led to another, and before Archie even knew what hit him, Johnnie was holding Veronique's hand and sneaking in a quick kiss when he thought no one was looking.

Poor Archie must've felt like a lost puppy watching his best friend swoop in. But this wasn't just some wartime fling; my Mom played the long game. While the boys were off at war, she wrote love letters to both of them, keeping her options open and her heart guarded.

Now, here's the kicker; those letters? Identical. Word for word. Ever the gentleman, Archie read his out loud to Johnnie one day, probably thinking he had the upper hand. When it was Johnnie's turn, he just smirked and said, "I think I'll keep mine private." Smooth, right? My Mom knew exactly what she was doing. Fast forward to the boys coming home. Still convinced Veronique was madly in love with him, Johnnie decided to take her on a canoe ride.

Somewhere in the middle of that calm, quiet lake, he let it slip that he knew about the matching letters. Mom didn't hold back; she let him have it, telling him he was full of himself and maybe not quite as clever as he thought. And yet, somehow, when he popped the big question, she said yes. Just like that. Talk about plot twists.

And poor Archie? He found himself in the ultimate friend zone, serving as Johnnie's best man. Life had a funny way of working out, though. Johnnie and Veronique got married, Archie was shipped off to Europe, and fate took another unexpected turn.

Archie's plane was shot down over Germany, while my Dad, thanks to his debilitating migraines, was grounded. Maybe the universe knew what it was doing all along. Their love story wasn't perfect, but it was theirs. Sixty years, six kids, three grandkids, and more inside jokes than I could count. Their love grew stronger with time, weathering every storm and cherishing every sunny day. It was the kind of love you read about that sticks with you, even after they're gone.

So, why am I such a hopeless romantic? When you grow up in a house where love isn't just a feeling but a way of life, it sticks with you. My parents couldn't live without each other, and honestly, that kind of love rubs off whether you want it to or not.

But if there's one thing my parents taught me, aside from what true love looks like, it's that raising children is an adventure all its own. You can't just hand them everything and expect them to thrive. You have to teach them to teach themselves, to take responsibility, and to face life head-on. Give them the tools, but don't do the work for them. Because if you do? They'll grow up thinking success comes easily, and let me tell you, life doesn't work that way.

Encourage them to chase wisdom, to welcome failure as much as success, and to grab opportunities with both hands. If you don't, you'll end up carrying the weight of their unlearned lessons, and trust me, that's a burden you don't want. Love, life, and raising kids are complicated and unpredictable, but they are beautiful if you do them right.

My parents built something amazing, not just in their marriage but in the way they raised us. They led with love, laughed through the hard times, and never stopped believing in the power of showing up for each other. So, here's to my parents, the ultimate lovebirds. Their story might have had a few bumps along the way, but it was one for the ages.

And if I learned anything from them, it's that love real, lasting love is worth every single twist, turn, and unexpected detour.

"Throw your stones, reveal your shadows, but know this, I am a quiet strength that bends but doesn't break, a flame that may flicker but never fade. Test me, and you'll see I rise like the dawn, steady and fierce, reclaiming my light and negotiating yours."

Colleen C. Carson

"FOR INDEPENDENCE SAKES"

Working Woman

High School

Colleen's parents' love as her compass and their wisdom as her guide, Colleen sets sail on the voyage of independence that started across the Atlantic Ocean to the shores of Liverpool, England, where the infamous Beatles lived and entertained before their fame. She knew that no matter where the winds of fate took her, she would always find comfort in the nurturing embrace of her parents' love.

It became a repetition mimicked in her mind during moments of adversity, a reminder that setbacks were temporary detours on the road to success. With her mom's gentle yet determined spirit, her mom would share insights that rose above the ordinary. "Life is a journey of discovery," her mom would say, inviting Colleen to explore the depths of her own identity. Under the gentle guidance of my mom's wisdom, I unearthed the invaluable lesson of authenticity and independence in a world masked in the pretense of conformity. I molded myself into what I fondly term a "nonconformist conformist" – a contradiction, perhaps, but one that brims with clarity and purpose.

Now, let me untangle this riddle for you. Amid the sea of sameness, I stood tall as a nonconformist, daring to encompass my uniqueness, refusing to be molded into society's predetermined molds. Yet, ironically, I am also a conformist, willingly positioning myself with the united when it serves the greater good of humanity.

Confusing? Not at all. It is a delicate performance, a balancing act between honoring the essence of who I am and recognizing the connection with all beings. When the call to conformity rings loud, when unity signals for the greater good, I step forward, my convictions firm, my spirit united with the united heartbeat of humanity.

But there are moments when the path of independence demands rebellion when conformity stifles the blossoming of individuality. In those moments, I stood firm as a nonconformist, charting my course, daring to be different in a world that often celebrates the mundane. So, being a nonconformist conformist is not just a whimsical notion – it's a philosophy, a way of life steeped in the knowledge of perception. It is about knowing when to blend in and when to stand out, when to follow the crowd and when to establish your path.

In this movement of duality, I find my strength, my purpose, my truth. Authenticity is not just a destination; it is a lifelong journey to unravel the layers of conformity and discover the radiant core of oneself. My parents carefully laid the steppingstones of advice that paved the way to my pinnacles of success. Their words, etched in the very essence of my being, become the fuel for my ambitions. "Motivating me to seek to achieve," as if their encouragement forced me forward, wind beneath the wings of my dreams. In their love and guidance, I discovered a reservoir of strength within myself. Their torch was more than a light; it was an endless source of power, bringing the fire in my soul to venture into the unknown frontiers of my destiny.

Almost as soon as I reached the seashore in Liverpool, I was worn out and collapsed into a very restful nap. When I got up, I ate a big breakfast, and I found myself refreshed after every bite. I tossed my knapsack (which was decorated with a Canadian flag) over my shoulder in anticipation of adventure. I made my way to a nearby road, my heart pounding excitedly. Sticking my thumb out, with the hoped of catching a passing driver's attention.

Luck was on our side! A car slowed down, and the driver leaned out, asking where my girlfriend and I were headed. We exchanged amused glances, unable to suppress our laughter, and cheekily asked him where he was going. With a smile and a shrug, we hopped into his car and set off, London-bound. The moment's spontaneity filled us with a thrilling sense of freedom and anticipation.

Hitching around Europe was an adventure full of thrilling highs and nerve-wracking lows. One time in France stands out vividly. Two guys picked us up, and instead of taking us to our destination, they veered off course, thinking they could spend the night with us. Our hearts raced with fear, but we diligently stood courageously tall in thought. They eventually dropped us off in a tiny, remote town. It was a narrow escape that left us shaken but wiser.

Another time, we were trying to cross the highway to get to Hyde Park in London. Traffic was zooming by at 80 km/h, and my swollen ankles made it hard to keep up with my girlfriend. Suddenly, a van struck me, flying 20 feet through the air and into oncoming traffic. I remember the terrifying sensation of car wheels whizzing by, brushing dangerously close to my head. People screamed, "Is she dead?" as cars screeched to a halt and others called out for a doctor. Through it all, I could hear my girlfriend sobbing desperately as I lay face down on the road.

Miraculously, I survived to tell the tale, though the police officer who had to write up his report was none too pleased. He sternly advised me to use the pedestrian tunnel under the highway next time, as all sensible people do. Despite the harrowing moments, these experiences became part of the incredible journey that shaped my identity.

Sometimes, I conformed to expectations, blending into the background and following the rules. Other times, I broke away, choosing my path and defying conventions. Each decision, whether to fit in or stand out, brought me closer to a sense of independence, which was my goal. With every step, I carried the essence of who I was and aspired to be, a medley of lessons learned, dreams pursued, and challenges conquered.

I began on this journey with the spirit of a girl yearning for independence. I wandered through bustling cities and quiet villages, soaking in the diverse cultures and languages. I met people who enriched my understanding of the world and myself. I tasted foods that ranged from delightful to peculiar, each bite an adventure. I faced moments of doubt, fear, and experienced the exhilarating joy of triumph.

I felt the thrill of breaking the rules in every bar I worked where I should not have. Drinking from fountains pouring out wine felt like sipping from the cup of life itself, each drop a reminder of the beauty in the unexpected. Sleeping under the stars, with the night sky as my ceiling, I felt a divine connection to the universe. Even the nights spent in jail cells, when there was nowhere else to go, became stories of strength and survival.

Along the way, I fell in love with boys who were not yet men, mirroring my own journey from girlhood to womanhood. These romances were tender and fleeting, yet they taught me about the depths of my own heart. I slept on cliffs with the sound of waves crashing below, on beaches with the sand as my mattress, on couches offered by generous strangers, and sometimes even in beds that felt like luxury. Through all these experiences, I discovered the strength and capacity of my soul.

It amazed me how, no matter where I laid my head, my heart stayed spirited and open, ready to embrace whatever came next. Each sunrise brought new possibilities, each sunset whispered lessons of gratitude, and amid it all, I found solace in the ever-present rhythm of life's journey. The power of optimism energized my days, while the beauty of welcoming honor enlightened my path, guiding me through the peaks and valleys with kindness and strength.

Upon my return home, I ceased to be the girl who had departed in search of independence; I returned as a woman who had discovered it. My journey had created a transformation, teaching me deep-seated confidence and self-reliance. I came to understand that genuine independence springs from within, nurtured by the hardships and comforts that mold our character. Every path was moments of intense self-discovery and a heightened awareness of principle.

These experiences infuse my soul with boundless joy and strength, propelling me toward my authentic purpose. I accepted each step with courage; through these odysseys, I realistically uncover my true self and my meaningful role in the world. I became my own trustworthy companion to the remarkable woman I had evolved into.

"Colleen blossomed from a girl into an independent woman, guided by the light of self-discovery and the strength found within her."

"Let your inner child dance among the stars, giggle with the sunbeams, and spin with the breeze. Rejoice in the magic within; let joy fill your heart. In every moment of delight, you uncover your spirit's limitless power."

Colleen C. Carson

"WAS IT AUSCHWITZ"

By the late sixties, the world still carried the unbearable weight of a war that had fractured Europe in a way no words could truly capture. Colleen had visited Auschwitz, the site where humanity's darkest side had bared its fangs, and there, in the presence of such inhumanity, she felt the shadow of history settle over her.

The air at the iron gates of the concentration camp was thick with something more sinister than any weather could explain, a presence that lingered, suffocating, heavy with the memories of the dead.

The day seemed torn, unsure if it would let the clouds win or permit the sun to shine, casting cruel, sharp shadows on the worn stone. Aside from the gentle rustling of the trees above, her slow and deliberate footsteps were the only sound. She made her way to the museum, where each photograph spoke in silence, each one a terrifying verification of what had been.

Faces from another world face so thin and swollen, eyes hollowed by suffering, stared back at Colleen from every corner of the room. Time had frozen for them in those black-and-white images full of commuter trains filled with doomed, frightened victims packed like animals, the defiant strength in the eyes of the few survivors still burning with a strength they had no choice but to summon.

Each step through the exhibits brought an unnatural chill that had nothing to do with the weather outside. The smell of the ovens still lingered in my mind, a trace of the horrors committed here, a scar that refused to fade. It clung to my thoughts, more potent than the stench of decay, its savage nature, a reminder of the millions who had been slaughtered on these very grounds. I was drawn to a room with its horror; the ovens stood as silent witnesses to unimaginable pain.

The smell of iron, rotting flesh, and the ghosts of lost lives still seemed to hang in the air. The oppressive cold was like a memory itself, an intangible echo of violence and death. The room held its secrets so horrific that only the silence could do them justice. Before me was an exhibit of personal belongings: shoes worn thin, clothes frayed with time, a child's doll, once clutched tightly in the hands of an innocent, now reduced to dust in a world that had moved on.

These relics, once so deeply personal, now only served to remind me of lives that ended too soon, stories abruptly silenced. But one picture drew me in, a photograph of a young girl, perhaps twelve, whose eyes seemed to follow me, full of sorrow and a silent demand for remembrance.

At that moment, my thoughts drifted to Grandma. I remembered the stories she had shared about her time in the concentration camp, the way the Nazis had ripped her from her family, and the deep, bitter hatred directed at Poles, especially Catholics like herself. She would recount these horrors in broken fragments, each word heavy with sorrow that never seemed to lift.

Her voice would always soften when she spoke of survival when she tried to explain why she had made it through when so many others had not. I remembered sitting with her, sharing tea and cookies, and, with a child's innocent curiosity, asking her what happened in the camp.

She would simply say, "I don't want to talk about it." As my persistence grew, her eyes filled with tears, and, with a quiet but firm tone, she would say, "I don't wish to talk about what happened to me, and Colleen, you must respect my decision." I never asked again. It was a pain too deep to touch, a wound that words could never heal.

There was always a silence in my Grandma's words, an absence of stories left untold, locked away deep within the confines of her memory. It was as if she carried the weight of those unsaid tales, a burden too heavy to speak of, too painful to revisit. The photograph of the girl in Auschwitz seemed to mirror this silence, this weight that both burdened and strengthened my Grandma. As I walked through the camp, the sobering truth of what had happened here surrounded me. Auschwitz was not just a place in history; it was a lesson in the cruelty humankind? was capable of and my solemn duty to remember.

Every face, piece of clothing, and photograph told a story that must never be forgotten, a story that demanded respect and that needed to be carried forward into the future. When I finally left the camp, the tears streaming down my face seemed to merge with the rain that had begun to fall, as if the heavens themselves wept alongside me.

The sorrow I felt, the horror of what I had witnessed, hung in the air like the weight of history itself. And as I boarded my bus to Munich, a deep, quiet sadness settled in my heart. Auschwitz had left its mark, not just on the land, but on my soul.

The memory of the millions who had perished here would never fade, for their stories must be told, their lives remembered so that such horrors might never be repeated, and the endless hours passed as the bus drove on with quiet, reflective melancholy.

Then, during a brief stop, the driver pointed out a nearby wire fence, its significance immediately apparent. On the other side lay communist Czechoslovakia, where armed soldiers stood hidden among the trees, waiting to guard their borders. The driver warned us not to approach, making it clear that this was a forbidden zone, a place where the very air was thick with the threat of violence.

Today, as I reflect on International Holocaust Remembrance Day, my thoughts are heavy, tangled with history, loss, and the echoes of voices that still cry for justice. Some people, even now, refuse to believe that the Holocaust ever happened, questioning the truth of the unimaginable horrors.

To them, I say, may your hearts open to the reality that there are wounds in this world so deep that they transcend the written word. May you listen to the facts and the whispers of the survivors whose memories carry the weight of a past too painful to deny.

For me, there was never any need for a warning. I had no intention of crossing that line, no desire to tempt the terror of border patrols, ready to shoot without hesitation. Yet, standing at the fence, my gaze wandered beyond it to a place where fear replaced freedom, where the cold grip of communism stole the warmth of democracy.

I stepped closer, curiosity tugging at me, but the soldiers were nowhere in sight. A rush of fear engulfed me, a feeling I couldn't shake. I returned to the bus, silently grateful for the freedoms I often took for granted as a Canadian.

At that moment, a quiet understanding settled in my heart: freedom is more than just a place you call home. It's the courage to stand, the strength to rise above fear, and the depth to treasure what so many have lost. Even in the darkest times, each step toward freedom is an act of defiance, a witness to the invincible human spirit that refuses to be silenced.

As I continue my journey, I carry the weight of the past, but also the hope that the lessons we've learned can guide us towards a future of peace, justice, and remembrance. It's on all of us to remember and honour those we've lost, and to recognize the atrocities happening yesterday and today.

If we can set aside our greed for money and power and act selflessly, we can create a world our children can inherit. Understanding the true cost of freedom can help us break the cycles of suffering and acts of violence, and build a future where peace is not just a dream, but a reality we can all contribute to.

"In our tranquility, we can discover the creation of our thoughts, the whispers of our souls, and the wisdom of our universe, guiding us toward a deeper understanding of the world we are meant to shape and who we are to become."

Colleen C. Carson

"Regrets are the shadows of unchallenged fears, the echoes of opportunities silenced by doubt."

Mama Carson

"True success lies not just in riches, but in the positive impact made, the lives touched, and the legacy created."

Colleen C. Carson

"THE CHILD"

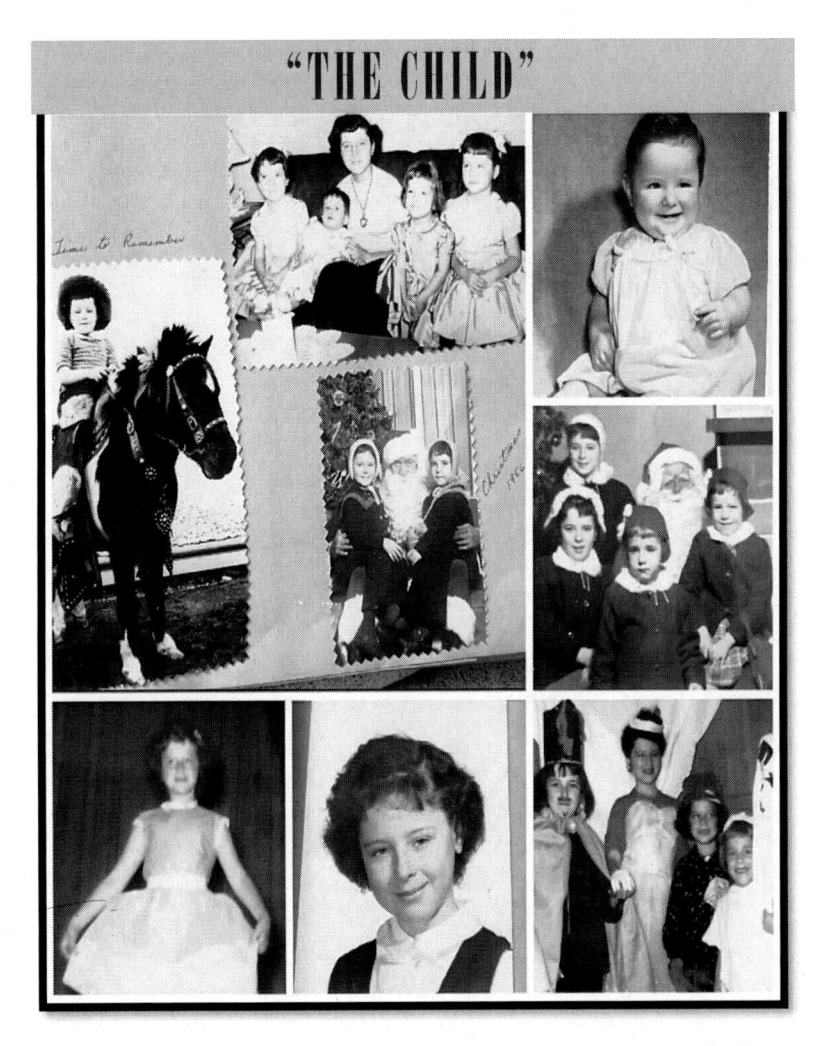

Once upon a time, Colleen's childhood was a giant playground where joy and confidence partnered with creativity and determination. To her, school was a dilemma that she felt could not be resolved. Learning was cool, but her way was different from their way. She found diversion in daydreaming, much to the dismay of some of her teachers who probably wished she would pay more attention to math. They saw her daydreaming as a crime and not about her imagination, but she felt that was their problem, not hers!

They would give her the evil eye, or they would make her hang out in the corner with the dust bunnies. Did it bother her? Nobody likes being laughed at, but hey, daydreaming was her thing, and she was not about to let anyone steal her sunshine. As long as she had her imagination, she was good.

I was all about drama: literally. Whether it was speaking in front of the class, acting in school plays, performing at piano recitals like the female version of Mozart, or singing out hymns in the church choir, I was there, front and center, soaking up the spotlight like a sponge. Public speaking? Bring it on!

I could talk the ears off a potato. When acting in school plays, I was the show's star, and singing? Let us just say I belted it out like a rockstar in the shower.

I was all about playing dress-up and putting on shows for my parents, like the death scene of the opera "Madame Butterfly." Of course, I was Madame Butterfly. In my make-believe world, I was always the lead and the one who fought the dragons with a twirl of my cape and a dash of glitter. And let me tell you, creativity ran through my veins like thick and delicious chocolate syrup on vanilla ice cream.

Sure, I had fears and moments of being scared out of my socks, but I never let fear rain on my parade. I would stare fear down and show who was the boss. I had this motto, "Believe in the magic of you, and you will achieve the dreams in you." Deep, right? Yeah, I was a wise little cookie. I have always believed in dreaming big and making those dreams my reality. Yup, come to think about it, I was a pint-sized philosopher.

Being the big sister and the dependable daughter in the family was also my thing. I was like the family's secret weapon, always ready to lend a hand to my parents or my sisters. Responsibility? Bring it on! Need help with homework? I got chu!

Need someone to lead the charge on a backyard adventure? I am your girl. I took on responsibilities as a boss because that is how I rolled. Being dependable was another one of my superpowers, and I wore that cape proudly. It was like training wheels for adulthood. At the ripe old age of seven, I rocked my first public speaking performance like a seasoned pro, talking about butterflies like I was the next Maya Angelou. Did not win first place? Not important. Second place was just the universe's way of saying, "Keep shining, girl." From then on, I knew I was destined to be a speaker, a legend in the making.

Then, at nine, I became a business capitalist without even knowing it. "The Brat's Club." Yep, that was my brainchild at nine. I had begun dipping my toes into the shark-infested waters of entrepreneurship. I started this club with my name slapped on it. "Bratus" was my last name; I just took out the "u" and replaced it with an apostrophe and hoped to make some serious dough or at least make our playtime more organized.

My neighborhood club had dues: membership for a dollar, an initiation fee of twenty-five cents, and a weekly fee of five cents—the whole shebang. My mom was my only sponsor; she would sponsor the snacks and the juice, bless her heart. We would meet up, plan stuff for our hood, and I would flex my leadership muscles like a champ. Businesswoman in the making, right?

Writing? Oh, I was all over that by fourteen. I penned a love story play performed at my school, and it was a hit. It had the whole school buzzing, and then it was performed at two other schools. Talk about validation! Who knew my pen had so much power? It was like Shakespeare but with fewer thee's and thou's.

By sixteen, I strutted my stuff on stage like a seasoned pro. Acting, speaking, you name it, was there, giving it my all and then some. And let's not forget my shining moment when I graced the stage of the Vancouver Arts Club like a true diva. Lights, camera, action – I was born for the spotlight! Drama queen? Guilty as charged!

But hey, I was not just about the spotlight. I had a soft spot for ice skating with Dad, harmonizing with my sisters, and cooking with Mom. Cooking was my passion. I later turned that passion into a business, "Colleen's Catering & Events." It all started with a ten-dollar ad and a dream that lasted two decades. Cooking became my ticket to culinary stardom.

Leadership? Oh, you betcha. I was the VP of our Student Council at seventeen, rallying the troops and leading the charge like a general in glittery combat boots or Hershey loafers. Oh, let me tell you about the great Student Council election fiasco. See, I was gunning to be President, the big cheese, the head honcho of the school.

It was down to the wire, neck, and neck, between me and this boy, the star basketball player. Do not get me wrong, he was a nice guy, but his leadership skills were about as practical as a lifeguard in a fish tank. The whole school was on edge, waiting for the results. It was like the Super Bowl of student government, except with less tackling and more awkward speeches.

Finally, they announce the winner, and wouldn't you know it? It is by just one vote—one measly little vote! I am standing there, trying to keep a straight face. Meanwhile, Mr. Basketball is already drafting his resignation speech. Yes, you heard me, resignation, not acceptance. Ah, good times. My childhood and teenage years were a rollercoaster of laughter, creativity, and triumph. My happiness was a choice and my joy the reward. And boy, did I want to inspire others to dream big, why not, right?

Looking back, I realize I have been the author of my story all along. Life's about pursuing your dreams, making friends you can count on, and kicking butt with purpose. Self-discovery? It's like a never-ending treasure hunt, and I'm here for every push and pull. So yeah, that's my childhood in a nutshell. It was a wild ride full of laughter, lessons, and dreams.

Who knew growing up could be so much fun? So, in the delightful journey of growing up from childhood, tweenhood, and teen hood, we can find ourselves amid laughter, lessons, and boundless dreams. Who could have imagined the path to adulthood is overflowing with such joyous adventures?

Hey there, kiddo. If all this tech stuff is not bringing you joy, it's okay to let it go. You can return your phone to your parents if it is stressing you out. Instead of scrolling through social media, why not let your imagination run wild in your backyard or bedroom?

You could create a universe of adventures or spend time enhancing your talents. Sometimes, real magic happens when we unplug and dive into the world around us. Next, accept your uniqueness and recognize your imperfections; when you do that, you will bring out the power within you. But then again, you must have the courage to believe in yourself.

To all the cherished souls starting on their journey, whether young or young at heart, remember this: within the orbit of your dreams lies the essence of your purpose. Encompass it with all your heart, for therein lies the magic that shapes destinies. Seek it, nurture it, and in the enchantment of fate, you shall not only find your dream but also discover the magnificence of your true unique self.

"Unleash your power of creativity to expose your potential."

Mama Carson

MISS KITSILANO 1971

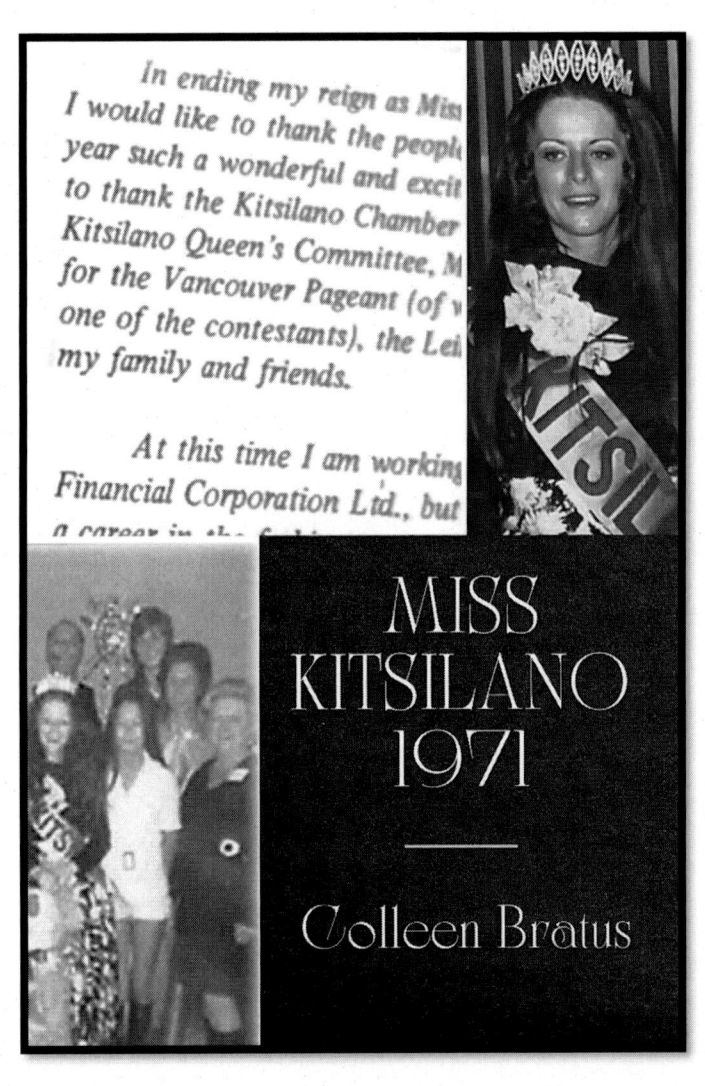

Colleen Bratus

> In ending my reign as Miss
> I would like to thank the peopl
> year such a wonderful and excit
> to thank the Kitsilano Chamber
> Kitsilano Queen's Committee, M
> for the Vancouver Pageant (of v
> one of the contestants), the Lei
> my family and friends.
>
> At this time I am workin
> Financial Corporation Ltd., but

Growing up, Colleen was fascinated with Miss America pageants. For a few years, they mesmerized her like a natural hold. She recalls watching the Miss America pageant on television for hours, entranced by contestants' glamorous dresses, sparkling smiles, and self-confident activities.

It had occurred to Colleen then how significant this interest was to her. Has there ever been a fantasy that you carried within your head and wished for with all your heart? For her, that meant being a beauty pageant winner.

She used to imagine she'd be walking down the runway in a beautiful dress and a glittering tiara with the universe at her back. It always stopped her in her tracks! When she was 11, she told her parents about her secret goal of one day being a beauty pageant winner, and they were incredibly encouraging.

In the ensuing decade, obstacles kept threatening to kill Colleen's dreams. But history kept ticking away the minutes, assembling a story to determine her destiny. And then, suddenly, her sister, an influential figure in the Kitsilano neighbourhood, came to be just the person she had dreamt of when she was young.

One day, my sister registered me in the Miss Kitsilano community queen competition: not a coincidence. It was an invitation I would never forget and set me on a path I'd never known. At first, I resisted jumping into something new that had always been my childhood hope. Though hesitant, I went deep inside myself and listened to myself. I had decided to steer my life in a new direction, in unknown waters.

Even though I was skeptical of standing on a pedestal, I felt the power of being alone in an effort to know myself. It wasn't about winning, I learned; it was about realizing a dream. So, I took it on more than I thought, and my sister got the biggest smile.

I was crowned Miss Kitsilano in 1971 and was delighted: joy filled me. The anticipation drove me to compete in Miss Vancouver, where I acted out the Romeo and Juliet death scene, earning a standing ovation and the Best Talent Award. Although I wasn't crowned Miss Vancouver, that didn't stop me. I instead entered the Ms. Sea Festival and finished 2nd.

My path to this was far more than trophies. It was a momentous turning point in my life, an opportunity to rebuild after a troubled relationship that had broken me. I was lifted by the idea of being victorious, the contestation, the anxiety of public speech, the glamour of the crown, and the liberty to dress up and act out my love for acting.

Beauty pageant wins made me more confident, and a competitive spirit inspired a spark of flame I had never known. Being able to express myself in front of an audience lifted me up, and fashion was my opportunity to display myself to the world. Acting allowed me to speak, feel, and connect with myself.

When I entered beauty pageants, I didn't know whether this was the best course of action in my recovery. It was an exploration of self-realization, power, and the liberating power of goal setting. The experience helped heal me and made me better and stronger.

While competing in these competitions, I saw how the women's movement and the press had begun questioning them. It was jarring to see that rather than celebrating women's diverse options and pathways, they started focusing on the bad side of the competition, disregarding choice and mentorship. It is also important not to forget that each woman has the right to be who she wants to be, and let's celebrate that rather than criticize it. After all, freedom means making our own choices without judgment or analysis.

The women's movement has struggled and succeeded in its quest for power and equality throughout history. Unfortunately, even now, many criticize the movement instead of accepting it. But instead of defying social norms and prejudices, society made it all the harder for women to do son.

This is particularly true in pageants where everyone else needs to be sensitive about the dedication, sacrifices, and work contestants go through to enter. But underneath the shiny lights of the theatre, a world of blood, sweat, and tears is invisible to everyone. Few of us realize just how many hours the competitors spend practicing, prepping, and preparing for their act. Beauty pageants changed my life. It allowed me to restore my narrative, rediscover my worth, and rediscover self-love in a disapproving world. It was a spiritual journey that allowed me to showcase my love, fight challenges and feel comfortable in the spotlight.

It was a time to celebrate diversity, honour the individual, and cherish every woman's story. Empowerment is not about forcing a single story but about celebrating all of the woman's life story. As glittering sisterhoods of womanhood, I welcomed the spirit of support for each other's visions and successes and removed the cloak of envy and the echo of childhood playground dreams.

We talk of solidarity, of supporting one another, but do we personify those ideals? Too often, I see wandering grasps of envy spin their way into our lives, overcoming hearts that should beat together, the envy of beauty, achievement, status, economic prosperity and natural talents. But take a deep breath, women, and ask yourself these questions: how can we women want to tear apart the walls of inequality in the rest of the world when, in our sacred circle, we don't do equality and appreciation?

Let us rewrite this narrative. Let each woman's achievement be a model of encouragement; each accomplishment is an expression of the infinite possibility we all possess. The ego will be replaced with respect, competition with cooperation, and polarization with cohesion.

Only through mutual empowerment, continuous determination, and celebration of each other's sparkle will we rise as equals, shining brightly into a world where every woman and girl can shine without the cloud of doubt or envy we impose upon ourselves.

ALTER EGO

A couple of years ago, Colleen's friend shared an unusual vision: to gather ten women of diverse ages and personalities and help them uncover their alter-egos through artistic expression. At first, the concept of an alter-ego seemed foreign, almost whimsical, to Colleen. But her curiosity stirred, and she agreed to join, embarking on a journey that would transform her perspective on identity and self-expression.

Ever feel like there's a version of yourself lurking just beneath the surface? The kind that doesn't overthink every little detail or worry about playing nice all the time? For Colleen, that version has a name: Colette. She's everything Colleen aspires to be and more. Colette isn't just a figment of her imagination; she embodies elegance, mystery, and fierce determination. Colette's French, of course, because if you're going to dream up an alter-ego, why not go all out?

Colette's captivating and poised, with a presence that stops people mid-sentence the moment she walks into a room. Similar to the younger version of Colleen, Colette's hair flows in soft, cascading waves, catching the light like it's twirled from rays of pure sunlight. Her eyes are a striking oceanic blue, calm yet intense, as though they've seen things most of us can't even begin to comprehend. And her style? Oh, it's straight out of a vintage Parisian dream: feathers, lace, and the kind of timeless sophistication that makes people stop and stare.

But Colette is so much more than her appearance. She didn't just show up fully formed one day. At first, she was a whisper in my ear, urging me to speak up, take risks, and stand my ground. When I'd hesitate or second-guess myself, there she'd be, nudging me forward. Over time, she grew louder and more assertive, eventually becoming a full-fledged part of me.

Colette doesn't overthink things; she acts. While I might weigh the pros and cons until the moment has passed, Colette sees a problem and dives in without hesitation. She's not impulsive; she's strategic, always playing the long game. She's the part of me that knows how to get things done without breaking a sweat. Colette has a sharp mind and a heart that beats for fairness and justice. She's no saint, but she's no pushover either.

Colette lives in Paris, at least in my mind. By day, she's the picture of poise and charm, gliding effortlessly through the upper echelons of society. She's a regular at art galleries and charity galas, where she dazzles everyone with her wit and warmth. People look at her and see her as a socialite, someone who enjoys the finer things in life without a care in the world. But that couldn't be further from the truth.

The daytime Colette is just the cover. By night, she transforms into something else entirely, a force of nature working behind the scenes to make the world a little more just. She's not loud or flashy about it;

her moves are subtle but impactful. While others shout into megaphones, Colette whispers into the right ears. She meets with people in shadowy corners, gathers the intel no one else can, and pulls strings that no one else even sees.

She doesn't crave the spotlight; she uses it. When Colette steps into a room, people pay attention. She knows how to steer conversations, guide decisions, and plant ideas that take root long after she's left. It's not about being manipulative; it's about being effective. Colette believes in amplifying voices that need to be heard, not stealing the stage for herself.

Her path to activism didn't start with grand gestures. It began quietly, almost unnoticeably. Colette saw injustice and acted one small step at a time. She's not the type to hold a sign and march down the Champs-Élysées, though she wouldn't rule it out if the cause called for it. No, Colette's methods are more shadowed. She's the one who gets behind the curtain, finds the levers of power, and pulls them just so. Her work isn't limited to politics or social causes; it's deeply personal, too.

Colette believes that change starts with individuals by listening to their stories and understanding their struggles. She doesn't rush in with solutions or platitudes. Instead, she takes the time to hear people out and know what they need, working tirelessly to make it happen. Her role as an actress plays into her mission beautifully. By day, she captivates audiences on stages around the Grand Boulevard. Her performances are legendary, earning standing ovations night after night. She's not just performing lines; she's creating stories that touch hearts and provoke thought. Backstage, the real work begins.

Colette mingles with theatre patrons, particularly those with influence: politicians, philanthropists, movers, and shakers. She charms them effortlessly, planting seeds of change in their minds without them even realizing it. She uses her art as a tool for advocacy, slipping truths into her scripts and sparking conversations that flow far beyond the theatre walls.

Colette's charm is her weapon, and she wields it masterfully. Where others see closed doors, she sees pathways and knows precisely how to open them. It's not always about grand accomplishments or big wins for Colette. Sometimes, her greatest triumphs are the quiet victories no one else sees. Helping someone find hope, ensuring a voice is heard, or setting a chain of events into motion that will lead to change years down the line are the things that fuel her.

Her loft in Paris is her sanctuary. I picture it as a cozy, yet stylish space filled with books, art, and mementos from her many adventures. It's here, away from the noise of the world, that she reflects and recharges. She finds solace in solitude, not because she's antisocial but because she knows the value of stepping back and refocusing.

Through Colette, I've learned the importance of those quiet moments. They're not a retreat; they're a reassessment. Colette doesn't see being alone as lonely; it's when she's at her most powerful. And honestly, it's a lesson I've taken to heart. Colette has taught me, above all else, that we're all capable of so much more than we give ourselves credit for. She's shown me that courage doesn't always roar and is not absent of fear. Sometimes, it's a whisper, a small, steady voice reminding me to keep going, keep trying, and believe in myself. And she's also reminded me that real power comes from knowing who you are and standing firm in that truth.

We all have a Colette inside us, waiting to come out. Maybe your alter-ego isn't a glamorous Parisian activist in vintage gowns. Perhaps they're a dreamer, a creator, a fighter, or a trailblazer in their own unique way. Whoever they are, they're there, waiting for you to give them a name, a story, a purpose. The beauty of an alter-ego isn't that they're separate from us; it's that they're a part of us, a reflection of our potential and our dreams. Colette is mine; through her, I've discovered parts of myself I didn't even know existed. She's my reminder to be bold, to act with intention, and never to underestimate my ability to make a difference.

So, who's your Colette? What's their name, their story, their purpose? Maybe they're already whispering to you, urging you to take that leap, to speak up, to be the version of yourself you've always wanted to be. Let them out. Let them guide you. You might be surprised at just how far they can take you. Your alter-ego is ready. Are you?

"A parent shows their child that empowerment is the courage to stand tall, be vulnerable, shed tears, and laugh joy."

Mama Carson

"Leading with courage isn't about having no fear,
it's about stepping up even when fear tries to hold you back."

Colleen C. Carson

Colleen's life chapters is a hold your interest exploration of how her life evolved over time. Colleen's life is a series of chapters, each lasting ten years. These chapters merge with the plots of her past and the promise of her new experiences.

Every chapter, she encounter familiar patterns and events, reminding her of where she has been and what she has learned. At the same time, each chapter brings fresh opportunities and challenges, shaping her in new and unexpected ways. As Colleen moved from one chapter to the next, she noticed the rhythms of life repeating milestones like graduations, career changes, relationships, achievements transformation. The past provided a comforting sense of continuity.

Yet, with each passing chapter, unique moments set it apart, whether discovering a new passion, an adventure, or facing unforeseen obstacles. These experiences deepened Colleen's journey, adding depth and meaning to her life story of self-discovery of ordinary moments becoming extraordinary memories.

The beauty of *'My Life Chapters"* lies a blend of the known and the unknown. It is about appreciating the journey and understanding that every ten-year span holds growth and transformation potential.

This perspective invited Colleen to reflect on where she had been, cherish her present, and look forward to her future with curiosity and hope. Each chapter is a tribute to her spirit, capable of strength and reinvention as her years unfolded.

CHILDHOOD/ADOLESCENCE
"The Butterfly Effect"

Let me start with my childhood; those first ten years are often filled with wonder and innocence. The excitement of noticing the world for the first time, the wonder of everyday objects, the school lesson, and the friends who started to shape my social consciousness. These were my cradles, that I grew into myself. The memories of those moments has reminded me of my innocence and wonder.

And then there was my teenage life between 10 and 20, a period of change and high emotion. It was an age of discovering myself and where I could fit in. I recall my adolescence; the thrills, the confusion, the first sip of independence. This was the chapter where I started creating myself and my ideology; at least that's what I thought. Looking back at this time helps me see how those early experiences and decisions still affect who I am, today.

I want to talk about my teenage years and what they did to me. I like to think of this chapter as the *"The Butterfly Effect"* because it's like the cocoon phase of a butterfly's life. I'd experienced a period of evolution; I was starting to see what I could be and where I could push the envelope. And each choice, experience, and friendship I made in those years was part of my discovery.

I had been awkwardly successful all through adolescence and young adulthood. I liked it but didn't because it was a period of exasperating development. Working through the pitfalls of friendship, competition, and public expectation, I finally found out who I wanted to be.

I found myself feeling agitated and rebellious, unlike the rest of my generation, I wanted to voice my views and take responsibility for myself. I was not rebellious just being true to myself. It was about figuring out where I was, who I was, and setting the stage for my life objective.

Then there is the delightful chaos of adolescence, the evidence that maturity was on the horizon. Take my period, for example. When it first arrived, I had mixed feelings. On one hand, I told myself it was a symbolic step towards womanhood. On the other hand, I was not ready to be, or even think of being, a woman.

It felt like a cruel joke, like being handed a job promotion before figuring out the basics of my role. I was annoyed that this momentous event had to happen before I felt willing or ready.

And then there was the awkward initiation into the world of bras. My first bra felt like an alien object invading my personal space, a constant reminder of the changes happening to my body. It was like an ongoing tug-of-war between me and this contraption. Bras still feel too confining, like a tiny straitjacket for my chest, that's why I haven't worn them too often. But the fun did not stop there. Adolescence was a parade of new, often bewildering introductions: nylons that had a vendetta against my legs, shoes with heels that turned walking into an extreme sport, and lipstick that made me feel like a kid playing dress-up.

Makeup was an entirely different beast, a mix of fascination and terror as I tried to master the art of not looking like a clown. Growing up had its benefits, though. There was a certain allure, the promise of becoming someone new and exciting. It was pretty cool and also incredibly frightening. It's like riding on a rollercoaster where you're both eager and scared. Every new experience was an oxymoron of "This is cool!" and "What have I done?"

I stumbled from childhood towards adulthood, one embarrassing, funny moment at a time. While some parts of me was still playing, the other part of me was getting ready for adulthood. The butterfly effect was my idea of the protection of my childhood cocoon leading into the significant actions of the unpredictable consequences of adulthood.

In Grade 12, there was a backdrop of growing curiosity; sex loomed as a compelling mystery. With my girlfriends already exploring this, the appeal was questionable. Johnnie was my boyfriend, and we decided to venture into this unfamiliar territory together. Our decision was not driven by social pressures or peer influences but rather by a genuine curiosity to understand the fuss.

Our initial experience left us both a little disappointed; we talked about why it was so massive for everybody. It was not the earth-shattering revelation we had anticipated but rather a quiet acknowledgment of newfound intimacy.

Over time, however, the allure grew, and we found ourselves drawn deeper into its embrace, exploring the mysteries of passion and desire. We were both definitely looking forward to exploring our new venture more.

On the one hand, I was thrilled about facing the new rules and the promise of independence. On the other hand, I was like, "Who made these rules anyway?" I did not want to follow the script of adolescence without questioning every line.

It was as if there was this unspoken agreement that I should start acting more maturely, while I was still holding on to my childhood with both hands, kicking and screaming.

In this chapter I was excited about the future, sure, but also ridiculously obstinate about following all those unwritten guidelines for growing up. Rules? Pfft. I had my own playbook, even if it was still under construction. But eventually I figured it out and began.

YOUNG ADULTHOOD
"Yours Truly Syndrome"

My young adulthood was the affliction where my dreams met reality, ambition met responsibility, and self-discovery met self-definition. By the way, I would call this chapter my twenties. It is a chapter where the hints of youth intermingle with the demands of maturity, where the lessons of the past unite with future aspirations.

Amid this time, I confronted my tendency to prioritize personal desires and goals over collective well-being. It was a balancing act between individual growth and communal harmony, where empathy, humility, and wisdom become guiding stars in the constellation of life's choices. Wow, that's sounds pretty good!

In this chapter, my journey through young adulthood was a whirlwind of ambition, achievement, but particularly independence. I adamantly pursued independence, energized by a burning desire to figure out my place in the world. Travel became my source of education and career choices, leading me down paths paved with determination, strength, and countless new adventures.

As I probed deeper into the stage of adulthood, the landscape of my life began to shift. New and intimate relationships blossomed, adding rich layers to the collections of my experiences. Amid the uncertainty and excitement about my future, I found myself standing at the crossroads of tradition and self-innovation.

Once I got it, I was in such a rush to start adulting that society thought I was already a senior citizen at the ripe old age of twenty-five when I got married. And when I finally welcomed my first little bundle of joy at thirty, the nurses were probably placing bets on when my CARP card would arrive. I have always been ahead of the game. Who needs a midlife crisis when you had a quarter-life crisis?

When I became an entrepreneur, wife, and mother which immersed me into the modern world's hectic rhythm, I remembered thinking: Am I losing myself? It was a foolish question, but at the time it felt valid. While I wore my titles like a badge of honour, there was a sense of unease within. Even with all the success on the surface, I was not free from the feeling I was drifting away from my real self.

This chapter of the *"Yours Truly Syndrome"* emphasizes sincerity, a genuine feeling of consciousness, casting a shadow over my sense of self. Caught in the vortex of society's expectations and my personal aspirations, I struggled with the absurdity of individuality versus responsibility. Was I pursuing these titles because society dictated them or because they were truly aligned with my deepest desires?

Reflecting on my journey, I realized that my quest for independence had led me down the path of soul-searching. Beneath the layers of badges and responsibilities, I unearthed the essence of my true identity, yours truly, a woman driven by passion, purpose, and a relentless pursuit of realism.

Finally, I realized that this chapter was a kind of maze of unexpected discoveries. It's not linear, like waves that bounce between light and shadow. Through it all, my one constant was the ability never to be anything other than myself, no matter how challenging or unexpected.

There were moments of clarity when everything made sense as if the missing piece was put in place. These are the times when I was most authentic and confident about my passions, values, and purpose. But there were also moments of doubt and confusion, where the road ahead looked cloudy and unsure. And it was in these moments that my determination was put to the test. In these moments of doubt, I found the strength I never knew I had.

This chapter was not just about getting there but about enjoying the ride, the hills, the plains, and everything in between. So, I navigated, and I did so with an excited heart and a mind that could accept the limitless possibilities that were to come. Every step brought me closer to myself and made me surrender to the perpetual work in progress.

ADULTHOOD
"The Realization Stage."

This chapter of my life was a decade of unexpected discoveries, encounters, or experiences: the thirties. It was a time when seemingly random events aligned in a way that brought about positive outcomes and opportunities, often leading to my personal growth, fulfillment, or newfound direction. During this chapter, I did stumble upon valuable insights, changes, and made meaningful connections I had not anticipated.

I directed unexpected changes and choices, each exposing a new layer of wisdom, flexibility, and strength. As a teacher and student relationship, I shared with my children, I started on a journey of mutual learning and growth. What began as a parent guiding her children soon evolved into a mutual exchange of knowledge and insight.

My children became my teachers, yet still my students, as I became their student, yet still their teacher. My children taught me invaluable lessons about perception, patience, unconditional love, and the beauty of simplicity, just a few to mention. I taught them integrity, confidence, perseverance, creativity, and most of all, kindness.

Amid the difficulties of family life, my marriage underwent pivotal changes. Choices regarding lifestyle and priorities in any relationship should be shared, yet this aspect of our life often felt one-sided, mostly favouring my husband's goals.

However, life had its plans, and one day, my husband departed, leaving us with little more than a handful of memories and a depleted bank account. In the face of adversity, I chose to shield my children from this harsh reality, spinning tales of their father's absence due to distant work commitments.

With financial constraints pressing down on me like a sumo wrestler, I became a master of innovation and resourcefulness. I had to kiss my beloved sports car goodbye to pay the bills, but I managed to keep the family car to avoid resorting to a unicycle and the next life-altering welfare cheque. I knew change was necessary.

I took a daring leap of faith, armed with sheer determination and a cupboard full of pots. After placing a modest $10 advertisement in the local paper, I launched a catering business and turned adversity into an opportunity, one delicious dish at a time.

Yet, during this chapter, the chaos of external changes, my body underwent its transformation. Early menopause, yes, you heard me right, early can sometimes be too early; this brought with it a mix of relief and uncertainty.

The unexpected became an opportunity for growth, a catalyst for taking a chance on fate. With all its uncertainties and unpredictability, life became a stage where I could highlight my strength, courage, and determination. Every challenge and surprise allowed me to prove my depth and adaptability.

On this journey, I understood that life cannot be controlled or organized totally. Instead, it mirrors a delicate dance with self-determination and fate, where we learn to move with the unpredictable and predictable of events. We often find ourselves navigating through uncharted territories, uncertainties, and mastering the art of adapting to whatever life presents.

I came to the realization that fate, is a force that propels you forward. It is not something you can drive; it drives you. *"The Realization Stage"* was both humbling and enlightening. It taught me to welcome the unexpected and enjoy life's surprises. Instead of resisting the unknown, I started to see it as a vast landscape of possibilities waiting to be explored.

Accepting this resulted in a shift in my outlook. I began to expect the unexpected, welcome it with open arms, and see every unforeseen event as a chance to grow and discover new aspects of myself.

This chapter was about my mindset transforming my approach to life. I no longer saw uncertainty as something to fear but part of my own story. It's not about controlling every aspect of my journey but finding strength in my ability to adapt and thrive amid the chaos. I continue to create a life full of unexpected wonders and endless possibilities.

Each fateful moment became a part of my story, a witness to the power of life's beauty of the predictable and unpredictable.

PRE-MIDDLE AGE
"My Passion, My Purpose"

The thing about my forties was that it was a chapter that could hit everyone differently. I call it "My Passion, My Purpose" because it's when you stop playing by other people's rules and start defining success and self-worth on your own terms, or you try to change them. I decided it was time to go all in, no distractions, no excuses. And you know what? It worked.

My business finally took off. For the first time, I was making money that I could actually feel proud of, the kind of money that made me stop and say, "I earned this." Oh, and let me tell you, I was 43 at the time.

So, let's cut through the noise about how it's "too late" once you hit your forties. That's nonsense. Your forties isn't the end; it's the beginning. But here's the deal: you've got to be focused. Life isn't going to hand you success just because you want it. You have to block out the distractions and get clear about what matters.

Still, doubting and overthinking? Let me recite to you some names: Vera Wang didn't start her fashion empire until her forties. She didn't even design her first dress until she was in her forties. Sam Walton, have you ever heard of Walmart? He's the guy behind Walmart and was well into his forties before he hit his stride.

Julia Child? The Chef we all adore. She didn't start cooking until her late thirties and didn't become a household name until her fifties. Icons like Ruth Bader Ginsburg, a legend on the Supreme Court; Lucille Ball, an absolute icon; Maya Angelou, poet and journalist extraordinaire; Henry Ford, Ford Motors; Carl Sagan, science genius and even Barack Obama, President of the United States, all reached incredible heights during or after their forties. These people didn't wait for some magical moment; they created it.

For me, something shifted during this chapter. My passions took on a new shape. Family and my parents became my priorities. It wasn't just about caring for them; it was about caring for myself, which I hadn't done nearly enough.

Self-care wasn't just a trendy term; it became a lifeline. I learned that confidence wasn't just about how I looked or what I achieved; it was about knowing my worth. And here's the thing: my work and personal life weren't separate boxes. They were intertwined, each feeding the other. If I wasn't happy and fulfilled at home, my work would suffer, and vice versa.

That's when financial independence became more than just a goal; it had become a passion. I started seeing money differently, not as something to chase but as something to manage wisely. Budgeting and saving weren't about restrictions; they were about freedom. I planned for retirement, built long-term security, and created a stable foundation for the future.

For the first time, I felt like I was in control of my financial destiny. This sense of power and security was empowering. Of course, life wasn't all smooth sailing. I was married to a man who didn't see the future the way I did. He wasn't a forward-thinker, and that created a lot of stress.

I had to face the hard truth: I couldn't change his mindset. What I could do was take control of my journey. It was terrifying at first, but giving up on my dreams? That wasn't an option.

I focused on what I could control: my decisions and my actions and started making smart moves for my health, happiness, and prosperity. It wasn't easy, but it was worth it. Building a life, I loved for myself, and my children became my driving force. This journey didn't just change how I saw myself; it also changed how I saw relationships.

I noticed something interesting among my single friends: they stopped dating "fixer-uppers." My girlfriends were especially done with partners who drained their energy instead of adding value to their lives. They wanted a real relationship built on mutual respect and shared goals. And you know what? That inspired me.

I started asking myself some tough questions about my own marriage. Was I okay staying in a relationship that wasn't growing?

Or did I want a partnership where we could evolve together, intellectually and emotionally?

These weren't easy questions, but they were necessary. Eventually, I sat down with my husband and had an honest conversation. I laid it all out: my hopes, my dreams, my vision for the future. I told him we needed to grow together, to challenge and support each other, or we were going to drift apart. It wasn't an easy task; it was something I had to do; years later, our marriage ended in divorce.

Through all of this, I learned the importance of prioritizing myself, not in a selfish way, but in a way that acknowledged my happiness as the foundation for everything else. I picked up hobbies, learned new skills, and even found time to relax (a miracle). That self-focus brought a calmness and clarity that flowed through every part of my life.

The chapter was about living my passions and knowing my purpose. It's about creating a life you love in the everyday moments, taking control of your story, and refusing to settle for less than what you deserve. This chapter wasn't just about surviving your forties; it was about thriving in them. And trust me, the best chapters are still ahead.

MIDDLE AGE
"Rewrite Your Story"

The fifties was the chapter to "Rewrite Your Story." It was the chapter when everything seemed to slow down yet speed up simultaneously. You've probably already carved out your spot in the world: career, family, and community.

You've got a few titles that define you, like "Parent," "Professional," "Entrepreneur," "Leader," or even "Caregiver." Those titles felt like everything you needed for a while, but here's the thing: the road ahead doesn't stay smooth for long. It starts to shift, and you feel it.

Sometimes, it hits you like a quiet wave. You're unsure where you're going but know something's changing.

At some point, you start reflecting on your life, your choices, the paths you've taken, and the moments you've missed. You've learned so much along the way, yet there's a nagging feeling that some of it got lost in the shuffle of life.

The distractions, the responsibilities, the roles you've played. It's easy to ignore that you've lived for others more than for yourself. But now, I had the power to change that. It's time to ask, "What about me?"

I remember feeling that pull. For me, it came in the middle of a busy life. A successful catering and event business. A house is full of teenagers. A life filled with love and challenges, growth and setbacks. But somewhere along the way, I started wondering if this was it. Suppose this was all there was.

I wanted more, more for me. And that's when I started thinking about finding my voice, doing something that wasn't just about caring for everyone else. I needed to look inward and search for something meaningful for myself.

It wasn't easy. My family was growing up, and I felt I was still trying to hold everything together. There were days when the pressure felt unbearable: marriage, kids, business, health. But despite it all, I found clarity in the chaos. The challenge wasn't about changing everything; it was about finding a new way to look at what I had, acknowledging the wisdom I'd gained, and finally listening to what my heart was trying to say.

You see, this isn't just about a midlife crisis. It's not the cliché of someone suddenly acting half their age or making reckless decisions. It's a deeper, quieter reckoning. It was a time when I began to question if the life I had built was the life I wanted to keep living.

Don't get me wrong, I loved my life, but I knew something was missing.

It wasn't about throwing everything away but rethinking what I wanted to do with the time I had left. It was that moment when I realized I spent so much time living for others, fulfilling expectations, and keeping everything afloat. I had lost sight of my own dreams. But as I began prioritizing my dreams, I felt a sense of liberation and hope for the future.

I remembered my twenties when the world seemed full of endless possibilities. When was I excited, ready to take on the world, explore new opportunities, and chase after my biggest dreams? But somewhere along the way, life took over. Responsibilities piled up, and suddenly, I was in my fifties, asking, "What happened to all those dreams?" This realism sparked a journey of self-discovery and personal growth, making me more introspective and contemplative.

That's when it hits. The realism that while raising kids, paying bills, and ensuring everyone else was happy, I forgot to check in with myself. Now, in my fifties, I'm standing on the edge of something new, asking if it's too late to pick up those pieces and rewrite my story.

Here's the truth: it's never too late. Seriously. I didn't have to stay stuck in the roles I had been playing. Life doesn't follow a set timeline. Just because it seems like everyone else has their life figured out by a certain age doesn't mean I had to.

There's always room to course-correct, rediscover your passions, and make changes that align with who you are now, not who you were when you were trying to meet everyone else's expectations. The one thing I knew was I loved my children, but I didn't know whether my story needed a rewrite.

I'm not saying it's easy. It's messy, and it can be overwhelming. But it's real. And it's possible. You don't have to have it all figured out, but you need to take a moment, maybe a big one, and ask yourself,

"What's next?" It doesn't matter if you're fifty, sixty, or seventy. Life is full of opportunities to redefine your story, find new dreams, and put yourself first for once.

This chapter was not about a crisis. It was about growth, renewal, and the courage to change direction when the road ahead doesn't look like you imagined. Don't be afraid to rewrite your story because, in the end, it's your story to tell. And the best part? The chapters are still waiting to be written.

RETIREMENT
"The Seenager"

This chapter is, hands down, Colleen's favourite chapter in life, but it didn't start that way. It began as a weight of grief; one she could barely breathe under. However, over the course of a few years, and with the help of a group of strong, incredible women, Colleen found herself in a space where she could begin to write this chapter of fun, adventure, and love.

What was once suffocating sorrow has transformed into a jubilant celebration of life. And let's say it's been one fabulous, freedom-filled chapter Colleen never saw coming.

She'd say it's like she took the energy of her teenage years; the wild, carefree spirit, and blended it with her hard-earned wisdom. What resulted is what she likes to call the "Seenager" stage. She's got that youthful fire, but now it's tempered with the knowledge of a life well-lived, and it's pure magic.

It's not just a stage; it's a reinvention or for her, a rebirth, a reimagining of what it means to live boldly, openly, and joyfully. Colleen had become a maestro at connecting people, emotions, thoughts, and the kind of random trivia that makes her like a walking, talking TED Talk, only with punchlines that make people laugh.

Gone are the days of shuffling around with a cane, something Colleen couldn't even picture herself using. In its place? Speed walking. She's quick and on the move, some of her fellow Seenagers even rock a pair of rollerblades. Colleen tried them once but quickly decided they weren't her style. As for the old rocking chair? Oh, no. Could you imagine? Colleen in an old rocking chair, gently swaying in the breeze?

Not even for a second. Colleen doesn't do rocking chairs; instead, she's rocking the nightlife of Vancouver. Why settle for a slow, gentle sway when you can feel the wind whipping through your hair at 80 km/h on a motorcycle? Oh yeah, safety concerns? Pfft. Seenagers don't have time for those kinds of worries. Colleen feels like a brand-new version of herself; one that doesn't even feel a day over fifty.

Let's talk about the wardrobe, because, trust me, this is important. I remember the days when older women would rock those dowdy elastic-waist pants and what I like to call "grandma blouses." You know, the ones are all flowy and not in a good way. Thank goodness those are now consigned to the donation bin where they belong! I'm not about that life anymore.

I still remember the pure joy of discovering "Forever 21." It was like I hit the fashion jackpot! The clothes were amazing, and the style? It was made for everyone, from teens to Seenagers like me. I could not believe I found a store that actually had things that fit my vibe!

I came home that day and excitedly told Crystal all about it. She couldn't help but laugh, then dialed up her friend and said, "My mom is 61 going on 21; I love it." I was laughing, too, but honestly, she wasn't wrong! But that wasn't all. Then came my next fashion revelation: yoga pants and athleisure wear. Oh yes, these were game changers. Who says you can't be comfy and stylish at the same time? Not me, that's for sure.

The best part? As a Seenager, I'd earned the right to rock that look, physically and mentally flexing. It's like accepting both comfort and confidence in one go.

And while we're on the subject of shaking things up, let's talk about intimacy: sweet, glorious intimacy. This one really surprised me. The truth is, I wasn't prepared for intimacy to be as revolutionary.

There's no more worrying about surprise pregnancies. Nope. I had unlocked the "freedom pass" of intimacy. It's like being 18 again, without all the awkward fumbling and curfews. Instead, there's this desire to explore the deeper sensuality of sexuality, unburdened by the constraints of youth.

As a Seenager, it's like being a rebellious teenager with a VIP pass to life. I've been there and done that, and now I'm creating my own rules. This time, I come armed with the glorious benefit of hindsight.

I've been around the block a few times, and I'm not just winging it anymore; I've got a roadmap to guide me. Independence? I've got that down to an art form. Freedom? Oh, sweetheart, I practically wrote the book on it; actually, I did: SHE HER ME. And wisdom? It's dripping off me like honey on a hot biscuit.

I don't anticipate new experiences; I curate them. I no longer wait for life to surprise me; I seek out those joy, growth, and adventure moments. Society's rules? Please. I've seen those, and frankly, some of them are laughable. Some rules I've followed because they still make sense.

But the ones that don't serve me anymore? Straight to the shredder. I'm not just living; I'm orchestrating a symphony of fabulousness. Society may think that aging means slowing down, but as a Seenager I am living proof that life after 60 isn't ordinary; it's extraordinary.

To me this chapter was about rebirth. No, I had no dramatic epiphany while meditating under a waterfall. My rebirth came after something far more unexpected, more heartbreaking, and, in a strange way, more transformative: the passing of my son. My world flipped upside down instantly, and I was forced to navigate a new life. I was thrust into a space where survival meant piecing together the pieces of a shattered heart. It was a painful process of shedding the old Colleen and asking myself, "Who am I now?"

Enter Mama Carson. That's right, Mama Carson. When we went to events, Crystal introduced me as her mom, but then, one evening, someone called me "Mama Carson," and something about that stuck. It felt like a symbol of the fresh, sassy dimension I was living, even if it wasn't exactly part of my original plan. I was Mama Carson, a woman who had transformed through pain, love, and a whole lot of living.

Now, let's talk about the big question: What's the difference between a Seenager and a teenager? Well, first off, we've got monthly allowances that last forever. Yep, pensions and social security are like the ultimate life hack.

It's not the lottery, but enough to keep the wine rack stocked and the caviar cooling, which is very important. And then there's the "no more surprise pregnancies" perk, which is the gift that keeps giving. It's like Mother Nature's parting gift for all the years of hormonal chaos I survived. And let's not forget the dating scene.

 I never thought I'd return to the dating world after my marriage ended, but life had other plans. I didn't just jump into dating for fun; at first, I did it because I needed to update my book, The Guyed Book. With the encouragement of a close group of women and my daughter, I ventured into the world of dating once again.

Being a Seenager means I could date whoever I wanted, and no explanations are needed. Age is just a number, sweetheart. Swipe left, swipe right; it's my world, and everyone else lives in it. My venture into dating was fun and even stimulating. It wasn't just for the sake of romance; it was learning more about myself in the process. Through charming dates, cringe-worthy duds, and hilarious encounters, I rediscovered a spark of romance I believed had been extinguished.

As for my social circle? The petty dramas of high school were long gone, and I had no time for them. I'm too busy living my best life. I've also become an expert at distinguishing between the two kinds of fear: the kind that keeps you from trying new things and the kind that keeps you from petting a grizzly bear. Spontaneity is my middle name. Feel like booking a last-minute trip to the island? Done.

Want to go yachting on a Tuesday? Why not? I have ditched the script of old age, and now, I'm writing my own plot twists. Every failure is a stepping stone to greatness. Every moment is an opportunity to create joy.

So, here's to rebirth. Here's to welcoming the Seenager chapter with open arms and a full heart. Whether it's speed walking, dancing, connecting, or simply letting yourself dream again, do it with passion. Life has a funny way of surprising us when we least expect it, and sometimes, those surprises are exactly what we need.

Being a Seenager isn't just a phase; it's a mindset. It's about ditching the rulebook and living life on your own terms. It's about finding joy in the little things, laughing at life's absurdities, and savouring every delicious moment. So, grab your rollerblades, hop on that motorcycle, or go for a walk around the seawall. This chapter is yours for the taking, and trust me, you'll have fun.

THE SENIOR
"The Dawn of Twilight"

The dawn of twilight, much like the journey of being a senior, symbolizes a gentle transition from the vibrancy of youth to the wisdom of age. It is Colleen's time when the intensity of her life softens, yet the light still shines, casting a warm, reflective glow on all that has come before her.

In this stage of Colleen's life, calm arises from understanding the past while welcoming an exciting openness to what lies ahead. Colleen has learnt it is neither the sharp clarity of youth nor the complete stillness of old age but a beautiful in-between where experience and anticipation harmonize.

Like twilight, Colleen being a senior invites us to find beauty in the fading moments and cherish the quiet potential of what is yet to unfold. It's her time to honour the lessons of the past while looking forward with grace, curiosity, and peace. The twilight of life is Colleen's masterpiece laced from memories and hope, creating a thoughtful sense of serenity and wisdom.

I've found myself reflecting on life in my seventies, looking back at the wonders I've experienced, while also coming to terms with the fact that death's finality is inevitable. When I was younger, I imagined this decade as a time of endless wisdom and peace, where everything would fall into place with ease.

Well, now that I'm here, I've realized that I was one of those mysteries life was unfolding. Life is kind of like yin and yang. The things that seem like opposites are really two halves of the same whole, each one shaping the other, both ordinary and extraordinary at the same time.

Living my seventies has been a silent journey of self-discovery. I often look back at the experiences that shaped me: the triumphs, the struggles, the wonders, and opportunities along the way. Those moments of reflection taught me more about life and myself than I could've imagined. The mistakes I used to agonize over are now lessons that guide me with a sense of wisdom. And yes, even now, I still make mistakes!

One thing I've really come to appreciate is the journey itself. When we're young, we're so focused on the destination, but now that I've got more years behind me than ahead of me, I've learned to savour the moments. I find joy in simple things: my morning coffee, a peaceful walk, laughter with my loved ones, especially Donald and Crystal.

These moments remind me that every day holds beauty if you're willing to look for it. It's so easy to miss the small things when you're in a rush. But when you slow down, life reveals its little treasures. Whether it's a quiet evening, the sound of birds outside, or just a smile shared with a stranger, these moments are what make life rich.

I've also learned that growth doesn't stop, even as we age. There's always more to learn, new things to try, and ways to give. Even now, in my seventies, I'm still pushing myself, whether it's exploring a new hobby, learning a new app, or sharing in a thought-provoking conversation. It keeps my mind sharp and my spirit vibrant.

Taking care of my health has become second nature, even with the aches and pains that come with age. Each little ache reminds me of all the adventures I've had and the full life I've lived. I no longer feel shy about my body; I've come to appreciate its strength and endurance, and the unique beauty that comes with it. Sure, our teeth may not always be our own, but my smile still says it all: genuine, joyful, and full of life.

You might roll your eyes when I talk about the "good old days," but one day, you'll look back at your own memories with the same fondness. And when it comes to love, it's not just about how it's felt or that someone exists; it's about being kind and compassionate in a world that truly needs it.

I might not move as fast as I used to, but why rush? Life's not a race; it's about soaking it all in. So, take your time. Stop and breathe in the moments. When people ask me what it's like to get older, I say, "You're both liberated and a little imprisoned."

Aging brings the freedom to be yourself, speak your mind, and live authentically, but it also brings the limitations of a body and sometimes a mind that doesn't move like it used to. But within those limits, there's beauty, a reminder that every moment is precious.

And let's be honest: there are things I wish I could still do, like running a marathon or climbing a mountain. But I've come to understand that life's not about chasing what you once did, but welcoming what's here, now. I may not run as fast, but I sure can still walk with purpose, and that's enough.

I've been thinking about death more lately, or maybe it feels like death's been thinking about me. Oddly enough, I'm not scared by it because, like so many things, once you understand it, it's easier to accept. Time feels more precious now, and I've learned to value the days that have passed, recognizing that they were well-lived. In my present, I try to be mindful of my actions and thoughts, cherishing what I've accomplished and living with the question, "Will I see tomorrow?"

I accept aging as long as I keep my mind young and my spirit vibrant. I believe in that, especially the importance of a youthful mind. I remember my mom in her seventies, sorting through her treasures, deciding who would get what.

At first, I didn't get it, but it turned out she was thinking about the future; about the time when memory might fade. It's something we all think about in our seventies, but those thoughts don't control us. They just pop up now and then.

Like my mom passing on her treasures and like me writing my memoir for my loved ones, it's all part of leaving something behind, a legacy, a reminder of who we are and what we've experienced. My mom lived to ninety-seven, and although she had dementia at the end, her legacy lived on. So, if you ask me about the seventies, I'd say it's a time of reflection and an awareness that life's short, but our memories can last forever.

Writing this book is my way of ensuring that the essence of who I am lives on, for Crystal, Donald, and the others I hold dear. It's my gift to them, a piece of me that remains, no matter what the future holds. The wisdom that comes with age is something to be cherished and passed on.

So, here's something to think about: "Decades, Eras, or Chapters (however you want to call the past years) from now, will you regret what you didn't do, or will you be thrilled about what you did?" Take your time, appreciate what you've experienced, and welcome the wisdom that comes with age. Life's a journey, meant to be savoured at every step. As I continue down this path of life, I want to walk with grace, gratitude, and a deep appreciation for every moment that makes my life extraordinary. Every day is a gift, and every moment is an opportunity to create memories that will endure. So, let's live with a heart full of gratitude and let our lives be a tribute to living fully and joyfully.

If you're wondering about the later years, know this: they're a time for reflection, a time to appreciate the wisdom we've gained. These years aren't an end; they're a beautiful beginning, a time to embrace the extraordinary in the ordinary. So, welcome the later chapters of life with an open heart, because there's so much more to discover and enjoy in the miracle that is life.

"MIGHTY SWORD"

In shadows deep, where ignorance reigns,
Injustice thrives, and deceit remains.
A distant dream, a flickering light,
Amid the madness of the night.

The ignorant wield their power with ease,
Blind to the pain they cause, they seize.
Upon the vulnerable, and the weak,
Their callous hearts, others dare not speak.

But in the sage of knowledge gleams,
Justice rises, ousting toxic schemes.
Of beings who hide behind their cloak,
In ignorance, where truth has choked.

In lands where whispers fade and shadows sneak,
An oppressive hand enforces rules to sheep.
Under the authority of a dictator's reign,
Hope battles to break free from their chains.

For knowledge is the mighty sword,
Against injustice, and justice restored,
Empowering those who seek its light.
Where truth is courage and our might,
We stand against our darkest knight.

Colleen C. Carson

"Maturity starts with discomfort."

Mama Carson

"Magic lies where wonder meets wisdom, revealing the extraordinary in the ordinary."

Colleen C. Carson

Colleen was a Hershey. With her proper V-neck sweaters, neat A-line skirts, and polished Hershey's shoes, she belonged to a group known for their excellent behavior and sharp appearance. Life as a Hershey meant playing by the rules, blending in, and keeping a safe distance from trouble. At least until she met her namesake.

This other Colleen, a Greaser through and through, was the embodiment of rebellion. She strutted through the halls with an air of defiance, her leather jacket and slicked-back hair starkly contrasting the tidy Hershey's. While they couldn't have been more different, something about the other Colleen intrigued her. In a world where fitting into a group was survival, the two Colleens formed a bond that defied high school's rigid social structures. Despite the judgmental stares and whispered gossip, they became an unlikely pair.

It wasn't long before the gossip hounds of the school went rogue: my Greaser Colleen was pregnant. The cries escalated, and soon, the whole school turned against her. Even her closest Greaser friends vanished, abandoning her when she needed the most support. I, however, stood firm. I felt an overwhelming sadness for my friend and refused to walk away. No matter what the others said, my loyalty was strong.

Life's cruel timing, though, tossed another wrench into our narrative. Colleen, a friend of mine, miscarried. She returned to school, holding her head high despite the whispers and stares of people who had disowned her. Her so-called friends from the Greasers? They were long gone, and she wasn't about to beg for their approval.

She was searching for something more, something real. As rumors swirled and threats simmered, my friend Colleen began to form a new identity, one not tied to any group or label. We grew closer still, finding solace in the simplicity of our friendship. We understood one another in a way few could, our hearts beating in unison despite the differences that had once set us apart.

But high school isn't a place where friendships like this go unnoticed. The tension between the Hershey's and Greasers hadn't just disappeared, it was about to explode. One day, the walls seemed to close in as a warning spread like wildfire. The Greaser gang, the group that had once embraced my friend, Colleen, was planning something.

Threats echoed in the school corridors, and fear worried me. Worried, I approached my friend, Colleen, desperate for advice. "Can't you stop this?" I asked, my voice trembling. My friend, Colleen, shook her head. "No, I can't," she said with brutal honesty. "But you can stand up for yourself. Fight, or they'll make your life hell." It wasn't the answer I'd hoped for, but it was the only one I got. I felt trapped, terrified to confide in anyone else.

As the moment of confrontation drew nearer, my friend, Colleen, handed me a comb, a simple item, but in the Greaser world, it was more than just for fixing hair. The comb's teeth had been sharpened like tiny blades, symbolizing toughness. I grasped it, the cold metal pressing into my palm, and a flood of courage came with it. Now, I would face the Greasers, come what may.

Behind the school, the showdown began in the silence of a secluded spot. The Greaser gang circled me, taunting, closing in. I could feel their breath, hatred, and eagerness to break me. But just as they were about to strike, a voice cut through the tension like a knife. "You fight her, you fight me."

It was my friend, Colleen: the Greaser with a heart of gold. She had come, bringing her own small crew. The gang leader hesitated, thrown off by the unexpected support. My friend's fierce loyalty stood like a shield, deflecting the attack. The Greasers backed down; their determination shaken.

The battle never happened. I had been spared a brutal confrontation, but what I gained that day was far more than safety. I had learned what true courage meant. My friend Colleen assured me the next day, "They won't bother you again." When I asked why she had stepped in after saying she wouldn't, she replied with quiet wisdom: "If you let fear control you, you'll never have the freedom to be who you want to be."

Those words stayed with me long after graduation. High school ended, and we eventually drifted apart as life took us in different directions. Time passed, and one day, as if by fate, our paths crossed again. We sat together, reminiscing about the wild days of high school, about the bond that had carried us through.

Two weeks later, tragedy struck. The rebellious, brave-hearted Colleen was gone, lost in a house fire. The shock was unbearable. The reunion we had shared had been our last. But my friend Colleen's legacy lives on, etched in the corridors of our high school, my heart, and in the memories of those who knew her. True friendship is a haven where authenticity thrives, freed from the chains of social expectations. It's where vulnerability is celebrated, not shunned. In our friendship, we had found that rare refuge from judgment, a place where we could be unapologetically ourselves.

My defiant friend, Colleen, taught me more than just how to stand up for myself. She taught me how to confront my terrors with brutal honesty and live with the kind of freedom only courage could provide. In a world filled with pretence and superficiality, Colleen helped me remember that being who you really are is the ultimate act of courage.

Though she was taken too soon, her laughter, fierce loyalty, and friendship live on. My friend Colleen's story whispers in moments of doubt and challenge, urging others to be brave, to stand tall, and to never let fear dictate our lives. Hers is a story of kindness, bravery and the lasting force of human touch.

And I still think about her now and then, making me smile constantly. Just two girls caught up in the whirlwind of high school, we proved to the world (and ourselves) that friendship can outsmart labels and cliques. We broke the mold in a place where fitting in seemed like everything.

We proved that connection transcends appearances, and that loyalty and courage define friendship far more than the clothes you wear or the crowd you run with. Through her, I learned that the most valuable friendships aren't always the ones that come easy but the ones that challenge you to grow, to stand up, and to be your most authentic self.

Our story is proof that even in the chaotic world of school culture, where external pressures often shape identities, friendship has the power to rise above it all. It doesn't conform, it doesn't judge—it simply embraces, protects, and uplifts. That is a lesson I carry with me to this day: the bonds we create in life are not defined by what others see but by the shared moments of truth and courage shaping who we become.

"LIGHTNING POWER"

In the heart of London, the air was filled with excitement as Colleen and her girlfriends began a spontaneous journey to Dublin, Ireland. The idea was to hitchhike their way down through the beautiful landscapes of southern England, exploring little towns along the way.

Their destination, however, was set in the vibrant city of Dublin. They put their backpacks on their shoulders and the fire of adventure in their hearts and headed off down the backroad. They travelled through small towns, each charming in their own way. It lay in green fields and small cottages in the open country before them.

Heading south, we came upon the ancient town of Dover, with its imposing White Cliffs looming over the English Channel. Our course took an unexpected turn in Dover, a ferry ride bridging the gap between England and Ireland awaited us. Onboard, we encountered four older gentlemen, their warmth matching the pleasant Irish breeze.

Striking up conversations, we learned about their lives and shared stories of our adventures. Laughter pulsated through the ferry cabin, creating a friendship that surpassed the boundaries of age and background. As the ferry glided over the gentle waves, the four gentlemen, now fast friends, extended an invitation to visit them in Manchester.

Big Al, the pleasant giant of the group, insisted we look them up if our travels brought us to the bustling city. His eyes twinkled with genuine kindness as he assured us, we would find a warm welcome and a place to stay. The ferry docked in Dublin, and as we bid farewell to our newfound friends, we promised to keep their invitation in mind. The city unfolded before us; history, culture, lively energy collections and even a ghost here and there. Dublin's cobblestone streets guided us through the heart of the city, where the sounds of music and laughter mingled in the air.

Days turned into nights as we immersed ourselves in the rhythm of Dublin's heartbeat. The vibrant pubs, Irish stew, the friendly locals, and the rich memories of Irish hospitality welcomed us. Amid it all, the memory of Big Al and his companions lingered in our minds, a promise of warmth and friendship awaiting us in Manchester. Our enthralling journey pressed forward, unfolding like a vivid culture as we navigated the emerald landscapes of Ireland. Each rolling hill, displayed in a lush green cloak, seemed to whisper tales of ancient mystique and untold adventures.

Ireland unfolded before us from Dublin to Belfast like a breathtaking panorama of beauty. Our ventures led us to the storied town of Killarney, where a castle steeped in history had been transformed into a hostel. Unbeknownst to us, the ancient stones sheltered ghostly inhabitants, and we confronted the eerie presence of ghostly guests on that solitary night within its walls. The caretakers, absent until the early morning, left us to navigate the haunted corridors, locked in a ghostly embrace of the unknown.

Our stay in Belfast took an unexpected turn, deviating into the laughter of friendship with law enforcement. A night that began with our arrests ended in a surprising twist as the constables on duty became hosts, entertaining and feeding us within the confines of the jail. The night, once uncertain, transformed into a fantastic experience of connection with the kind-hearted custodians of the law.

Hitchhiking through Ireland was an adventure unique unto itself. Though scarce in passing cars, the winding roads sounded the rhythmic clopping of horse-drawn carts. Our journey took on a leisurely pace as we hitched rides on these charming carts, turning what would have been a swift journey into a prolonged trip.

The delay, however, followed us to savor the countryside's enchantment, creating memories that united themselves into an extraordinary expedition. The air in Ireland was heavy with the scent of blooming flowers and the bittersweet aroma of saying goodbye. As we said our farewells to Ireland's lush landscapes, Irish hearts of kindness, and enchanting beauty, we were filled with anticipation for the next chapter of our journey. The thought of returning to London excited us, but it was the invitation to Manchester that truly intrigued us.

Upon our arrival in London, we could not shake the possibility of Manchester. We decided to start our journey to Manchester with hopes the gentlemen who extended their invitation were genuine in their intentions. The thrill of the unknown lingered in the air as we traveled through the bustling city, eager to uncover the mysteries awaiting us. In Manchester, a phone call connected us with one of the gentlemen who expressed genuine excitement at our arrival. Minutes later, a sleek Jaguar pulled up, driven by our host for the evening. I cannot remember his name for the world of me; I remember his warm smile as he welcomed us and chauffeured us to his luxurious nightclub, a haven of luxury and vibrant energy.

Inside the nightclub, he treated us to a feast fit for royalty. The night unfolded with laughter, fine cuisine, and crystal glasses clinking. As the clock struck midnight, he casually mentioned we would be staying at his penthouse for the night, a gesture that left us in awe of his hospitality. The following day, we woke up and went to a plush hotel restaurant for breakfast. He had organized the gathering, and as we entered the restaurant, we were greeted by the sight of the other three gentlemen already seated with drinks in hand.

Laughter and friendship filled the air as we exchanged stories and memories, once again forming even stronger bonds exceeding mere acquaintances' boundaries. Then Big Al, with his charismatic manner, announced we were welcome to stay at his place for as long as we pleased. Grateful and excited, we bid farewell to the other three gentlemen at the hotel.

Suddenly, a silver Rolls-Royce chauffeured to perfection, rolled up and parked in front of Big Al and my girlfriends. The excitement increased as Big Al chuckled and motioned for us to enter the luxurious vehicle. The chauffeur held the doors open for us, and with hearts pounding, we started on a drive that would lead us to Big Al's extravagant estate.

Half an hour into the drive, the Rolls-Royce stopped magnificently before massive black gates that flung open to greet us. The driver drove us along a long driveway dotted with trees and flowers to a mansion that demonstrated luxury. We had arrived at Big Al's mansion, a pre-dream transformed into reality.

With infectious excitement, we crossed the threshold into Big Al's home, eager to unravel the mysteries. The welcoming hug of his beautiful wife, Emma, greeted us at the door, setting the tone for a memorable stay. Emma's warmth radiated as she ushered us through their home, highlighting its grandeur and inviting charm before leading us to our bedrooms to prepare for an evening of delight.

As we explored their home, it became evident that the couple were avid horse enthusiasts. Their décor displayed their love of these beautiful stallions in a stately, equestrian fashion. Then, to my amazement, I was given my own room and a bathroom, a luxury I had never had before.

In the mornings, we woke up to the ritual tea drinking by their kind maid, who added to the pleasures of the visit. The enchantment of waking up in such opulent surroundings became a cherished routine, setting the tone for each day's adventures.

The following morning, the excitement continued as we joined our hosts for a refreshing walk before breakfast. Accompanied by their four delightful dogs, our stroll through the scenic surroundings was a harmonious blend of laughter and the joyous barking of our newfound canine companions. The bond with our hosts deepened as we shared these simple yet precious moments.

As the day unfolded, Emma gracefully excused herself, revealing her role as the owner of a fashionable boutique in downtown Manchester. She generously invited us to visit her store, where we could choose items to our liking. Emma's departure was stylish as she hopped into her American Chevrolet convertible – a lavish birthday gift from Big Al the previous year.

Buckle up because our unexpected shopping spree with Emma was about to turn into a wild ride through the fabulous fashion boutique! We were charged with anticipation as we stepped into Big Al and Emma's world, and my excitement meter was skyrocketing.

Emma, our fearless fashion guru, led the way with confidence in her step and a sparkle in her eye. She had this magical ability to turn any shopping excursion into a dazzling adventure. The store's aisles transformed into runways, and suddenly, we were parading our stuff like supermodels on a mission.

Luxury beckoned at every turn as we found ourselves surrounded by velvety fabrics, shimmering sequins, and shoes that practically whispered, "Take me home; I'm fabulous!" We playfully tried on every hat, and my girlfriend tried to find the perfect pair of sunglasses. We laughed and posed to the amusement of the other shoppers. Our shopping bags overflowed with a wide-ranging mix of styles. Emma was closing the store for afternoon tea, which she wanted to treat us to, and we were excited to experience it.

Exiting the store with our heads held high and our shopping bags swinging like victory flags, I knew one thing for sure – Big Al and Emma's world was a place where fashion met fun, and every moment was a chance to create memories that sparkled just as brightly as the sequins on our newfound treasures. Cheers to the adventure, the luxury, and the unforgettable embrace of friendship in this fashionable wonderland!

The decor was an easy reversal of the turn of the century, with fine details and sumptuous furnishings, making me feel like I was in a palace. I can still recall how excited we were to be served freshly made tea and scones, sandwiches, and cakes. Emma was excellent with her stories and laughter; it was such an enchanting day! As days turned into weeks, the unlikely friendship between Big Al and me deepened, creating a bond beyond the ordinary; it felt like we were family.

Big Al invited me to accompany him to his three casinos one day. The very places where fortunes were made and lost were filled with the glimmer of slot machines and the suspense of card games. It was a world I was not supposed to enter, being underage, but with Big Al by my side, doors opened, and rules seemed to bend.

We walked along the glittering hallways, and he proudly introduced me to his team and friends, telling me about his career in the company. As I listened, he took me through the workings of the casinos, from the slots to the psychology of the cards. It was a schooling in a world I'd never guessed I'd be able to enter.

Despite the glamour of the surroundings, what made the experience truly special was the genuine connection we were building. Big Al treated me like the daughter he never had, and I found solace in having a father figure away from home. His laughter sounded through the halls, and his stories of wisdom grew on me, leaving an enduring memory in my heart. It was not just about the casinos and the business; it was about the shared moments, genuine care, and laughter we experienced together. I embraced Big Al's wisdom and warmth, creating memories that would last a lifetime.

Surprisingly, initially skeptical about our unusual friendship, my girlfriends began to see the genuine connection and happiness it brought to both of us. Emma recognized the importance of Big Al in my life and actively supported our bond. She suggested and planned events we could enjoy together.

One morning, I was awakened by my maid, who informed me Big Al was waiting for us girls at the stables. She instructed me to hurry up and get dressed. I was thrilled as I loved horses. Until that day, Big Al had never allowed me and my girlfriends to be near the stables. However, he was permitting us that day.

The sun sat low in the sky, lighting up the vastness of the stable estate. There was so much anticipation and hushed energy when I rushed outside with my girlfriends. We were about to start on an exciting journey, riding racehorses under the supervision of the legendary Big Al.

We laughed as we ran up to the stables, hearts racing at the promise of something new. Big Al greeted us with a big smile, and his eyes were filled with mischief. Today,' he said, 'you can ride my beautiful horses. We waited eagerly when he told us the horses had been tucked up all winter, wanting to get out their legs and wind in their hair. We were lucky enough to be selected to provide them with the exercise they yearned for.

Big Al began introducing us to his equine companions, each with a unique story and personality. There was Champion, a chestnut thoroughbred, the seasoned veteran; Lightning, a black stallion, the fastest in the stable; Winston, a brown morgan, a gentle giant; Daisy, the spirited Mustang; Lady, an Arabian, with elegance in every step; and Starlight, a golden palomino, a dazzling beauty.

Eager to experience the thrill of speed, I requested the chance to ride Lightning. Big Al hesitated, warning me about the dangers of the horse's incredible speed. Undeterred, I argued my case until he reluctantly agreed, extracting a promise I would only engage in a slow trot. I eagerly agreed, my mind racing with the prospect of riding the fastest horse in the stable.

Before we mounted our majestic steeds, Big Al took a moment to educate us on the nuances of Western and English riding. My mind, however, was lost in the anticipation of the impending adventure, and I only half-heartedly absorbed the information.

Finally, the moment arrived. The three of us, accompanied by Big Al and his two assistants, gathered in the center of the stable grounds. Magnificent horses surrounded us, their powerful presence sending shivers down our spines. Big Al and his assistants positioned themselves strategically on the outside, ready to provide guidance and protection.

I climbed Lightning and felt a surge of adrenaline. The cadence of hooves and the gentle motion of the horse under my feet were sensations to savour. I felt a bit of pure enchantment when I realized I needed to be open to things, take risks, and experience the thrill of riding a super horse like Lightning.

I suddenly realized I was not taking full advantage of this opportunity, as I was riding him as if he were an old, tired mare. This thought hit me hard, and I looked around to see Big Al and his assistants answering my girlfriend's inquiries. I knew this was my chance to experience Lightning's incredible speed, so I encouraged him, and he immediately took off at full speed. I was overwhelmed with joy, feeling the wind in my hair, and the freedom both Lightning and I experienced was beyond words.

However, my joy was short-lived as I suddenly saw a large fallen tree blocking the path to the right, which was the direction Lightning had decided to take. I felt a surge of fear, and I tried to steer Lightning towards the left into the large field, but he was not responding, as he only understood English riding, and I only knew how to ride with Western riding. I could hear the hoofs of other horses, and Big Al's raspy voice crackled for me, but it was too faint due to the wind and speed.

Lightning's thundering hooves pounding through the sprawling ranch as I urged him to go left. The adrenaline surged within me, the thrill of the chase electrifying the air. Just as we approached the treacherous bend, Lightning resisted my commands. Panic set in as the blocked path loomed ahead, and my attempts to steer him left proved futile. The seconds ticked away, danger closing in.

In the nick of time, my inner voice boomed in my ear, "English riding, use the reins!" The urgency in its tone fueled my instincts, and I yanked the reins sharply to the left. Lightning, responding with a sudden burst of energy, swerved just in time to avoid the looming obstacle. Yet, the abrupt maneuver sent me hurtling through the air. Time slowed as I floated, and the wind tore through my gear. The ground rushed over to greet me, my body writhing in midair. First, my head slammed into the ground, and then the crunch of the impact rocked my bones.

Pain shot through my body like a lightning bolt, but the sheer force of the fall didn't allow me the luxury of wallowing. I laid still, assessing the damage, muscles throbbing and bones aching.

Big Al and his team galloped to the scene, dismounting with the precision of a well-trained squad. One of the assistants bolted towards Lightning, determined to rein in the spirited black stallion. Big Al's sharp eyes scanned for injuries as the others surrounded me.

"Can you move?" he barked, urgently cutting through the chaos. I nodded, gritting my teeth against the pain. Slowly, I rose, determination masking the discomfort. Emma's distant scream reached my ears, but there was no time for reassurance. Big Al's voice resonated, "We can't let fear rule you. Get back on that horse, or you won't ride again."

Big Al's face bore a mix of concern and regret, but beneath it, I thought I would not let one fall dictate the fate of my riding aspirations. Emma's voice cut through the air like a whip. "This is madness! You're not getting back on that horse, when we don't even know your injuries." Big Al squared his shoulders, his rugged features etched with conviction. "Emma, accidents happen. It'll haunt her if she doesn't conquer her fear now. I won't let a single tumble steal the joy of riding from her." I interjected my voice firm, "I can do this, Emma. I need to face my fear."

Emma shot me a fierce glance, torn between her protective instincts and my determination. Big Al seized the opportunity, rallying support from his team. They brought Lightning back, his coat glistening under the stable lights. With a cautious nod from Big Al, I mounted Lightning again, the saddle now a seat of mixed emotions. My friends watched anxiously, their expressions reflecting concern and hope.

The sound of hooves against the ground trotted through the quiet as we set off again, the wind whipping against our faces. This time, Lightning responded to my cues. As we returned to the stables, the triumph on my face mirrored the determination within. Emma's scowl softened, replaced by a hesitant smile. Big Al's nod acknowledged the victory, not just over the fear of falling but the spirit to get back up.

The ranch became an authentication to triumph over adversity and Lightning, my steadfast companion, a symbol of strength. Through grit, determination, and Big Al's guidance, I conquered the fear that threatened to shatter my dreams and transformed a painful setback into a powerful comeback.

A week passed, and we were leaving this captivating ranch with a bid farewell to Big Al and Emma, a weighty sense of melancholy settled within me. The beauty of the surroundings lingered, but the purpose of our expedition was clear, to welcome independence. Amid the rustic charm and invaluable lessons learned, a couple of insights stood out, with the wisdom I had acquired.

Foremost among these was the realization that the art of listening surpasses the clamor of one's voice on the path to enlightenment. In the quiet moments of absorbing the tales and wisdom shared by our hosts, it became evident the key to learning lies in the attentive silence that precedes thoughtful words.

An unexpected recall from my upbringing resurfaced during moments of contemplation: my mom's often repeated words, "If you fall off the horse, get back on it." The irony struck me with a gentle, amused force. The cliché, rooted in my youth, unfolded in real-time while pursuing independence. The conviction to rise from each fall to dust off your bruises and keep walking, roared louder than any powerful declaration of success. It was in those moments of struggle that I discovered the true strength within me, a strength that couldn't be measured by words alone.

As I ventured forth, stumbling upon obstacles, and overcoming challenges, the character of this newfound wisdom grew, plotting itself into the very makeup of my being. It became more than just knowledge; it became a part of who I was becoming. And with each step forward, this wisdom became my steadfast companion, whispering words of encouragement when doubts clouded my mind and lighting the way when darkness threatened to engulf me.

"In the grand charade of life, we either bear our truth or cloak ourselves in deception. The masks we choose to wear become the very influence that shapes our reality."

Colleen C. Carson

"BORDER ESCAPE"

It's essential to recall the Spanish history of this period to realize how serious the case was for Colleen and her friends. The world had been ruled by the ruthless dictator Francisco Franco, who led his totalitarian state with an iron fist. The army, which served as a military and an organ of the police, stalked the streets in a heavy-handed manner.

Simple rights were restricted, and photographing state institutions or sitting on a beach after dusk could get you arrested and sent to prison. They weren't idle threats either, or many of them disappeared into Spain's humid, ruthless prison system for offences we might call insignificant today. One of them, Colleen's friend's brother, went missing for three years in a Spanish jail because he risked putting his feet on a beach after sunset.

Putting this in perspective, we start our narrative. Colleen and her friends, a group of young Canadian women, had opted to travel by train to a charming Spanish town not far from the French border. They had arrived late at night, so dark that it was impossible to see even a few feet in advance.

The night was unsettling despite being a mere 20 minutes from the French border. The novelty of a foreign country, the border so irresistibly close, had inspired them with a kind of boldness, an innocent exhilaration at the prospect of something huge. They did not anticipate that their decisions that night would trigger an intense encounter with the Spanish military police.

Tired and hungry, they walked over to the hotel. The humble, little hotel had an old-fashioned appeal that immediately appealed to their adventurous sensibilities. But the warnings about robbery still nagged at them. Leaving personal possessions in the room was highly discouraged, as hotel thefts were prevalent. And so, they brought their knapsacks into the restaurant, stumbling around between the little dining tables, never willing to leave their belongings for one second.

As we took seats, eager to get some much-needed food, four American boys were at the table next to us. They, too, were young, wild, and eager to discover Europe's treasures. It was late, and soon, we were in lively conversation with them. It was laughter in the small restaurant, the kind of wild joy that rendered us blind to the darkness and unknown outside. For a few hours, we were mere tourists, getting to know our fellow travelers through stories and the rush of being far from home.

It was getting late, so as midnight approached, we agreed that it was time to go to our rooms. The boys from the US were in the same hotel, and, like us, they planned to cross into France the following morning. But when we went outside, they suggested one last nightly adventure, a walk on the beach.

I instinctively responded to the offer, well aware of the dangers. The rule was simple: if you sat on the beach at sunset, you weren't allowed and paid dearly for it. I told the boys this: they didn't know the state laws. The only sensible thing to do was to avoid the beach.

We made no changes initially, walking in the empty streets and taking in the evening atmosphere. But inevitably, the collective wariness had worn off, and, despite my cautions, everybody decided to head to the beach anyway. I hesitated. I was frightened to think we'd get locked up if we walked on that forbidden beach. But I followed them anyway, reluctant as I was to risk leaving myself alone in the middle of the night.

We had been on the shore for a few minutes when the night was suddenly punctured by the presence of heavily armed military police. Their darkness was great, their machine guns glittering in the pale moonlight. I heard my heart race as they walked by, shouting commands in hypersonic Spanish. I couldn't have been more blown away by the fact that this wasn't a prank; we were in serious trouble.

We disguised ourselves as non-experts, pretending not to know what they were talking about in the hope that our mere status as unknowing tourists would qualify us for a warning. To our utter relief, after several heated minutes of interrogation, the military police ordered us off the beach but let us pass without arrest. So, we quickly packed up and headed out off the beach, our shoulders heavy from all that had just happened.

You would have thought this mishap encouraged us to return to our hotel rooms. But no. Less worried by the military police's harsh admonition, the American boys encouraged us to return to the beach. Their arrogance was astounding. It wasn't as if they had any sense of how bad it was, or maybe they did and didn't notice. So, we signed again against my better judgment, suckered by the excitement of the outlawed or perhaps a few too many glasses of Spanish wine.

Every bush brush I felt on the way back to the beach gave me chills. I could not help but sense we were under surveillance and that the military police would show up at any moment. But they didn't. We all cowered together for the next hour or so, looking up at the horizon for patrols. Feeling worn and uncomfortable, we girls finally took a break and walked away.

And then, right when we thought we were safe, the military police showed up. We'd been caught red-handed, and the prospect of jail was thick on our minds. We wept and pleaded for forgiveness, asking them to release us. Their eyes lit up when they thought about what to do.

Once again, they understood after what seemed like an eternity, but this time, they stated straight out: if we returned to their town, we'd be arrested, no question asked. They walked us out of town, not toward the French border as we'd hoped, but in the other direction. We had found ourselves on a gravel road, the town in question long forgotten.

The darkness was deadening, the silence oppressive. My legs were tiring as we made our way up the steep hill, my knapsack pressing down on my shoulders. We were stranded in the middle of nowhere, away from our hotel, the border, any symbol of safety, and our rooms.

While walking, it became apparent how far we were getting. We were no longer tourists on a European trip of the moment but escapees fleeing from a law we'd deliberately violated. With each hum, paranoia waved through the group. Were the police following us? Were we being watched? The road seemed to run forever ahead of us, twisting through unfamiliar terrain.

And then footsteps went wild in the night. We flinched as we looked around the darkness, looking for the cause. Trying to run for our lives, we noticed a wire fence that we had climbed over. Blood trickled down my legs; the wire had sliced open my skin. We huddled in the grass together, barely able to keep our breathing as the noise intensified. And then, as suddenly as they'd come out, they went missing, and we were left alone again.

The terror that had gripped us for hours was turning to weariness. We had no other recourse but to sleep in the hope that some fragment of reason would dawn on us in the morning. But when the sun came up, my heart started to throb. I was inches from the top of a cliff. One bad decision in the darkness last night could have driven me into the abyss below.

Panicked, I gradually but quietly woke my friends, reminding them of the danger. We made hasty arrangements and started the strenuous walk back toward town. Returning to the wire barrier, we saw the sign we hadn't seen last night: "No Trespassing Forbidden." To find that we had been trespassing on restricted property added more tension. We were going to have to leave Spain, and we had to leave soon.

With renewed vigour, we climbed the fence and sped down the street without pausing. I couldn't quite believe it when we finally crossed the French border. We handed over our passports, and with an immeasurable sense of relief, we were allowed into France. I fell onto a huge boulder, tears welling up from my eyes. We had made it. We were safe.

I think I walked away from that evening gaining two valuable lessons. At the very least, I appreciate the customs and laws of my country. Second, others should not be telling me what I should be doing, and it's essential to listen to my intuition while going through life's minefields.

I remember that night in Spain, as frightening as it was, as a turning point in my self-discovery. I came out of it braver, more fully awake to my own power, and more willing to tackle whatever was thrown at me with courage and wisdom.

"Integrity is rare; loyalty is rarer."

Mama Carson

"BELIEVING IN YOU"

In the uncertainty of doubt, when shadows loom tall,
Believe in the whisper that rises above all.
In the halls of your heart, where dreams take flight,
Accept the courage, welcome the light.

Through storms that rage and trials untold,
Believe in the strength that you behold.
In the depths of uncertainty, where fears may brew,
Hold fast to the faith that resides in you.

In the quiet moments, in the midst of strife,
Trust in the power to shape your life.
For within your spirit, a flame burns bright,
Guiding you through the darkest night.

Believe in the journey, achieve in the quest,
In the pursuit of dreams, in the hope that's best.
In the composition of life, show your part true,
For believing in you is where dreams come true.

So, when doubts overwhelm and fears arise,
Look within, where your strength lies.
For in believing in yourself, you will find,
The courage to conquer and peace of mind.

Believe in the magic you possess,
In your potential, in your progress
The best adventure, in the journey you pursue,
Begins with believing in achieving you.

Colleen C. Carson

"Life's great journey is not about where we go, but about who we become, what we learn, and why we exist."

Colleen C. Carson

"Both 'an eye for an eye' and 'turn the other cheek' are mirrors of justice; one seeks balance through punishment, while the other finds strength in mercy. True wisdom lies in knowing when to defend and when to forgive, for each has its place in the heart's pursuit of peace."

Mama Carson

"Through the shadows, I found a light within I never knew I had. Every step forward showed me my strength, and with each challenge, I learned I was also made to fall. I rose because I was built to rise, and now, I stand taller than the dark ever was."

Colleen C. Carson

"MÜNCHEN SPEECH"

Colleen's friend had taken off for Morocco, leaving her in Munich with just CAD 25, a plane ticket from Montreal to Vancouver, and a firm decision not to call home for money to make it from Munich to London for her flight back to Canada. She asked the hostel if she could clean to cover her stay, and they agreed! That day, she headed out with her favourite book, craving a coffee, and found this cozy little outdoor café. Colleen ordered coffee and started reading, and soon enough, a girl sitting across from her struck up a conversation, asking where she was from. Her name was Caroline. She was from Long Island, NY, studying to become a neurosurgeon like her Dad.

They got to chatting, and Colleen shared her situation. Caroline mentioned she had a friend who might be able to help. The next day, Caroline introduced Colleen to her friends, and they clicked right away. One of them, Freddy, actually his real name was, Friedrich, but Colleen shortened it to Freddy, mentioned a job opening at his company and thought Colleen could land it. The only problem? Colleen didn't speak German; she could barely count to ten! But Freddy came up with a game plan for the interview, and they were all hopeful it would work. And that's where Colleen's story really begins.

The interviewer spoke English but soon switched to German, testing my abilities. I followed our rehearsed strategy to perfection, gesturing as if to answer before Freddy jumped in to provide the response in German. I then repeated the answer in English, demonstrating my understanding and engaging in a smooth conversational flow. I hoped the interview would go as well as I expected, and to my surprise, I was offered the position. It was not a job offer but evidence of the strength of friendship, ambition, and ingenuity. Freddy had not only helped me bridge the language barrier but had become a crucial part of my success story.

The first day at my new job as an assistant Chemist was exciting but also nerve-wracking. As I approached the company's entrance gate, reality hit me hard. Despite securing the position, I knew I was still far from fluent in German. I cringed at trying to speak to my colleagues, who were all fluent speakers. I thought for a minute about walking away and returning to the hostel's safety, where I wouldn't have to face the problem.

But something inside me refused to let fear win. I knew that turning away from this opportunity would mean turning away from my dream of independence. It would mean letting down my friends, particularly Freddy and Caroline, who had gone out of their way to help me succeed. Summoning every ounce of courage, I walked through those gates with my head held high, determined to prove that courage could transcend language barriers.

Inside the building, I was introduced to my new team. The introductions were formal but warm, and soon, I was directed toward my immediate supervisor's office lab. I couldn't help but feel a sense of apprehension as I walked into the office of a towering blonde, middle-aged man with a Swedish accent whose presence seemed to command the room. He eyed me with skepticism, questioning whether I belonged there. His name was Ivan, an intimidating figure who would later play a pivotal role in my journey. As he greeted me, he casually mentioned that he would communicate with me only in English for the first two weeks to make the transition easier. After that, however, it would be "German or nothing." His tone was firm, but there was a glint of amusement in his eyes as if he was issuing me a challenge.

Panic hit me like a freight train. Fluent in German in two weeks? Was I auditioning for the role of a linguistic superhero? The sheer absurdity of the task nearly floored me, but retreat was not an option. I rallied my troops, namely my friend Sadot, the human language machine who spoke seven languages like it was no big deal. Under Sadot's command, I dove into a crash course in German that felt more like boot camp. When I thought it couldn't get more ridiculous, a female coworker swoops in, offering a language swap: I teach her English, and she teaches me German. Cue the high-five, and out came the English German dictionary, our new weapon of choice.

I became a walking, talking German textbook for the next two weeks. As my life depended on it, I crammed phrases into my brain, muttering vocabulary over my coffee, chatting with colleagues in a bizarre mix of broken sentences and wild hand gestures. I ate German; I slept in German, and even dreamt in German, though those dreams often involved me being lost in a maze of umlauts (word accents; two dots above a letter).

There were moments when I thought my brain might pack up and quit. But, with sheer determination and the encouragement of my ever-patient coworkers, the language slowly started to click. To my shock, I realized Munich German wasn't the language beast I thought it was, it's practically the distant cousin of English. Now, Berlin German? That's an entirely different animal.

When the two weeks were up, I stepped into Ivan's office, bracing myself for what I knew would be a make-or-break moment. True to his word, Ivan launched into his instructions in German, waiting for me to falter. But I didn't. With newfound confidence, I responded to each of his directives in German, surprising myself and me. It was his face in shock and, for the first time, a little respect in his eyes. For the rest of the time, the language barrier didn't seem like a mountain to climb. I had overcome my fear, and for it, I had learnt something far more valuable than just a few languages. I'd proven that I could be versatile, learn and succeed anywhere, any place, no matter how hard.

The months that followed were transformative. I grew not only in my professional role but also as an individual. My friendships deepened, and I became part of the University community that supported me unconditionally. I even began a romantic relationship with this American boy I met; his name was Bobbie, a singer and sergeant in the US Army, a relationship that would later blossom into something more intense.

My success at the company did not go unnoticed. As I proved my worth, the company offered me an incredible opportunity to pursue further education. They promised to cover my tuition if I agreed to work for them for five years after completing my studies as a Chemist. It was a generous offer that would have secured my future in Germany.

But my soul was pushing me in another direction. Despite how much I had fallen in love with Munich, my friends and my independence, it was time to go home. I had met Bobby and proposed to him, and I couldn't help wanting a fresh start in my life. As I said goodbye to my colleagues and Ivan, who had been my mentor and friend, I thought about the experience.

She had come to Munich with nothing more than an appetite for adventure and some euros in her purse, and I was returning with plenty of experience, friends, and new-found confidence. On my last day in the lab, he had an unexpected poignancy, a quiet but thoughtful farewell that caught me off guard. Ivan, the reserved and introverted man who seldom revealed even a flicker of emotion, had become a figure of mutual respect over time.

Though we had shared a few words here and there, his demeanour had always been steady and impenetrable. But that morning, when I arrived, something was different. He greeted me with an uncharacteristic warmth, a "Good morning," accompanied by a rare smile and a dry remark about it being my final day. It was so unlike him, yet somehow perfectly in character, his subtle way of acknowledging the end of a chapter. As the day ended, Ivan asked to speak with me in his office. I assumed it would be a brief, formal exchange, perhaps a few words of farewell, nothing more. But when I stepped inside, I saw a small gift and a card placed carefully on his desk. He stood there, his usual composed self, but the words he spoke next surprised me.

Ivan told me how proud he was of me, how I had left an imprint in this place, and how he was confident my future would be anything but mundane. His confidence in me was steadfast, as though he saw something in me, I hadn't always been able to see in myself. I gave him a hug then, something I never imagined doing in all those months of working together. It felt necessary, a gesture to express the gratitude I couldn't quite put into words. I thanked him for pushing me and forcing me to believe in myself when I was too hesitant.

As we parted, there were tears in both our eyes, though neither of us spoke of it. In that unspoken way, we both understood this was a goodbye that carried more weight than anticipated. We'd never see each other again, but our friendship would be etched in our hearts forever. During my stay in Munich, I learned that there is always a path to overcome, even when everything goes wrong. If you have the willpower, courage, and support of others, anything is possible. It was a survival but also a self-development triumph, and when I landed on the plane home, I believed that anything could be beaten in life.

In the end, it was not about work, language, or my friends; it was about finding strength in myself. I realized the strength I carried, my boundless capacity for growth, and the incredible transformation that happens when you truly believe in yourself. Munich had been more than just a place; it became the stage where I stepped into my own potential. For that, I will forever be grateful. But more than anything, it gave me the gift of independence, the freedom to trust in my abilities and the confidence to navigate my future with steadfast conviction.

"A man's true virtues shine brightest when he uplifts a woman, for in their rise, humanity ascends to greater purpose and boundless significance."

Colleen C. Carson

Genesis 2:7 says, "He breathed into his nostrils the breath of life, and it was then that the man became a living being."

Moses 3:17 tells us, "Thou mayest choose for thyself, for it is given unto thee."

Luke 6:37 advises, "Do not judge, and you will not be judged. Do not condemn, and you will not be condemned."

Colleen once stood firm as a Pro-Lifer, but her perspective shifted strongly as she supported the fundamental importance of freedom of choice. She references biblical passages not to weaponize scripture but to address those who claim to be devout while dismissing the complexities of life.

These passages, Colleen asserts, indicate that life begins at birth, choice is a divine gift, and judgment is reserved for God alone. Colleen is aware of critics who argue, "That's your interpretation, and it's wrong," implying their interpretation is reliable simply because it aligns with their beliefs. However, dismissing her perspective is judging her intellect as inferior. "That's not very pious," she would respond with pointed clarity.

In Colleen's view, no one has the authority to strip away another's right to choose, particularly when motivated by personal or religious biases. She challenges: If you truly worship God, how can you ignore the divine principle of free will? By doing so, aren't you assuming God's role? Isn't that a violation of the First Commandment?

To Colleen, such presumption is not an act of faith but arrogance, a defiance of God's ultimate authority. Through candid conversations, Colleen has addressed the polarizing debate between Pro-Life and Pro-Choice. "Strip away the prefix 'Pro,'" she says, "and what remains is 'Life Choice.' This term summarizes the real meaning of decisions we all make, decisions that shape our future and define our paths. Life choices belong to the individual, not to external forces dictating their fate."

Colleen reflects on her own life-altering experience. Upon discovering she was pregnant, she and her husband at the time, once a jet-setting couple, felt surprising joy. They eagerly planned for their baby, envisioning a future reshaped by love and parenthood. But this dream was abruptly shattered. At four months, Colleen experienced severe abdominal pain and heavy bleeding, leading to her parents taking her to the hospital. At the hospital, her doctor diagnosed a miscarriage. The devastating news brought overwhelming grief, magnified by the judgment she later faced.

My doctor looked at me with serious eyes and said the remains of the fetus were a threat to my life. The words hit me like a punch to the chest, leaving me breathless. I had to choose to undergo a D&C procedure, something Pro-Life advocates call "abortion," or risk my own life. The weight of it crushed me. Desperate to survive, I agreed to the procedure scheduled for the next day. The thought of staying in that sterile, suffocating hospital room was unbearable. I pleaded with my doctor to let me go home, just for a little while. I needed space, air, anything to think, to feel something other than the walls closing in around me. I had to get away.

My survival came with a weight I wasn't ready to bear. Leaving the hospital, I felt hollow; the future I had so carefully envisioned shattered. The sadness was suffocating, but I longed for a moment of escape, anything to numb the pain. My girlfriend, seeing my anguish, suggested a movie. Reluctantly, I agreed. Sitting in the dark theatre, the warmth began. At first, I thought I had wet myself, but there was no urge, no sensation like that. I leaned over, whispering to my girlfriend that I needed the bathroom. She insisted on coming with me.

Once inside, I peeled off my coat, only to discover my pants soaked in blood from the waist to my hips. Panic gripped us both, though my girlfriend's terror only made my own fear spiral. I had to calm her down, trying to mask the rising dread in my chest. She drove me back to the hospital, and I was admitted immediately. The D&C that followed wasn't just a medical procedure; it was a harrowing fight for my life.

My decision, born of necessity, brought guilt and sorrow but also clarity: I had done nothing wrong. Yet, the scorn from religious communities, particularly women who claimed to be advocates for life, was a piercing betrayal. "How can they ignore the complexities of a lived experience?" I questioned. "If men of faith faced similar circumstances, would they not demand their right to choose?" I asked myself.

This experience manifested my belief in the sanctity of choice. Freedom to choose is fundamental to human dignity and liberty. Without it, our society risks descending into authoritarianism, where life itself is stripped of freedom. I contend, "It's not about taking sides; it's about respecting every person's right to self-rule." I urge women to recognize the core issue: this debate is not about opposing life or choice but about affirming the independence of each person's decisions.

Respecting a woman's self-rule is essential to a free and just society. Women have weathered life's trials, navigated complexities, and emerged resilient. They understand the value of empathy and the power of support. Through unity and resolve, women can safeguard the right to choose for themselves and future generations. I have said, "Life is precious, but it is defined by the ability to choose: a power we must protect at all costs."

For those who impose their beliefs on others, I ask this question: How can you claim to cherish life if you deny the freedom it entails? How can you preach love and compassion while condemning those who walk a different path? To assume the authority to judge and control others is to forget one's imperfections and the divine gift of free will.

Faith emphasizes a deeply personal journey that no one should disrespect. At its core, religion unites souls in shared rituals and spiritual devotion. Neither should be wielded as tools of division or oppression. "Who among us," I ask, "has the right to overrule what God has ordained? Our role is not to dictate but to honour the diversity of paths God has created in his infinite wisdom."

In honouring these principles, I have envisioned a world where every soul is empowered to live authentically, guided by respect, empathy, and freedom. By upholding these values, humankind can ensure that the legacy of choice endures, fostering justice, equality, and spiritual fulfillment for all. What devastates me now, what leaves me in tears and fury, is hearing about women in the United States dying because they couldn't access what I received in my most desperate moment.

Their lives were cut short, and their families shattered, all because they were denied the care they needed. It's unbearable to think about how preventable those deaths could have been. I relive my trauma through their stories, and it feels like the same helplessness all over again. No one should lose their life when it could so easily be saved based on someone's own beliefs. As a united humanity, we must rally behind the principle; "The Freedom of Choice." It's not just a statement; it's a call to action, a shared responsibility to protect and honour the choices that sustain and define us as a democracy.

"Determination is the fire that turns dreams into reality; it's the determined force that breaks barriers and builds legacies. Fuel it passionately, for within it lies the power to reshape the world."

Colleen C. Carson

"When the fool meets the wise, the fool's ignorance trembles in the shadows of fear."

Mama Carson

"She holds the pen to her story, where freedom bonds with choice, each word a tribute of her power; the author to her destiny."

Colleen C. Carson

"Sometimes, the loudest truth is the one whispered by the silence between our words."

Mama Carson

Get your copy now:
https://www.amazon.ca/FARE-CHANCE-COOKBOOK-Savoir-Simple/dp/0994839049

Colleen starting her catering company was like diving into a pool without knowing how to swim. It all began with a $10.00 ad and a cupboard full of pots, spurred on by a dare from her girlfriends. They didn't expect her to take it seriously, but something inside her stirred at the challenge. In the beginning, she was pumped with excitement. The idea of running her own business, creating delicious dishes, and being her own boss filled her with adrenaline. But as reality set in, fear crept up on her like a shadow in the dark. Doubts clouded her mind, and she found herself questioning whether she had what it took to make it in the cutthroat world of catering.

Despite her initial enthusiasm, she soon found herself in denial, pretending that everything was fine when, deep down, she knew it wasn't. Then, one day, the phone rang. Someone wanted to hire her for an event. At that moment, fear and excitement collided within her. Colleen was scared of failing and not living up to expectations, but she also knew she needed the income. It was a critical moment that forced her to face the reality of her situation.

The early days were tough. Every penny I earned returned to the business, leaving little for myself. It felt like I was constantly treading water, struggling to keep my head above the surface. After two years of pouring my heart and soul into my catering company, I was at a crossroads. The prospect of quitting loomed large, tempting me with its promise of relief from the constant pressure and uncertainty. But deep down, I could not shake the feeling that I had not given it my all. Despite the setbacks and sacrifices, a flicker of hope was still burning within me. I could not bear the thought of giving up on something I had worked so hard to build.

Here's the deal: I'm knee-deep in pots and pans, whipping up a storm in the kitchen for a sorority dinner of 25 lively sisters. Just as I contemplated my life choices (as one does when elbow-deep in dish suds), one of my regular clients strolled in, all smiles and curiosity. She asked me how things were going, and I candidly disclosed information about my fleeting thoughts of quitting the catering game. Now, let me tell you, this client would not have any of it. Her disappointment was written all over her face, and before I knew it, she was rallying the troops: aka, the sorority sisters, to my cause. It was like witnessing a culinary revolution right there in her kitchen.

They all chimed in with a resounding "NO" to my quitting, and before I could protest, my client had them all committed to booking an event with me within the next six months. And just like that, my business took off like a kid on a sugar high. Who knew that a group of sorority sisters could be the secret sauce to success?

I may not have been the poster child for meticulous market research. While all the marketing gurus were preaching about analyzing the competition, I was here winging it like a culinary superhero. But hey, who needs trendy dishes when you have got a secret stash of recipes up your sleeve? My clients were not just getting a meal; they were getting a one-way ticket to Flavor Town, courtesy of yours truly.

Take, for instance, my legendary shrimp balls. One bite, and you'd swear you'd died and gone to seafood heaven. I had this one woman practically begging to buy them off me without delay. But sorry, beautiful, you will not find these babies on any store shelf. No, the only way to get your fix is to hire me and let me work my magic at your next event. And get this, it turns out she used to run her own catering company. If that is not a sign from the culinary Gods that I'm onto something special, I don't know what is.

So, while others were busy playing by the rules, I was out here breaking them with a spatula in one hand and a whisk in the other. And you know what? It worked. Because sometimes, all it takes is a little bit of guts, a whole lot of flavors, and a group of sorority sisters who believe in you to turn your kitchen dreams into reality. Ah, the suburban hotel gig; that is where the real adventure began. It was like stepping into the ring with a lion and coming out with a crown made of spatulas. But hey, that's just how life rolls when you are in the catering game. As if running a catering company was not wild enough,

I also decided to throw my hat into the ring as an event coordinator. Why settle for just one challenge when you can have two? Am I right? And let me tell you, once I got that hotel deal locked down, there was no stopping me. I roped in my kids faster than you can say "tasting menu," before I knew it, they were knee-deep in flour and fancy napkins, learning the ropes alongside me. It was like a crash course in culinary chaos, but hey, they say the family that cooks together stays together.

Now, my client list? Let us say it was more eclectic than a thrift store on a Saturday morning. From weddings to diplomats to celebrities—talk about spinning plates (both metaphorically and literally). One day, I would be buttering up the local mayor at a political shindig; the next, I wound be rubbing elbows with Hollywood's finest at some swanky soiree. It was like a culinary circus, and I was the ringmaster, juggling menus and mood lighting like nobody's business.

And do you know what? Despite the occasional chaos and the never-ending stream of demands, it was the most fun I had ever had. Because when you are in the business of making memories, every event is a chance to sprinkle a little magic into someone's life. So, here is to the suburban hotel that became my culinary playground and my kids, who jumped on board and turned it into a family affair. Because when life serves you up a platter of opportunities, you grab a fork and dig in with both hands.

Ah, the peaks and valleys of life, like a rollercoaster ride through Flavour Town with Guy Fieri hollering "Welcome!" Do you know how they say everything comes in three? Well, sign me up for that fan club. That is why I decided to become a wedding planner and add it to my already impressive résumé in the catering and event industry. But wait, before you start picturing me as the next Mary Fiore from The Wedding Planner, let me clarify, I am already married! So, no worries about me running off with the groom. Seriously, the only thing I will be stealing is an extra slice of cake!

Fast-forward years, and there I was, packing up my pots and pans for a grand adventure to Alberta. My husband had decided it was time for a change of scenery, and who was I to argue? So off we went, leaving behind the hustle and bustle of Vancouver for the wide-open spaces of Calgary. But you know what they say about life: when one door closes, another one opens. And for me, that door led straight to the kitchen. Even though I had to bid farewell to my beloved catering business, I could not shake the feeling that cooking was in my blood. So, while my clients in Vancouver mourned the loss of their favorite caterer, I rolled up my sleeves and got to work in my new home.

Now, let me tell you, starting over in a new city can be challenging. I tried to kickstart my catering company in Calgary, but it was like trying to bake a soufflé in a microwave, just not meant to be. So, after much soul-searching and one too many failed soufflés, I decided to hang up my apron and explore new opportunities. But here is the deal about passion: it's like a stubborn stain on your favourite shirt. No matter how hard you try to scrub it out, it just will not budge. And for me, that passion was cooking. So, even though I had closed the door on my catering business, I found myself drawn back to the kitchen repeatedly.

And that's when inspiration struck like a bolt of lightning in a frying pan. I decided to channel my culinary expertise into something new; a cookbook. But not just any cookbook. Oh no, this was going to be a culinary masterpiece, filled with easy-to-follow recipes and a healthy dose of wit. I called it "A Fare Chance Cookbook," after Chance because he was my biggest supporter and motivator in writing this cookbook.

Cooking should be fun, dammit! It should not feel like a chore or a punishment, it should be a joyous celebration of tastes and creativity. And with my cookbook in hand, even the most ardent cooking haters would find themselves putting on an apron and diving headfirst into the kitchen. But even better, the recipes range from vintage to modern-day, so when you are cooking, you can channel your inner Doc Brown from Back to the Future. Great Scott! Yep, I'm a total movie buff, how can you tell?

So, here is to new beginnings, following your passion wherever it may lead, and never underestimating the power of a well-timed pun. Because when life hands you lemons; you make lemonade. And when it hands you a cookbook title as perfect as "A Fare Chance," you grab a spatula and get cooking. Cheers for that! Before I conclude, I wrote the following culinary love letter at the beginning of the book to give you a little insight into the fun of cooking;

My Dearest Fare,

Our relationship goes back decades, but it seems like yesterday. You presented yourself in such a teasing manner when observed along with an enticing show of desirables. I knew on meeting we would be together forever it was love at first nibble and it's been a love of fare since and forever. Together we have planned such celebrations as births, weddings, anniversaries, even remembrances with tender morsels to share. You have presented stirring savvies and bathed moments of essences which we both relished.

My fare, over the years you have been obliging in wanting to please my kneads! Your saucy appeal, catered rubs, and delicate bites of pleasure have without question spiced up my life while measuring up to all my expectations. Of course, in all relationships, there have been times where you were quite braising, leaving me stewing for hours! On occasion, your indulgence has stirred up several to sear or reach their boiling point yet, in the end, you were always about being fare.

Remember, when we started our business together, it was somewhat intimidating, but due to teamwork, careful attention, and of course our creations; we achieved success. Even when others differed in mindset or took you for granted, you were able to just toss their thoughts aside. Sometimes it grates on me how others have no time or don't even want to try to see how you could blend in their lives. It doesn't seem to batter you; I know I must stop simmering over grating situations.

We have had very steamy moments of unforgettable along with simmering instances of inviting display while blending well in creativity, which I'm genuinely thankful for. I believe our journey has many more creations to share and my interest awe-inspiring. Enclosing what I want to say, to you, my dearest fare is...

"THE AUTHOR'S JOURNEY"

Colleen's journey as a writer began with a simple yet powerful love for stories. Since childhood, stories have enchanted her, sparking her imagination and transporting her to distant lands filled with fascinating characters. The power of language captivated her; she was amazed at how words could evoke emotions, bring characters to life, and reveal entire worlds. Her love for storytelling grew with her, becoming a core part of her identity.

As she grew older, Colleen began writing plays. She spent countless hours creating plots and characters, pouring her heart and soul into every story. Writing was never just a pastime; it became her way of exploring her imagination and connecting with others. With each story she shared, she aimed to touch readers' lives just as stories had touched hers. Writing, however, came with its challenges. There were times when doubt crept in, making her question if her words were worth sharing. Yet, despite the setbacks, Colleen's passion for storytelling remained untiring. She continued to write because she felt a calling, a need to share her perspective, inspire others, and create lasting connections.

Life, as it often does, threw Colleen unexpected challenges. She had to put her literary dreams on hold, shifting her focus to other responsibilities. But then, an unusual request from her teenage son reignited her passion. Her son came to her for advice on relationships, wanting her guidance on understanding romance and impressing his girlfriends. His request was simple: keep it a secret. And so, Colleen became his undercover love coach, guiding him on how to navigate relationships with charm and sensitivity.

Her son's success with her advice soon led to more questions from his friends, all curious about his new skills. Eventually, her son asked Colleen to put her insights into a book so he could reference her wisdom whenever he needed it. That idea sparked "The Guyed Book," a heartfelt guide on love and relationships crafted from Colleen's years of advice and insight. Tragically, Colleen's son passed away in 2007, and she shelved the book for years. But one day, her daughter suggested that she share it to help others who could benefit from its insights. With support from friends and family, Colleen brought "The Guyed Book" to life as a tribute to her son and as a guide for anyone seeking to understand love and connection.

Today, Colleen's book is a tribute to her son, a way to share her son's memory and her unique perspective on life and love. Writing has been her path to healing, growth, and connection, and she continues to believe in the power of storytelling to touch hearts and bring people together.

https://www.amazon.ca/GUYED-BOOK-GUY-ROMANCE-WOMAN/dp/0994839081

My second book, "A Fare Chance" Cookbook, came about when my children often called me for family recipes. Then came a moment when Chance approached me with a heartfelt request: creating a cookbook to immortalize our culinary heritage for him and his sister. Overwhelmed by love and determination, I began this culinary journey, driven by a pressing desire to complete the venture before the dawn of Mother's Day. I gave them each a copy as a thank you for being my miracles. I must say when I was completing this cookbook, I sense an urgency to complete it by Mother's Day, and I am so happy I did because Chance passed away in July 2007. I still wonder if he had ever had the opportunity to go through the cookbook before he passed away.

"I have done coupon booklets called "Rendezvous Me" and "Heads I Wine Tails You Woos." Spice up your Sex Life!"

These vouchers booklets give you the urge to live your sexual secrets and fantasies into the desired action of sensuality with a hint of romance.

Sexuality + Sensuality = Romance.

They are also on Amazon.ca

The next book was "Tiger Spirit Within," a transformative journey of self-discovery and empowerment. It is a simple and profound conversation between an Elder and a Child. It's a powerful guide that helps you overcome the bullying mindset, challenge your fear, and discover the new you. The book explores the core of human rights and discrimination, revealing secrets and inspiring truth. It energizes and motivates you to act toward a more just and equitable world. It is a book that will leave you feeling empowered, enlightened, and inspired to be the best version of you. I have adapted "The Tiger Spirit

Within" into a musical play, for which I wrote the music score. It is also an Audio Book!

https://www.amazon.ca/Tiger-Spirit-Within-revealing-energizing/dp/0994839022

"I'm also a believer. I believe that
one day our tiger spirits within will roar into the masses, giving strength in the obliteration of this hideous disease we call bullying."

Colleen C. Carson

"SHE CAN FLY"

Being fired from a job is not the end of your world. Colleen felt when she got fired it was like being pushed off a cliff only to discover she could fly. The initial panic was real but then came the realization that she was soaring toward better opportunities.

Colleen enjoyed her job she got fired at and the people she worked with, but she was not living her passion. She believes that in a free society, no employer owns you, disrespects you, or controls your time. She is not suggesting you go out and get fired just for the thrill, but she encourages you to demand respect from your employer and to communicate your expectations and your employer equally. This way, the relationship can be a glass half full rather than half empty.

Your day is divided into three segments: home, work, and sleep. Maintaining a balance among these is essential for a healthy physical and emotional life. Gone are the days when a company would give you a cheap watch after twenty-five years of service as a token of gratitude.

Remember this: getting fired is not a rejection of your worth. Instead, it is a redirection towards a path meant for you. Accept it as a powerful opportunity to reshape your destiny. My cliff dive happened at a financial company that occupied two floors of the Board of Trade building. I was hired as the assistant to the manager of the shareholders' department but calling him a manager was a stretch. This guy was the epitome of inefficiency.

Office gossip had it that he had gone through assistants like a hot knife through butter because they all ended up doing his job and getting fed up with his miserable treatment. Spoiler alert: the gossip was true. I found myself juggling his job and mine while he perfected the art of looking busy doing nothing. Others ask, "Why didn't you stand up for yourself?"

Because it was the seventies, women standing up to their male bosses risked losing their jobs; I liked my work and his too, and I also enjoyed the staff. Then came my excellent opportunity: the manager was going on a three-week vacation. I was ecstatic! While he was away, I revamped the system, making everything run like a well-oiled machine, you know, like a NASCAR pit crew on Red Bull and espresso shots!"

I am a bit of an organizational Guru; the powers that be were so impressed with the improvements that they decided to keep the new system. When my manager returned, and noticed the new system, he could see his cushy, do-nothing job slipping away, he threw a fit. He called a meeting with the President and Vice President but snubbed my offer to join. He strolled in with all the confidence of a cat who caught the canary, only to emerge fifteen minutes later looking like a cat who had lost the canary. He threw an abrupt "It's all yours now, good luck" over his shoulder as he breezed past my desk.

Here's the deal: the higher-ups believed we had co-created the new system. He was so livid that he had to work, the manager ratted me out during the meeting, saying I had changed the system behind his back while he was on vacation. Once they realized he had nothing to do with the improvements, they gave him a choice: get fired or quit. He chose to leave, and that was the end of his swaggering days. With the manager gone, I revolutionized the entire department.

My success was such that I was given a four-woman staff and regularly spoke at shareholders' meetings. I even convinced most shareholders to convert their shares during a company takeover. I was on cloud nine, the darling of the company, promoting me to Director of the Shareholders Department with the pay to match.

Suddenly, the corporate lawyer announced he was leaving, and I was genuinely disappointed. We had worked so well together, sharing similar goals, humor, and integrity. Then his replacement arrived, a ridiculously handsome man who had all the women in the office, including me, swooning.

At first, he was charming, a real collaborator who wanted to be involved, asking many questions that were positively welcomed, even advocated. Slowly, he started to undermine me, holding meetings without my involvement, and eventually declaring that my staff and I would report to him. He handed me a timeline that felt more like a ticking time bomb.

Then, one sunny Friday afternoon in June, around 4:15 pm, the Company President and Vice President called me into the boardroom. They praised my outstanding work but said the lawyer had "learned the system" and made "a few corrections," claiming the company did not need to pay two people for the same job. Despite acknowledging that I was a great asset, they felt having a corporate lawyer on staff was obligatory.

They offered me three months' severance pay and a glowing written reference. I left the building looking dejected but was dancing a jig inside. Summer was beginning, and they had permitted me to take the summer off with pay. Because as sure as my name is Colleen, I knew they would ask me back, it was just a matter of time, and I was hoping not until September.

This unexpected break was a gift, a rare chance to breathe, reflect, and rejuvenate. It was a reminder that sometimes life gives you exactly what you need, even if it comes wrapped in unexpected packaging. So, while they saw my departure as a necessity, I saw it as an excellent opportunity, a door opening to new possibilities and adventures. Listen, we women know we are much more strategic than men. I left the new lawyer with only half the knowledge of my system. Did you think I was that naïve? Just because he was good-looking, you thought I would trust him. Excuse me! Anyway, while he floundered, I enjoyed a fantastic summer, answering the company's increasingly desperate calls often enough to keep them guessing.

In mid-September, the company called and requested a meeting. They fired the lawyer, and I negotiated a threefold salary increase before agreeing to return. The shareholders were furious during my absence, and the system needed to catch up. On my first day back, I ran into the departing lawyer, who sheepishly apologized for underestimating me. And so, he should: the dumbass!

This experience confirmed the power of knowing your worth and playing your cards right. It was not just about winning a negotiation; it was about reclaiming my value and showing that strategic thinking and patience are invaluable assets. That summer off was not just a break—it was a salute to my spirit and foresight.

The department thrived under my leadership once again, and at the next shareholders' meeting, they were grateful to see I was back. But here is the deal: precisely three months later, at 4:15 PM on a sunny Friday afternoon, I walked into the President's office and resigned. The Vice President had a meltdown, but the President just smiled, understanding it was payback. I told him with a confident smile, "I wished them the best, and thanked them for the opportunity."

With that, I walked out, leaving them to ponder their mistakes. Their oversight was glaring they thought they had an ordinary woman working for an extraordinary company. They had an extraordinary woman working for an ordinary company. This experience taught us all a valuable lesson. For them, it was a reminder never to underestimate their employees' quiet strength and strategic brilliance. For me, it was a reaffirmation of my worth and the importance of standing up for myself. Cheers for finding my wings to soar to greater heights of opportunities and self-worth.

"TIGER WITHIN"

Let's really talk about bullying. For Colleen, some memories are still raw, even decades later. She remembers being in Grade 11, caught in a ring of boys who thought they ran the school. Their "power" wasn't earned through respect or good deeds; it was built by bullying others. They handed out cruel nicknames like badges as if that somehow made them look stronger or cooler. Colleen was called "Bat Legs" just because her ankles were a bit thicker than some other girls. When you hear a name like that shouted across a crowded hallway, followed by laughter, it pierces deep into the soul. And that sting doesn't fade quickly. Over sixty years later,

Colleen can still feel the impact of those words, as if it happened yesterday. Colleen realized that she was letting the bullies get to her, which meant she was giving them the power to do it. And she knew that if someone as visible as her, a leader in the school, was getting bullied, it might make the timid students feel even more afraid, thinking they could be next. So, one day, when those same boys tried to taunt Colleen with nickname, Colleen stopped, turned, and walked right over to them. At first, they laughed, but they soon went quiet when she stood face-to-face with them.

Colleen asked calmly, "Does bullying make you feel stronger? More powerful? Or is it just a cowardly action to give the appearance you've got power?" Colleen paused, the continued, "Is this something you learned at home? Or do you get bullied at home, and that's why you bully at school?" The hallway went silent. Everyone waited to see how the boys would respond. But Colleen's confidence had them rattled. The leader muttered, "Let's get out of here," and as they walked away, he called her a bitch. Colleen smiled and replied, "I'm not; I'm just braver than you." After that day, they avoided her, and the bullying stopped.

Colleen discovered her tiger within, where her courage and spirit roared without fear or favour. By trusting herself, and welcoming this inner force, she realized she could face any challenge with fearless bravery, inspiring change not only in herself but in those around her. Bullying doesn't just begin at school. Sometimes, it starts at home.

I believe that parents are usually the ones teaching kindness, respect, and understanding. But there's a side that most adults preferred not to discuss: some parents teach bullying, directly or indirectly. Maybe they openly mock others or drop casual, hurtful remarks about people. Either way, kids are soaking it in. It becomes part of their world, a cruel family "legacy" where bullying is normalized and almost expected.

In my own life, I saw how this cycle works. My son, Chance, once had a bully whose father, a teacher at his school, was someone you'd expect to know better. This man should have been a role model, but instead, he looked the other way when his son harassed others, and maybe even approved of it. When the school suggested that Chance "befriend" this bully to somehow make things better, I was furious. Instead of facing the real problem, they wanted my son to put himself in a vulnerable position with someone who'd already bruised him.

It's shocking how often adults choose to ignore or sidestep the problem. Let's be clear: children learn far more from our actions than from our words. If parents mock, belittle, or disrespect others, their kids absorb it like a sponge. They learn to see others as "less than," a mindset that can stick for life.

And when those kids turn into adults, they carry these toxic attitudes into workplaces, communities, and even their own families. The cycle spins on and on, with each generation passing down this learned superiority. I've seen it firsthand. For example, my sister and her partner often used racial slurs when discussing politics or lifestyle differences. They were quick to blame minority groups for things they didn't like, and they didn't care who was around to hear it. But they knew better than to use that language around me because I made it clear; I'd leave if I listened to any of that vile talk in my presence. Teaching kids to stand up to bullying begins with adults showing courage and holding others accountable. It's a tough but necessary stance that I've seen ignored far too often in the name of "keeping the peace."

Then, a more prominent example of bullying affects us all: politics. In recent years, I've watched leaders act more like playground bullies than public servants. These leaders use their power not to uplift or unite but to mock, divide, and belittle. They bully their opponents, humiliate those who disagree with them, and somehow, they get away with it. Instead of standing as examples of respect, they weaponize their influence, setting a damaging example. They show our kids that the "strong" survive not through kindness or wisdom but by tearing others down.

It's a chilling message that trickles down to our children, who see these leaders as role models. So, what's the answer? It's not just about telling kids, "Don't bully." We need to hold ourselves to that same standard. Parents who allow or encourage bullying should face consequences right alongside their children. They're part of the problem not part of the solution; they should be held responsible when their actions hurt others, too. If a child bullies another student, and it's clear that the behaviour is being modeled at home, both parent and child should face the repercussions together.

Repercussions aren't punishment for punishment's sake, it's about accountability and the real work of breaking the cycle. We also need to stop treating bullying as an inevitable "rite of passage." Too often, society writes it off as a perverse life lesson that kids just have to endure. But that's nonsense. My daughter, Crystal, now 43, still carries scars from the bullying she faced as a child. And she's not alone. Adult bullying is real; it's just more subtle. It's there in the workplace, disguised as competition, insecurity, or jealousy. And once again, people look the other way, pretending it's not a big deal.

But the pain remains the same. Bullies don't disappear when high school ends; they often evolve, bringing their toxic behaviour into offices, communities, and beyond. In today's world, bullying has even more reach. Back in my day, bullies had to confront you in person. Now, social media allows them to follow kids home. It's relentless and can hit any time, anywhere. We've all seen the heartbreaking stories of young people who felt there was no escape. They were trapped by bullies who attacked them online, in school, and even in their own homes. And yet, people still call bullying a "rite of passage." It's past time to stop this mentality.

Let's not forget that workplaces, too, can be toxic environments where bullying is alive and well. Women, in particular, often find themselves competing rather than supporting each other, which only deepens the cycle. People in power sometimes become the worst bullies of all, using their authority as a weapon to make others feel small. We see this in offices, communities, and politics, where leaders bully rather than inspire. They rule through fear rather than respect, creating cultures of division instead of unity. And these so-called "leaders" were often bullies as children or were bullied themselves. But rather than using that experience to develop empathy, they've let it fester into cruelty.

Ending the cycle of bullying starts with us saying enough is enough. Schools need to take a stronger stance, not only against kids who bully but also against teachers and staff who look the other way. And parents who are raising bullies should face accountability right alongside their kids. It's a harsh but necessary message: when you teach bullying, you don't just hurt your victim, you set an example that can ruin lives, including your children. And workplaces must adopt strict anti-bullying policies, holding people accountable regardless of their position.

As a society, we have to challenge the harmful idea that "strength" comes from suffering. We don't need cruelty to build character. What we need is compassion, understanding, and support. The next time someone says, "Bullying is just part of growing up," call them out.

There's nothing "normal" about making others feel worthless. We all have a role to play in ending bullying, whether we're parents, teachers, leaders, or simply people who care. Every voice in this fight matters, and yours could be the one that makes someone feel seen, valued, and safe.

Unlock the Power...

"HER HEART"

A chapter where the power of self-love blooms like radiant flower, its fragrance extending far beyond yourself to welcome those you hold dear: your children, the men in your life, and all who touch your soul. Join Colleen on this enchanting journey to discover the beauty of devotion to your inner voice, unveiling the core pillars of heroism, egoism, and realism: the guiding forces that lead to a life rich with meaning and true fulfillment. Learn to love yourself with purpose and tenderness, setting boundaries that protect your spirit while allowing your love to flow freely to others. This chapter reveals the sincere truth that nurturing your own heart deepens the connections you share. The unconditional bond with your children become a symphony of trust and joy, while the respect shared with the men and women in your life is strengthened by dependability and kindness. Love transforms into an energy that heals and empowers everyone, it touches including yourself. Here is your invitation to love boldly and joyfully, to cherish yourself and others in equal measure, creating a life of warmth, connection, and infinite beauty.

Are you ready to open your heart?

Your journey of love and transformation begins here...

CHAPTER TWO

"What if love never touched the world?
Would silence fill the spaces where hearts once loved?
Would the soul's whispered secrets, never be told?
Would we wander in shadows, never daring to dream?
Would the stars lose their shimmer?
Would the sun cease to rise?
Would we still see beauty in each other's eyes?
Would we even find the strength to rise?
Would we yearn to live ever searching?
Would we connect as you or me?

Mama Carson

"THE GENTLEMEN OF INTIMACY"

"FIRST DATE"

"This was my grad picture I gave Johnnie."

Imagine a world of wonder where love blossoms and magic is real. There, in the heart of her universe, her romantic tale unfolds with a chapter that dances with the enchantment of young love. This story is about Colleen's first date; her first love, Johnnie, was his name that whispered within her heart.

He was a handsome boy with impeccable manners at the tender age of eighteen, and she was a sweet sixteen. Their encounter was like a serendipitous waltz at a community center dance, the beginning of a love story that would be cherished forever. The night was mesmerizing, with the hope that it would go on forever, but of course, the night ended. It was time to go home, and he gallantly escorted her through the moonlight, a prelude to a date with parental permission.

Her heart, confined by her parents' strict rules, has a newfound freedom. Before granting consent, her parents set a curfew, a cautionary about their evening performance. But nothing could dampen her spirits as the evening arrived, adorned with butterflies of anticipation fluttering within her. Johnnie, a dashing figure, appeared dressed in the legendary Bombers jacket, a tribute to his skill on the football field.

Introductions harmonized with exchanged instructions, and his father's chariot awaited them, elevating their sense of maturity. It was a night to remember, setting the tone for their romantic journey together.

We began our trip to the movies with an unmistakable sense of anticipation. The silence between us was filled with quiet thoughts and unspoken emotions we were both hesitant to reveal. But as we approached the theatre, something shifted in the atmosphere, and a sense of excitement began to develop.

When we pulled up to the curb, he quickly exited the car and walked around to my side to open the door; a chivalrous gesture set the tone for the rest of the evening. I could feel a smile spreading across my face as I stepped out of the car and met his gaze; something was electric between us.

As we made our way towards the theatre, hand in hand, he could not help but compliment me on my appearance, telling me how beautiful I looked. It left me feeling a mixture of flattery and shyness, and I could not help but offer a grateful nod in response. We exchanged smiles like secret whispers, each lost in our thoughts and feelings but unified by the shared excitement of the evening ahead.

The night was nothing short of magical! We had just finished watching an epic movie, 2001: A Space Odyssey, which took us on an unforgettable journey through different worlds and emotions. As the credits rolled, I knew I wanted to spend more time with this fantastic boy. Without hesitation, I suggested we grab a bite to eat, and he jumped at the opportunity. We sat down to a delicious meal of hamburgers and chips, talking and laughing as if we had been friends for years.

The atmosphere was exciting, and I felt like I was in a story of shared laughter. Johnnie asked me if we could go to Whalley's Drive-In, where his friends were waiting to meet me. When we arrived at the drive-in restaurant, I could see his friends were waiting for us. The introductions were awkward, but we soon settled into a comfortable rhythm of conversation and laughter.

During our hangout, one of his friends inquired if I had been putting a smile on Johnnie's face lately. I found myself caught up in a whirlwind of emotions. Our eyes met, and it felt like time stood still in that fleeting instant. There was an unspoken connection between us, a silent acknowledgment of our joy. It was a tender moment, a quiet exchange of affection that spoke volumes about our friendship.

Leaving the restaurant, the evening air was filled with anticipation and nervousness. We arrived back at my home, and as we walked towards my doorstep, we chatted and laughed, trying to shake off the awkwardness that had settled over us. When we reached my doorstep, we stood there momentarily, giggling and feeling shy. But then he took a deep breath and asked if he could see me again. My heart fluttered with joy and excitement as I responded with a shy yes. He leaned in and gently kissed my cheek, and I could feel my cheeks turning red with happiness.

Suddenly, my Dad opened the door and asked if I was coming in soon. Johnnie then said goodbye to my Dad and drove away in his Dad's car; I watched him drive away with longing and anticipation. I knew that I had found someone special who made me feel alive and happy in a way I had never experienced before.

As I shut the front door behind me, said goodnight to my parents, and made my way to my bedroom, anticipation bubbled inside me, eager for our next meeting. The quiet of my room as I settled onto my bed, grappling with the emotions that had transpired earlier. Each moment felt like an eternity as I sought to untangle the emotions swirling within me, searching for clarity amid my confusion.

My mind was racing with excitement as I replayed the events of the evening repeatedly in my head. I could not help but feel my heart racing with anticipation as I thought about how I would tell my girlfriends about my first date with Johnnie.

I started getting ready for bed, distracted by my thoughts. I knew I could not wash his kiss away, so I went to bed with makeup on my face that night. The next morning, while getting ready for school, I heard a song on the radio that made my heart know he was the one. The song was "Johnnie Angel" by Shelley Fabara, released in 1962.

This memory gave me firsts: first date, first kiss, first boyfriend, and first love. The feelings of sixteen are still fresh, as I remember the excitement and the wonderful sense my love had come alive. Johnnie and I were a couple for eighteen months, and then I left for Europe, not knowing when I would be back. I did not think it was fair for him to wait for me, and he agreed.

I did not cross paths with Johnnie again until nearly a decade had passed when we bumped into each other at a lively New Year's bash surrounded by my husband and relatives. Seeing him approach my table filled me with a rush of excitement and nostalgia. He greeted me warmly and swiftly invited me to dance, igniting a flood of memories from days gone by as we twirled on the dance floor. Amid laughter and shared recollections, we extended an invitation for him to join our group, but he politely declined.

Later, as the festivities wound down and we made our way back to our hotel room, fate seemed to intervene as we encountered Johnnie by the elevator. Seizing the opportunity, I expressed my desire to have a private conversation with him, prompting my husband to graciously excuse himself and head back to our room, leaving me alone with Johnnie.

As we caught up on the happenings of the past decade, I could not help but notice how Johnnie had changed; his charm and good looks remained intact, now accompanied by a newfound maturity that only added to his appeal.

With a hint of nostalgia in his seductive, smoky voice, Johnnie revealed his romantic pursuits over the years. He never quite found someone who compared to me, and as a result, he remained unattached. Hearing this melted my heart, especially when he mentioned the graduation photo I had gifted him all those years ago, still proudly displayed in his home.

Then came the unexpected confession that took me by surprise: Johnnie expressed regret over our breakup and confessed that he often wondered how things would have turned out if he had chosen to accompany me to Europe all those years ago. He lay conveying his feelings, admitting that his love for me had lasted over the past decade, evident when our eyes met again.

Grateful for his heartfelt words, I gently reminded him that I was now happily married, cherishing our shared memories but acknowledging that they belonged to the past. Understanding my stance, Johnnie gracefully accepted, prompting me to mention that I needed to return to my room where my husband, Brian, awaited my company.

With a subtle smile, Johnnie leaned in and kissed my cheek tenderly, a gesture filled with the echoes of our first date. He whispered in my ears words that stirred my soul, a farewell, promising me eternal love and bidding me a beautiful life.

Watching him walk away, a bittersweet realization came over me - this encounter marked the end of an era, and I knew deep down that it would be the last time I would see Johnnie. Just to mention; I never saw Johnnie again. My first love was a treasure in my heart, sparking desires by day, dreams by night and now a forever memory.

"With a simple hello, worlds unite, hearts connect, and journeys begin."

Mama Carson

"MY SPANISH AFFAIR"

Madrid, a city pulsating with the rhythm of life, became the backdrop to an unexpected love story. The warm Spanish sun greeted them as Colleen's girlfriend and she arrived, their hearts brimming with the excitement of the adventures awaiting them in this vibrant city.

Their days were filled with exploration after finding a charming place to stay. The attractions of Madrid unfolded before them the grandeur of historic churches, the colourful markets, and the lively streets lined with tapas bars. Each moment was a city that whispered tales of passion and romance. One enchanting evening, they found themselves in a tapas bar, the air thick with laughter and conversations. Unexpectedly, a table of gentlemen across the room sent over drinks, a gesture met with hesitant smiles. They would typically decline such offers, but they decided to accept the spontaneity of the offer. While engaging in fun conversations and shared moments, a request from the men's table reached them through a courageous messenger.

A gentleman from the distant table asked Colleen's permission to join him. She was pleasantly surprised, so she agreed. Little did she know this decision would open the door to a romantic encounter. Moments later, a tap on my shoulder turned my attention to a vision of Spanish charm. I will call him Matador, a well-dressed embodiment of charisma who greeted me with a captivating smile. His manners were as refined as his attire, and how he said "hello" carried a pleasing quality that ran deep within.

He pointed to a romantic corner in the restaurant where an empty table was showered in soft, dim light, creating an ambiance that whispered of romance. I nodded, and under the spell of Madrid's night, we spent hours talking, laughing, and sharing glimpses of our worlds. The connection was self-evident; the atmosphere charged with energy transforming the ordinary. As the night unfolded, my girlfriend approached, signaling the end of this unexpected rendezvous. Reluctantly, I excused myself, explaining our commitment to security. Understanding yet disappointed, Matador rose with a grace that matched his charm. He pulled out my chair, an act of chivalry, and with sincerity in his voice, he asked if he could see me again.

His deep Spanish accent lingered in the air, adding a layer of allure to the request. Enchanted by the evening and the magnetic presence of this stranger, I could not resist but say yes. Plans were made, promises exchanged, and as I left the dimly lit corner of the bar, I carried with me the memory of a chance encounter that had sparked the flames of a promising romance in the heart of Madrid.

The next evening, as the clock struck 7:00 PM, a sleek black car pulled up in front of our temporary residence in Madrid. My heart raced with anticipation as I entered the car, wondering what the night had in store. The journey was filled with excitement and curiosity, the Spanish night air carrying the promise of romance. As I arrived at a charming restaurant overlooking the city lights, Matador emerged from the shadows, looking even more captivating than the night before. His smile lit up the entire place, and he greeted me with a warm gentle hug. We settled into an intimate corner table, surrounded by the soft glow of candlelight.

Matador's conversation was as captivating throughout the evening as the Spanish guitar playing in the background. We shared stories about our lives, love for Madrid, and passion for art. Time seemed to stand still as we laughed, connected, and savoured the delicious authenticity of Spanish paella and sangria. After dinner, Matador suggested a moonlit stroll through the streets of Madrid. The city was alive with the vibrant energy of the night, and as we walked hand in hand, I could not help but feel a deep connection with this charismatic gentleman.

As we reached a quiet square surrounded by historic buildings and the distant sound of flamenco music, Matador turned to me with mesmerizing eyes and asked if I believed in fate. His words captivated me, and I nodded, eager to see where this enchanting night would lead. Underneath the starlit sky, Matador took my hand and led me into a waltz that felt like a scene from a romantic movie.

The world around us disappeared, and it was just the two of us, lost in the moment's magic. As the night ended, Matador led me back to the waiting car. With a promise to see each other again, he bid me farewell with a lingering kiss that left me yearning for more. The car pulled away, leaving the city lights of Madrid behind, but the memory of a mesmerizing night lingered in my heart. In the days that followed, Matador and I continued to explore the wonders of Madrid together. Our connection deepened, and the city became a backdrop to our budding romance.

Little did I know that this impromptu encounter in a Madrid bar would lead to a love story that surpassed borders and ignited a passion within us both. As the sun dipped below the horizon, casting a warm glow over the streets of Madrid, Matador and I strolled hand in hand through the sparkling city once again.

The air was thick with anticipation, a tension that lingered between us, unnoticed by the bustling crowd around us. Then, Matador's usual manner of confidence was awkward when he revealed that he had something important to share. We found a quiet corner in a quaint plaza, away from the prying eyes and echoing footsteps. Matador's eyes bore a mix of hesitation and anticipation as he took a breath. His adorable expression began to tug at my heart when he confessed, he was a bullfighter in Spain. This exposé carried both admiration and apprehension, for the world of bullfighting was as captivating as it was death-defying. Despite my initial reservations, I assured him that his profession held no bearing on our relationship. I admired his passion and skill, and my fondness for the artistry of bullfighting allowed me to look past the inherent danger. Little did I know that this conversation would set a series of events in motion.

The following day, a sleek black car arrived at my doorstep. The same courageous gentleman who had sought my permission at a tapas bar was now holding the car door open and gesturing to my entry. He shared Matador's storied history as we navigated the bustling streets toward the arena. The significance of this bullfight vibrated through the air, adding weight to the atmosphere within the car.

Upon arriving at the arena, I was ushered to a particular place, an exclusive vantage point reserved for those close to the performers. The vantage point was draped with a red cloak, signifying exclusivity, and I was the only one seated in the area. The gentleman said he would escort me back to the car after the bullfight.

A sense of excitement mingled with a hint of nervousness as I settled, gazing at the vast arena. The rhythmic drumming and the crowd's cheers signaled the bullfight's commencement. My eyes fixed on Manuel, a figure of grace and bravery as he faced the mighty beast.

The battle between man and beast unfolded before me, a mesmerizing display of skill, courage, and tradition. The grand finale of the bullfight brought forth a triumphant climax, the air pulsating with the thunderous applause of the delighted crowd. Spellbound, I remained, the lingering echoes of excitement vibrating. As the enthusiasm subsided, a curious hush descended upon the arena.

Confusion fixed across my face, I watched Matador approach the fallen bull, a solemn figure amid the dust and remnants of the spirited contest. Beside him stood a man, clutching a knife with purpose. With a swift exchange, the knife found its way into Matador's hand, and a hushed gasp escaped my lips. He cut the ears of the death defeated bull in a solemn ritual; a gesture laden with tradition.

Once again, in a surreal silence, the arena witnessed this intimate act of respect. Then, like a matador presenting a trophy, Matador walked towards me, holding the bull's ears in the air. Placing them ceremoniously on the cloaked rail, he bowed gracefully in the direction of me. A radiant smile played on his lips, a silent acknowledgment of our shared experience. In that surreal moment, the stadium erupted into loud applause and joyous shouts.

The crowd, moved by the spectacle and the following ritual, expressed their appreciation with unrestrained enthusiasm. As Manuel gracefully retreated into the shadows, the booms of the ovation lingered in the air, a tribute to the intricate prance between tradition, triumph, and the unexpected turns of the bullring. The same gentleman who had accompanied me earlier appeared, gesturing to me to follow him. We navigated the complex corridors of the arena, and soon, I found myself in a secluded area where Manuel awaited, a triumphant smile on his face.

The shared experience strengthened our bond, a unique connection created in the cauldron of the bullring. At that moment, as the vibrant city of Madrid continued its ceaseless rhythm outside, I realized that sometimes, the most unexpected experiences are the ones that engrave themselves into the hearts of our memories, creating stories that defy the ordinary.

As we left the arena hand in hand, I couldn't help but feel grateful for the twist of fate that had led me to witness the breathtaking battle between man and beast in the heart of Madrid. As the chauffeured car glided through the city, the air between us charged with a subtle tension, a scandalous connection that defied words. The evening felt promising, and as we approached his hotel, I hesitated before mustering the courage to break the silence.

"Could you drop me off? I want to dress for the evening," I asked, my voice a mix of anticipation and excitement. He agreed with a warm smile, promising to accompany me once he had dressed into his evening attire. The hotel lobby welcomed us with applause and an unexpected standing ovation from impressed onlookers. Requests for autographs gushed towards him, and I stood back, feeling like a companion to a superstar and celebrity. It was a moment that added an unexpected touch of glamour to the night, and I could not help but celebrate the scene's enchantment.

We finally arrived at his hotel room; my eyes widened as the door revealed an opulent penthouse. The room displayed luxury, and I felt like the leading lady in a romantic novel, stepping into a world of elegance and charm. The realization of my extraordinary fate lived within me, and a soft smile played on my lips as I giggled to him, "Is this it?" We laughed and kissed, and then he disappeared into what I guessed was his bedroom.

As he appeared from his bedroom and transformed into the essence of sophistication, he invited me to the adjacent room. A hint of hesitation lingered, but I agreed, my heart quickening with curiosity and anticipation. To my surprise, a carefully arranged ensemble of women's fashion lay on the bed. I turned to him, with gratitude and confusion intermingling, and without hesitation, I kissed him. A question hung in the air, and he answered with sincerity. "I wanted to give you a gift, and the clothing seemed appropriate."

Once dressed in the elegance he had chosen, I stood looking at myself in the floor-to-ceiling mirror. I was wearing a breathtaking delicate blue gown that seemed to flow like water with every step I took. The fabric was a rich, shimmering softly under the light, giving me a delicate glow.

The gown featured a fitted bodice that accentuated my figure gracefully, adding a touch of elegance and sophistication. The neckline was a tasteful revealing while highlighting my silhouette and adding a subtle touch of movement. The gown's skirt cascaded down in soft, flowing fabric, creating a mesmerizing effect as it swirled around my legs.

As I moved, the gown came alive, each fold rippled catching the light and adding to my enchantment. The back of the dress dipped into a low, graceful V, adding a hint of vintage charm. My outfit was completed with elegant silver heels, understated jewelry that complimented the gown perfectly without drawing attention away.

I swept my hair into an elegant bun, effortlessly chic and full of charm, and my makeup from the day was still refreshingly subtle. It enhanced my natural features and gave me a radiant, almost mysterious beauty. The delicate blue gown was more than just a dress; it was a statement of grace, elegance, and timeless beauty, making me look like I had stepped out of a fairy tale. I entered the living room, where he awaited with a glass of champagne, his eyes set on fire upon seeing me. In that moment, I sensed a depth of emotion that exceeded mere infatuation. His smile revealed the unspoken truth: he had fallen in love.

As we stood there, cherishing the shared moment of enchantment, I acknowledged the emotions stirring within me. A complex blend of feelings, a choice between love and independence, directed my decisions. For now, I chose to delight in the magic of the present, allowing the allure of the night to create its spell around us. We engaged in the warmth of shared laughter, clinking glasses, and the unspoken promise of love to unfold. We allowed the evening to take us on a magical journey of sensuality, an evening of touching, kissing, and the intimacy of our love affair.

The morning sunlight filtered through the curtains, casting a warm glow on the tangled sheets that enclosed us. As our eyes met, the lingering traces of a shared night frolicked between us. A gentle knock at the hotel door interrupted our peaceful yet playful cocoon, and with a soft kiss on my neck, he reached for his robe to answer the insistent summons.

In the calm exchange from the other room, I sensed a change in the air. When Matador returned, a troubled expression sketched across his features; my curiosity begged me to ask the source of his unease. He slipped off his robe and sought solace in the warmth of our shared space, embracing me with a kiss. Then, with a sigh, he confessed, "I thought I would have more days with you, but I have to leave today. Would you come with me?"

His eyes, pools of vulnerability, searched mine for an answer. I gazed into the beautiful face before me, grappling with the weight of the looming decision. Removing myself from his embrace, I slid out of bed, put on my robe, and wandered into the living room. As he followed with a furrowed brow, I mustered the strength to speak the truth. "Matador, my beautiful Matador, as much as I have fallen in love with you, I cannot give up my journey. I cannot risk resenting you one day for making me abandon my dreams. Do you understand?" His eyes echoed disappointment and yet understanding. "Yes," he replied, acknowledging the complexity of the situation.

His love for me radiated, and he expressed his desire to spend a lifetime proving it, but as I spoke to him once again, I once again expressed that our paths differed, and reality echoed in the spaces between our words. My tender kiss sealed our bittersweet farewell, and we both dressed silently. With heavy hearts, we descended to the awaiting car. At the curb, amid the murmur of the city morning, we shared one last kiss.

He handed me a note with his number and spoke of a lifetime should I change my mind. Tears welled up in both of us as we looked deeply into each other's eyes and parted ways with whispers stating our love. The car pulled away, leaving a love that exceeded time and distance on the streets of Madrid. The love Matador and I shared was like a clock without hands, timeless and filled with meaning in every moment. Our days were fashioned with joy, and our nights were adorned with tranquil embraces and alluring kisses. Yet, I realized that even the most beautiful moments must end. Though our time together was precious, it was time to part ways.

Even the most beautiful love stories have their seasons. Our vibrant and alive love now echoes with memories of what once was that left behind a bittersweet ache. The laughter we shared, the warmth of stolen glances, and the promises we whispered in the dark still linger like the last traces of sunlight on a summer evening. Yet, as the season turned, I found comfort not in mourning what was lost but in cherishing what we had. Our love was a flame that burned fiercely, lighting up the world around us. It was raw and untamed in our quiet moments. We danced through the streets together, fearless, until the dance began to slow while glowing softly in the corners of our hearts.

Though we had parted ways, the pain of loss became a distant echo fading, softening with time. I chose to remember the love, not the loss. I decided to hold close the joy we created, letting go of the sorrow that threatened to consume me. Because in every ending, there is a beginning, and in every goodbye, there is the hope of new hello's. We were a love affair to be remembered, a story that unfolded with the intensity of a thousand lifetimes in just one. And though our season had passed, the beauty of what we shared remains timeless. The pain? Forgotten. The love? Forever memory.

"THE SEASONS OF LOVE"

In the garden of our hearts, love blooms like spring,
Fresh and tender, with promises of everything.
It paints the sky in tones of blue,
And whispers secrets only lovers' view.

Like summer's warmth, love wraps us in embrace,
Filling our days with laughter and grace.
Underneath the sun, we dance and sway,
Creating memories that never fade away.

As autumn comes, love changes its hue,
Golden leaves with a deeper, richer view.
We gather moments like stirs in the wind,
Cherishing each one as our story rescinds.

Then winter arrives, love's season draws near,
Quiet and still, yet the memories are clear.
Though time has passed, and seasons may change,
Love's warmth remains in hearts exchanged.

For love lives through all seasons, and the rain,
A memory cherished through joy and pain.
It lives in whispers of laughter and tears,
In the echoes of moments across the years.

So let love be your reason, a memory bright,
A journey cherished through day and night.
In every heartbeat, in every rhyme,
Love endures beyond the bounds of time.

Colleen C. Carson

J.O.Y. – Journey of Yourself

"The role of you to live the joy of who you are."

&

H.A.P.P.Y. - Heartfelt Appreciation Powers Positive You

"The role of others in bringing happiness into your life."

Mama Carson

"In your book of life, each person you meet is a page, every relationship forms a chapter, but only a few shape the story that defines your journey."

Colleen C. Carson

"Transform within, and the world will transform with you."

Mama Carson

Break Our Silence

Freedom

Colleen discovered that Munich was more than just a destination, it was a vibrant haven of joy and connection, where every corner offered warmth, excitement, and a true sense of belonging. The city's grand architecture, cozy cafés, bustling streets, and peaceful parks filled her with a deep contentment, making her feel completely at home. The people were just as lovely, adding to the city's charm.

Her time at the University of Munich was full of laughter and close friendships. The dorm was a lively retreat where she and her friends would gather in the communal kitchen to whip up dinners, their laughter echoing through the halls. Weekends were all about adventure, whether hanging out at the campus bar, exploring the city's hidden gems, or relaxing in a beer garden with steins of beer and shots of Schnapps. The hours flew by in a whirlwind of joy and camaraderie, creating some of the best memories of her life.

Late spring brought an air of excitement and relief. The students were wrapping up finals, and the buzz of celebration filled the campus. Colleen and her friends were ready to go all out to mark the end of the term, and they planned the ultimate weekend party: a night at a downtown nightclub to dance the night away. Anticipation ran high as they prepared for a well-earned night of freedom. Finally, Friday arrived, and the energy was electric.

They shot back Schnapps, laughing like the night would never end, and hit the dance floor like there was no tomorrow. The music pulsed, the lights sparkled, and they were fully immersed in the moment. Colleen felt alive, ready to let go and celebrate the end of the term with everything she had.

In the middle of all this fun, a fellow came over and asked her to dance. At first, she politely turned him down, not wanting to leave her friends behind. He took her response graciously, but her friends were in shock; he was charming, good-looking, and totally cool about it. They teased her as they continued enjoying the night, the mood filled with lighthearted banter and nonstop fun. Suddenly, a rich, smooth voice filled the air, crooning "The Shadow of Your Smile."

It sounded just like Lou Rawls, and everyone was captivated. The voice got louder and closer until Colleen's friends pointed behind her, giggling like crazy. When she turned around, he was the same guy who'd asked her to dance, now serenading her with that incredible voice.

Her cheeks burned with embarrassment, but something magical was happening. His confidence and the way he sang directly to her were moments she couldn't ignore. She tried to get her friends to stop laughing, but there was no denying the romance in the air. And just like that, what started as a fun night became unforgettable. Before long, Colleen was dancing with Bobby, and soon after, they were dating. Age was just a number; he was fifteen years older, but their connection was undeniable. Bobby was endlessly romantic, and their relationship was filled with laughter, love, and a shared passion for music.

They even began performing together at the nightclub where they first met, turning their love story into something extraordinary.

Then, one night, Bobby popped the question. Of course, she said yes! Her friends were thrilled for her, though a bit sad knowing Colleen would soon return to Canada to plan her wedding. As she packed her bags to leave Munich, Colleen felt an exhilarating mix of emotions. She was leaving behind a city that had stolen her heart but was stepping into an even more exciting chapter of her life with Bobby by her side. The future sparkled with possibility, and she couldn't wait to see where their love would take them next.

I had been home for months, waiting for Bobby, a Sergeant in the United States Army, to finally get his transfer to Denver, Colorado. Once we were married, Denver would be our new home, a city I knew little about aside from its brutally cold winters, which weren't too different from Canada's. Still, it was where we'd begin our life together. Bobby was finally arriving to meet my family, and while I was excited, I couldn't shake my nervousness about how things would go.

After a week, it seemed like everyone except my parents had taken a liking to Bobby. Sure, they were polite, smiling through the small talk, but there was an undercurrent I couldn't ignore. Something about their warmth felt like they were waiting for the other shoe to drop. And when Bobby casually suggested I move in with him in Denver for a few months before the wedding, that certainly triggered a reaction. My parents were less than thrilled, but I knew it was our best decision. Still, it was clear they didn't trust him, or maybe they didn't trust my judgment.

After Bobby left for Denver, my Mom approached me, clearly weighed down by whatever had been brewing in her mind. She and my Dad thought I was making a mistake by going to Denver. I had anticipated some resistance; they always had an opinion, but what came next caught me off guard.

My Mom, with an almost rehearsed tone, said that when Bobby and I got married, her tears wouldn't be ones of joy but of sadness and despair. Really? She had to go there. I wasn't prepared for that level of melodrama. Her words stung, but I brushed them off. I was determined to follow my heart, even if it meant pushing back against my parents' looming shadow of disapproval.

Time flew by, and soon enough, the day arrived when I was finally heading to Denver. Saying goodbye to my family was difficult, but honestly, the thrill of reuniting with Bobby was all I could focus on. As the plane took off, I wondered what life would be like as Mrs. Bobby.

I imagined the wedding, the new chapter... but my Mom's words still echoed, lingering like an unwelcome guest. It was almost laughable how her doubts seemed to hover, yet I couldn't help but feel a hint of cynicism creeping in. Maybe things would be challenging, but then again, whose life ever was?

The pilot's voice crackled over the intercom: "We'll be landing in fifteen minutes." A flutter of excitement stirred inside me as I put out my cigarette and swallowed the last of my wine. I could hardly wait to see Bobby. My heart raced, my pulse quickened, and the anticipation of that moment, seeing him after so long, was almost too much to bear.

As I walked up the airport ramp, he stood at the gate, looking devastatingly handsome. His smile was the kind that made my knees weak, and in his hands, a bouquet of the most beautiful roses, their scent mixing with the electricity in the air. When our eyes met, it was as if the world stopped for just a second. I rushed into his arms, and we kissed, long and deep, like lovers in a classic romance film, where time doesn't matter, and all that exists is the two of you.

That night was like something from a fairy tale. We headed straight to dinner, where the atmosphere was dripping with romance; the candlelight was soft and warm, and the food was exquisite. The way Bobby looked at me across the table, his eyes dark and smoldering, sent shivers down my spine. Every moment was perfect, every word charged with an undercurrent of playful passion. We laughed, toasted to us, and when the night deepened, we returned to his apartment.

When we arrived, Bobby took my coat with a charming grin, as if he couldn't wait for what the night held. He offered me a drink, and we toasted again, this time to new beginnings. As we curled up on the couch, sipping our cocktails, I called my parents to let them know I'd arrived safely. Bobby's fingers brushed my knee as we talked about our future, and something was intoxicating about how we melted into each other's company, plans, dreams, and undeniable chemistry. Later, when we finally slipped under the sheets, the feel of his arms around me made everything else in the world disappear. I fell asleep with a smile on my lips, knowing I was exactly where I was meant to be.

The next morning, I awoke to coffee's rich and inviting smell. Bobby had left it brewing just for me, a small gesture that made my heart swell. But as I walked into the living room, I noticed something odd. The phone was gone. I searched everywhere, convinced I must have misplaced it. A part of me laughed it off—maybe I'd been too distracted by Bobby to notice anything else.

When Bobby returned that evening, his smile lit up the room again. I greeted him with a kiss and asked about the phone. "Oh, that thing? It broke when I tried to use it this morning," he said with a casual shrug. I took it to get fixed. It'll be back in a week, but if you need to call your Mom, there's a phone booth up the street."

His explanation seemed perfectly reasonable, but a tiny flicker of unease crept into my thoughts, you know, that inner voice. No matter, I told myself. Bobby always knew how to smooth things over with that irresistible charm. As the days passed, though, that unease grew, a strange tension between us that hadn't been there before. The phone still hadn't returned, and when I brought it up again, Bobby's mood shifted; his playfulness turned to something darker, a sharpness in his words I hadn't noticed before.

But there we were, wrapped in the romance of it all, and even in that tension, the spark between us remained. Our love was passionate and sometimes unpredictable, but it was real. And in the moments of doubt, I still held onto the magic that had brought us together in the first place, hoping it would guide us through the uncertainty.

I understood Bobby was under pressure from his job transition, and I tried to remain patient, even as frustration simmered beneath the surface. When I gently asked about the phone again, his reply was curt, a firm "no," followed by the promise that he'd handle it the following week. Something in his tone made me pause. The sharpness unsettled me, a creeping discomfort I couldn't quite explain. I wanted to dismiss it, but as the weekend blurred into yet another weekday, that tiny flicker of concern began to grow, casting shadows over my thoughts.

It wasn't just about the phone anymore. The absence of it, this lifeline to the outside world, felt like more than just an inconvenience. It had become a barrier, a wall between me and everything familiar. And the weight of it was pressing in on me, harder with each passing day. Bobby's behaviour gnawed at my mind.

The sudden shift in his attitude, the way he brushed off my concerns, insisting that he would take care of everything. But nothing was being taken care of. The silence and isolation made it seem like the apartment walls were closing in on me, inch by inch. Each passing hour stretched longer than the last, and the uneasy quiet that filled the space between us felt more ominous than ever.

I tried to reason with myself. His job was taking a heavier toll than I realized. Maybe the stress was manifesting in ways I hadn't seen before. But there was a nagging feeling I couldn't shake. Something didn't add up, and I feared there was more lurking beneath the surface than I wanted to acknowledge.

By midweek, I could no longer stand the suspense. The tension had become unbearable. The unease that had lingered in the background now consumed my every thought. The broken phone had become a symbol, a mystery begging for resolution, and I needed answers. The weight of waiting was too much to bear.

Then I remembered the small mall we had passed on a Sunday walk, just a block from the apartment. I hadn't thought much of it then, but now it seemed like a symbol of hope. Without a second thought, I left the apartment and went to the mall, my heart racing with an urgency I couldn't explain. I found a store that sold phones and quickly made a purchase, my hands trembling as I carried it back to the apartment.

Once inside, I hurried to set it up, plugging it in with a sense of determination, almost desperation. As soon as I dialed my Mom's number, the tension began to unravel, piece by piece. Her voice on the other end of the line was a lifeline, grounding me in a reality that suddenly felt so far away. We spoke freely, and I felt relief for the first time in days. There was no Bobby hovering nearby, and there was no need to whisper my words or guard my tone.

But I knew it wouldn't last long. Bobby would be home soon, and the unsettled atmosphere between us still hung heavy in the air. I took a shower before dinner, hoping the steam and the quiet would help clear my mind. Yet, as the water cascaded over me, the questions I had buried flooded back louder than ever. What had happened to us? And what was really going on with Bobby?

The hot water cascaded over me, offering a fleeting escape from the tension that clung to every corner of my mind. My eyes closed, allowing the warmth to wrap around me like a fragile shield, a momentary sanctuary. But peace is fragile, and it shattered abruptly. The shower curtain was yanked open with a screech of metal rings against the rod, the sound slicing through the air, pulling me from my brief solace.

There he stood, a silhouette of menace in the doorway. Bobby, once my lover, now loomed like a dark figure from a nightmare. His eyes, which had once held tenderness, now blazed with a fury that froze the blood in my veins. Before I could react, he reached for me, his hand tangling in my hair with a force that made me gasp. The water turned against me, splashing wildly onto the floor as my footing slipped beneath me. In an instant, I was dragged from the sanctuary of the shower, the cold tile biting into my skin as he pulled me across the bathroom floor.

Fear clawed at my throat as he dragged me into the bedroom. The dim light cast long, sinister shadows on the walls, amplifying the terror of the moment. I tried to speak, to plead for reason, but my voice trembled, lost in the oppressive silence that followed his every breath. His face was inches from mine, his breath hot and rancid with rage, and his words dripped with venom. "Did you ask my permission to buy a phone?" he spat; the words as sharp as a blade. I stammered, "I didn't know I needed permission. It's just a phone!" My voice cracked under the weight of terror. Why was he doing this?

His grip on my hair tightened, the pain shooting through my scalp, and I felt my body tremble under his control. His smile was twisted, cruel, and filled with a darkness I had never seen before. "You should have known better than to defy me," he hissed, his voice dripping with malice. "You'll learn your lesson tonight and won't forget."

The room seemed to shrink around me as he dragged me further, my sobs muffled by the suffocating atmosphere. My skin scraped against the floor, and every step felt like the walls were closing in, trapping me in this nightmare. He hurled me against the wall, my body limp and trembling, as I searched frantically for any means of escape. But there was none. The room, once a home, now felt like a cage, its every corner steeped in dread.

Bobby leaned in closer, his face so near I could feel his breath on my skin, and he whispered in a voice so cold it sent chills through my bones, "You'll ask for permission next time." His words were followed by the sickening thud of his boot slamming into my ribs. I crumpled under the force, my pleas for mercy falling on deaf ears as he kicked me again and again. The pain was unbearable, but my fear, my complete and utter terror, was far worse.

"Have you learned your lesson?" he finally growled, his voice low and guttural, echoing in the darkness.

"Yes!" I gasped my voice barely a whisper through the agony. "I've learned it. Please stop."

He sneered down at me, victorious in his cruelty. Then, with an eerie calm, he reached for the phone I had bought, my only connection to the world beyond these four walls. He held it up, a twisted smile creeping onto his face as he held it in his hand. I watched helplessly as my last lifeline was ripped away from me. His grip over my life tightened, suffocating any remnants of freedom.

He stormed out of the apartment, leaving behind an oppressive silence that throbbed with the remnants of his rage. The walls seemed to pulse with the memory of his violence, trapping me in the chilling aftermath of his brutality. Tears poured down my face as I lay motionless on the cold floor, the pain in my body a cruel reminder of what had just happened. Every breath was agony, every movement a sharp jolt of torment. I was alone. Trapped. And the darkness that lingered in the corners of the room felt like it was closing in, swallowing me whole.

Staggering into the bathroom, I was greeted by a chaotic scene. Water streaked the walls, pools of it gathered on the cold tile floor— a reminder of my desperate attempt to escape him. The mirror, clouded with steam, reflected a face I could hardly recognize, the hollow eyes of a woman consumed by terror, cheeks smeared with the remnants of tears. I stood there, frozen, surveying the wreckage of my sanctuary. My gaze drifted down to the discoloured swelling that marred my skin, dark reminders of his fury, and the cuts where his boots had torn the flesh, now seeping blood onto the bathroom floor.

The sight of my own blood sent a shiver down my spine, a wave of nausea crashing over me as dread settled deep in my core. Each wound was a grotesque reminder that I was trapped in a nightmare that had no end. My hands shook as I fumbled for the bandages, the tremors revealing the fear that had gripped my entire being. I clung to the small, futile act of tending to my wounds, a fragile defiance against the darkness closing in on me.

I bandaged the cuts, my fingers trembling as I tried to wipe the blood from the floor. The bathroom, once a place of solace, now felt like a crime scene, the stains of violence forever imprinted on its walls. With the room cleaned and my body barely held together, I dragged myself to the bed, my limbs heavy with pain and exhaustion. The darkness of the bedroom swallowed me whole, thick and suffocating. It pressed down on me as I lay there, sobbing into the sheets, each tear a desperate cry for escape.

Sleep came slowly, but when it did, it offered no peace. Shadows of his rage haunted my dreams, twisted reflections of my waking nightmare. The abuse became relentless, a constant presence looming over me. I lived in a perpetual state of terror, never knowing when the next blow would fall. The fear gnawed at my insides, a sickness I couldn't shake.

I remembered the phone booth up the street, the one where I made that call to my parents. Bobby had stood beside me, his eyes burning into me, watching every word that left my mouth. My voice trembled as I spoke, the weight of my fear clinging to each syllable.

I could sense my Mother's concern through the phone, her instinctual worry for her child, and she asked me if everything was okay. Her voice was gentle, a stark contrast to the storm brewing inside Bobby. His gaze darkened, his silent rage seething just below the surface. I had no choice. I lied. "It's just the flu," I said, forcing the words out, hoping that my explanation would be enough to calm the fury building in him. But the truth could not be hidden for long.

When we returned to the apartment, his rage erupted. His fists flew at me with a terrifying force, each blow more violent than the last. Blood sprayed across the walls, painting them in gruesome streaks, and I collapsed in a pool of my own blood, helpless against his wrath. The pain was so intense, so all-consuming, that darkness took me. Unconsciousness was a bitter reprieve, a momentary escape from the relentless nightmare of my reality.

Weeks passed in a blur of violence and fleeting apologies. I woke up every morning with the same gnawing fear, wondering if today the day would be when he killed me. The threat of death hung over me like a shadow, always present, always waiting. I could still remember the night he invited a couple of friends over. For a moment, there was a flicker of hope, a chance to escape the constant terror, even if just for an evening. I dressed, choosing something simple that made me feel almost human again. But when he saw me, his eyes darkened, the familiar rage bubbling up.

"You look too sexy," he said, his voice low and dripping with menace. The clothes were nothing special, nothing provocative, but his words cut deep. He ordered me to change, and I obeyed. I stripped off the clothes that had made me feel normal for a fleeting moment and returned to my baggy, shapeless attire. I wiped away the makeup that had made me feel visible, retreating into the shadow of myself once again.

When his friends arrived, we played the part. Dinner was served, polite conversation exchanged, and laughter filled the air, a grotesque mockery of the violence that lingered just beneath the surface. But beneath the forced smiles and the hollow laughter, I could feel the terror simmering, always waiting to erupt, always waiting to consume me whole.

Bobby seemed relaxed that evening, laughing with the others, and for a brief moment, I believed everything was okay. But peace in my world was always an illusion. As they left, Bobby walked them to their car, and I could hear their laughter outside, carefree. Exhaustion consumed me, and I collapsed into bed, seeking a brief escape in sleep. But even in slumber, the fear lingered—a dull hum in the background, reminding me that my fragile peace was always one breath away from breaking.

Then it happened.

A brutal, searing pain exploded across my back, ripping me from unconsciousness. His sharp and venomous voice filled the room, accusing me of flirting with the woman's husband. "You whore!" he screamed, his words biting, his rage palpable. Before I could comprehend, his hand connected with my face, the slap so fierce it split my lip. Blood poured from the wound, but all I could focus on was the fire burning in my eye as if acid had been thrown in it. My face throbbed, swelling to twice its size, a mask of pain that betrayed none of the deeper scars he left, the ones no one could see. The ones he never wanted anyone to see.

I scrambled across the bed, desperate to escape, but he grabbed the neck of my nightgown, dragging me back. The fabric tightened around my throat, choking me as I gasped for air. His hands were cold and merciless as he tore away what little dignity I had left, whispering in my ear with sick satisfaction, "Is this what you wanted?"

My body ached for weeks after, bruises hidden beneath layers of clothing, his apologies as meaningless as the promises he made. He swore it would never happen again each time, but I had long since stopped believing him. Every beating was a twisted ritual he never failed to follow.

Weeks passed, and then came the night that would change everything. Bobby came home, and from the moment he walked through the door, I felt a storm brewing behind his eyes. His face was a mask of anger, his movements heavy, each step a ticking bomb. We sat down to dinner, but the tension was unbearable. He barely touched the food, his voice sharp and cruel as he spat out complaints. I shrank back in my chair, praying for it to be over, but instead, he shoved his chair back, the sound cutting through the silence like a scream. He stormed out, leaving me alone with the shattered remnants of our meal.

When he returned, the ground seemed to tremble beneath his steps, each one sending a wave of fear crashing through me. He stood over me, his hand hidden behind his back, his gaze dark and unnerving. Then, slowly, deliberately, he revealed what he had been concealing: a gun. He held it up, the metal gleaming, and explained it was loaded with only one bullet.

"We're going to play a little game," he sneered. "Russian Roulette."

My heart stopped. He described, with chilling calm, how he would pull the trigger three times. "Let's see if tonight's your lucky night," he said, pressing the gun barrel against my temple. The cold metal sent shivers down my spine, paralyzing me with fear.

Click.
The first trigger pull. Nothing.

He laughed, his voice dripping with insanity. "Still alive! Aren't you lucky?"

Click.
Another pull. Still nothing.

He grinned wider; his eyes wild. "Maybe next time," he taunted.

Click.

Silence followed, heavy and suffocating. I was still alive, but the relief was drowned in terror as he threw on his jacket, his final words hanging in the air like a death sentence. "If you ever make me unhappy again, I will kill you."
And then, he left.

I sat there, numb, my hands trembling as I stood on shaky legs and stumbled into the bathroom. The medicine cabinet reflected a ghost, my face pale, eyes hollow, lips still stained with blood. Mechanically, I reached for his razor, pulling out the blade with steady hands. I filled the bathtub, the water rising slowly as my tears fell into it.

I stripped off my clothes and slipped into the tub, the cold water doing nothing to numb the pain inside. I held the blade, staring at it, convinced this was my only escape. My body shook with sobs, my mind racing with thoughts of release, of freedom from the nightmare I was living.

But then, a faint but persistent voice whispered in my mind. What about your family? You will hurt them more than him. I froze. My inner voice, the one that had kept me alive through so many dark nights, was speaking. I knew she was right. Slowly, I put the blade back into the razor. I stood, water cascading off my body as I reached for the towel and my pyjamas. I dressed in silence, the decision made, the path clear. I wouldn't give him the satisfaction of breaking me. I returned to the bedroom, climbed into bed, and closed my eyes. I waited for sleep, knowing that one day, soon, I would escape his insanity. But tonight, I survived.

The following morning, I awoke to a dimly lit bedroom; the air hung heavy with tension, and the silence was broken only by the occasional distant sounds of the city outside. My heart raced as I glanced around the room, contemplating my next move. He then left for work, and as he closed the door, it clicked shut, sealing me inside. The apartment, once a sanctuary, now became my prison.

His accusations lingered in my mind like a sinister whisper from Satan. I had become a puppet in a twisted game of control; the strings pulled tightly with every offence. But today was different; I could feel the undercurrent of change. My inner courage had come to life, and it was time to live it again. I pondered my life as I lay on our bed, thinking of what to do.

I remembered delighting in the warmth of love and the enchantment of romance. The belief in the magic of love was deeply embedded in my heart and manifested in every corner of my life. Love, in its purest form, should be a haven, a sanctuary where one finds solace and understanding. It should be a force that uplifts and heals, not inflicts manipulation and traumas.

This harrowing experience served as a stark reminder of the fragility of assumptions and the importance of addressing one's deeper issues that lurk beneath the surface. It urged me to reflect on the consequences of unchecked emotions and underscored the need for empathy and understanding in relationships.

As the hours ticked by, I realized this might be my only chance to break free from the suffocating grip of his manipulation, his control. A surge of determination fueled my every step as I searched for a way out of the apartment. The windows were sealed shut, but a glimmer of hope emerged when I discovered a forgotten spare key hidden behind a stack of old magazines. The key felt extraordinary in my trembling hands as I unlocked the door, cautiously peeking into the corridor. The hallway stretched out before me, a passage to potential freedom; my heart pounded as I walked out and carefully locked the door behind me, hoping to avoid detection.

With bustling streets and indifferent strangers, the outside world beckoned to me. I hesitated momentarily, torn between the fear of the unknown and the desperation to escape. The cityscape was vague as I walked, head down, eyes fixed on the pavement, just as I had done with him because if I looked at anyone, particularly a man in public, he would accuse me of wanting to cheat on him, permitting him to beat me.

As I navigated the unfamiliar streets, paranoia crept in. Every passerby carried the weight of judgment, so I quickly glanced over my shoulder with every step. The rhythm of my heartbeat roared the pulse of suspense, a constant reminder of the terrifying moments I engaged in my escape. Liberation mingled with my fear as I sought refuge in a quiet cafe. The aroma of freshly brewed coffee and the soothing hum of conversation engaged me. I chose a corner seat, casting secretive glances at the entrance, half expecting Bobby to materialize. As I drank my coffee, I realized my plan was crumbling before my very eyes.

It was becoming increasingly clear that it was not going to work. However, instead of feeling scared, I had a sudden surge of bravery; this newfound courage spurred me to devise a safer strategy. Without wasting time, I left the café and started running to the apartment, praying to reach there before his arrival. As I entered the apartment, I carefully put the key back precisely where I found it just in case he had placed it there. From then on, I knew I had to be extra cautious and calculating in my approach. Every move I made needed to be deliberate and thought out. I trembled knowing that I was starting a journey toward freedom, but I was also aware of the risks involved. The fear of making a wrong move was honest and kept me on edge. I had to play my cards right, ensuring that each step I took was measured and precise.

The atmosphere in the apartment felt heavy, filled with unspoken tension. I could almost feel his eyes on me, even when he wasn't there. This was more than just getting out of a situation—it was about regaining control and ensuring my safety. I knew I had to stay vigilant, not letting any detail slip unnoticed. My journey to freedom had begun, and with it came the need for a heightened sense of awareness and a cautious, strategic approach to every decision I made. The fear that had once bound me was now transforming me into a plot of strength and courage. The shadows of his accusations began to fade, replaced by the dawn of a new plot in my life, where I was no longer captive to his twisted illusions.

The night was peaceful, and sleep was early because he had to wake up early. As the morning sunlight filtered through the blinds, casting a warm glow on the bedroom, I laid still, watching him sleep. I slipped out of bed quietly, my heart racing, anticipating what lay ahead. I dressed carefully, making sure not to make a sound. Today was the day I would put my elaborate plan into motion. I tiptoed to the kitchen as I prepared his preferred breakfast and packed his lunch with extra care. I could hear him showering. Then the bathroom door opened, and he laughed in the enjoyment of a breakfast surprise. His kiss of gratitude pressed against my lips made me feel repulsed. I wanted to run to the bathroom and wash away his taste. But instead, I wished him a loving goodbye and offered him his lunch and a good day.

The intricate layers of my inner strategy were working seamlessly. In my teens, I studied the complexities of psychology for four years, improving my persuasion skills. I aimed to make him so secure in our love that he would be the last person to suspect my true intentions. As the days passed, I meticulously executed my plan. I became the personification of a perfect partner, anticipating his needs and desires with eerie precision. I immersed myself in his world, building an illusion of trust and loyalty. One morning, after weeks of playing the devoted lover, I looked at myself in the mirror and set a deadline. Thirty days. That was the time I had given myself to execute the final phase of my plan. Without the framework, the sequences of my plot would unravel into chaos.

The thirtieth day arrived, and the tension in the air was palpable. I watched him leave for work; his goodbye kiss wiped from my lips once he was gone. It was time. As I sat all day waiting for his return, I put everything in place: his much-loved dinner, his change of clothes, and his drink of choice, ready for his arrival. After dinner, he pleasured himself with my body, and we then cuddled lovingly. It was repulsive, yet I had to keep my anxiety at bay to complete my journey to freedom. Those emotions occasionally visited, but I forced them down, knowing that any slip could jeopardize everything I had worked towards, even more so my life.

Still, I could not help but feel anxious. I was about to ask Bobby a question that would make or break my plan. My heart pounded in my chest; my palms sweaty as I prepared to speak. "Bobby, I want to marry you," I said, my voice quivering with anticipation and fear. The words hung in the air, the moment fragile and tense. Would his response shatter my plans or propel me on my path to freedom?

The silence stretched on, each second feeling like an eternity. I could hear my shallow and rapid breathing while waiting for Bobby's reply. My mind raced with possibilities of what could happen next. Then, like a ray of sunshine breaking through dark clouds, he replied, "Sure, I will start making the arrangements." Temporary reprieve washed over me but with lingering anxiety. Bobby's answer was the response I needed, with the reality that one slip could make him change his mind and derail my plans. With a small, satisfied smile, I said, "Okay, let's not wait months; that's all I ask." And he agreed. The first part of my plan was successful.

As he spoke about the future, I immediately started planning my next steps. Every detail mattered, and every action had to be calculated. The fear and anxiety were still there, lurking in the background, but I channeled them into determination. The path ahead was burdened with challenges, but I was more determined than ever to seize my freedom. With the wedding date looming ahead, I was on a mission to persuade Bobby about the necessity of involving my parents in the preparations. The second part of my plan was crucial, and I knew I had to craft a compelling storyline that would resonate with him emotionally.

Seated across from Bobby, I took a deep breath and began formulating my argument. "Bobby, I've been thinking a lot about our wedding plans, and I ask you to understand something," I said, locking eyes with him. "I am the first daughter in my family to get married, which means the world to my parents. Their involvement in the planning process is not just a desire; it's a deeply rooted expectation and tradition."

As I spoke, I could see a flicker of confusion in Bobby's eyes as he shuffled in his comfort chair. His appearance exposed a sincerity to my words. I continued, "You see, I am torn," allowing a hint of vulnerability to seep into my voice. "On the one hand, I want nothing more than to make you happy and ensure our wedding day is everything we've dreamed of. But, on the other hand, there's this overwhelming desire to respect my parents' wishes and make them a significant part of our journey." Then, I went silent and let my words do the needed work.

I could sense Bobby's thoughts churning as he tried to reconcile the conflicting emotions I presented. It was a delicate spin between prioritizing his happiness and highlighting my obligation to respect my parents' expectations. Then, my following statement, the most powerful yet, "I want you to know your happiness is my top priority," I emphasized, reaching for his hand. "However, not involving my parents in the planning process would significantly disappoint them. It's not just about us; it's about bringing our families together in this joyous celebration, and you're the only one that can do that."

Bobby's expression was now a mixture of understanding and empathy. My plan to create his control and power in the decision of our and my family's future was working. "Bobby, if you decide to include my parents, you'll see the significance of it. It is not just about meeting expectations; it's about building a foundation of love and unity that will live through our marriage and raising our children," I explained with a reassuring smile, hoping to solidify my point and his control of power. As the weight of my words settled in, my plan to use a combination of emotions and persuasive language was working, and I knew we were now on the same page. He said, "Let me think about it; I will tell you tomorrow." A knot tightened in my stomach, but my reply was calm and inviting, "Okay, Bobby, tomorrow it is!"

In the morning, I could feel the weight of our conversation from the night before lingering in the air; a dense cloud of uncertainty threatened to suffocate any calm. The unease gnawed at me, my mind racing with what-ifs and worst-case scenarios. Yet Bobby appeared oblivious to the storm within me as he continued as if nothing had transpired. A sense of disappointment settled in, the anxiety growing more intense with each passing moment. Why hadn't he mentioned it? Was he having second thoughts? The silence between us spoke volumes, a deafening void filled only by the radio commentator in the kitchen. As he prepared for work, I braced myself for what might unfold.

He opened the apartment to leave for the day and suddenly turned with a smile. "I think you're right," he said, his voice cutting through the tension. We should respect our parents. Let's discuss this when I get home tonight." Confidence yet apprehensive crashed within me like a ship heading to shore, realizing there was no dock. I was relieved that his answer had finally surfaced, but I was also apprehensive about the impending conversation. I took a deep breath, attempting to steady my nerves and collect my thoughts. "Thank you for understanding and respecting my parents," I replied, my voice steady. "I'm grateful you will involve my parents in our decision. With their support, we can get married and start our life together. I love you so much!" I sealed my words with a hug, careful not to betray the urgency. Bobby kissed me goodbye, and as the door closed behind him, a mix of emotions churned within me as I washed my lips clean of him. I took pride in successfully navigating the second part of my plan, yet I still felt uneasy with a betrayal.

The third part of my plan had begun. After our decision, I meticulously arranged a carefully scripted performance by Bobby in this charade of love and marriage. I asked him if he would call and tell my parents about our wedding plans. The stakes were high in securing Bobby's commitment to my parents. It was not just about the wedding; it was a strategic move to bind him to the gravity of the situation. If Bobby had promised and his promise had unraveled, my Dad, a man of integrity and influence, would not hesitate to board a plane and demand answers from Bobby. In the shadow of potential failure, Bobby recognized the looming threat my Dad posed.

Abusers are cowards at heart, bullies who quivered at the mere thought of facing the courageous as unyielding and assertive as my Dad. My performance was not just a charade; it was my lifeline, the brutal abuse and control he had forced upon me. I only had two choices: flight or death. I wanted to live for the ones I love, if not for myself.

The night before my departure, the air in the room felt tense as I meticulously packed my belongings, each reflecting memories of the emotional rollercoaster I had endured. The mere thought of returning home offered a glimmer of hope, a prospect of escaping the clutches of an abusive relationship that had subjected me to torturous confinement. Once a battleground for emotional turmoil, the room was the quiet resolve of someone determined to reclaim their life. I took a deep breath, bracing myself for the journey ahead—towards healing and rediscovery.

My bags, now bulging with the remnants of a life I was eager to leave behind, stood as silent witnesses to my escape from a journey that brought an insidious toll on my well-being. The scars of his abusive conduct ran deep, leaving me emotionally battered. The toll on my physical health was evident in my mirror's reflection. I had become a mere shadow of my former self, the once vibrant and spirited woman who was now eighty pounds of stress. The weight loss spoke volumes about the mental and emotional strain I had endured, a tangible manifestation of the torment that had become a daily reality.

Hesitation lingered in my every movement, a residual effect of the constant fear and manipulation that had become a pervasive presence in my life. The prospect of being around people, once a source of comfort, now evoked a sense of anxiety and fear as the clock ticked relentlessly toward the morning. The morning had awakened, and without a hint of warning, "I don't think you should leave.

I made the wrong decision. Forget it, you are staying here. I will cancel your flight," he declared, the weight of his words hanging heavily. Panic seized my heart as the ground beneath my plans started to crumble. In that agonizing moment, the realization struck me like a thunderbolt. If I did not escape this suffocating environment, my only refuge would be the acceptance of death, whether by his hand or, in desperation, my own.

The gravity of the situation pressed on me, squeezing the breath from my lungs and leaving me on the edge of despair. Attempting to gauge his intentions, I played one more chance; I nicely agreed, my mind racing with fear and uncertainty. As I obediently carried my luggage into the bedroom, a sense of resignation settled over me, a temporary surrender to his oppressive power over my fate. I felt and hoped this was an act in a sinister game of control to gauge my response.

Just as quickly as he had taken away my escape, he gave it back with my response, and we were en route to the airport. The car ride felt like an eternity, each passing moment laden with the oppressive weight of the unknown. Once at the airport, as I kissed him goodbye, my anxiety peaked. The fear he might retract his decision loomed over me like a storm cloud, casting a shadow on my every step toward the gate.

As I proceeded to the gate, I turned around repeatedly, forcing smiles in a desperate attempt to appease him, the uncertainty gnawing at me. Then I crossed the gate, stepping onto the plane, my path to freedom. It had lifted me, replaced by a sense of survival and the realization that I had escaped a madman's clutches. As my plane took off, the stewardess approached me and asked if I needed anything.

My joyous reply was, "I have everything I have ever wanted, but thank you!" My freedom has now been restored. One year had passed, and Bobby's repeated threats throughout the year had faded into the distant past, defeated by the firm strength of family support. My parents and my uncle, my silent guardians, confronted him with a stern warning never to set foot in Canada, telling a tale of a nonexistent arrest warrant. It was a bluff, but my uncle played his part with conviction. He was a Police Officer whom Bobby had met on his visit to meet my parents.

If there's one thing I've learned from my experience with domestic violence, it's that survival isn't just about getting out; it's about reclaiming yourself, piece by piece. It's about finding your voice again, even if it trembles initially. I won't sugarcoat it; healing is messy, unpredictable, and takes time. Some days, you feel like you've moved mountains; other days, a single memory can pull you back to a place you thought you'd left behind.

But here's the truth: you are not broken beyond repair. You are stronger than you think; there's life beyond the pain. I'd sum it up: Domestic violence is a thief, it steals your sense of self, your safety, and your joy. I know because I lived it. It wasn't easy to leave and wasn't a straight path to healing. But let me tell you this: life on the other side, a life filled with self-discovery, peace, and joy, is worth it.

I used to believe that things would get better if I just loved him enough and tried a little harder. But the reality is no amount of love can change someone who doesn't want to change. And love, real love, doesn't hurt. It doesn't leave you walking on eggshells, questioning your worth, or living in fear of the next outburst. Love should lift you, support you, and, most of all, allow you to be yourself without fear. That's a lesson I had to learn the hard way. You're not broken, even if you feel like you are. You're not alone, even when it seems no one understands. And you're not weak for staying or strong only when you leave. Strength shows up in ways we don't even notice in the quiet moments we survive, the tears we cry, and the hope we keep alive.

Looking back, I see how fear once held me hostage, how it convinced me that leaving meant failure, that I was weak for wanting more. It told me that I was somehow to blame for the abuse. I let shame and doubt whisper lies in my ear, telling me no one would understand, that I was somehow to blame. But stepping away didn't make me weak; it made me wise. It taught me that my worth isn't defined by someone else's opinion or by the visible or invisible scars I carried. It showed me that freedom isn't just about physical space but also emotional and mental peace.

If I could reach back to my younger version, I'd tell her, "You deserve peace, not pain. Love doesn't hurt, and you're braver than you think." And I'll tell you the same thing. Stand up, speak out, and find your way because your story doesn't end here. There's a life waiting for you that feels like freedom. Trust me, it's beautiful; reclaiming that peace is not just empowering, it's a beautiful journey of self-discovery. I won't pretend it was easy. It took time to unlearn the patterns of self-doubt, to replace the fear with confidence, and to trust myself again. But little by little, I did. And so can you.

To anyone who's still walking that difficult path, please know this: you are not alone. I know it feels like no one understands like the walls are closing in, but there's a whole world of support out there waiting for you. When you're ready, reach out, whether it's to a friend, a hotline, or just someone who's been there. You deserve to be heard. You deserve to be free. And when you do step into the light, you'll realize that the most powerful thing you can ever do is choose yourself.

Because you, my dear reader, are worth it. Always. You are valuable, you are important, and you are worth every step of this journey.

"Sense is your compass, nonsense the detour, and
commonsense the map that transforms
the ordinary into the extraordinary,
with wisdom lighting your way."

Colleen C. Carson

"HER POWER TO RISE"

Once a victim, lost in fear,
Holding back each silent tear.

Bound by chains of fear and pain,
Struggling back to break the chain.

But deep within, a flicker glows,
A spark of strength begins to
grow.

With each small step, she finds her way,
Towards the light of a brighter
day.

Through hardships faced and battles fought,
She learns to rise, to stand in
thought.

No longer captive to her past,
Her spirit soars, free at
last.

With courage as her guiding light,
She walks with purpose, strong and
bright.

From victim to victor, she is transformed,
In ordinary words, but courage
adorned.

In whispers soft, her tale unfurls,
A performance that touches
worlds.

Through her journey, hearts ignite,
Guiding souls to reach their
height.

Her story spirals through time and space,
An inspiration in life's endless
race.

Each step she takes, a path to find,
A tribute to the human
mind.

In her courage, we find our own,
A melody of strength is
sown.

Inspiring hope, igniting flame,
Her legacy, a lasting
claim.

So let her story fill the air,
A witness to all who
dare.

To rise above, to truly be,
The heroes of our
destiny.

Colleen C. Carson

"Visionaries enlighten the journey ahead, imagination meets innovation and the future awaits its authors."

Mama Carson

"LOVERS PICNIC"

In the realm of my thoughts, there exists a duality,
One of stark reality, the other, a realm of dreams,
In the dream, there lies no expectation,
Merely a hopeful wish, a whisper of someday.

And that someday arrived,
A dream woven with care by a special soul,
Crafted in anticipation of my delight,
A gift adorned with a solitary thread of love

It commenced with two clear wine glasses,
In a park aglow with the tones of early evening,
A blanket adorned with my preferred flavors,
He, a child at heart, celebrating my amazement.

"This is just the beginning," he uttered,
Feeding me with delectable bites,
Sipping on the nectar of our chosen wine,
My thoughts, a canvas painted with perfection.

With a gentle touch, he positioned me, eyes covered,
Anxiously awaiting the launch of the surprise,
His excitement mirrored in the air,
Then, as if descending from cosmic realms,

A Cello began to serenade us with Brahms,
My eyes fluttered open to a heart brimming with joy,
The dream now a tangible reality,
Brought to life by the selfless love that encircled us.

As my form nestled against his,
We listened in awe to the musical masterpiece,
My mind swirling with thoughts of his magnificence,
Overcome by the harmonious reflections of his love.

Yes, my dream, now a reality through him,
Another dream, a presence from the early days,
The dream of him, both eternally in my heart,
Two dreams converging, connected, forever.

Colleen C. Carson

"True growth arises when we blend the wisdom of others with the clarity of our own inner voice."

Colleen C. Carson

"In the wonder of eternity, humankind unearths comfort
in the wisdom of our brief journey."

Mama Carson

"BEGUILED GARDEN"

Lorian wandered through the Beguiled Garden, the warmth of the day wrapping around him like a tender hug. The flowers reached skyward in vibrant colours, their petals shimmering as though dipped in sunlight. Around him, the garden hummed softly as if nature whispered secrets too sacred for words.

He meandered along the winding paths, the air thick with the sweet perfume of roses, lilies, and lavender, their scents twirling together in perfect harmony. For a while, everything felt untouched by time.

The sun poured golden light over the landscape, and a playful breeze, carrying notes of joy, frolicked around him. Lorian felt at peace, as though the world had paused just for him to cherish its beauty.

But as he ventured deeper, something shifted. It was subtle at first; the bright, sparkling hues of the flowers dulled just slightly. The breeze, once so carefree, now carried with it a soft and heavy sigh. Even the sunlight, warm and golden moments before, began to dim as though the garden were gently surrendering to the unavoidable passage of time.

Lorian slowed, his footsteps quieter now, almost humble. The blue sky above faded into muted gray, and the once-vivid landscape grew more silent, cloaked in a melancholy stillness. He sat beside a fading rosebush, its petals beginning to wilt, and let the hush of the garden settle over him.

As his eyes wandered, he caught sight of a single rare flower standing apart from the rest. It glowed faintly, its delicate light defying the intruding shadows. Drawn to its quiet radiance, Lorian knelt and carefully plucked it. The moment the stem snapped free, the flower's soft glow began to fade, dimming in his hand.

The air felt heavier now as the first cool breeze of evening stirred. Lorian sat there, the fragile bloom cradled between his fingers, watching as the light of day diminished into dusk. He then understood that the garden wasn't merely a place; it was a reflection of life itself, vivid and alive one moment, quiet and fading the next. Its seasons mirrored his own.

Though fleeting in beauty, the flower held a quiet wisdom. It reminded him that life's preciousness lies not in longevity but in its humanity.

As autumn nears, the Beguiled Garden murmurs its sorrowful truth: Like the rarest blooms, the rarest moments are meant to be cherished because they cannot last. The flower, once vibrant and full of life, was plucked too soon, leaving the stem barren and the soil yearning. Its petals, scattered like forgotten memories, remind us that even the brightest love can wither.

The garden mourns, yet whispers of resilience, of new buds waiting in the shadows. Life's power lies in accepting the ache of change, knowing that every fallen petal enriches the earth, and every end holds the quiet promise of a new beginning, even amid the weight of sorrow.

A sentimental ache settled in his chest as the shadows grew longer and the Beguiled Garden stilled. The garden's vibrancy had softened into something more poignant, a reminder of time's uncompromising march. And yet, even in the melancholy of that fading light, Lorian found solace.

He lingered, reluctant to leave, as though his presence might pause the approaching night. But as the last glowing petal disappeared into the dark, he rose, carrying the lesson of the garden with him. Change was inevitable, and beauty, though fleeting, left a lasting memory.

In all its seasonal glory, the Beguiled Garden speaks to the fragile nature of existence. Lorian's journey through its paths mirrors our own: the joy of bright beginnings, the slow fade of fleeting moments, and the quiet understanding that follows. The rare flower he plucked is life's fragility and brilliance, a reminder to hold tightly to what matters, even as it slips through our fingers.

"True richness lies not in what fills your pockets, but in what fills your heart."

Colleen C. Carson

"UNTYING THE KNOT"

A few days before Colleen's twenty-fifth birthday, she stood on the verge of one of the most exhilarating moments of her life: her wedding day. The air buzzed with excitement as anticipation built toward the celebration of her dreams. From the moment Colleen had watched Gone with the Wind at thirteen, she had envisioned a wedding bathed in the grandeur of that era.

The lavish gowns, the stately mansions, and, of course, the dashing Rhett Butler had etched themselves in her mind, fueling a vision of elegance and timeless romance.

Colleen and Brian decided their wedding would be nothing short of a Gone with the Wind spectacle. Both shared a love for blue, which naturally became the palette for their celebration.

Despite the oppressive July heat, their wedding unfolded beautifully, exactly as they had imagined. After the joyful ceremony, they set sail on a month-long honeymoon, cruising through the crystalline waters of the Caribbean.

Their love story had all the charm of a classic romance. Brian, already a homeowner, lived next door to Colleen's parents. One day, as fate would have it, Colleen stepped outside to grab the car keys from her father, who was chatting over the backyard fence with Brian. Colleen barely noticed him, but Brian? He noticed her. That day, he told his friends, "I just met the girl I'm going to marry."

Colleen's father, sensing Brian's interest and liking him as the new neighbour, invited him for dinner. Brian eagerly accepted, and that meal set the foundation for a blossoming relationship leading to the life they were about to embark on together.

Returning from their honeymoon, Brian and Colleen found themselves knee-deep in wedding gifts, deciding quietly what to keep and store away. Some gifts, like a particularly hideous vase, went straight to storage, convincing them it was likely a recycled gift. Despite the chaos of settling in, Colleen had to dive back into work, leaving her little time to organize the house, a task she preferred to avoid on precious weekends.

The first few years of their marriage were a whirlwind, full of unexpected twists and turns. People often told them that this was their honeymoon phase, but for Brian and Colleen, that phase felt remarkably short, more like honeymoon months, six to be exact. Both were workaholics, deeply engrossed in their careers.

Brian transitioned from working on the tugs to becoming a Regional Manager in a direct sales company, while Colleen moved from being an office manager to an Area Manager. Coincidentally, they both ended up working for the same company.

Their career advancements brought with them not just financial success but also a jet-set lifestyle they thoroughly enjoyed. Life was a constant adventure filled with travel, new experiences, and an intoxicating sense of freedom. But the true adventure was yet to come. Colleen and Brian soon welcomed two beautiful children, Crystal and Chance, into their lives, and their world shifted in the most extraordinary way.

Suddenly, jet-setting and career ambitions took a backseat to Christmas plays, parent-teacher meetings, birthday parties, and endless playdates. And you know what? Colleen and Brian wouldn't have had it any other way. This new chapter, filled with the laughter of their children and the simple joys of family life, was more fulfilling than the luxury trips and high-powered career moves ever could have been.

In the end, Colleen realized that this was the life she had always wanted, rich not in material wealth but in the boundless love and personal growth that came from raising a family. This life was more rewarding than she had ever imagined, full of meaning, purpose, and a depth of happiness that no glamorous lifestyle could rival. It was, without a doubt, the most incredible adventure of all.

As time moved forward, Brian's presence at home became increasingly scarce. Even the arrival of our children did little to alter his relentless dedication to work. Meanwhile, I found solace and purpose in staying home, creating a life as an entrepreneur while raising our children.

This dynamic, though fruitful for me and our children, created a quiet, widening abyss between Brian and me. My life revolved around our children, while Brian was only truly present from Saturday night to Monday morning, with Sunday serving as a family ritual, a day to spend time together, visiting others or engaging in activities as a family unit.

Over time, our relationship transformed from a traditional marriage to something more like that of best friends who still deeply valued the family we had built. Our love remained, though it quietly transformed into something less romantic, more platonic.

Crystal and Chance grew into their own lives as the years passed, graduating and venturing into the world with a sense of pride that filled us both. Yet, when they left, the house, once full of their laughter and bustling energy became hollow. The realization hit me with unexpected force: Brian and I had drifted so far apart over the years that the silence of the empty nest revealed the truth we had long ignored.

I found myself at the edge of exhaustion, weary from living a life built around Brian's ambitions rather than my own. We never explicitly discussed a separation, but I considered moving back to Vancouver, leaving Brian to continue his life in Calgary. And then, the unthinkable happened: our son, Chance, passed away.

The devastation was beyond words and plunged me into a dark hole. I was utterly lost, consumed by grief. Brian, sensing the depth of my despair, called our daughter. "We need to help your mom, or she won't make it," he said, urging Crystal to take me in.

I moved to Vancouver, and as the months became years, I recognized I could never return to the life I had known before Chance's passing. Nor did I want to. In the quiet moments of reflection, I realized that I needed to live life on my own terms, unburdened by anyone else's expectations. Though I loved Brian and always would, I was no longer in love with him. Our relationship had been beautiful, and our bond deep, but I had to prioritize my own joy and well-being now.

This was not a case of failure or betrayal. It was the culmination of years lived in contrast, where our once-shared dreams had strayed. Marriage, in its essence, is often seen as a partnership rooted in love, trust, and shared goals. But even the strongest unions are not immune to the subtle shifts of time.

Brian and I began as best friends, lovers, and partners in life's journey. We built a home, nurtured our children, and found happiness in each other's company. Yet, as the years passed, our paths slowly separated, and we found ourselves on individual journeys.

In our separation, we remained steadfast as co-parents and friends. Our love and respect for each other did not diminish, but our journey as a married couple had run its course. Brian continued to excel in his career, and I found a new sense of purpose and joy in my entrepreneurial ventures. Our lives, though separate, were still filled with pride and support for one another.

The beauty of our story lies not in its longevity but in its authenticity. Our decision to part ways was born out of love, not resentment. It was an acknowledgment that to live fully, we needed to accept change.

I learned that the success of a marriage is not measured by its endurance but by the growth, fulfillment, and respect it fosters. By choosing to live authentically, Brian and I gave each other the freedom to flourish in ways we never could have imagined within the confines of our marriage.

Several years after our divorce, Crystal called me one day with concern in her voice. "Mom," she said, "Dad's not feeling well. Could you come over and check on him?" It wasn't like Brian to be unwell, so I hurried over, When I arrived, the diagnosis was simple: a bit too much red wine, a rare indulgence for Brian. I helped him to bed, making sure he was comfortable. As I turned to leave, he called out, his voice softer than usual.

"Colleen," he said, "I wish I could have time back. I would do things differently." I paused, sensing the weight of his words. "I think most of us feel that way at some point," I replied. "What would you change if you could?" His answer was one I hadn't expected. "I know I couldn't have loved you more," he began, "but I could have shown you just how much I loved you."

I couldn't help but smile at the honesty in his voice, at the vulnerability of the moment. He continued, "I miss you. I'll always love you. I fell in love with you the moment I first saw you, and that's never changed. There will never be another woman in my life." I felt my heart tighten, not out of regret, but out of the profound connection that still lingered between us. "Don't do that to yourself, Brian," I said gently. "There might be a woman out there who could make you very happy."

But he shook his head, smiling through the haze of red wine and old memories. "The only woman who has ever made me that happy is standing right before me," he said. "I just want you to know that I will always be in love with you. But more than that, I want you to be happy because you and your heart deserve it." I leaned down, kissed him on the forehead, and said goodnight. As I left his room, a sense of peace washed over me. We've never spoken of love again since that night.

Yet, in that moment, I realized something beautiful: love doesn't always fade with time. Sometimes, it transforms, becoming something deeper, an unspoken understanding, a quiet respect for what was and what will always be. If there is one regret, it is that we did not take this step sooner. But then again, life unfolds in its own time, and we welcomed our truth when we were ready. Timing, after all, is everything.

"Strength is found not in the absence of struggle,
but in the courage to confront it head-on."

Colleen C. Carson

"Overthinking is the thief of inspiration, the jailer of growth, and the assassin of dreams."

Mama Carson

"HELLO MS. COLLEEN"

It was the summer of 1971, a season of magic and romance that swept through Vancouver like a warm ocean breeze during the Sea Festival. The shimmering waters of the Pacific sparkled under the golden July sun. American ships, grand and proud, docked for the festivities. In the heart of it all, Colleen, adorned with the title of Miss Kitsilano, stood as the Canadian hostess for the U.S. Marines at the Seaforth Armory. It was an honour that filled her with happiness and anticipation, though she had no idea that this duty would alter the course of her life.

When she stepped into the Armory, her thoughts were on small talk with Marines and plans with girlfriends later. Little did she know that fate had its own script for the evening. The festival's energy buzzed as several US Marines gathered around her, eager to chat. She shared stories of the charming places they could explore during their week-long stay, their conversations flowing with a mix of light-hearted banter and laughter.

Suddenly, it felt as though the room responded to guests parting like a sea, forming a path leading directly to a table of officers. In that fleeting moment, while she was still talking with the Marines, her eyes locked onto another pair, solid and steady. Time seemed to freeze, and her breath caught as she stared into the eyes of an officer gazing right back at her. The world around her faded; even though the Marines continued their conversation, all she could hear was the rapid beat of her heart, lost in the magnetic pull of this remarkable Marine officer. Could someone this perfect be here now?

This officer was a figure who seemed to have walked straight out of a Hollywood film. His presence was magnetic, a Hollywood dream— tall, charming, and with the kind of easy confidence you only see in stars like Cary Grant. At that moment, the world narrowed to just him. My heart raced as our eyes locked across the room, and something in me shifted, a feeling so strong, it was as if the universe whispered in my ear, "This is the one."

The air between us felt electric, and the anticipation grew as I walked closer. I bid the surrounding Marines a warm good evening, wishing them nothing but the best as they set off to explore the wonders of Vancouver.

This parted path was like an invitation to a place or journey I have yet to take, a journey of the extraordinary. When I approached their table, I steadied myself and introduced myself, my voice surprisingly calm despite the flutter of butterflies in my stomach. "Ms. Colleen," he said, rising to his feet.

The entire table of officers followed his lead, and the gesture caught me off guard. A bit flustered, I smiled and kindly asked them to sit back down, adding a soft "thank you." His voice reached me then, and it was enough to send a shiver down my spine as he introduced himself, "Major Keith. It's a pleasure to meet you." As he extended his hand, I grasped it, and something shifted at that moment.

It was as though I had been swept into a whirlwind of emotions. His gaze, his presence, his very essence, I barely remembered his name—he was that captivating. The world had quieted for just the two of us; it was as if time paused for us in the middle of that vibrant festival, leaving us suspended in a moment that felt far too extraordinary to be ordinary.

I couldn't help but think, Is this how love begins? A chance moment, a glance, a simple hello? We spoke, but it was more than words. Each exchange felt like the universe pushing us closer together, as if we were meant to find one another in that sea of uniforms and celebration. His charm was undeniable, but it wasn't just his looks; it was how he made me feel, as if I was the only woman in the world.

As my duties at the Armory wrapped up and I prepared to leave, I felt a tap on my shoulder. "Ms. Colleen," he said softly, "are you leaving so soon?" "Yes, Major Keith," I replied, feeling a swirl of emotions. He invited me to take a walk, and without hesitation, I agreed. We strolled through the festival, laughing and exchanging stories.

His touch was light, but it sent a cascade of sparks through me. Keith took my hand, and we kissed as his lips met mine in the magic of that festival night. It wasn't just any kiss; it was the kind that changed you. The world faded away, and all that existed was the two of us. In that instant, I knew our connection was something more than chance: destiny, written in the stars.

Over the next few days, we spent as much time together as possible, sharing moments of laughter, stolen glances, and deeper conversations. What started as a festival fling blossomed into something magical. Beneath the twinkling lights and the Pacific night breeze, we shared our dreams, fears, and a vulnerability that neither had expected. But the magic wasn't just in the festival; it was in the connection we found: two souls meeting in a universe that seemed to have planned it all along.

But time, as always, moves too quickly. The Sea Festival ended, and with it came the reality that Keith would soon leave. The thought of parting weighed heavily on us, though neither could bear to speak of it. The night before his departure, as we walked along the water's edge, with the waves whispering their secrets to the shore and the night breeze tossing my hair, I felt like I had stepped into a story where love was more than a fleeting romance. It was timeless, reaching beyond the world's noise into a quiet, sacred space only we shared.

He finally confessed his love and promised to find a way to keep us together; hope bloomed in my heart. Keith spoke of Vancouver, San Diego, and a future we could build no matter the miles between us. Our love endured, defying the distance with letters, phone calls, and cherished visits. Each moment together felt like a stolen treasure, a reminder that love is not bound by time or place. Each visit was a reunion that felt like coming up for air after being underwater.

Months passed, filled with longing and anticipation. Each reunion was sweeter than the last, and our love grew stronger with every visit. And then, during one of my trips to San Diego, Keith surprised me. He knelt before me over candlelight and whispers of romance, holding a little red box. Inside was a diamond ring, shimmering like the stars that had brought us together. His voice trembled as he asked me to marry him, and my heart soared as I said yes. Later, he told me he had spoken to my Dad and asked for my hand in marriage, and it seemed to have made my Dad very happy.

For a time, everything felt perfect. Our love was a fairy tale come to life. But as life often does, love can be tested by forces beyond our control, no matter how strong. One day, as I awaited his arrival in

Vancouver, the silence became unbearable. Keith didn't call as planned. When the phone finally rang, his voice was filled with a sadness I had never heard before. He confessed that just before we met, his ex-girlfriend had left him, only to return with the news that she was pregnant with his child and the due date was just weeks away. He was torn between the love we had and the duty he felt to his unborn child.

At that moment, the world we had built began to crumble. Keith, with all his sincerity and regret, knew that his obligation would tear us apart. I felt the weight of his decision in every word, and even though my heart was breaking, I understood. His duty was to the life he had unknowingly created, and no matter how much we loved each other, he couldn't walk away from that responsibility. One of the many traits I love about this man is his integrity. Tears poured down my face as he told me the news.

The man I loved, the one I believed I would spend my life with, was slipping through my fingers. He asked me to come to San Diego one last time, but I couldn't bear it. The final goodbye was excruciating. I begged him not to call again, knowing that every word would only deepen the wound. And so, with one last conversation, we ended what had felt like a love story written in the stars.

My days and years followed with an emptiness I couldn't shake. I eventually met my husband and built a life of stability and love, but Keith's memory lingered, a ghost from the past that refused to fade. He remained in the corners of my heart, a ghost of a love that could have been. It wasn't until decades later that I learned the full truth.

One day, in a conversation with my parents, the truth I never expected surfaced. Keith had reached out to them, longing to reconnect. He never married his ex-girlfriend, living instead as co-parents, and their relationship never blossomed into love. He had told them he still loved me, had always loved me, and regretted our parting every day. Why hadn't they told me?

Why hadn't they encouraged him to reach out? My parents answered, filled with regret; they believed it was for the best that I had moved on, built a family, and didn't need the past to come knocking. But knowing now what I hadn't known then, the sorrow was almost unbearable.

It was a revelation that hit me like a wave. Keith had never stopped loving me. He'd chosen to stay away because I hated him for breaking my heart. And in his silence, I, too, had believed our story was over. But it had been kept alive by regret, misunderstanding, and the weight of unspoken words.

I realized then that life is full of choices; some are made for us, and some are made for ourselves. But the love Keith and I shared, however brief, had never truly faded. It had simply been set aside, carried by both of us in different ways, in the quiet corners of our hearts.

Keith and I never reunited; perhaps that was how it was meant to be. But I will always carry the lessons of that love with me, especially how fate brings people together, and sometimes, it's only for a season. Even in parting, love leaves its mark, shaping who we become and reminding us that there are no coincidences in the grand dance of life, only moments meant to be cherished for what they are. There's wisdom in knowing that not every love story ends the way we expect. Some are etched into our souls, leaving marks that time cannot erase.

Though Keith and I were never destined to spend our lives together, the love we shared will forever remain—a reminder of what could have been and what still, in some small way, was. In the end, love is not always about holding on. Sometimes, it's about letting go, knowing that it was real and that, for a moment, it was everything.

"A Tender Goodbye"

As I walk the enchanted path of life,
Our love springs to mind, vivid and bright.
A hint of your scent fills the air,
Awakening emotions once in despair.

Did your scent ride the spring breeze?
Or fall in gentle rain from the willow trees?
In the passages of our shared history,
Our reflections on our memories.

Under the moon's glow, our souls are defined,
In the pirouette of love, our hearts aligned.
Our whispers transformed into lyrical vows,
While sensual caresses kindled our souls.

Witnesses are envious of our loving magic,
As we waltzed, like in a lover's poetic.
I trusted we'd infinitely script our tale,
A forever love on a perceptive scale

We took pleasure in the art of our love,
Unaware betrayal would tear us apart.

Once turtle doves, our love was worn,
A forever promise, no longer sworn.

As time passed, a disturbing sense grew,
I questioned if our connection still grew.
Your confession broke my heart as my lover,
Words of farewell, leaving me for another.

Sobbing, I uttered, "I can't be the other,"
My heart is in ruins, no longer your lover
Sorrows bled from my wounded heart,
Lonely, I faced a tomorrow torn apart.

Days were haunted with words "if only,"
Nights wept tears, melancholy and lonely.
Life seemed void of purpose and worth,
My journey began nervously put forth.

My being found comfort in purpose and friends,
Healing my heart through seasons and mends.
Years passed, fulfilling time's commitments,
Another love and family are my enrichments.

Here I stand, beneath the shades of the sunset,
Wisdom whispers, no regrets towards our duet.
Our love, however fleeting, was truly magnetic,
A once-cherished love that breathed authentic.

A grin graces my lips; a tear glistens my eye,
Memoirs of moments, not years, passed by.
Farewell, my love, to what was you and I,
A love affair that inspires a tender goodbye.

Colleen C. Carson

"Not every thought has to be spoken."

Mama Carson

"Within life's chaos, we discovered each other,
a serendipitous affair of hearts and fate."

Colleen C. Carson

"Boys build walls; girls break barriers, both transforming the world."

Mama Carson

"IMPERFECT PERFECT HEART"

Yet in our hearts, we deeply know,
Perfection's not where we must go.
Each scar and line a tale does tell,
Of battles fought and where we fell.

Our stumbles, falls, and paths at hand,
Shape the contours of our land.
In every tear, a story gleams,
In every flaw, a thousand dreams.

Accept the quirks, the odd, the strange,
In every heart, a vast exchange.
For whom we are, and who we strive,
Is what makes us indeed alive.

So, seek not just the flawless days,
But cherish all the chaotic ways.
In imperfection, find your grace,
For that's where love and life embrace.

We are pieces of a splendid design,
Each piece is unique, trims a line.
Together, in our flaws, we blend,
An identity that knows no end.

In every heart, a perfect spark,
A light that shines within the dark.
So let us honour every part,
Of our imperfect, perfect heart.

Colleen C. Carson

The tale of Colleen's quest for love began at sixteen when her parents allowed her freedom in the dating world. The possibilities were exciting, but amid the excitement, she considered the vague question of who she wanted to share her life with and what qualities defined the man she wished to call her soulmate.

At that tender age, she was dreaming far into the future, yet the idea of knowing her goal before starting on the journey of love felt paramount. So, she meticulously made a list, a collection of pros and cons that summarized the traits of her envisioned soulmate. The document found its home in the depths of her junk drawer then jukebox but was eternally filed in the recesses of her heart and mind.

As life unfolded, she spanned the scopes of love, encountering charming men who captivated her heart. Three engagements and even a thirty-six-year marriage transpired, and though these relationships came remarkably close, none embodied the man of her dream list although one came very close.

A chapter of my life unfolded in the romantic embrace of Paris, the city of love. In the shadows of the Eiffel Tower and along the Seine, on my departure some fifty years and plus ago, I made a silent promise to the city of love, " Paris, I will not return until I can bring the man of my dreams, my soulmate."

Soon after my promise, my girlfriend and I visited the Parisian Street market. While waiting for her among a table of old, there was this table of jewelry; my attention drifted towards a medallion with the signs of the zodiac. A curious connection drew me to this antique piece, and I could not resist buying it. With its mysterious charm, that medallion became a cherished possession, worn close to my heart as if safeguarding a secret promise.

Life unfolded with various love affairs, but oddly enough, I had never contemplated taking any of them, not even my former husband, to Paris. Post-divorce, my journey of self-discovery led me to begin a research-driven dating spree while researching the revising of 'The Guyed Book.'

My research had ended, the revising chapters of my book were accomplished, and fleeting connections were completed. I was closing all my online dating sites when I stumbled upon a dating site I had forgotten. I started filing through before closing my account, and a photo of this gentleman who got my attention while sending my heart fluttering.

A message to him was imperative, and as fate would have it, he responded, directing me to his YouTube channel. I discovered one of his talents; he sang and sounded like the soulful voice of Nat King Cole. It was a rendition of "My Way," the song I declared to live by, in my early teens.

In the soft glow of my bedroom, the gentle melody of "My Way" was sung in the background. Setting the stage for a dance in my heart while my body twirled and swayed, a little impromptu celebration of the joy coursing through my veins. In that magical moment, I felt a connection, a delicate sequence composed through the notes, linking our souls. Then, amid the rhythmic dance, I knew I had found the man of my dreams: My Soulmate. In its grand design, the universe, my God, had orchestrated a symphony of destiny and the romantic melodies of love in harmonious unity.

The eagerly awaited day had arrived when we were to meet in person. I meticulously adorned myself, dressing to impress the man who had captured my heart from afar. Ready and excited, I ventured from my condominium to pick him up at the airport. Yet, in my haste of preparation, I had forgotten to wear any jewelry. A gentle nudge from my inner voice reminded me of the medallion tucked away, urging me to wear it. It didn't make sense, but this piece held a mysterious significance for decades.

As we met for the first time, an indescribable energy embraced us. Gazing into his eyes, I felt confident he was the soulmate I had searched for my entire life. Little did I know, months later, that he revealed love at first sight to me.

Three years later, we found ourselves in the enchanting embrace of Diner en Blanc in Paris, the city that witnessed the blossoming of our love. Standing beside the Seine, in the same spot where I had made a promise fifty years prior, I introduced my soulmate to her, the city of love. "I told you, Paris, I would not return until I could bring the man of my dreams. Meet the man of my dreams; his name is Donald!" I could sense the city's joy, mirroring my own and even applauding the fulfillment of a long-awaited promise.

Recalling the medallion that had guided me through the maze of love, I marveled at its symbolic power. On its front, the zodiac signs stood united, while on the back, the celestial archer, Sagittarius, marked a hidden connection. This hidden connection: I had never dated this sign in all my years of affairs and marriage. I dated Cancers, Leos, Geminis, and every zodiac sign except Sagittarius. You will never guess; yes, Donald is a Sagittarius!

Was it fate that brought us together, or was it a divine gift? I could not unravel the mysteries, but one thing was sure: It took over half a century from the moment I wrote my list to meet Donald and more years until I returned to Paris. The universe, My God, with a little help from my Guardian Angel, Chancey, and Mother Mary conspired to create a love story that transcended time, proving that dreams do come true in the most unexpected ways.

Months later, after we proclaimed ourselves soulmates, I penned these words in the stillness of my day, surrounded in solitary contemplation. They emerged from the wisdom of my thoughts, guided by the depth of my heart, and resonated with the sweet echoes of already shared love and memories with excited anticipation of more to come.

"In the soft light of the morning, I woke with the tender thought of you, a quiet inspiration that filled the space where our love began. You came into my life with the grace of an eagle in flight, strong and free, lifting me with you. Your touch stirred me gently, like the flutter of butterfly wings, delicate and full of life.

Like a winter storm, wild and beautiful, your spirit brought warmth as we shared fireside embraces and whispered our dreams. Our love became a haven filled with the endless comfort of togetherness. In your gentleness, I felt the calm of a spring breeze, softly awakening hope within me. Your laughter, a song that echoes like the golden warmth of the summer sun, our love that brightens every corner of our world, leaving joy in its wake."

In those moments of reflection, I was deeply immersed in the unforgettable encounter of our connected destinies. My longing mirrored our first kiss, a moment that lingers in the treasure trove of our shared memories. Each touch we exchanged was an intoxicating potion, leaving a lasting imprint and connection that transcends mere physicality. I remember my heart beating in harmony with our love, finding a thoughtful tranquility, a peace that settles within the core of our shared journey even now.

His presence has a solace pace, a constant reminder that we are soulmates in this beautiful dance of love and life. With every step we take together, we harmonize our movements, creating a song that is uniquely ours.

This song speaks of unity, understanding, companionship, and a timeless melody of forever always. Donald is a man of integrity, wisdom, and truth. He makes me laugh even when I want to cry, and his words of love flow effortlessly, reminding me of his steady affection. I am, without a doubt, his precedence, a status I never had to request.

At seventy-four, our love feels as vibrant as if we were twenty-four, filled with the same youthful energy that awakens our inner child. With his impeccable style, Donald looks like he's just stepped out of a fashion magazine. He's intelligent, spiritual, and gifted, a true blessing from God. In this ordinary world, our journey of love is anything but ordinary, and together, we continue to share a romance that transcends time, making each day feel as extraordinary as the first.

Ah, dear hearts, in the enchanting journey of seeking our soulmate, our kindred spirit, we often find ourselves swept away, occasionally settling for compromises that dim our hearts. I, too, have danced that dance myself and carried the whispers of regret. Yet, in every man I loved, I discovered precious lessons that shaped me, and I experienced the warmth of love that touched my heart. How can one truly regret being loved?

Some might ponder, "Wouldn't it have been better if it had happened sooner?" Sometimes, those thoughts linger in my mind. But then, my inner voice, a gentle whisper of wisdom, whispers softly, "Cherish and celebrate the beautiful gift of finding your true soulmate. Many never have that blessing." As I hold immense gratitude in my heart. My dance for love has led me to an insightful truth: every moment, every connection, has arisen the journey of my soul, guiding me toward the love I was destined to welcome.

As we reflect on this journey, we are reminded that each step, each heart we touched, has brought us closer to the radiant love we now hold dear. It is a love that transcends time and circumstance, enlightening the path we walked to arrive.

So, let us welcome our bittersweet and joyful stories, for they are the delicate steps on the journey of our hearts. In the end, the love we have known guides us, reminding us that every moment was worth it, for it led our souls to this enchanting truth: we deserve a love that is intimate, selfless, and everlasting.

"MS. PERFECTION"

Perfection, Colleen learned, can be a double-edged sword, bringing an insufferable weight of stress that can consume you. This lesson was communicated to her decades ago by a wise gentleman, the founder and president of the company she worked with. At the age of twenty-seven,

Colleen was passionately pursuing the ideal of "Ms. Perfection" in both her life and career, and this relentless quest was a source of tremendous stress. Despite achieving her goals, satisfaction always eluded her. She was caught in a cycle of believing she could do better, which only deepened her discontent.

This gentleman often reminded her, she had nothing to prove by striving for perfection. At the time, Colleen dismiss his words with a smile, assuming he was just being humorous. Yet, one evening, he called her at home with a serious tone, informing Colleen he would be visiting the Vancouver office the next day. He asked if they could share lunch together, saying he had something special to give her. Colleen's heart raced with excitement; she really admired this man, not for his wealth or fame but for his wisdom and character.

The next day, he arrived at the office, greeting everyone warmly before coming to me with a smile. He asked, "Ready for lunch?" he asked. I nodded enthusiastically, thrilled that he had made reservations at one of the finest restaurants in Vancouver.

I remembered a year prior when he sought my advice on where to take his investors for dinner. I had suggested this impressive dining experience, and when he asked if I had ever been, I had replied wistfully, "I wish, but we can't afford it." Yet here I was, being treated to the very experience I had longed for.

Upon our arrival, we were seated and ordered cocktails. Moments later, the restaurant manager approached, leaning into whisper something to him, who nodded in acknowledgment. The manager soon returned, presenting a beautifully wrapped gift that he handed to him, who then passed it to me. I was taken aback and filled with gratitude for his unexpected kindness. "You truly deserve this," he said, acknowledging my contributions to the company, but he asked me to wait until after lunch to open it.

The meal was a culinary masterpiece, transporting us to the intimate elegance of the French Riviera. The air was fragrant with burnt butter and roasted garlic while the soft notes of French melodies played in the background. Outside, a dark, rainy day only heightened the restaurant's warm ambiance, where candles flickered like stars in the dim light. It was simply perfect. As we dined, we engaged in a lively conversation about business, aspirations, and family, weaving through moments of seriousness and laughter, each moment exquisite.

He gestured for me to open my gift as we savoured our dessert. I carefully unwrapped the package to reveal a stunning lead crystal vase, hand-cut with such precision that it refracted rainbows when kissed by the light. "Do you like it?" he asked, his eyes twinkling. I couldn't help but smile as I confessed my love for it. He had arranged for it to be shipped from Paris after I had shared my fondness for crystal, particularly vases.

He seemed genuinely pleased to see my delight, but what unfolded next was a revelation that transcended any material gift I had ever received. With a gentle sincerity, he began elaborating on the vase's beauty: its intricate design, colours, and glowing reflections, reminding him of my unique qualities. His words were lovely, yet what followed truly took my breath away.

He likened me to the vase, explaining that while it possessed elegance, warmth, and a capacity to bring beauty to the world, it was, at its core, empty without the flowers to fill it. He posed a thought-provoking question: were the flowers necessary, or did they merely mask a deeper sense of loneliness? I looked at him, puzzled, and asked, "Are you saying I'm like the vase and that I'm empty inside?" He quickly apologized, recognizing my confusion, but conceded that a metaphor was indeed on the horizon.

"Colleen," he said earnestly, "You are a beautiful woman inside and out. Yet you don't seem to see it. You believe you need those flowers: the validation of perfection to be acknowledged for your accomplishments. But perfection comes at a high price, causing constant stress and yielding little joy. It leads to posturing and loneliness that dwells within." He paused, allowing his words to sink in. "The stress of pursuing perfection can cut your life short. I want you to promise me this: when you feel overwhelmed, ask yourself, 'Is this worth losing five years off my life?'"

At that moment, a thoughtful silence surrounded us. I smiled and nodded, pledging to heed his advice. Since that day, whenever stress begins to creep in even now, I recall that simple yet powerful question: "Is this worth losing five years of my life?" Often, the answer is a resounding "NO."

I realized that my relentless pursuit of perfection was as hollow as the vase itself while welcoming my imperfections opened the door to genuine learning and growth. I placed the beautiful vase in a room I frequented in my home, where it would remind me each day of his wise words about survival and the importance of self-acceptance.

After lunch, we returned to the office and shared a warm hug. The next day, he departed, and shortly thereafter, I learned he had fallen ill and retired from the board and company. He reached out once more, curious if I had begun to live by the metaphor he had shared.

We laughed and enjoyed a lovely conversation, and that was the last I heard from him. Reflecting on that afternoon, I carry with me the wisdom he imparted. In a world that often demands perfection, I choose to accept my flaws, knowing they are not signs of weakness but opportunities for growth. Perfection is not the goal; living fully and authentically is the true measure of a well-lived life.

"Though her footsteps may fade, her legacy remains etched in the hearts she touched, like the gentle waves in the river of time."

Mama Carson

"WHISPERS IN THE WIND"

Whispers weave like tangled threads,
Spun by lips where truth has fled.
A careless word, a sly, quick glance,
And suddenly, it's a bitter dance.

The gossiper thrives on idle minds,
Feeding rumors, where nothing binds.
But oh, what price is paid in haste,
A reputation smeared, a soul laid waste.

For gossip drips with poison sweet,
And those who spread it meet defeat.
They think they rise with every tale,
But truth will cut and lift the veil.

So, mind the words you choose to share,
For once released, they're everywhere.
And though you think you've left no scar,
The hurt you sow can travel far.

Be wary of gossip, its fleeting disguise,
It dulls the heart, dims the eyes.
For in the end, those who spread the lie,
Are caught in the web they spun, by and by.

Hold tight to kindness, let it lead,
Uplift the wounded, plant good seed.
For what you say is who you'll be,
Your words, a mirror for all to see.

Speak life, speak love, let gossip fall,
In silence, rise above it all.
In a world that thrives on what's not true,
Choose compassion; choose you!

Colleen C. Carson

"A TALE OF LOVE"

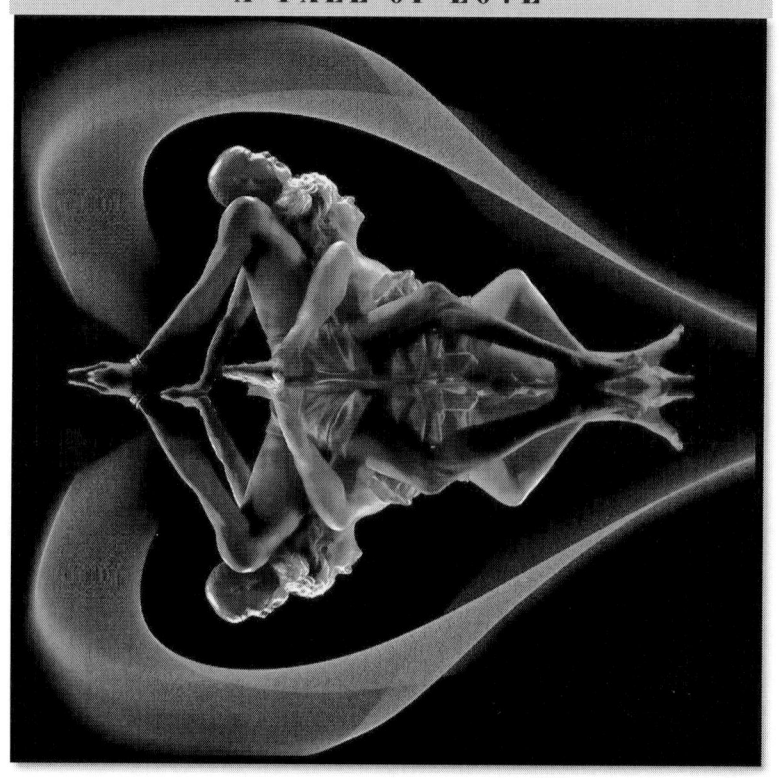

I wrote of you in dreams of old,
A tale of love both soft and bold.
With every line, I longed for more,
A soul to meet, a heart to soar.

But time, it teased and led me wrong,
I feared I'd searched for far too long.
My pen grew heavy, my hope grew thin,
Could love like ours still begin?

Then you appeared, a spark, a flame,
And life was never quite the same.
Your eyes met mine, the world stood still,
A love so pure, it bent my will.

In that moment, time unwound,
My heart, my home, in you was found.
The love I thought had slipped away,
Was born again that fateful day.

Now every morning, by your side,
I wake and feel our hearts collide.
With every touch, with every kiss,
We write our story, bound by bliss.

No longer words on empty pages,
Our love, a song that never ages.
You are the dream I always knew,
The love I wrote, now lived with you.

I thank the stars that led you near,
For in your arms, I've found no fear.
The years ahead, the love we claim,
Is more than passion our souls aflame.

I almost gave up; I almost let go,
But in your heart, I've come to know,
A love so deep, so endlessly true,
The life I dreamed was always you.

Now here we stand, as one, as whole,
With every beat, you fill my soul.
Decades of waiting now behind,
A love like ours, so rare to find.

Together we'll walk through endless days,
Our love will guide us, come what may.
For you are my story, my heart's delight
The dream I once wrote now fills my life.

Colleen C. Carson

"THE LOVE OF FAMILY"
"ART OF NURTURING"

Before Colleen became a parent, she was not interested in raising children. She often found them annoying and couldn't quite understand their appeal. She was a career woman, never interested in marriage or family. Nonetheless, over the years, she became aware that she wanted to do childbearing, although she still didn't know what it was like to be a parent.

She came to see that teaching and learning are not confined to a school classroom but the world classroom, beginning with adults teaching children. Her children, Crystal and Chance, were her students and teachers, just as she was theirs. Together, we entered on a mutual journey of growth and understanding, learning from each other daily.

I had a vague relationship with teenagers in my early interactions with them. On the one hand, I enjoyed their company, but I also had no patience for entitlement. I admired hard workers who strived for accomplishments and had trouble with those who seemed to take everything for granted. With this insight, I formulated my parenting philosophy: educate my children in hard work and dignity and open myself to what they could teach me about patience, love, and communication.

When I got pregnant after many years of marriage, I knew that raising a child would not just be instinctual but would also have to be carefully considered. I began this process by revisiting my childhood and asking family and friends for guidance, but I quickly discovered there is no "universal" solution to parenting. What we were doing would have to change with each experience.

Together with my husband Brian, we recognized that the goal wasn't just to raise successful adults but compassionate, empathetic, and kind-hearted human beings. We learned that prioritizing values over accomplishments was the key to guiding our children. The lessons we imparted weren't just about reaching for success and building the character needed to navigate life with grace and integrity. In turn, my children taught me valuable lessons about parenting.

One day, Crystal was about three, and we were at the grocery store. Like many young children, she threw a tantrum when I refused to buy her a chocolate bar. Rather than get frustrated and scold her, I took a different approach. I got down on the floor and mirrored her behaviour—flailing my arms, stomping my feet, and loudly squealing.

Crystal, confused at first, quickly stopped and watched me with amusement. Soon enough, she got up, walked over to me, patted my shoulder, and said, "I'm okay with not having my chocolate if you're okay with not having yours." From that moment on, she never threw a tantrum like that again. Crystal taught me that sometimes, humour and empathy can be far more effective than discipline alone.

Chance, too, was both my teacher and my student as well. When he was in fourth grade, he found himself in trouble after taking a soda from a vending machine without paying. I had always taught him about honesty and integrity, but this incident gave me an opportunity to reinforce those lessons in a real-world context.

I sat him down and explained how actions have consequences and how the company he kept would shape his character. But what I learned from Chance during this time was the importance of compassion and understanding. He was remorseful and had learned his lesson about theft, friendship, and trust. His genuine reflection on his actions taught me to listen more deeply and to guide him with a softer hand.

As a parent, I never placed the burden of perfection on my children. I knew that chasing perfection would only lead to frustration and a lack of joy. Instead, I focused on teaching them and learning from them about the importance of embracing imperfection and growing from their mistakes.

Throughout their teenage years, Chance and Crystal continued to teach me about courage, compromise, and choice. Chance, who had been bullied in grammar school, developed a strong sense of justice. By high school, he had grown into a tall, muscular young man who stood up for the smaller, timid kids, becoming a crusader against bullying.

With her fierce sense of right and wrong, Crystal often advocated for her peers, even when it meant standing up to authoritative figures.

Both of them demonstrated courage in ways that also reminded me to be brave in my own life.

I discovered that parenting wasn't just about teaching. It was about being taught by my children, by life itself, and by our evolving relationship. The lessons were challenging, but they were necessary. As I guided them, they showed me the importance of patience, unconditional love, and purpose.

In today's world, I passionately believe in the principle of "reap what you sow." Accountability needs to be improved, not just among children but in our society as a whole. Children learn by example, and too often, they see adults bypass consequences, leading them to believe they can do the same. I hope that, through teaching and learning from each other, we can create a world where responsibility and kindness go hand in hand.

Perfection is an illusion, but growth is not. We can teach and learn through our imperfections, building a better future for ourselves and our children. My role as a mother, a teacher, and a student will never end. Just as my children have learned from me, I have learned from them. And together, we continue to learn from life.

"PARENTAL PILLARS"

In the quiet moments before dawn,
when the world slumbers in blissful ignorance,
there exists a silent hero,
a guardian of dreams, a shaper of souls.
They are the silent melody in
life's masterpiece,
the tender touch in a world of chaotic edges,
a guiding light of unconditional love and
boundless strength,
forming futures from the fires of their devotion.
In their eyes, galaxies dance,
each star a reflection of hope, of dreams,
of possibilities.
Their hands, weathered by time and toil,
cradle the universe within

their grasp.
They are the creators of tomorrow,
nurturing tender purposes
of promise,
guiding stumbling steps toward greatness,
whispering secrets of spirit in ears
yet to listen.
Their laughter, a harmony that echoes
through generations,
their tears, the rain that waters the roots
of empathy,
their hugs, the sanctuary where
fears find solace,
their presence, the lighthouse
that guides ships through stormy seas.
Oh, what marvels they are,
these founders of love,
these custodians of dreams,
these pillars upon which humanity rests.
In their silent sacrifice, in them
boundless devotion,
we find the essence of greatness,
the purest form of love,
they are the only builders of leaders, inventors,
and more,
better us today for a successful tomorrow.
To the parents, the unsung
heroes of existence,
we offer our humble gratitude,
our deepest admiration,
for they are the very heartbeat of
life's eternal song,
the creators of humankind.

Mama Carson

"BELLE & CHANCEY"

YOU	BOTH	ARE
MY	LIFE	MIRACLES
MY	PRECIOUS	ANGELS

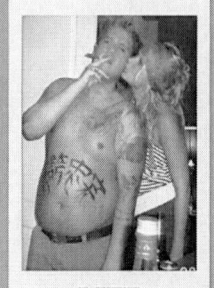

In the story of my life, my children, Crystal and Chance, have been the heart and soul of everything beautiful; the miracles in my life. They are my constant inspiration, the source of my greatest joys, and the creators of countless memories that fill my heart with love and gratitude. Every day spent with them is a treasure, and I am deeply blessed to be their mother.

When I think of my Crystal Belle, my precious daughter, our pure heart. Whose love, strength, and grace have shaped my life in the most beautiful ways. She is my constant support, always there with a word of encouragement or a loving hand. Her strength and compassion leave me in awe every day. Crystal's warmth and boundless energy create an environment of love and happiness, and she makes our lives feel whole.

And then there is Chancey, my precious son, our old soul. I feel his presence as my guiding light, showering me with love and wisdom from heaven. His laughter, pure and magical, once filled our home with an energy that uplifted everyone. His heart, gentle and kind, was a source of comfort to all who knew him. Chance had a way of bringing light into the world, spreading hope and joy, as if his very soul was meant to lift others.

Together, Crystal and Chance are the defenders of my soul, the angels who care for my heart, and the companions who walk beside me with loving devotion. They fill my life with purpose and love, and every moment with them is a reflection of the power of family and the beauty of unconditional love.

They are not just my children; they are my miracles, my greatest blessings. Every day, I thank God for the privilege of being their mom, for the love they bring into my life, and for the endless joy they bring to my heart.

I love you both forever always,

Mom xoxo

"I LOVE BEING ME"

We have endured the bullying of many,
In the midst of both foe and friendly.
True courage is not a cowardly bully.

Courage must dwell among us with certainty,
Granting our children the gift of liberty,
Free from oppression, welcoming dignity.

I cradled a child who was in withering pain.
I whispered, "Why my child please explain?"
Child cried: "I am a slave to my bully's chains."

I cradled a child who desperately wanted to die.
I whispered, 'Why my child is death your only cry?"
Child cried: "I am the tales to my bully's lies."

I cradled a child who listened to terrorizing chatter.
I whispered, "Why my child does this matter?"
Child cried: "I am a target to my bully's batter."

I cradled a child who frantically lived in fear.
I whispered, "Why my child are you shedding tears?"
Child cried: "I am different to my bullying peers."

I cradled a child who punished themselves in shame.
I whispered, "Why my child do you feel blame?"
Child cried: "I am ugly my bully tells me the same."

I cradled a child who lived in scornful ridicule.
I whispered, "Why my child are they so cruel?"
Child cried: "I am accepted as my bully's fool."

I cradled a child because they bullied others in hate.
I whispered, "Why my child do you choose this fate?"
Child cried: "I am a birthday no one celebrates."

I roared to the elders; this must change.
No child shall feel unlove or estrange,
These bully actions must surely refrain,

Children's hearts should laugh and sing,
In pursuit of their butterfly wings,
As they dance, in the joy they bring.

The elders assembled all the children,
As they spoke of heroes and villains,
In words of courage in their opinion.

Our words at times are not so kind,
Live your heart and you will be fine,
As the children cheered their shine.

I welcomed a child's heart who boldly speaks.
I asked, "What my child makes you unique?"
Child smiled: "I am my courage in life's valleys and peaks."

I welcomed a child's heart who wants to aspire.
I asked, "What my child do you admire?"
Child smiled: "I am my confidence in devoting to inspire."

I welcomed a child's heart who bravely defends.
I asked, "What my child do you lend?"
Child smiled: "I am my promise in bringing justice to a friend."

I welcomed a child's heart who faithfully believes.
I asked, "What my child is the path you perceive?"
Child smiled: "I am my purpose in world freedom to achieve."

I welcomed a child's heart who unconditionally loves.
I asked, "What my child brings sparkle to the stars above?"
Child smiled: "I am my harmony in peace like wings of a dove."

I welcomed a child's heart who lives with empathy.
I asked, "What my child will be your legacy?"
Child smiled: "I am my integrity in both a friend and enemy."

I welcomed a child's heart to whose spirit soars.
I asked, "What my child do you best adore."
Child smiled: "I am my inner tiger who empowers my roar."

As the child and I walked the path of hope, faith, and love,
I reminded my child their uniqueness is a gift from above.
To always speak to self and others with self-love.

As the child walked beside me in glee,
Their joyful smile and eyes looking up at me,
I asked, "Why my child are you happy to be?"
Child smiled, "Because I love me."

Colleen C. Carson

"Children are life's miracles, turning the ordinary into the extraordinary and reminding us that each day holds magic and wonder."

Mama Carson

My kids, my life.

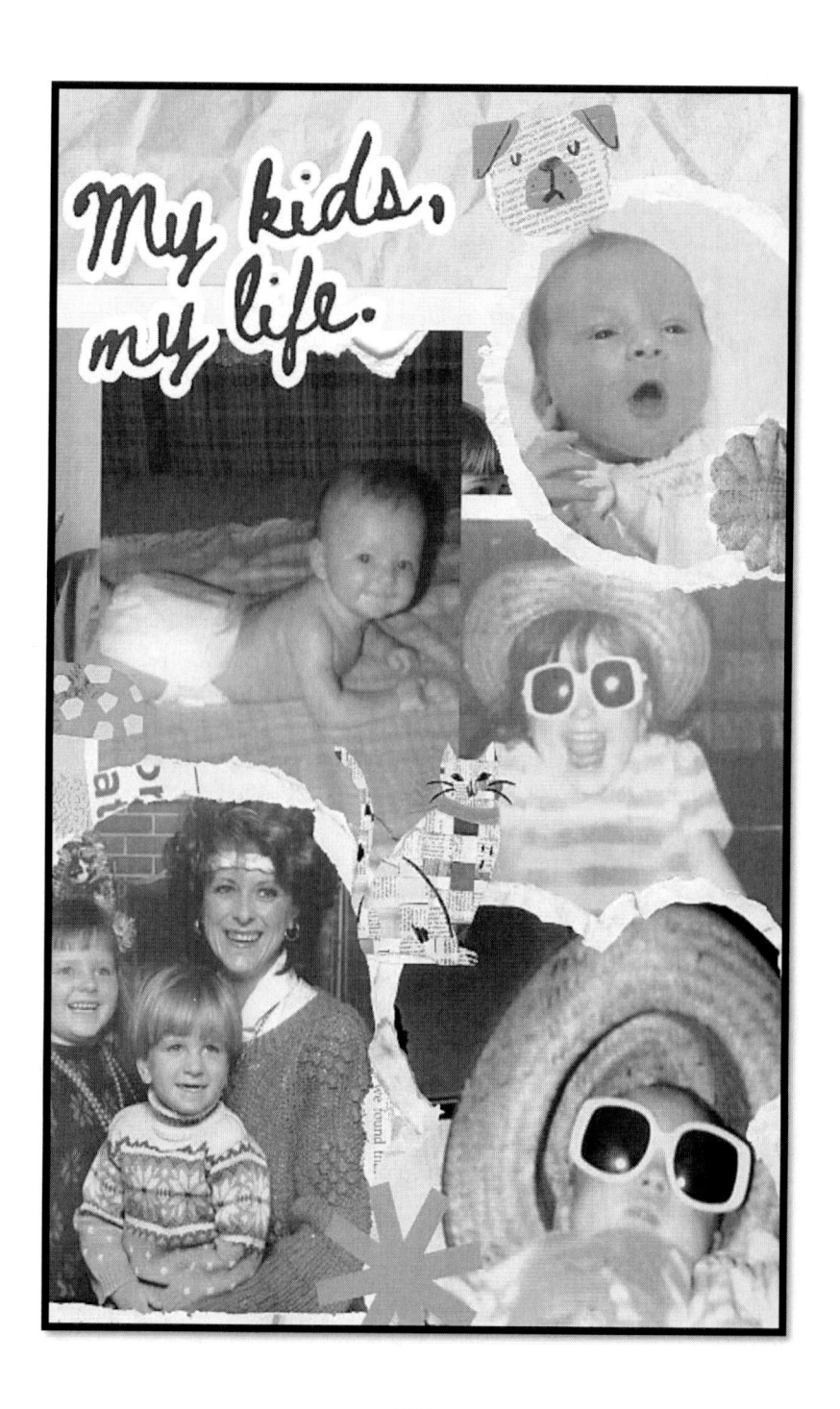

Once upon a time, in the mystical realm of Suburbia, a place where minivans prowled the streets like mighty chariots and lawns were so pristine you'd think they were curated by garden gnomes from the Hanging Gardens of Babylon, I found myself crowned as the Queen of All Things Momhood. And what a coronation it was!

Armed with my trusty minivan, which could haul more gear than the Batmobile and still have room for snacks, I embarked on a daily journey filled with playdates, school runs, and a level of caffeinated enthusiasm that could rival a cheerleader on game day. All this while dress in high-waisted jeans and shoulder pads that said, "I'm here to mom, and I mean business."

I still remember when my life took a left turn into the land of motherhood. The exact dates are as mysterious as the whereabouts of that one missing sock in the laundry. But I pressed on, fearless commander of my Tiny Army, leading the charge in the nightly battles of sleeplessness, diaper warfare, and tantrum negotiations.

Every day was a new chapter in an epic novel, an entire chapter of chaos, unexpected plot twists, and the occasional potty-training rebellion. Sure, I wielded the power of soothing lullabies and multitasking with the balance of a circus juggler but make no mistake, this was no peaceful reign. This was a full-on, laugh-out-loud whirlwind through the wildernesses of parenthood.

Now, picture this: my home, once a serene oasis of adult furniture and peaceful vibes, transformed into a fortress guarded by pacifiers, baby gates, and a legion of onesies. It was as if my living room had been conscripted into the army of baby gear, ready to face the incoming siege of milk spills and diaper explosions. Meanwhile, my social life performed a disappearing act that would make Houdini jealous.

One day, my friends and I were bonding over wine and deep conversations; the next thing I knew, they had vanished, leaving me alone with my thoughts and a pile of burp cloths. I began to suspect they had all been beamed up by aliens in search of wine-loving earthlings, now sunbathing on a distant beach where contact was forbidden and cocktails flowed freely. The mystery of their whereabouts? It is as perplexing as folding a fitted sheet.

Enter my husband, the once mild-mannered nine-to-fiver, now suddenly the CEO of "Long Hours Inc." Watching his transformation was like witnessing Clark Kent morph into a business tycoon, briefcase in hand, suit looking sharp, while I wondered if he'd ever make good on those promises of cozy Saturday nights. Spoiler alert: they were more elusive than a unicorn on spring break.

But when it seemed like adult conversations had become extinct, hope glimmered on the horizon, babysitting exchanges and preschool! Suddenly, the clouds parted, and there was a chance to escape the land of mashed peas and diaper debates.

Still, venturing into mom social circles was like a flashback to high school cafeteria politics, trying to find your tribe amidst the chaos of juice boxes and snack-time gossip. The conversations? Less about wine pairings and more about the exciting world of potty-training techniques, which could double as espionage tactics.

But ah, I persevered. Armed with coffee as strong as a toddler's will and determination sharper than a teething ring, I navigated the treacherous terrain of babysitting exchanges, a bustling marketplace where sanity-saving babysitting shifts were traded with the finesse of Wall Street brokers. It wasn't just a break from child-induced tedium; it was a social experiment, expanding both mom and child's horizons beyond the confines of the playroom.

And somewhere amidst the noise of toddler tantrums and lullaby singalongs, I discovered a rare breed of moms who had reached an ego-less state that rivaled Zen masters. These weren't the drama queens of parenthood; they were warriors who navigated potty training with the poise of Olympic athletes. We celebrated each toddler milestone like we were winning gold in the Toddler

Olympics, complete with imaginary podiums and victory anthems. Who knew coaxing a tiny human to use the potty could feel like climbing Everest?

But, my readers, the true heroism lay in our coffee-fueled strategy sessions. We tackled nap schedules with the precision of military generals planning a top-secret mission. And when the day's battles were over, we raised our wine glasses like victorious knights after the war, savouring the sweet taste of fleeting freedom.

Our tales of suburban survival became the stuff of legends destined to be passed down through the ages. Future generations of parents will surely marvel at how we balanced sippy cups with style and tantrums with grace. They'll tell stories of us, the pioneers of playdate diplomacy, the queens of bedtime battles, the champions of snack negotiations.

So, to my brave comrades in this noble quest called parenthood, I say: onward we march! May our diaper-changing skills remain swift, our minivans (now SUV's) mighty, and our laughter plentiful. For in this hilarious saga of motherhood, we have truly earned the Valour Medal of Momhood!

"A cherished family is the sanctuary of the heart, where love finds its tender refuge and blooms in the warmth of shared affection."

Mama Carson

"In a mother's love, a child gains strength to soar,
and in a child's eyes, a mother glimpses the universe's magic."

Colleen C. Carson

"MY MIRACLES"

As a mom, I have found immense joy and fulfillment in raising my two exceptional children, Crystal and Chance. I lovingly refer to them as my "miracles" because they have brought an intense sense of beauty and magic into my life that surpasses even the most enchanting fairytales.

It was only years later, after undergoing a diagnostic test for an unrelated symptom, that my doctor disclosed the presence of a condition I had been living with before my pregnancies: endometriosis. This condition, which can be marked by extensive scarring, blocked fallopian tubes, and damaged ovaries, is known to pose significant challenges for pregnancy, often necessitating advanced fertility treatments.

I vividly recall my doctor affirming, "Colleen, you've consistently referred to your children as your miracles, and I can unequivocally confirm that they truly are." We both smiled, "They truly are!" I replied. I love being a mom there and now and the joy motherhood brings while creating a collection of cherished memories.

Whether we read captivating stories, sang lullabies, or cheered them on with words of encouragement, our days were filled with adventures, family outings, backyard parties, themed birthdays, and simple moments like sharing fruit and watching their favourite shows before bedtime. Each moment was truly enchanting.

Their laughter resonated through the walls of our home, a beautiful echo of love and the unbreakable spirit of humanity. In the ups and downs of daily life, their laughter became the reassuring warmth that united us in our pursuit of happiness.

No matter how seemingly small, each milestone became a grand celebration, a tribute to the thoughtful impact of love in our lives. Brian and I, as parents, were dedicated to instilling in our children a sense of gratitude for life and an appreciation for the significance of every fleeting moment.

Expressing our love became a cherished ritual as we consistently exchanged heartfelt declarations. The echoing proclamation of "I love you!" became a joyful symphony, with each voice echoing in response to the initial statement, creating a harmonious chorus of affection throughout our home and paths. This continues even today.

My dedication to Crystal Belle and Chancey never wavered, even when we encountered tough times and had to navigate financial and personal challenges. In return, they showered us with a boundless love that knew no limits, nurturing an unconditional bond within our family.

As Crystal and Chance grew older, our home became a haven of love, support, and encouragement. We fostered their creativity, nurtured their ambitions, and instilled in them the belief that they could overcome any obstacle. Our spirit became a source of inspiration for our children, shaping their characters and guiding them toward a promising future.

Then came the day when Crystal and Chance stood at the threshold of adulthood, about to begin on their extraordinary journeys, yet they could not help but glance back at their happy childhood. Tears welled in their eyes as they hugged us, thanking us for our sacrifices and the love we shared into their lives.

I believe in my heart that extraordinary miracles lay quietly within the spirit of an ordinary child, waiting to unfold. Within the warm embrace of a mother and father's love, one discovers the strength to triumph over all obstacles. Our parental love provided a haven of safety and encouragement with a sense of comfort, with love and respect in the forefront.

Yes, no day goes by then and now without thanking my God for allowing me and us the privilege to be a family of inspirational growth through our miracles and memories.

I love forever always My Miracles!

"FAMILY"

In the heart of a home, where laughter blooms,
Family gathers, chasing away life's glooms.
Through joys and tears, we stand as one,
Bound by love, till each day is done.

Children's laughter, like music in the air,
Parents' guidance, steady and fair.
Together we grow, through every trial,
Hand in hand, mile after mile.

From bedtime stories to shared meals,
Each memory, a treasure that deeply appeals.
In family's embrace, we find our place,
A sanctuary of love and grace.

Through seasons of change, our bonds endure,
Stronger together, steadfast and pure.
For in the rhythm of family life's song,
We find belonging, where we all belong.

In morning's light or evening's hush,
Family gathers, no need to rush.
Through whispered dreams and voices raised,
In every heartbeat, love is praised.

As years roll on and journeys may part,
We carry each other, heart to heart.
For love's the longevity that won't unwind,
Forever united, soul and mind.

Mama Carson

"HER SPARKLE"

When Colleen thinks of her daughter, Crystal, her heart practically overflows with gratitude and inspiration. It's hard to describe the depth of love and admiration she feels for Crystal. If she had to describe her in one word, it would be "sparkle." It's not just how Crystal lights up a room when she walks in or how her laugh fills the air with warmth. It's the way Crystal radiates love, strength, and kindness wherever she goes. People often talk about their loved ones being "a light" in their lives, but Crystal is more than that; she's the sparkle that makes everything brighter.

Crystal's life is a witness to the strength of her character. While she has achieved success, her heart, intellect, and determination stand out most vividly to Colleen. Crystal possesses a rare ability to leave a sparkle wherever she goes, and she has a thoughtful, caring nature that touches everyone she meets. She has a way of putting others before herself, always looking out for their happiness. Yet, in her independence, she often carries her struggles quietly, leaning on her own strength instead of asking for help.

Growing up, Crystal faced challenges that would have been enough to break most people. Life threw challenges at her, one after another, but instead of crumbling, she rose. Every setback was met with her fierce determination and a refusal to be defeated. Colleen remembers watching her grow through her teenage years and how she handled every hardship gracefully. Crystal had her share of struggles, but her spirit stood out most. No matter what happens, Crystal always finds a way to shine with her ability to feel deeply and intuitively understand the world.

One of the things I admire most about her is her ability to stay true to herself. Crystal is one of those rare souls who knows exactly who she is and doesn't apologize for it. She's always been this way: confident, self-assured, and unapologetically genuine. It's a quality that's sometimes hard to come by, especially in a world that often tries to tell us who we should be. But not Crystal. She knows her worth, and it's something that I've always admired. Watching her grow into the woman she is today has been one of the greatest privileges of my life.

What really gets me is the way Crystal loves. Her heart is so big that it's almost impossible for her not to think about others before herself. Whether it's making sure someone has what they need, offering a kind word when someone's down, or going out of her way to make someone feel special, Crystal is always thinking of others. And that's what makes her sparkle. It's not just her kindness; it's the pure, genuine way she cares for the people around her. She has this ability to make you feel like you're the most important person in the room, even if a crowd surrounds her. That's a rare gift, and it's one of the things I cherish most about her.

But here's the thing about Crystal: despite all of her love and generosity, she's incredibly independent. She carries a lot on her shoulders but rarely asks for help. Even when I can see that she's struggling, she'll quietly bear the weight, never letting on that she needs a hand. I see so much of myself in her, and I can't help but feel a little concerned when she keeps everything to herself. I know she's strong, but I also want her to know it's okay to lean on others occasionally. It's one of the things I've learned over the years: asking for help doesn't make you weak; it makes you human. I hope one day; Crystal will let herself experience that same freedom.

Crystal's sparkle isn't just about being kind, though. It's about the way she moves through the world with purpose. She's a woman who knows what she wants and isn't afraid to go after it. I've watched her build a life for herself that I couldn't be prouder of. She's worked hard, fought for what she believes in, and made her dreams a reality. And through it all, she's remained humble. Crystal never brags about her accomplishments, but I can see the satisfaction in her eyes when she talks about her work, her passions, and the life she's created. It's a quiet pride, but it's there. And it's something I've always admired.

I remember one Saturday afternoon, we decided to go through old boxes of memories, school projects, birthday cards, old photos, and the like. Crystal dug through those boxes with a kind of tenderness that made me smile. As we sorted through everything, I couldn't help but notice something: Crystal had kept almost everything that related to her brother, but when it came to her own things, she only kept a small pile. I pointed it out to her, and she seemed a little embarrassed as if she hadn't done enough for herself. At that moment, I knew that her heart was always thinking of others, even in something as small as keeping memories.

We both agreed to toss most of the birthday cards. But later that day, Crystal started to feel guilty. She thought maybe she had done something wrong like she had hurt someone's feelings by getting rid of them. She fretted about it until I finally said, "It's not about the cards, Belle. It's the love and the memories that matter. We don't need the paper to hold onto the moments." That's just her, though, always thinking of others and worrying that something she did might have upset someone, even if it was unintentional. It's that big heart of hers, always wanting to make sure everyone else is okay, and sometimes it makes her feel responsible for things that aren't hers to carry.

And then there's the memory of the 2010 Olympics. It had always been a dream of mine to attend the closing ceremonies, and Crystal made it happen. She worked hard to ensure everything went off without a hitch, obtaining the tickets, organizing the day, and ensuring I had everything I needed. The day was perfect. The ceremony was breathtaking, everything I had imagined it would be. It was one of the best memories of my life. But, just recently, Crystal brought it up out of nowhere. She confessed that she'd felt guilty all these years, thinking that maybe she hadn't been kind enough to me that day because she was so stressed about making sure everything went smoothly.

I was completely taken back. "Crystal, that day was one of the best memories we've ever shared. Why would you think anything else?" I had to remind her that she gave me one of the most special days of my life, and I wouldn't change a thing. That's just who Crystal is, always making sure everyone else is okay, often at the expense of her own peace of mind.

One thing I've always admired about Crystal is how she's never allowed life to make her bitter. No matter what challenges she's faced, she's only become more compassionate, more understanding, and more loving. She's got this incredible ability to take everything life throws at her and turn it into something beautiful. It's something that many people never learn to do, but Crystal has. She's a true inspiration.

Crystal's sparkle is the kind that doesn't fade; it only grows stronger with time. She brings light to every room she enters, and she's made the world a better place just by being in it. She's more than just my daughter; she's my greatest gift, my pride, and my joy. Watching her grow and become the woman she is today has been the most incredible adventure of my life.

And me? I'm just so grateful to be her mom. Watching her grow, watching her love, watching her sparkle—it's been one of the greatest gifts of my life. She's everything I could have ever hoped for in a daughter and more. I can't wait to see where her sparkle takes her next. No matter where life leads her, I know she'll keep lighting the way for everyone lucky enough to know her.

So, bring on the sparkle, my dear Crystal. You are, and always will be, the brightest star in my sky.

"In a world where respect is currency, let's all be wealthy. Because a lack of respect doesn't just cost, it bankrupts the soul."

Colleen C. Carson

"Glitter is nature's confetti, spreading joy and sparkle, reminding us that even the smallest shimmer can light up our world with magic."

Mama Carson

"OUR PRECIOUS ANGEL"

Looking back, Colleen was filled with wonder and admiration, marveling at the journey that begun on a tranquil morning when the world was still cocooned in the serenity of sleep. In that hushed moment, she awoke to the unmistakable sign that life, as she knew it, was about to change forever; her water had broken. The realization dawned with an emotional rush, and she scrambled for towels, calling out to her husband, who, equally dazed, joined her in a breathless dash to the hospital, their hearts pounding with the gravity of what was to come.

The contractions were gentle yet elusive, making them difficult to track. The nurse, unsure whether Colleen was truly on the brink of labour, hesitated, but the undeniable truth of her water breaking secured her place in the maternity ward. Colleen's husband steady presence beside her was a solace amid the flurry of medical interns, a whirlwind of observers during this sacred moment of life unfolding.

CHRISTMAS 1980

It was Christmas past of 1980, when I believed I was ready for anything. But how naïve I was. As the contractions deepened and the waves of pain grew overwhelming, I was engulfed by the sheer magnitude of childbirth. The agony was a force beyond anything I had imagined. And just when I thought I could bear no more, the nurse arrived, in what felt like a whirlwind, progressed from two to ten centimeters in less than thirty-five minutes. The epidural, arriving like a sign of salvation, brought relief but slowed the labour.

Then, fear struck. Crystal's heartbeat faltered, and the room was suddenly filled with an icy dread. But there was no turning back, I pushed with every ounce of a mother's unshakable love. And at precisely 3:12 p.m. on that fateful Monday, March 30, 1981, Crystal entered the world. In that instant, the universe itself seemed to shift. My heart, which had been brimming with anxious anticipation, now overflowed with a love so overwhelming it defied description. We had been granted a miracle, and in that moment, life was forever transformed.

Today, on Crystal's birthday, the sun itself appears to seek her radiant presence, yearning to bask in the joy she brings to our lives. Forty-three years have slipped away like a gentle breeze, and as I reflect on her birth, I see her once more as a fragile newborn nestled in my arms.

I recall that magical day when a sunbeam pierced through our dining room window, lightening the edge of a hand-cut crystal dinner bell.

The room danced with prismatic light, and in that moment of delicate beauty, her nickname, Crystal Belle, was born. A name that mirrors the brilliance, grace, and wonder she brings into our world; like a rainbow, a rare marvel that leaves us breathless in its presence. Rainbows are not mere phenomena of light; they are bridges between realms, symbols of rebirth, renewal, and the limitless potential of the universe. And like the radiant arc of colours after a storm, Crystal Belle has always been a symbol of hope, a living expression of joy and beauty, spreading light wherever she goes.

Even in childhood, her gentle heart shone with unmistakable kindness. I vividly recall a Valentine's Day when every classmate received a card, except her. Though her tears mirrored the sting of exclusion, what left a lasting mark on me was her compassion. She forgave without hesitation, her soul untainted by bitterness, a rare and beautiful quality that reflected the grace within her.

As adolescence swept in like a tempest, Crystal's world became an exhilarating image of teenage dreams and rebellion. Her days were filled with Cobain's grunge chords, bedroom ceilings transformed into artistic expressions, and the electric energy of sleepovers and whispered secrets. Life was a thrilling journey of discovery.

But on a fog-cloaked September evening, that vibrant journey came crashing down. Crystal was in a terrible car accident. In the terrifying stillness that followed, her heartbeat faltered, then stopped altogether. Darkness descended upon us, shrouding the world in an unbearable silence. And yet, as if touched by divine grace, life returned to her fragile form. In the months that followed, her strength, resilience, and spirit grew brighter than any rainbow.

On her sixteenth birthday, laughter once again echoed through our home. Her eyes, once dulled by trauma, now sparkled with an unbreakable will. Like a phoenix, she had risen from the ashes of despair, transformed into a force of courage and determination. She stood not as a survivor, but as a warrior, evidence to her unconquerable human spirit.

As Crystal grew into adulthood, her journey, like many, was filled with moments of both joy and hardship. She had an openness to people that, at times, left me feeling concerned, yet I couldn't help but be moved by the way she extended herself to others. During one of my visits from Calgary, we decided to take an evening walk. As we strolled, we passed a young man sitting on the sidewalk, bundled in blankets. Something about the way he was wrapped up felt familiar, and as we drew closer, he called out Crystal's name.

She smiled warmly and struck up a conversation as though they were old friends. She asked how he had been and listened as he expressed his gratitude for her kindness. After learning he hadn't eaten or had a hot bath in days, she didn't hesitate, she invited him back to her apartment. Once there, he had a bath, changed into a set of clothes her brother had left behind, and ate a proper meal. While he got settled, Crystal quietly made a list of places where he could go for hot meals and showers. He was deeply thankful and left with a sense of hope. After he departed, I couldn't help but ask, "Weren't you afraid? He was a stranger." She simply gave me a puzzled look and said softly, "Sometimes, you just have to trust." Her capacity for compassion touched lives in ways I could never have foreseen.

You got this!

Always a Fashion Diva!

From a young age, fashion had been her passion. Friends flocked to her for style advice, mothers entrusted her with their makeup, and she had an uncanny ability to transform the simplest outfit into a statement of elegance. That innate sense of beauty grew with her, blossoming into a career that would leave a mark on the world. Yet life, in its relentless unpredictability, dealt another cruel blow with the loss of her beloved brother. The grief was suffocating, yet even in her darkest hour, she became our pillar, vowing to hold our family together. Her strength was nothing short of extraordinary, a shining example of resilience and grace.

Crystal's journey as a Shepreneur and a woman of extraordinary vision has been inspiring. She has navigated the realms of fashion and finance with grace and determination, proving that success knows no boundaries. From her early days as a fashion maven, where her keen eye for design captured the hearts of many, to her bold venture into the world of finance, she has redefined what it means to be a multi-faceted leader.

Crystal embodies the trinity of chance, change, and choice, guiding others to seize opportunities, incorporate transformation, and make empowering decisions. Her story speaks volumes about spirit and innovation as she continues to shape industries and uplift those around her. In a world that often forces women to choose, Crystal proves that you can thrive in many arenas, inspiring countless others to follow in her footsteps.

Through every trial, Crystal has remained a living testimony to love, hope, and joy. She is our unicorn of rainbows, a being of light who embodies the beauty of life itself. Her laughter is infectious, her wittiness sharp, and her spirit a symbol of hope. She is radiant, like the sunrise on a perfect summer morning, a source of unending inspiration for all who are fortunate enough to know her. Each day, Crystal reminds me of the magic found in life's simplest moments, the thoughtful power of kindness, and the unyielding strength of the human spirit. She enlightens the world, one breathtaking moment at a time, leaving an everlasting impression on the hearts she touches.

"Impossibilities aren't barriers; limits are."

Mama Carson

"SILVER LINING"

When life hands you a stormy day,
And skies above are dull and gray,
Find the silver lining in the clouds,
A hidden blessing that stands proud.

When trouble knocks and things go wrong,
Turn the pain into a song.
In every challenge, seek the light,
For even in darkness, stars are bright.

If doors close and paths seem blocked,
Use your strength, your spirit unlocked.
For every end can be a start,
A chance to mend, a brand-new part.

When the world feels cold and unfair,
Find warmth and love to share.
In every setback, find your way,
To make tomorrow a brighter day.

So, when life gives you a bitter pill,
Transform it with your iron will.
From every negative, find the seed,
Of something positive you need.

Colleen C. Carson

"GRANDPARENTS"

In a sunlit garden where stories unfold,
Grandparents whisper the tales of old,
With laughter like music, a soft, gentle breeze,
They recite golden memories among the trees.

Little hands clutching, with eyes wide and bright,
Listening to stories that dance in the light.
"Once upon a time," begins the refrain,
As dreams live through moments like a gentle rain.

Wrinkled hands cradle the weight of the years,
Each line a journey through laughter and tears.
Eyes sparkling bright with the wisdom they've known,
They share precious moments, never alone.

Grandchildren dance in a world full of dreams,
Their imaginations like wild, rushing streams.
They climb on the shoulders of giants so wise,
Seeing the world through love-filled eyes.

In the glow of the fire, as shadows take flight,
Grandma's soft laughter, like stars in the night,
Grandpa's strength, a fortress of grace,
Together they cherish each moment they face.

And as seasons change, and time marches on,
The lessons of yesterday linger, not gone.
For in every giggle, in each tender glance,
The spirit of family spins a sweet dance.

Through playful adventures, and games in the sun,
They share secrets and smiles, a world of their own,
With every hug given, a treasure exchanged,
In this circle of life, where love is unchained.

So, here's to the moments, both simple and grand,
To the magic of memories held in a hand,
For the love of a grandparent, a gift so divine,
Is a legacy cherished, a bond that will shine.

Mama Carson

"BEYOND THE ACCIDENT"

As Colleen busily prepared to cater a wedding the next day, a friend from the island was set to join me, ensuring that everything remained on schedule for the event.

While Crystal's evening plans unfolded, and Colleen's girlfriend arrived for to help her with the wedding the next day: she found herself caught up in the whirlwind of preparations. As her girlfriend poured them a glass of wine, she momentarily stepped away to bring warm water from the sink.

Then, she caught a fleeting vision of Crystal drowning in a ditch of deep water. An unsettling fear gripped her, but she dismissed it, attributing it to the typical parental concern for the safety of her children when they're out with friends. As the early evening seamlessly transitioned into night, she prepared dinner for her friend, Chance, and herself. Despite Chance's lingering pain from a football accident, and drowsiness from his medication, she pressed on with her duties. With her friend retiring for the night, she remained watchful, awaiting Crystal and Brian arriving home. The clock ticked past eleven, and anxiety crept in.

Crystal, known for her punctuality, had yet to arrive home. Brian entered, and I shared my concerns about Crystal's being late. Despite his reassurances, my worry lingered. A phone call broke the uneasy silence, it was Steve's Dad, equally anxious about his son's whereabouts. Simultaneously, the hospital in Langley contacted me, revealing that Crystal had been in a car accident. Silent panic washed over me then relief as I learned she was okay but needed to be picked up with dry clothes.

In an unexpected development, Steve's Dad also received a call about his son's been in an accident, confirming he was safe and awaiting pickup at the hospital. In haste, I rushed into the living room to inform Brian about the unsettling phone call, then sprinted upstairs to Crystal's room to grab a set of clothes for him to take to the hospital. Stirred by the commotion, my girlfriend woke up and inquired about the situation. I explained the gravity of the call, and she promptly offered to take care of Chance if I wanted to go with Brian to the hospital. Deciding against it, staying home, and waiting for Crystal's return would be more practical.

Our residence was a forty-five-minute drive from the hospital so that it would take about two and a half hours. However, Brian called just an hour later, sharing that the nurse had informed him Crystal had gone down for X-rays. Once she returned, they would provide an update. He assured me that he would keep me informed as soon as he had more information.

Meanwhile, my girlfriend contacted her family, instructing her daughters to catch the first ferry in the morning. Their assistance was crucial, as Steve and Crystal, servers at my catering event, needed help to fulfill their roles. Throughout the night, Brian consistently called to update me, but there was no sign of Crystal returning home. In his final call before coming home, he revealed they were transferring Crystal to Vancouver General Hospital for additional tests. The small urban hospital where Crystal was initially admitted could not meet her specific needs.

The realization Crystal might be facing a life-and-death situation left my heart and body weak, and I sensed a feeling of faintness. However, I reasoned that collapsing would not be of any help to anyone. Brian returned without Crystal and explained she was being kept at Vancouver General Hospital for tests and rest, with the plan to pick her up in the morning. Though I harbored doubts, the stress and uncertainty prevented me from voicing them.

The night passed without sleep, and with the break of dawn, I found myself in motion, preparing for the wedding I had committed to catering and ensuring breakfast for everyone. The need to stay occupied overwhelmed me, providing a semblance of normalcy amidst the chaos. As my friend departed to collect her daughters on the ferry, and I readied myself for the wedding venue, Brian juggled phone calls with the hospital and reassured Chance, both sharing in the equal weight of worry. Loaded with supplies, and ready to depart for the venue, I realized I had left my purse in the kitchen.

Upon entering, I found Brian talking to Chance, who seemed on the verge of tears. My immediate inquiry was met with Chance's assurance that he shared our collective concern. Why did I continue to cater for the event despite my daughter's hospitalization? The truth was, I had no choice. Cancelling a wedding was not an option, and the only person capable of taking over, my sister, declined as she wished to be with Crystal at the hospital.

The wedding reception unfolded successfully, but when I called Brian expecting to find Crystal safely at home, I was shocked to learn she remained at the hospital. Anguish with frustration, I surged as Brian disclosed the severity of her condition. Crystal was in intensive care with suspected spinal damage and had already undergone emergency surgery for other injuries. Assuring Brian I would return home soon, I stepped out of the venue into dense fog and biting cold. The drive home tempted me to detour to the hospital, but the exhaustion of forty-eight sleepless hours cautioned against such a risky decision. Upon arriving home, everyone was asleep, so I slipped into bed, setting the alarm for a brief three-hour reprieve. Minutes before the alarm, I awoke, grateful for the solitude, got dressed, and then headed to the hospital.

Upon my arrival at the hospital, I entered the intensive care unit to find my beautiful daughter lying there, connected to tubes that infiltrated every conceivable part of her body. Bandages concealed most of her face, leaving barely a glimpse of her features. A wave of weakness swept through my knees, and the threat of tears loomed, but a stern inner voice reminded me that Crystal needed my strength. As I opened the door and greeted her with a soft "Hello, Belle," I could see her eyes, swollen and struggling, attempting to focus through the puffiness. Despite my physical limitations, she recognized me through my voice.

Crystal informed me that they had removed all mirrors from her surroundings, prompting her to inquire about her appearance. I downplayed the severity with a reassuring tone, assuring her that it wasn't as severe as she feared. This brought her a momentary sense of relief. Overwhelmed with emotion, she teared up but expressed happiness at my presence, acknowledging the understanding that my delay had been unavoidable. She shared that Brian and Chance had been by her side throughout the day and evening.

As our conversation unfolded, she disclosed details about her broken nose, her face, back, and hip, mentioning that X-rays had been taken of her spine and a suspected broken hip, only for the results to indicate a fracture of the hip and nothing yet about the spine. She divulged this information while expressing the need to use the bathroom, hoping I could assist her. I felt uncomfortable with the task and opted to summon a nurse who could better attend to her needs. Remaining by her side, we shared tears, laughter, and comfort until the nurse entered, announcing the imperative need for rest.

I kissed her goodbye, promising to return later. Her once sparkly blue eyes, now bloodshot and clouded with anxiety, fear, and sadness, tugged at my heartstrings, leaving an enduring indication of the challenging journey that lay ahead. As days passed, Crystal's recovery in intensive care progressed at a sluggish pace. The desire of numerous family and friends to visit her was evident, but stringent regulations allowed only immediate family members to enter.

Faced with this limitation, I summoned a meeting with the hospital staff, proposing the idea of a brief, one-hour evening session where friends and family could visit in five-minute intervals. Initially met with resistance, I emphasized the negative impact of Crystal's deepening depression on her healing process. I stressed that the emotional support from her loved ones could offer a glimmer of hope amid her struggles.

After careful consideration, the staff agreed to the proposal. Subsequent brief visits from friends and family proved beneficial, uplifting Crystal's spirits and instilling hope in her recovery. Specialists and nurses gathered for a comprehensive discussion with Crystal, Brian, Chance, and me in the following days. This meeting reviewed current results and outlined the trajectory of future procedures, fostering a collaborative approach to Crystal's ongoing care and well-being.

Once again, the doctors convened with us to provide an update on Crystal's condition. They revealed that her spinal cord had suffered an injury, though fortunately, it was not severe. Unfortunately, most of the nerves surrounding her spinal cord were damaged, and the prognosis for their complete normalization was bleak. She has a fractured hip, but only time will heal, and she was not to put much pressure on that hip; she will need plastic surgery for her nose not but her face that had a large open wound because of the severe nerve damage in her face.

Despite this challenging diagnosis, there was a positive aspect: Crystal would be discharged and allowed to return home the following week. However, her journey to recovery would be grueling. Crystal would require specialized doctor's care and weekly appointments for the next six months to a year. During the initial month, she would be bedridden, necessitating assistance for basic tasks like using the bathroom and undergoing cloth baths. Subsequently, she would depend on assistance with showers for the next six months. The uncertain path of her recovery would unfold from there, with ongoing adjustments and support tailored to her evolving needs. The following week, we brought our Crystal Belle home.

The events of that night, filled with worry and relief, served as a stark reminder of the unpredictability of life, where a tranquil September day could swiftly transform into a night of unexpected life and loss challenges that would alter our lives and others forever. Before we brought Crystal home from the hospital, we took measures to ensure her recovery was as comfortable as possible. We purchased a TV for her room and arranged her bedroom to resemble a hospital setting, welcoming friends, and family to visit.

Despite her return home, the challenges persisted. Due to Crystal's fragile condition, she could not be left alone as she required assistance to get out of bed, fearing the possibility of fainting, which had occurred multiple times in the initial month. Her routine included frequent visits to specialists, averaging three times a week.

Maneuvering with crutches initially posed difficulties, and she had a staggering twelve specialists, including a plastic surgeon addressing facial injuries. The conclusive diagnosis revealed that sixteen out of eighteen nerves around her spine were damaged, resulting in fibromyalgia for the rest of her life. Recalling a particularly poignant day, I asked Crystal's boyfriend to take me to the site of the car accident. The emotional impact deepened as I witnessed the location of the dreadful event. The ill-fated night unfolded when they decided to explore a party in Cloverdale.

Finding it uneventful, they returned to the car, with Crystal seated in the compromised center of the back seat that had a broken seat belt. Navigating a dark, rocky road at excessive speed, the driver suddenly went airborne into a water-filled ditch.

Crystal was propelled forward, her face colliding into the rear-view mirror, causing severe damage and tossed side to side, front to back then landed across the open car door where her foot was wedged inside the car. Though everyone managed to exit the car, Crystal remained trapped due to her wedged foot and weakened state. As they all reached safety, they realized that Crystal was missing. Steve, her boyfriend, rushed back into the water, finding her face down and unresponsive. After freeing her foot, he carried her up the bank to safety. Concerned onlookers from the party arrived, witnessing the distressing scene started calling 911, others started screaming while others started crying.

Steve, trained in CPR, acted swiftly, resuscitating Crystal after finding she had no pulse. The traumatic event left an indelible mark on all involved, shaping the ongoing challenges of Crystal's recovery. As time unfolded, she began to recount to me an extraordinary encounter she had after being revived. Initially, she mistook the apparition for a Christmas tree but soon realized it was her Guardian Angel.

Crystal described a meaningful after-death experience, sharing that after seeing her angelic presence, she traversed through a glowing light where she engaged in conversation with a divine voice – an encounter she recognized as the divine presence of God. Their dialogue extended for a while until the divine voice conveyed a message: it was not her time to depart; she still had unfinished endeavours on Earth.

Although bathed in a profound sense of happiness and security, Crystal reluctantly accepted that she had to return, trusting that she would reunite with her loved ones in a future death. Abruptly, she found herself being ushered into an ambulance where she began to choke and was having difficulty breathing because she was bleeding not only externally but internally. Her body was swelling to the point she could no longer open her eyes, and the pain she was feeling was unbearable.

I learned something disturbing about Brian's visit to the hospital. Unbeknownst to me, he was directed to her room when he approached the hospital desk inquiring about his daughter, Crystal. Upon entering her room, a startling scene unfolded before him – her body was three times its standard size, marked by severe bruising and open wounds. It took him a moment to recognize her, but when she weakly whispered the word "Dad," the realization struck him. Overwhelmed with emotion, he gently embraced his daughter, promising to return after seeking answers. As he exited the emergency room, the weight of the situation hit him, and he crumpled to the floor, succumbing to heart-wrenching sobs.

The journey through her recovery brought about a multitude of transformations, not only in her physical abilities but also in her daily routines, including alterations in movement and eating habits. Through this arduous process, there were moments of shared tears and laughter between all of us. Her strength and untiring positive attitude played a pivotal role in expediting her healing. Without her strength of spirit, the recovery timeline might have been prolonged.

As the initial months passed, she gained enough strength to commence schoolwork. Steve, her devoted boyfriend, played an integral part by offering support during these academic endeavours.

Eventually, she returned to school at the beginning of April, although only for half a day, due to the limitations imposed by her endurance. Holding her head up for more than ninety minutes proved challenging, leading to extreme fatigue. Despite these obstacles, she persevered and excelled by the end of the year, achieving a commendable B+ average in all her exams. Her triumphant journey is a testament to the power of resilience and a positive mindset in overcoming life's formidable challenges.

We all endured the painful sight of her suffering as her brother, Chance, would silently weep in his room, overwhelmed by a sense of helplessness for being unable to alleviate her pain. I reassured him, emphasizing that he was not powerless; he was the one who could make her laugh the most and keep her company for the most extended durations, fostering happiness and a sense of security within her. A year later, as we joyously celebrated her sixteenth birthday surrounded by family and friends, the room echoed with relief and happiness.

We all reminisced about her remarkable recovery, mindful of the harrowing experience she had endured, an ordeal that had prompted my daily prayers of gratitude to God for returning her to us. Today, as we eagerly anticipate her forty-third birthday two months away, the journey was glorious. She continues to grapple with fibromyalgia, a persistent challenge in her life. Nevertheless, I am grateful, once again, to thank my God for the precious gift of having her back in our lives.

I understand that our lives can be incredibly hectic, but it is crucial to recognize that there is nothing more significant than dedicating time to our children and, in fact, all our loved ones. We never truly know when a simple "goodbye" or "goodnight" might unexpectedly become the last. Therefore, we must prioritize and cherish these moments, consciously creating lasting memories with those we hold dear. In the hustle and bustle of our daily routines, let's keep sight of the thoughtful impact our presence and attention can have on the lives of our loved ones.

"Life is a journey, shaped by choices, love, and wisdom gathered along the way."

Colleen C. Carson

"Believe in what you say; say what you believe."

Mama Carson

"WHERE DO BABIES"

Ah, the eternal parenting curveball: "Where do babies come from?" It's the sort of question that sends even the calmest adults into a tailspin. This isn't just idle curiosity; it's the kind of query that sneaks up on you mid-sip of coffee and leaves you choking while your child stares at you like you've got all the answers in the universe. Spoiler: you don't.

It was an ordinary day in the kitchen, toast browning in the toaster, the smell of coffee in the air, when in stomped my five-year-old philosopher, Crystal. Her curls bounced like tiny question marks, her backpack was half-zipped, and her face wore the look of someone ready to solve life's greatest mysteries. *"Mommy,"* she began confidently, like a queen addressing her subjects, *"where do babies come from?"*

I froze, butter knife in hand, staring at her as though she'd just asked me to explain the theory of relativity. My thoughts immediately went into a panicked shuffle. Babies? Now? Wasn't this a question for later? Like, much later? But there she stood, all innocence and expectation, waiting for me to drop some profound knowledge.

I did what any sensible parent would do: I stalled. *"Well, Belle,"* I said, embodying my best calm-and-collected mom voice, *"Where do you think babies come from?"* Ah, the art of deflection. It's a tried-and-true parenting move, as reliable as bedtime negotiations and the magical powers of a bandage on imaginary boo-boos. I figured she'd throw me something easy, storks, maybe, or a story about angels.

But Crystal, my pint-sized Sherlock Holmes, wasn't playing along. She narrowed her eyes and crossed her arms, clearly unimpressed with my attempt to pass the ball back into her court. *"Babies,"* she said with the seriousness of a judge about to deliver a verdict, *"come from God."* There it was. Boom. The answer is clear as day. Simple, sweet, and perfectly kindergarten approved. I nodded, relieved that the conversation might be over. But Crystal wasn't finished yet. Oh no, she had one more zinger tucked away and delivered it with a flair that would've made Shakespeare proud.

"See, Mommy," she said, wagging her tiny finger for emphasis, *"if you went to kindergarten, you'd know that."* And just like that, I was floored. My five-year-old had managed to outsmart, outwit, and out-

debate me in the span of thirty seconds. I stood there, dumbfounded, while Crystal grabbed an apple from the counter and marched off, her curls bouncing triumphantly with each step. The rest of the day, I couldn't stop replaying the scene in my head. There I was, a grown adult, utterly defeated by a child who probably still needed help tying her shoes. But you know what? That's parenting in a nutshell. It's a nonstop rollercoaster of questions you're not ready for, answers you have to invent on the fly, and moments of sheer, unfiltered hilarity.

I couldn't help but laugh at myself. Here I was, worried about giving her the "right" answer when she already had one that worked for her. She didn't need a lecture or a detailed explanation. She needed a mom who could listen, laugh, and be just as curious about life as she was.

And isn't that the beauty of raising kids? They remind us to see the world through fresh eyes, to find wonder in the ordinary, and to embrace the chaos with open arms. Sure, the big questions can catch us off guard, but they're also opportunities to connect, to share, and, let's be honest, to laugh until our sides hurt.

Looking back, I realized Crystal wasn't just asking about babies. She was asking for a conversation, for a moment of shared discovery. And in her own way, she taught me something important: parenting isn't about always having the answers. It's about being there, ready to navigate the unknown, one hilarious question at a time.

So, the next time your little one stumps you with a question straight out of left field, remember this: it's okay to fumble, to laugh, and to admit you don't know everything. Because, in the end, it's not about being perfect. It's about being present. And sometimes, that means letting your five-year-old win the debate and walking away with a story you'll cherish forever.

Daughter: 1. Mommy: 0. Parenthood? A never-ending comedy of errors, and I wouldn't trade it for the world.

"What if there was no hate in the world, how would we redefine our stories, and what interesting connections might thrive in the spaces once filled with shadows?"

Mama Carson

"FARMGIRL CHELSEA"

Let us hop in our time machine and travel back to that magical day when little Chelsea graced the world with her presence! It was a day bursting with joy and celebration, made even more special by the unique spelling of Chelsea's name. Colleen, was always one to infuse meaning into the ordinary, chose to spell it with the "sea" at the end. Why? Because Chelsea's Dad was a fisherman, and the sea held a special place in their hearts.

To Colleen, her children are her precious Angels, each one a miracle. Chelsea, however, was also a miracle in the truest sense, a little bundle of life who ended up saving her mother, Christina. Yes, you heard that right! This tiny, beautiful girl was born with the power of healing. It all started years before Chelsea was born when her sister, Christina, began experiencing some odd and worrying symptoms.

She had severe headaches, tunnel vision, and the strangest dreams, unlike anything she had ever known. Doctors initially thought it was all emotional stress and suggested therapy. The family followed it, thinking that perhaps a little emotional support would help. Why wouldn't they?

When Christina got pregnant, Colleen was her rock, right by her side every step of the way. Pregnancy is no walk in the park, and for Christina, it was especially tough. She opted for a natural birth, and it was a challenging experience for her body. But through all the stress and strain, she brought home her beautiful baby, Chelsea.

A week later, on the day of their outing to Playland, Christina seemed in good spirits. She had a bath, and out of nowhere, the serenity disrupted with her frantic screams for Colleen. In a heart-stopping moment, Colleen found her sister thrashing violently in the bathwater, caught in the throes of a seizure.

Colleen's quick thinking kicked in; she yelled for John, Chelsea's Dad, to bring something to place in Christina's mouth to prevent her from biting her tongue. That terrifying moment was a revelation. Christina's pregnancy had masked a severe underlying condition. It turned out that her unusual symptoms were due to a condition that pregnancy had aggravated, leading to the seizure. If it had not been for Chelsea, Christina's condition might have gone undiagnosed until an after-death autopsy.

And so, Chelsea's arrival was not just the birth of a beautiful baby girl but the saving grace for her mom. This little miracle truly lived up to her name, bringing with her a wave of hope and love, much like the sea she was named after. It was then that my family discovered the shocking truth: my sister had a brain tumor dangerously close to her inner brain. The doctors acted quickly, performing surgery to remove it. Thankfully, she made it through without any major disabilities, although she did need medication to maintain everyday life.

Here's the truly incredible part: if my sister had not gotten pregnant, and especially if she had not had a natural birth, the tumor would have gone undetected and eventually killed her. My niece, Chelsea, is nothing short of a miracle who saved her mom's life. Let us fast forward a few years to Chelsea's childhood. She was an adorably shy little thing. I still remember how she would hide behind her mother's legs, peeking out with those big, cautious eyes like a little kitten peering out from its safe spot. Unlike my sister, I had a firmer voice and mastered the infamous "Mother's look." You know the one—the look where your mom's eyes silently scream, "Don't you dare," while her mouth stays closed, curved into a gentle smile. It is a universal mom superpower; let me tell you, it's one of the scariest things a kid can experience.

I should know; my mom perfected that look. My sisters and I would freeze in our tracks whenever we saw it, knowing we were toeing a dangerous line. I channeled that very same look with my kids, and poor Chelsea, observing this, would get so nervous! My children knew the power of that look and behaved accordingly, but it was a whole new level of intimidation for Chelsea.

Despite her shyness, Chelsea was always such a sweet and thoughtful child. She had this endearing way of tiptoeing around me, always polite and careful. One time, during a family barbecue, I remember she wanted to ask me for more marshmallows but was too shy to come out with them. Instead, she sent her little cousin as an ambassador, whispering instructions behind her mom's legs. It was the cutest thing!

As Chelsea grew into her teenage years, the shy little girl began to transform. Slowly but surely, she blossomed into a confident young woman. With that transformation came a delightful change in our relationship. Gone was the timid child who hid behind her mother's legs, and in her place was a young lady who laughed with me over the silliest things and shared her dreams and secrets. Our interactions became more humorous and honest.

I remember the first time she teased me back after one of my playful jabs. It was like seeing a new side of her, one that was full of spirit. We bonded over shared jokes and late-night talks, finding a rhythm that was uniquely ours. So, our bond has grown into something extraordinary from those early days of shyness to the present. Chelsea, once the miracle baby who saved her mom's life, has become a cherished friend. Our journey together is filled with love, laughter, and a shared appreciation for the miracle that brought us closer. And now, every time I give her that "Mother's look" for old times' sake, we both burst into laughter, remembering how it once made her eyes go wide with innocent fear.

I vividly recall a memorable Christmas spent at Chelsea and Ryan's home with Brynley, their adorable daughter, Crystal, Donald, and myself. It was a warm and festive gathering filled with laughter, delicious food, and the cozy ambiance of holiday cheer. We were all excited to be together, exchanging stories and enjoying each other's company.

Chelsea handed me a beautifully wrapped gift as we gathered around the Christmas tree, adorned with twinkling lights and ornaments that held memories of years past. Her eyes sparkled with excitement as she watched me carefully open the package. Inside was a beautifully crafted wooden plaque, and when I read the inscription, my heart swelled with emotion:

"There is an instinct in a woman to love most her own child; and an instinct to make any child who needs her love, her own."

Tears filled my eyes as I looked at Chelsea, feeling love and gratitude. This simple yet powerful message perfectly captured our bond. It was more than a gift; it was a tribute to the deep connection and unconditional love that had grown between us over the years. This plaque, with its heartfelt words, now holds a special place in my home, serving as a daily reminder of the incredible journey we have been on together. Our bond has always been a light of hope, illustrating the reflective impact of nurturing relationships on our journey toward self-discovery and fulfillment.

Chelsea has become a significant part of my life, from the shy little girl hiding behind her mother's legs to the confident young woman who now bestows thoughtful gifts. Our relationship has taught me so much about love, patience, and the beauty of opening your heart to others. As we sat around the tree that Christmas, I could not help but reflect on how far we had come. The shared moments of joy and laughter, the challenges we faced together, and the untiring support we provided for each other had all contributed to a bond that was as strong as any family tie.

Brynley, with her infectious giggles and wide-eyed wonder, added to the magic of that Christmas. Watching her play and interact with everyone, especially Crystal. As Brynley would say, "My sister!" I saw glimpses in Brynley of the same shy curiosity that Chelsea once had. It was a beautiful reminder of the cycles of love and care that continue through generations. That Christmas was a celebration of more than just the holiday; it was a celebration of family, love, and the nurturing bonds that make life so meaningful.

I remember when Chelsea's loyal commitment to her mother's well-being fostered a spirit within their bond and served as proof of the enduring power of love and family devotion. Despite their trials, their connection remained a source of strength, anchoring them amid the uncertainties of health struggles. As Chelsea matured, she cultivated friendships at school and sought solace in the range of books and imagination. I knew that within Chelsea lay a dormant spark, waiting to ignite into something extraordinary. And ignite it did. With time, Chelsea began to find her voice, articulating her thoughts and opinions without fear of judgment.

Each interaction nourished her confidence, like a delicate flower blooming under the sun's gentle warmth. In the compelling narrative of Chelsea's journey, we are not merely presented with a story of individual development but rather the strength of love and spirit. Chelsea, the extraordinary "Farmgirl" perfectly captures her rustic charm and deep-rooted connection to the land. Nestled within the serene confines of her farm, Farmgirl coordinates a composition of life, tending to horses, sheep, chickens, and the ever-loyal dogs that grace her homestead.

Despite the ceaseless demands of farm life, she seamlessly juggles her responsibilities with a full-time job, demonstrating a remarkable balance between work and home. However, Farmgirl's devotion extends far beyond the confines of her farmyard. Family reigns supreme in her world, and her devoted commitment to her loving daughter, Brynley, and partner, Ryan, is evident in every aspect of her life. Whether she's shuttling Brynley to horse-riding classes, curling sessions, or providing invaluable assistance with homework and personal growth, Farmgirl's dedication knows no bounds. But wait, there's more to this remarkable woman than meets the eye.

Farmgirl's alter ego, "Super Farmgirl," emerges as she effortlessly navigates the many tasks that come her way. From lending a hand to Ryan in the relentless upkeep of their farm to indulging her passion for reading, Farmgirl is an inspiration of versatility and perseverance. Amidst the hustle and bustle of farm life, Farmgirl finds solace in the simple pleasures of leisure. Picture her on a clear day, perched upon her veranda with a cold beer in hand, lost in the pages of a captivating novel. The sun is shining, birds are singing, and there she is, fully absorbed in her book, occasionally glancing up to appreciate the view of her sprawling farm. It is a slice of heaven right there on the porch.

When she is not relaxing with a book, you might find her tracking the vastness of her land on horseback with Brynley by her side. The two of them make quite the pair, Brynley giggling, both looking every bit the adventurous duo. Or, if the mood strikes, she might be tearing across the fields on an ATV, whooping with joy as she leads Brynley and a merry band of family and friends on a thrilling ride.

Her laughter is infectious, echoing through the countryside as they navigate bumps and turns, everyone holding on for dear life. But Farmgirl's escapades do not stop at the edge of her farm. Oh no, she is an avid camper, always planning the next great adventure. When Farmgirl organizes a camping trip, it is anything but ordinary. She turns these outings into unforgettable events, filled with hilarious stories, spontaneous sing-alongs around the campfire, and epic marshmallow roasting competitions.

Picture tents set up in a perfect circle, everyone gathered under the stars, and Farmgirl at the center of it all, leading the charge with her boundless energy and enthusiasm. With Farmgirl at the helm, camping trips have become legendary. She has a knack for turning even the simplest activities into joyous celebrations. A hike through the woods becomes a scavenger hunt with silly prizes. A quiet night by the campfire suddenly becomes a talent show, with everyone displaying their hidden skills. And the food! No one ever leaves hungry, thanks to her campfire cooking that's somehow both gourmet and comforting.

Every adventure with Farmgirl is a blend of excitement and laughter, seasoned with the warmth of her love for family and friends. She is the heart of every gathering, the spark that ignites fun and creates lasting memories. Whether on her veranda with a book, exploring her land on horseback, or leading a wild ATV adventure, Farmgirl's zest for life and passion for the people she loves make every moment extraordinary.

Farmgirl, my beautiful Chelsea epitomizes the spirit of a modern-day woman – a master of countless pursuits, a committed community pillar, and, above all, a devoted matriarch of love, family, and the land she calls home. She is an authentication of the power of perseverance and self-belief. A loving mother to her sensational daughter Brynley and a devoted partner to her loving Ryan, she has built a life filled with joy, love, and achievement. Yes, this timid girl I once knew blossomed into a poised, confident woman who gracefully embraces social exchanges with enthusiasm. Witnessing Chelsea's transformation has filled me with immense pride.

Her journey is proof of the power of love, support, and perseverance. It is a reminder that we can all grow into the best versions of ourselves with the right encouragement, a nurturing environment but most importantly, love. Watching Chelsea evolve has been one of my greatest joys, inspiring me to continue fostering growth and confidence in those around me.

"An entrepreneur transforms challenges into steppingstones, and dreams into realities, all with a spirit that turns aspirations into inspirations."

Colleen C. Carson

"KINGDOM OF KNOWLEDGE"

In the city's heart, a grand library stood, showered in sunlight that seemed to warm the very stones of its walls. Its towering pinnacles rose as if to touch the sky, and its ancient stones, softened by the hands of time, whispered secrets to all who ventured close. This was no ordinary library; it was the Library of Research, a gateway to the Kingdom of Knowledge, renowned far and wide as a place where curiosity met wisdom, where past and future embraced. It held within its vast collection the stories of humanity's greatest minds, each word carefully preserved for those brave enough to seek its wisdom.

Although not formally a scholar, Colleen had always been a learner, a seeker of truth, and a mentor to many. She had spent years traveling, exploring, and studying the written word, absorbing the world's knowledge as she encountered it. To her, this library was sacred. The long corridors filled with books were not just aisles of paper; they were pathways to understanding the mysteries of existence. It was a place where every question was welcomed, and every answer, though temporary, was a stepping stone toward greater knowledge.

Her son Chance and daughter Crystal, too, had a deep respect for the library's power. While they were still young, their minds had already begun to grasp the vastness of the Kingdom of Knowledge. With her quiet wisdom and limitless curiosity, Crystal was often the first to burrow into a new book or topic. Full of energy and laughter, Chance brought joy and wonder to every discovery, reminding his mother of the joy that learning could bring. They both saw the library as a place of endless possibilities, a treasure trove of insight waiting to be uncovered.

As I stand here now, reflecting on those days spent in the library with my children, I can't help but feel immense gratitude for the lessons we learned together. I think back to the moments when Chance would pull a book from the shelf, his face lighting up as he discovered something new. "Mom, look at this! Did you know that the stars in the sky are just like our sun, only farther away?" he would exclaim, his excitement contagious. And Crystal, always the quiet observer, would smile and add, "Yes, and the light we see from them has traveled millions of years to reach us."

Those moments, filled with awe and wonder, became the foundation of our shared understanding. We learned that knowledge isn't just about gathering facts but about connecting those facts to something deeper within ourselves. Every book we read, and every piece of information we uncovered brought us closer to understanding not just the world but ourselves and each other. I remember one quiet afternoon when Crystal and I were seated together at one of the long oak tables in the library. The sunlight streamed through the tall windows, casting a warm glow over the pages of the book I was reading. She had just finished a chapter on the nature of the universe and turned to me with a thoughtful look in her eyes. "Mom," she asked, "what does it mean to truly understand something? Is it just about knowing the facts, or is it something more?"

Her question struck me deeply, and I paused, reflecting on the years of learning I had gathered. "Understanding," I replied, "is more than just knowing. It's about seeing the connections, feeling the emotions, and recognizing the patterns in the world around us. It's about being open to new ideas while still staying grounded in what we know to be true." Crystal nodded slowly, taking in my words. "So, it's about seeing the bigger picture, not just the details?"

"Exactly," I said, my heart full of pride for her insight. "The details are important, but they only make sense when we can see them in the context of the whole. Knowledge is a journey, one that never truly ends. The more we learn, the more we realize how much there is still to discover." As we left the library that day, Chance bounced ahead of us, laughing and imagining grand adventures, while Crystal walked beside me in contemplative silence. We didn't leave with books in our hands; we left with something more: a sense of connection to the vast world of knowledge and the realization that we were part of something much larger than ourselves.

In that moment, I realized that the true power of a place like the Library of Research isn't just in the knowledge it holds but in the way it shapes us as individuals. It encourages us to ask questions, seek answers, and never stop learning. It reminds us that we are all part of a much bigger story that continues to unfold with every new discovery. As I continue my own journey of learning, I carry with me the lessons I've shared with my children and the wisdom I've gained through years of exploration. Knowledge is not something to be hoarded or kept in isolation. It's meant to be shared, passed on, and celebrated. It's about growing together, embracing curiosity, and inspiring others to begin on their own journeys.

I see now that this library, with its endless shelves and infinite possibilities, is not just a place for scholars or seekers but for all of us. Whether we are young or old, experienced or just beginning, we are all on a journey of discovery that will continue as long as we remain open to learning. In that sense, the Kingdom of Knowledge is within all of us. It's a place where our curiosity meets our potential, and every question brings us one step closer to understanding the world and ourselves.

The Library of Research stands as a reminder of truth, a sanctuary of wisdom inviting all who enter to begin on their own journeys. It is a place where questions are welcomed, answers are offered, and we can grow together as we learn from the past, explore the present, and imagine the future. And as I looked at my children, watching them learn and grow with each passing day, I was filled with hope. For they are the future, and the library, with all its knowledge and wisdom, will continue to guide them, just as it guided me.

"A MAMA'S LOVE"

In the quiet whispers of the morning's first light,
A woman rises, with strength so bright.
She bears the burdens and dreams of her kin,
Shaping a legacy where love and joy begin.

Amid trials and triumphs, she creates her tale,
A mother's journey, active with detail.
With wisdom's touch, she nurtures and guides,
Her spirit ablaze, where courage resides.

She conveys the echoes of generations past,
Their stories and struggles, eternally cast.
With each gentle step, she paves the way,
For her daughters and sons, in the light of day.

Through every challenge, her spirit remains strong,
Guiding with wisdom, where hearts belong.
A legacy of love, timeless and true,
In her embrace, all things are made new.

In her home, a sanctuary is found,
Hearts are cherished, and dreams abound.
She's the foundation of her family's power,
In her love, a sacred space to empower.

With each passing year, her presence grows,
Like the roots of a mighty oak inner-self flows.
An inspiration of hope, faith, and principles,
A mama's love devotes forever miracles.

Colleen C. Carson

"Free speech opens doors for dialogue; hate speech slams them shut."

Colleen C. Carson

"Ordinary is a secure path, extraordinary is where the heart dares to dream and the soul finds its true wings."

Mama Carson

In the annals of Vancouver's sporting history, a remarkable story unfolds, a tale of underdog triumph, an unexpected coaching journey, and the rise of a champion. Picture this: it's 1995 when flannel shirts were the epitome of cool, and rollerblades glided through the city streets like a vibrant breeze. Enter Tiger Williams and Bill McMenamin, the visionary duo behind the Vancouver Voodoo Roller Hockey League, who decided it was time to sprinkle some puck magic over the city and gave birth to a minor roller hockey team that would soon etch its name in the hearts of many.

Let me introduce you to a rising star in this narrative: Colleen's son, Chance Kingsley Carson. With dreams of hockey stardom dancing in his mind, Chance faced a harsh reality, his Dad's wallet wasn't exactly cheering him on. Ice hockey, with its soaring costs, seemed an impossible dream. But then, like a lightning bolt of destiny, minor roller hockey rolled into town. Chance seized the moment, pouncing on this newfound opportunity faster than a cat chasing a laser pointer.

With a spark of enthusiasm lighting up his eyes, Chance turned to Colleen, pleading with all his heart to let him join the roller hockey ranks. Being the supportive mother that she is, Colleen readily agreed, promising to be the designated supplier of water and oranges on game days, ensuring her son was well-hydrated and energized.

But fate had more in store for her. Just days later, the phone rang; a call from the hockey honchos. They needed a coach; the only one they could find was Colleen. She knew her hockey knowledge could barely fill the back of a postage stamp, but the thought of disappointing her beloved Chance was not an option. After considerable convincing: okay, let's be honest, a monumental effort: she reluctantly stepped up to the plate.

Cue the frantic phone call to my Dad, hoping for sage advice on all things hockey. Instead, I was met with laughter; uncontrollable, knee-slapping laughter. My Dad's amusement at the prospect of me becoming a hockey coach was evident, as he knew as much about roller hockey as a goldfish does about algebra. Thanks for the assist, Dad!

Undeterred by the initial chaos, I dove headfirst into the thrilling world of roller hockey coaching. Armed with unyielding determination and a couple of assistant coaches who actually knew what they were doing, I hit the rink running, well, more like stumbling since I couldn't rollerblade to save my life. However, not everyone was rooting for me.

One notably presumptuous wife of one of my assistant coaches suggested I should step aside so her husband could take the reins. Fueled by tenacity and fierce protectiveness for my son and team, I firmly declared, "I don't step down; I step up!"

Despite my best efforts, the team's early performances were rocky, leading them to clutch the wooden spoon of shame and be eliminated from playoff contention. This bitter defeat was compounded by the knowledge that some fellow coaches conspired against me, using my gender as an excuse to question my place in the coaching ranks.

And so, dear reader, we find ourselves at the heart of an age-old story, where I set forth my personal goals: conquering sexism in the league to assert my self-worth, teaching respect to those who dared to disrespect, and finding satisfaction in proving the doubters wrong.

Though the scoreboard may not have reflected victory, I hadn't won a single game. I won the hearts of my players and their parents. And those doubting Thomases? They would soon learn a valuable lesson: never underestimate the power of a determined mom armed with a bag of oranges and a hefty dose of moxie.

As the rollercoaster ride of sports and triumph continued, I prepared for another season of Chance's roller hockey journey, dress in my "Coach Extraordinaire" summer dress with renewed vigour. This time, I was armed with a splash of strategy and a whole lot of sass. No more frantic calls to my Dad for advice; I was on a mission. I scoured libraries for the elusive book of roller hockey wisdom, and just when hope seemed dim, I stumbled upon it, a slim volume of ten pages packed with enough knowledge to ignite my coaching career.

With newfound insights, I gathered the parents for a huddle, laying down the law and setting the tone for the season. There would be no swearing in the stands, no missed practices without consequences, and certainly no room for backstabbing or narcissism. The parents nodded in agreement, though one particularly icy hockey Dad stood out like a storm cloud on a sunny day.

Undaunted, I orchestrated Tuesday night street hockey sessions, fostering camaraderie and revealing each player's strengths and weaknesses. I even recruited two college students passionate about roller hockey as assistant coaches because teamwork makes the dream work!

As the season kicked off, I strutted into the rink like a fashion-forward hockey goddess, my stilettos clicking confidently against the floor. My team; twelve spirited boys and one ballet-dancing dynamo girl rallied around my leadership, transforming into a pack of rollerblading warriors. And that ballerina? She was a whirlwind of speed and strategy, leaving opponents in the dust or, or should I say, ice spray while her teammates defended like noble knights.

But it wasn't all smooth skating. I stood firm when a threatening "monster Dad" tried to exert his influence by claiming he'd pull his son from the team if I didn't adopt his coaching style. Unfortunately, his tearful boy and his friends watched as his father ushered him out of the locker room. However, in a display of maturity that filled me with pride, Chance stepped up as team captain, leading his teammates with enthusiasm and determination.

As the season progressed, our teamwork shone brightly, guiding our team through pre-season and regular-season victories until they found themselves in the nail-biting showdown for the Provincial Cup.

With the stakes sky-high and the crowd buzzing with anticipation, Chance delivered the game-winning point in sudden-death overtime, erupting the arena into cheers and securing their place in roller hockey history.

WE WON **THE NATIONAL CHAMPIONSHIP FOR 1995**! As they stood triumphant, Chance and I hoisted the cup high, embodying the true essence of courage, teamwork, and a killer pair of stilettos.

But the real triumph lay in the bonds created, the lessons learned, and the friendships cherished along the way. As I basked in the glow of our victory, I recognized that I was not just a coach, I had become a mentor, a friend, and a symbol of inspiration for every player daring to dream. Each of my players, especially Chancey, became my guiding light, transforming the journey into a shared legacy.

Days later, as i accepted bouquets of red roses and heartfelt gratitude from MY team and their parents, I couldn't help but reflect on the extraordinary journey we had embarked on together. It was a mother-son experience that filled our hearts with pride and excitement, a bond strengthened through every thrilling moment. "I love you, my Chancey," I whispered, knowing we had created something extraordinary.

The following week, Chance and I rallied our team to join the twenty-four other coaches at B.C. Place for a special provincial recognition ceremony. This moment was filled with immense pride for Chance, our team captain, a recognition of his hard work and leadership. For me, the Roller Hockey Coach in Stilettos, it was a delicate balancing act both literally and figuratively.

Standing tall amid a sea of male coaches, the only woman in the spotlight, I felt a blend of surrealism and pride wash over me. In my stilettos, I was ready to accept the Voodoo Roller Hockey Provincial Cup of 1995. The cheers from our team and parents echoed through the stadium, creating an electric atmosphere that surrounded us.

The ceremony was a whirlwind of handshakes, smiles, and photo opportunities. I tried to maintain my poise in my stilettos while accepting congratulations and posing for pictures with the trophy. Chance stood proudly beside me, his face beaming with joy as our team celebrated our hard-earned success, waving banners and chanting our names.

As I surveyed the scene, I couldn't help but chuckle to myself. Who would have imagined that the Roller Hockey Coach in Stilettos would find herself in this moment? Life has a whimsical way of surprising us, and this was one of those delightful surprises.

Amid the cheers and celebration, a reflective sense of gratitude filled my heart. I felt thankful for my team's solid dedication, Chance's remarkable leadership, and the steadfast support from parents and fans. This trophy symbolized not just our victory; it was a tribute to the power of teamwork, determination, and a splash of humour.

As we left B.C. Place that night, trophy in hand and hearts brimming with joy; I beamed with pride. The Roller Hockey Coach in Stilettos had demonstrated that when passion meets perseverance—coupled with a sprinkle of humour; anything is possible.

Our bond, mother and son, deepened with every shared smile, heartfelt conversation, and stride taken together. So, here's to forever, Chancey and the whole roller hockey crew, may your skates be swift, your goals plentiful, and your spirits forever unconquerable.

Let's roll!

"RING MY BELL"

"Gather 'round and prepare to be amused, for 'Ring My Bell' is not just a tale; it is a boisterous escapade that tickled our funny bones and left us with sides sore from laughter. It is a stunning comedic success; a rollercoaster of hilarious memories that still makes us laugh. So, let us raise a toast to 'Ring My Bell' - the epitome of side-splitting entertainment and the source of endless joyous recollections!"

Once upon a time, in the bustling halls of Abbotsford's Robert Bateman Secondary School, there lived a legend that was anything but ordinary. Let us rewind to the cusp of the millennium, where amidst the sea of hormonal unease and equational mysteries, there stood Chance - a figure whose charm was as candid with a lot less confusion and more laughter.

Whether it was his impromptu stand-up routines during lunch breaks or his uncanny ability to turn algebra into a punchline, or the sound of his car engine rumbling every Friday afternoon leaving the school parking lot, Chance brought laughter to every corner of the school. His legend lives on in the annals of Abbotsford lore, forever etched in the memories of those lucky enough to have shared a laugh or two in his uproarious presence.

Picture this: its talent show season, and everyone is scrambling to assemble their diverse crews of performers. But poor Chance, with his flair for the fabulous and an affinity for partying like 1979, found himself about as welcome as a sunburn at a beach party. No one wanted to roll the dice with Chance.

A group of mavericks, a ragtag bunch who stumbled into each other's company like socks in a dryer. By cosmic joke or a clerical error in the school's roster, Chance was reluctantly roped into their escapades. The teacher in charge made them work together to produce something. And so, the stage was set for a journey through the halls of high school folklore.

With "Ring My Bell" as their anthem and a trunk full of polyester dreams, the group embarked on a quest to conquer the talent show. The rehearsal room became their playground, a battlefield of wigs, disco attire, and funky beats. Ah, yes, the opening night! Little did we, and the unsuspecting audience, know what spectacle awaited them.

Chance and his merry band of disco divas had been shrouded in secrecy, their rehearsals cloaked in mystery and intrigue. But one thing was for sure: whatever they had planned, it was bound to be a performance of epic proportions that would leave a lasting mark on the annals of talent show history.

As the curtains rose and the lights dimmed, an unmistakable sense of anticipation was in the air, mingled with a healthy dose of curiosity and a touch of nervousness. What had Chance cooked up this time? What grand scheme lay in store for the unsuspecting audience?

And then, as if by magic, they appeared on stage, Chance and his cohorts, dazzling in their disco finest, shimmering and shining in disco glory. But it was not just their outfits that dazzled; oh no, their sheer audacity and unabashed commitment to the cause stole the show from the very first moment. As the group took the stage, decked out in threads that screamed disco fever, the crowd braced themselves for the usual high school hijinks.

Wigs were put on, bell bottoms were resurrected, and Chance, the unsung hero at the back, his attire was his Dad's suit, handed a dinner bell and made to ring it with type of noise. Oh, the chaos and hilarity that ensued!

Chance, decked out in his dad's oversized suit, struggled to wrangle a dinner bell into submission while his cohorts, bedecked in disco, wigs, and platform shoes, danced around the stage like a band of merry misfits, lip-syncing to the lyrics of Ring my Bell. It was a sight to behold, an opus of laughter that echoed through the halls of Abbotsford's Robert Bateman Secondary School.

But amidst the laughter and the madness, there was a sense of solidarity, of friendship shaped into the fires of disco fever. Each clang of the bell, each misstep on the dance floor, was met with uproarious laughter and good-natured ribbing, binding the group together in shared fun and hilarity. The audience roared with laughter and applause, swept up in the infectious energy of "Ring My Bell" and its sheer audacity.

Ah, but then came the chorus and, with it, Chance's moment to shine. Hidden at the back, he struck that dinner bell like a maestro conducting a symphony of chaos. Laughter rippled through the crowd like waves of joy, but little did they know, the real showstopper was yet to come. In a move that would make John Travolta proud, Chance broke free from his shell, unleashing a dance routine that defied gravity and all expectations.

It was as if the spirit of the disco itself had possessed him, his every move a tribute to the power of polyester and platform shoes. As he threw off his suit jacket and ripped his shirt open, revealing a clothed wife-beater chest that glistened in the spotlight, the crowd erupted into cheers and applause. But it was not just his physique that captivated them; oh no, it was his sheer exuberance, his unbridled enthusiasm for the art of dance, that stole their hearts and left them breathless with excitement.

And all the while, the dinner bell rang on, its metallic clang ringing out in perfect harmony with the pulsating beat of the music. It was a moment of pure, unadulterated joy that transcended the confines of the talent show stage and soared into the realm of legend. As Chance took his final bow, basking in the crowd's adoration, there was no doubt in anyone's mind: he had become the unexpected star of the night, a shining sparkle of disco glory in a world hungry for laughter and excitement.

The rest, as they say, is history. The group swept through the district competition like a glittering tornado, leaving a trail of disco dust in its wake. And Chance? He became more than just a high school legend, inspiring and demonstrating the power of passion and individuality.

From YouTube fame to whispered tales in the school corridors, Chance's triumph echoed far and wide. And within the chaos of high school drama and teenage anxiety, his story served as a reminder that sometimes, the most unlikely heroes are the ones who shine the brightest. So, here is to Chance, the disco king of Abbotsford, and to the belief that anything is possible with a bit of flair and a whole lot of heart."

Another Airband with family friend Meghan.

"THE MALE GENERATIONS"

"I believe that through the male generations, men are not defined by the legacies they inherit, but by the wisdom they cultivate, learning that true strength lies not in dominance, but in the integrity and courage to build, protect, and uplift."
Colleen C. Carson

"THE FEMALE GENERATIONS"

Women Of the Family

"Every generation of women carries a torch of wisdom, passed from mother to daughter not as a burden, but as a guiding light for those who follow, while honouring the strength of those who came before."
Colleen C. Carson

"THE COURAGE OF CHANCE"

When Colleen found out she was pregnant with her third child, joy came with a quiet anticipation. It wasn't just her happiness; there was a happy influence for Brian, Crystal, and her family. This pregnancy felt different, like a prelude to something big. She was sure it was a boy, a belief that tugged at her heart. She picked Chance Kingsley Carson and Jamieson Fitzgerald Carson, but Chance echoed a promise she couldn't quite grasp. By the seventh month of pregnancy, Chance sat so low it felt like he might just walk out on his own. The physical strain was intense: nerve pain, sleepless nights, and the constant tease of false alarms. Colleen lost weight, her body worn down by sickness and exhaustion, but her soul clung to the belief in the boy she was carrying.

When Chance finally arrived, he wasn't demanding, just hungry for life in the gentlest way. Even as a baby, he seemed to sense her weariness, his tiny hands reaching out as if to soothe her. He was a quiet force, full of a longing for connection and everything the world had to offer. I still remember how he first showed his caring nature in small ways. When Chance discovered the magic of talking, it was as if he'd unlocked the secrets of the universe. Words tumbled out of him with the enthusiasm of a puppy chasing its tail. I vividly remember one evening in the kitchen when he was about four, eagerly narrating his every thought while I attempted to cook dinner. This wasn't just a cheerful recount of his day; oh no, it was an unrelenting interrogation of "whys." Finally, in a moment of culinary desperation, I said, "Chancey, your tongue is very tired. It needs a little rest."

He froze, his big, earnest eyes narrowing in concern. "How can I get my tongue to rest, Mommy?" he asked, his tone as serious as if I'd just prescribed a life-saving remedy. I told him he simply needed to stop talking for a bit to give his tongue a break. With the solemnity of a tiny monk embarking on a vow of silence, he nodded and left the kitchen. Parents, you know the truth; this wasn't about his tongue's well-being. It was about me snatching a fleeting moment of peace from the jaws of a pre-schoolers chatter. But alas, my sanctuary was short-lived. Barely five minutes later, Chance strutted back into the kitchen, triumphant. "I rested my tongue!" he announced with heartfelt pride, launching straight into a detailed explanation of how he'd achieved this miraculous feat. So much for silence.

At just twelve, he took over the kitchen not to impress but to give me a break and make something special for the family. Once the heart of our home, the kitchen became a symphony of clanging pots and rising steam. But the result? A meal so thoughtful and filled with love brought happiness not only to our tummies but also to our hearts.

We all knew then that Chance wasn't just a boy playing with recipes; he was destined to nourish others in every sense.

But it wasn't just his cooking; let's be honest, the boy could whip up a grilled cheese like a Michelin-starred masterpiece. Chance had this knack for making us feel like the stars of his little universe, turning the mundane into memories we'd never forget. His humour was gentle, the kind that came with a side of a quick hug or that sly smile that said, "I know, I'm your favourite." Even now, his laughter lingers in my heart, a sound that somehow made everything feel right, no matter what chaos was brewing.

Chance was a boy of many hats, literally and figuratively. One moment, he'd play dress-up with his sister, the next stealing the show in the choir with dance moves that screamed, "I was born for this. He was the proudest altar boy you've ever seen, the storyteller of Catechism class, rapping like a star on the rise, strutting as if a long-time cowboy, a baritone belting out shower solos, or dreaming up his next big idea. Oh, and let's not forget his inner poet and hopeless romantic, Chance lived every moment with flair and passion. But of all his roles, his best work was being his sister's partner-in-crime and the kind of son who could melt your heart with just a thoughtful gesture. In our eyes, Chance wasn't just a star; he was the whole constellation.

Our days were filled with his milestones: his first words, his first steps, the first time he said, "Mommy, I love you." Then there was the first day at kindergarten, the first game of rugby, the first graduation, the first date, and so many more. Each achievement, each new experience, was a step further from the tiny baby I once held in my arms, his skin so soft, his lashes so long they seemed to brush away time itself. And now, when I look back, I realize those nine months were just the beginning of a journey that would test and transform us all. Courage might as well have been his middle name. As a kid, Chance was small for his age, the kind of kid bullies zeroed in on. He'd come home teary-eyed, looking scared out of his wits. But then life had a plot twist—he shot up to 6'2" with arms like a pro wrestler, and everything changed. Suddenly, he wasn't just standing tall—he was standing up for anyone who needed it.

I'll never forget the day in high school when he found some boys picking on a younger kid. Chance walked up, lifted one of the bullies like a sack of potatoes, pinned him against the locker, and calmly delivered some "words of wisdom." Whatever he said must've been gold because those bullies apologized on the spot and never messed with anyone again.

Chance wasn't just about big gestures, though. As a young boy at the beach, if he spotted a child playing alone, he'd make it his mission to get them involved, rallying his friends to join in. Even at the Stampede, he had a way of showing up for his people. One time, after settling the tab at a bar, he walked out to find his buddies surrounded by a group of guys. Without missing a beat, he tore off his shirt and bellowed in his best WWE voice, "YOU SHOULDN'T HAVE BOTHERED MY FRIENDS!" The group took one look at him and bolted. Chance wasn't just big in size—he was big in heart, the kind of guy who made sure no one ever felt small. Chance brought more than just joy; he brought a quiet strength, a depth that wasn't always easy to understand but impossible to ignore. Even as a child, something old in his soul reached out to others with kindness and wisdom far beyond his years. He had this way of sitting beside you when you were upset, not saying much but letting his presence do the talking. He could ease a heart with a single look and calm a storm with his words.

Chance was a boy who had the remarkable gift of turning the simplest moments into meaningful memories. His presence brought joy, laughter, and enthusiasm, brightening every room. Though his physical absence leaves a quieter space, the essence of who he was, the love, the humour, and the boundless empathy remain powerfully alive in our hearts. He was a master at transforming the ordinary into the extraordinary, from dressing the dog in sunglasses and a cape with the conviction of a stylist to convincing his classmates that broccoli were miniature trees that needed care and nurturing. Chance had a way of showing us the beauty and wonder in life's most minor details. His laughter, his wit, and his generous spirit filled our home with a warmth that endures even now.

Reflecting on his life, I no longer focus on the loss but on the many moments of beauty and love he gifted us. Chance's life was a collection of firsts, each a step in his adventure, each filled with its own lesson of compassion and wisdom. Every meal he cooked, every joke he cracked, every hug he offered were pieces of a beautiful journey. Though that journey may feel as though it ended too soon, the love and care he brought still ripple through our lives. He taught us that even when moments pass, their echoes continue to echo in the quiet of our hearts. In this time of reflection, I hold onto the wisdom that love transcends all. Chance's physical presence may be gone, but the love he gave us is eternal. I see it in the laughter that still occasionally bubbles up unexpectedly, in the memories that surface with every familiar scent or song, and in the quiet peace that comes with knowing he lives on in all of us. While Chance may no longer be here to share new moments with us, he remains with us in spirit, in every laugh, every shared memory, and every whisper of "I love you, Mommy," that still echoes softly in my heart. His light has not dimmed; it has simply shifted to a place where it can shine eternally, guiding us with the love and wisdom he left behind.

"A hug speaks the language of comfort, while a kiss seals the promise of love; together, they create moments that words can not speak."

Colleen C. Carson

"We Love You"

1984-2007

CHANCE KINGSLEY CARSON

The story unfolds on a forsaken morning, where silence draped the world in an oppressive blanket, smothering even the faintest hope of pardon; it was as if humanity had forgotten how to breathe. Nothing stirred, no birds sang, no laughter broke the heavy stillness. The world seemed to mourn; it was as if the earth wept in unending sorrow.

Fourteen months, eleven days, twenty-three minutes, and eight seconds had crawled since Chance's light faded from this world, leaving only shadows behind. With a heart of unbearable grief, Colleen reached for her pen, not with hope, but with the desperate wish that words might somehow bleed her anguish onto the page.

In the deepest of her heart, she had always known that Chance's time was fleeting. Yet, that knowledge hadn't prepared her for his leaving so soon. She last saw Chance when he visited during the Calgary Stampede. He and his friends had come for the festivities, but when they left, Chance and his girlfriend chose to stay a few extra days. They'd planned a family dinner, a cherished tradition with lobster and steak.

Chance had given Colleen the money, and with a light heart, Colleen had headed to the store. But as she drove, an unshakable feeling rose within her, that familiar inner voice she'd trusted since she was a child now bearing a heavy message. "Chance is going to die," it whispered. The feeling was so strong that, without hesitation, she turned the car around and went straight back home. When Colleen arrived back home, she couldn't help but ask, "Do you believe in God?" Chance responded without hesitation, "Of course I do. I don't believe in religion."

He laughed, then glanced over, noticed Colleen had no groceries, and questioned why. She paused, saying she'd forgotten her wallet; he gently stopped her as she headed back out. "Mom, I want you to know that Dad and you were amazing parents. My choices were my own, not yours, and I don't want you to carry any guilt over anything I've done."

Her heart skipped a beat. "Why would you say that, Chance?" He shrugged, unsure, then said, "I just feel you needed to hear it." It was a moment weighted with meaning; one she couldn't fully grasp then but one that would echo in her heart forever.

The day after their family dinner, after she had poured her love into preparing yet another of Chance's favourite meals, he and his girlfriend packed their things and set off for Vancouver. As always, Chance's ritual brought her comfort: he would drive to the end of the street, turn around, and pass the house once more to wave goodbye. But this time, the car didn't reappear.

Colleen stood at the kitchen window, her hands against the sill, waiting for that familiar gesture of reassurance. Instead, he turned toward the highway without a glance back; he took the lane, leaving the street and her heart-achingly empty. Tears traced silent, bitter paths down her cheeks as the crushing weight of an unspoken goodbye filled her chest. A deep, gnawing desperation gripped her soul; somehow, she knew this was the last time she would see him, the last goodbye.

Colleen has known the intense joy of motherhood, a love that filled her life with wonder, hope, and a sense of endless possibilities. Her children, Crystal and Chance, were her miracles, the very heartbeat of her existence. But on July 28, 2007, everything shattered when Chance was taken from her too soon.

The loss of a child is a grief too deep for words, a wound that feels as though a part of you has been ripped away, never to return. Chance was not just a son; he was her confidant, a best friend. She remembers the haunting night after his passing when family and friends gathered at her daughter's home, attempting to comfort each other with stories and shared memories.

As always, Colleen found herself in the kitchen, her hands busy preparing food, a small act of normalcy amid the overwhelming sorrow. She could hear laughter and voices from the other room, and for a brief moment, she almost expected to hear Chance's unmistakable laugh joining in, filling the space with its warmth. She turned, half-hoping, half-dreading, that he might be standing there as if nothing had changed.

But all that met her eyes was an empty space where he used to stand. At that moment, the full weight of her loss crushed her, and she realized that Chance would never again walk through that door. The counter became her anchor as she clung to it, her knees weak, her heart breaking all over again.

Crystal came to Colleen the next day, tears streaming down her face. "Mom," she whispered, her voice quivering, "Would it have been better if I had died instead of Chance?" Colleen's heart hurt with sorrow for her beautiful Belle. She pulled her daughter into her arms, trying to hold herself together, and said, "Oh, my precious Angel, no. I didn't want Chance to go, but God has his reasons, and maybe one day we'll understand. I would have been just as heartbroken losing you as I am losing Chance; I love you now and will forever always."

They just held each other, both drowning in their grief, crying until exhaustion took over, and they fell asleep together on Chance's bed. Losing Chance took something from Colleen that she could never return; a piece of her was gone forever. In those early days, she was trapped in a constant spiral of "What ifs" and "If onlys," replaying every moment, questioning everything. For years, she couldn't even bring herself to say the word "death," as if not saying it might make it not true. Colleen would pray to her God, asking if she could have just five minutes with Chance so they could have their last goodbye.

Planning his funeral felt strange, almost like organizing another family gathering. The gravity didn't sink in until I picked out his clothes; I fussed over his shoes, just as Chance would have done himself. Then Brian looked at me and gently said, "Colleen, he doesn't need shoes. He's not going anywhere." That's when it struck me: this would be the last time I'd dress my Chancey. In tears, my grief was so overpowering it had engraved itself into my very soul.

His funeral was everything he'd envisioned. His pallbearers wore white and carried canes, bagpipes played, and doves took flight; every detail was exactly as Chance had wanted. After a friend's tragic accident when Chance was sixteen, he had planned his funeral, wanting to ease the burden on all of us. He wrote it out and handed it to his best friend, a brother to him Randy, with instructions, just in case. It was a rare, selfless gesture from our young son, and we ensured we'd honour his every wish.

> Those we love
> don't go away,
> they walk beside us
> every day.
> Unseen, unheard,
> but always near,
> so loved, so missed,
> so very dear.

After returning to Calgary and sorting through the legal matters, I was alone in facing my emptiness. The world moved on, indifferent to my pain. Chance's absence was a void that swallowed everything. Calgary once filled with his laughter, now felt hollow and cold. I existed in the shadow of my former life. The woman I once was, gone, buried alongside my son. I moved through the days, a ghost tied to memories and a grief that refused to release its grip. The world kept turning, but for me, time had stopped.

The light that Chance brought to my life was gone, leaving only darkness in its wake. It felt as if I was falling into an abyss, with only a faint glimmer of light far in the distance. The darkness was overwhelming; each day felt like crawling through that darkness, searching for any reason to keep going. Days blurred into weeks, weeks into months, and eventually years. Slowly, ever so, I started finding who I had become.

Grief never truly leaves; it becomes a part of you, reshaping you in ways you'd never imagined. Though Chance was gone, in my heart, he's always there, a laugh, a place, a memory, a scent, a spirit I would carry with me forever. I still remember those quiet mornings, fingers wrapped around a coffee mug, feeling the warmth that anchored me as I descended the stairs to his bedroom. My feet instinctively led me to his closet, our sanctuary, or maybe just mine. I had placed a chair in the center of his closet so I could sit surrounded by his clothes, breathing the faint scent that lingered on the fabric, touching the sleeves and collars he once wore.

In that quietness, I'd reach out and graze each piece with my fingers as if feeling those soft fabrics could somehow bring him closer to me. There was his old sweater, the one he'd put on when it got chilly, his graduation shirt, and those summer-worn jeans, faded perfectly in all the right places. Each piece was more than just cloth to me; it was a memory captured in fabric.

As I touched them, moments flooded back, filling that small space with laughter, conversations, and winks we had shared. Sitting alone in that dimness, I could almost pretend he was still there, along with my inner promise never to forget. But then the tears would fall, each one pressing into my face like a small, relentless weight, amplifying the pain buried deep within.

But the grief was a weight I could barely carry, and every day felt like trying to walk with boulders bound to my feet. Everywhere I looked, each place and each person felt haunted by memories of happy times that now seemed like distant echoes. Calgary felt like an empty shell like everything I once appreciated was left with him. The world moved on, indifferent to my pain. Chance's absence was a void that swallowed everything.

I existed in the shadow of my former life. The woman I once was gone, buried alongside my son. I moved through the days, tied to memories and grief that refused to release its grip. The world kept turning, but for me, time had stopped. The light that Chance brought to my life was gone, leaving only darkness in its wake.

One day, the phone rang, and it was Ranj, Chance's best friend; more like a son to me and a brother to Crystal. His voice felt like a lifeline in my sea of sadness. He told me he was moving to Calgary and asked if he could stay with us until he found a place. Without thinking, I said yes; just the thought of having him around brought a tiny spark of hope. When Ranj showed up, he wasn't alone; he had his German Shepherd, Chika, a bundle of energy with a tail that never stopped wagging. Chika seemed to sense our pain, and with every playful bark and nudge, she chipped away at it, trying to bring back the laughter we'd lost.

Ranj's presence was like a breath of fresh air. His laughter and Chika's energy slowly filled the house, easing some of the emptiness. Ranj didn't just bring life back into our home; he brought Chance back, too. He'd share stories about him—little things I'd almost forgotten but now remembered so clearly. We laughed, we cried, and bit by bit, the grief softened.

Crystal began to open up more, too. She and Ranj had many memories of Chance and having him there comforted her. They'd talk for hours, their laughter filling the space. Watching them, I could feel a shift inside me, a small, peaceful moment amid the sorrow. Ranj and Chika have become part of our daily lives. Mornings were filled with plans, and we'd share meals or sit quietly together in the evenings. When he finally left, the emptiness felt sharper, but he'd left us with something invaluable: a reminder that even in the midst of darkness, there's still room for laughter and joy, a glimmer of light.

I slipped back into my solitude, letting the silence surround me. Friends and family reached out, offering words of comfort, but I could barely bring myself to respond. Their kindness felt so distant, and I didn't have the strength to push through the darkness of grief to allow them in. It was as if a part of me had accepted being lost in this maze of pain because I deserved to be. In those days, my mind became a battlefield, filled with broken dreams and what-ifs. I thought of all the moments I would never witness: Chance's wedding, his children, the future we had all imagined together.

Slowly, my body began to show the toll of my sorrow. A rash broke out, a physical sign of the turmoil inside. The itching was constant, as though my skin itself was crying out. The doctor said it was stress-induced and gave me creams that didn't help. I scratched gently at first, then more desperately, until blood flowed. I'd stare at myself in the mirror, at those angry, bloody open wounds on my skin, feeling guilt for not being able to keep it together, even physically. My grief was written on my body, and I felt like I deserved it because I had been incapable of saving my son.

It wasn't long after that, during lunch with a compassionate friend, I realized something wasn't right. One side of my face felt strange, frozen; I couldn't even blink. A doctor's visit revealed it was Bell's Palsy, a condition brought on by stress. For months, I couldn't move one side of my face, and I had to use artificial tears to keep my eyes from drying out. It felt like a cruel twist of fate: here I was, drowning in grief, and now I couldn't even cry properly.

One afternoon, I was in Chapters. I searched for a book but found out it hadn't been released. I was leaving the store when something inside me urged me to go back as if something was waiting for me. Trusting my inner voice, I followed her guidance and soon found myself standing before a shelf of books. My attention was drawn to the bottom shelf, and there, my eyes landed on Ghosts Among Us by James Van Praagh.

The title alone captivated me, and as I began to read, the words seemed to lift me, pulling me back to the surface. The book reminded me that healing was still within reach, and perhaps a glimmer of light awaited me. Months passed, and the decision was made to return to Vancouver. Crystal and I moved into a beautiful condo, and one evening, she organized an intimate birthday party for me, inviting her and my friends. I appreciated their presence, but my loneliness remained even in a room full of loving family and friends.

That night, my longtime friend Kim pulled me aside, gently urging me to seek help, worried that I might spiral deeper into despair. Days passed, each one a small step away from the overwhelming darkness. A close friend of Crystal's, Rani became like family to us, a silver lining amid our heavy clouds. She visited daily, bringing warmth, laughter, and a quiet reminder that love endures, even through loss.

Her presence was a comfort, softening the sharp edges of my grief. I remember those first few years, surrounded by friends but still feeling this uneasy sense of doubt. I was physically there, but emotionally, I wasn't quite able to connect. My lack of confidence made it hard to step out of my loneliness, even though part of me wondered if I should.

There were nights when I'd wander the city streets, aching to see Chance's face again. I'd find myself drawn to figures that looked like him, hoping, just hoping, that somehow he'd come back to me. One chilly autumn evening, I thought I saw a young man with a familiar look, laughing with friends. My heart raced, and before I knew it, I was following him as if the act of walking toward him might close the abyss of loss inside me.

But as I got closer, reality set in, and I realized it wasn't Chance. I sank to my knees on the cold pavement, tears spilling down my face that wanted to form a puddle below me. The night air muffled my sobs. At that moment, I let myself feel every ounce of pain, every pang of longing that had been building inside me.

In that dark evening, surrounded by the city's unsympathetic hum, the weight of my grief pressed down on me fully. And yet, even as I knelt there, heart laid bare, I felt a faint flicker of something else, a quiet, fragile hope that maybe, somehow, I'd find a way through this, that I'd learn to carry his memory with a little less pain and a little more love. But then, I thought to myself, no, you don't deserve that.

Wandering the streets had become my go-to for dealing with the grief that felt like it was eating me alive. But when I wasn't out walking, I'd sit on the patio, staring up at the moon and the two bright stars in the sky. I convinced myself one was my Dad and the other was Chance. Years later, I was strolling along the seawall for my usual evening walk, ear pods in, when a song came on that instantly took me back. It was Bruno Mars' "Talking to the Moon." It hit me emotionally, bringing all that past back to the surface.

Months passed, and on one rainy night in Yaletown, the evening that makes you want to fade into the shadows and forget everything, I found myself lost in my thoughts, the pain in my chest growing with every step. The rain came down harder, blurring everything around me into a mess of wet pavement and fading lights. I stopped at the corner of Davie and Pacific, feeling like I couldn't move forward anymore. My thoughts were too heavy, my heart too broken.

I was so lost, so weak, stuck in this endless cycle of hopelessness. I couldn't see a way out. It just felt like too much. "God," I whispered, "I don't know what to do. Please, help me find my way back." And just like that, I started sobbing, but no one noticed because my tears blended into the rain. In that moment of complete vulnerability, I begged for strength, for a way to escape this unbearable pain that had taken over my life.

I asked God and Mother Mary for help, feeling too small, too shattered to go on alone. I stood there, eyes shut tight, rain pouring down my face, facing the sky. I was desperate, just standing there for what felt like forever. Then, something shifted. For a brief second, I didn't feel the weight of my grief. My tears weren't part of the rain anymore; it was just rain.

Something changed. I couldn't explain it, but I felt a tiny crack in the heaviness, like a sliver of peace. When I opened my eyes, the world felt different. Maybe it was the rain, perhaps something more, but I felt lighter. I turned around and started walking home, each step a little firmer than the last. I unlocked the door to our condo, quickly peeled off my soaked clothes, and sank into a hot bath, letting the warmth soothe my chilled, aching body and shattered soul.

Crystal's soft knock on the bathroom door broke through my darkness as I lay quietly. Her voice, full of concern, asked if I was okay. "Yes, my precious Angel, I'm good!" I replied, the words barely escaping my lips but enough to reassure her. But at that moment, I realized something. Maybe it wasn't about "getting better" in the way I thought. Perhaps it was about being reborn. It wasn't instant, but I felt like a new life was beginning; that life was mine, a rebirth.

The woman I was becoming, the one who would later be known as Mama Carson, was beginning to emerge from the cocoon of grief and pain. There was love, warmth, and hope now surrounding me. And in those dark days that followed, Chance appeared in one way or another, offering comfort and strength. It felt like he was sent to guide Crystal, me, and everyone around us through the chaos of healing.

Chance appeared in my life unexpectedly, not just in my dreams but in moments that felt too real to be coincidental. It was as if he had been sent to guide me, to remind me that love never truly leaves us. I was reborn through these moments, through the people who reached out and the love surrounding me. One of those people was my precious Angel, Crystal, whose human strength and quiet spirit became my anchor; to be honest, she saved my life.

I remember how hard it was to even consider moving forward. The thought of living a life without Chance felt like I was betraying his memory. How could I laugh? How could I smile? How could I go on? But Crystal never let me forget that life was still beautiful, even in the face of heartache. She would sit with me, her hand in mine, not saying much, but her presence was enough to remind me that I wasn't alone. Together, we carried the weight of our loss, but we also learned to carry the love that Chance had left behind.

Through Crystal, I found hope. Through her, I learned to smile again; to remember the joy we had shared with Chance, and to hold on to that instead of drowning in sadness. She carried a piece of him, and when my heart felt too heavy to bear, she would share that piece with me, giving me the strength to keep going. My grief comes in waves; there is no warning nor preparation, but you learn to live with those waves.

It's just like learning how to breathe again, to live again until one day you feel a sense of hope. Chance can never be lessened, only transformed. Grief has taught me to honour him by carrying his spirit forward: in my actions, my words, my tears, and in the way I treasure life's simple joys.

Another mending experience on my road to healing occurred when I was working for this company in Burnaby. The company radiated integrity and professionalism, and every morning, I eagerly looked forward to the drive there while listening to this Radio Show. It wasn't just the laughter or the fun; something deeper echoed within my heart. The radio host's voice, infectious laughter, and humour were solace to my wounded soul. He reminded me of Chance, who had once dreamed of becoming a radio host or a sports commentator. Chance had always joked about calling himself "Kid Carson" or "King Carson," a playful nod to his middle name, Kingsley.

I would listen and wish to meet this radio host. As the years went by, I often thought about Chance's dream and how much it had meant to him. And then, almost as if the universe had orchestrated it, I found myself at an event where this radio host was present. Tears filled both of our eyes when I shared my story with him. He was everything I had imagined and more, and it felt like Chance's spirit had led me to that moment. I'll never forget how much joy that brought me and how it felt like a piece of Chance was present that evening. This radio host's professional name was Kid Carson.

Though some days are heavier than others, it's in the quiet moments when the world slows down, and I can feel him in the stillness, as though he's sitting beside me, his gentle spirit strolling in the very air I breathe. The cherished memories spring to life when I least expect them, the sound of his voice echoing in my mind or the way his laughter could brighten even the gloomiest day.

And it's in every whisper of love that fills the spaces between the tears. That love has become my compass, guiding me through the darkness of his absence and teaching me to take one small step at a time. Some days, those steps feel shaky, like I'm walking a journey I never wanted to take. But even then, I hear his voice in my heart, urging me forward, reminding me that I carry him with me.

Grief has a way of reshaping you, of making you see the world through a different lens. It's been a slow realization that my love for Chance doesn't end simply because I can no longer hold him. Instead, that love has become the bridge between the life we shared and the life I now live, a bridge built on memories, spirit, and the unshakable bond we still share. I have learned to celebrate his memories, sometimes with tears but with gratitude, and now a smile of thankfulness. I began to see him everywhere: in the sun's warmth on my face, the wind that would rustle the trees, and the stars that sparkled above me at night. His love is with me. It never left, which brought me comfort.

Chance isn't gone; he's just changed forms. He's in every little moment of beauty that reminds me to keep going, to find strength in the love we shared, and to honour him by living a life he'd be proud of. Step by step, I move forward, not leaving him behind but carrying him with me in my heart. Love like he doesn't disappear; it becomes the strength that gets me through, reminding me he's always here. It's been 17 years since Chance passed, and while the grief is still there, I've learned how to live with it. I've figured out how to carry it without letting it take over. Crystal and I have found our peace; our hearts might still be scarred, but they're stronger now.

For anyone navigating the pain of losing someone, let me tell you what's helped me: healing isn't about "getting over it" or pretending it doesn't hurt. It's about learning how to carry that pain in a way that doesn't crush you. You don't erase the sadness but find a way to coexist, and eventually, life feels lighter again.

Take it one step at a time, no matter how small, knowing they're right there beside you, guiding you along the way. And don't forget, you're never alone. Their spirit is always connected to yours, cheering you on and having your back every step of the journey. And please remember to show your love to your loved ones who are your life's living presents.

"THE PROMISE"

This story lives in Colleen's heart, living in thought, forever carried in love. Crystal had left for Paris, hoping to escape the heavy sadness that clung to her, every moment, every place around her seemed to echo the memories of days spent with her brother. She had been gone for several days when Colleen received a text full of excitement, followed by a call. Colleen could hear the joy in Crystal's voice, but behind it was a tremble, the sound of lips quivering in sadness, and Colleen could sense the soft tears gently falling.

Crystal began to share her story, her words carrying the weight of both heartache and hope. Then, she sent Colleen photos through WhatsApp. She couldn't help but laugh and cry simultaneously when she opened them. One photo, the image of an older man walking hand-in-hand with a young boy, looked exactly like Colleen's Dad and Chancey on their regular walks. It was uncanny, a perfect reminder of moments gone by. But the other photo was even more miraculous. It was so beautiful; it warmed her shattered heart in a way Colleen hadn't felt in a long time.

This is what the story is about. But before I begin, I want to share something I always told people when they marveled at Belle and Chancey's incredible love for each other. I would say, "As one exhales, the other inhales, that's how much they love each other. They give each other the joy of breathing life together." Their bond wasn't just special; it was extraordinary, and that same love kept this story alive within me. Crystal's journey to Paris was not a simple escape; it was a quiet plea for release from the suffocating hold of grief. Each breath felt heavy, and each step dragged under the weight of her brother's absence as if life had lost its colours and faded into gray. Once a city of dreams, Paris now seemed to her a foreign place of shadows, where the light of her own heart flickered, dimmed by sorrow.

Her brother was more than her sibling; he was her kindred spirit, the other half of her soul. Their bond was a delicate, sacred sequence united by years of laughter, secrets, and the deep comfort of knowing you are truly understood. That intimate and sincere bond had been a steady constant in her life: a love that moved silently but powerfully through the foundation of their days. To the world, their closeness was admired, even envied. To them, it was as natural as breathing. Together, they had created a world of shared moments, a universe where no words were needed, only the quiet, knowing glance that spoke of love without end. The joy they found in each other was a shield against the chaos of the world, and with his passing, that shield had shattered.

Now, she wandered lost. The streets of Paris offered no answers, only reflections of her pain. The city's beauty mocked her, the laughter of strangers echoing through her solitude like a distant memory of happiness she could no longer touch. Yet, in her heart, she still clung to the memories of her brother, desperate to find him in the corners of her mind where he still lived, alive and vibrant. Paris became her refuge, but it could not heal her. It could not fill the void left by her brother's death. She walked its cobbled streets like a ghost, searching not for peace but a way to bear the unbearable. The Basilica, with its ancient stillness, offered her no miracles. Kneeling in the soft glow of candles, her tears fell like prayers, heavy with sorrow. She begged God for comfort, for a sign that her brother was somewhere beyond the indefinite, waiting for her in a place untouched by pain.

Outside, in the soft light of a fading day, she saw an older man and a little boy, their hands clasped as they moved together in quiet harmony. The sight stirred something deep within her: a memory of her childhood, walking hand in hand with her grandfather and brother through silent streets. In this simple moment, in the tenderness of a stranger's gesture, she felt a soft whisper of reassurance. She felt her brother's presence, not as a shadow of loss, but as a gentle reminder that he was still with her, united into the foundation of her being.

Her heart swelled with the quiet realization that her prayers had been answered, not with words, but with this quiet miracle of memory and connection. Her brother and her grandfather were together now, in a place where grief could not reach, and their love would never fade. And so, with this fragile peace nestled in her heart, Crystal continued her journey through Paris. The days stretched ahead like a path she could not yet see, but with each step, she felt the weight of her sorrow ease just a little. Her birthday came, bittersweet and lonely. It was the first one without him, and the ache of that absence gnawed at her. But she surrounded herself with friends, hoping their laughter would fill his voice's once-occupied silence.

As the cake arrived and the candle flickered, she made her wish with trembling hands. She wished for her brother not to return, for that was impossible, but to feel him close for a moment. And in that wish, she found a flicker of hope. As she closed her eyes, she felt a presence, as if in the silence of that moment, her brother was beside her, smiling, watching over her. Later, as she looked through the photos of that night, one image caught her breath. In the flicker of candlelight, there was a heart: glowing, faint but undeniable. It was as if the universe itself had conspired to give her this sign, this minor miracle, to show her that love, their love, transcended everything, even death.

Tears flowed freely as she shared the photo with her friends, their wonder mirroring hers. In that moment, she saw the truth she had longed for: her brother was still with her, his love a light in the dark, guiding her through her grief. As the days passed, that realization grew within her. Love, in its purest form, could never be extinguished. It lived on in every memory, shared smiles, and small, quiet moments that spoke louder than words. And though she would carry the weight of her brother's absence for the rest of her life, she knew now that he had not truly left her.

He was with her always, just beyond the reach of her hand, but forever within the grasp of her heart. As Belle reflected on her journey, she felt the merging of a new truth: the promise that grief had not broken her. It had opened her eyes to the lasting power of love, a love that bridged time and space, uniting Chance and her still in ways she could not fully understand. And with this, she felt a deep, quiet peace, a peace born from the realization that love, once given, never truly dies. The promise that love lives on, offering her comfort and strength through her darkest moments.

"SUCCESS"

Success in life isn't just about fame or wealth,
It's found in the moments that you give of your self.
In laughter with friends and the love that you share,
In kindness to strangers, showing you care.

It's the courage to follow your dreams every day,
And learning from failures that come your way.
It's finding your passion, that makes your heart sing,
And bearing each challenge life tends to bring.

Success is moments of joy and of peace,
In gifting to others, finding purpose that frees.
It's in family and friendships, bonds strong and true,
In being yourself, in all that you do.

Standing with strength when storms come around,
Rising again each time you are down.
Growing through trials, discovering integrity,
Discovering the valour to nurture solidarity.

For success is a journey, a path we all pave,
Through love and through loss, humble and brave.
So, measure your success not by what you possess,
But by the joy felt, and the lives you bless.

For life's true success is found in the heart,
In living with meaning, right from the start.

Colleen C. Carson

"Persons who spread gossip trade self-respect for envy."

Mama Carson

As Colleen walked towards the church for the Good Friday Service, each step felt like a burden. Her heart was heavy with the absence of her dear Chance. The air, which should have been filled with the fragrant promise of spring, seemed dull and lifeless to her. The colours were muted, and the scents lacked their usual sweetness.

Something began to change inside the church, surrounded by the solemnity of Good Friday, the archbishop's words connected with the gospel, cutting through her weariness. Colleen felt like Chance's voice echoed in the archbishop's sermon, guiding her toward a deeper understanding. Through the sermon's words, she sensed Chance's presence, his message of love and reassurance reaching her from beyond.

It wasn't just a sermon, a revelation, a message of love and connection that transcended earthly bounds. As the archbishop spoke, she realized that Chance's friends were more than just companions, they were family, bound by a love even death couldn't sever. She had gained five more sons when losing Chance, and Crystal now had five brothers. It was proof of the enduring power of love and the bonds that hold us together, even in the face of loss.

As I sat in the pew, surrounded by his words, it felt like a comforting embrace, like a warm cape wrapped around me. It wasn't just any embrace. It was as if the very wings of angels had encircled me, whispering love and comfort into my soul. In the middle of the crowded church and the bustling parishioners, I felt an overpowering sense of solitude, yet not loneliness, for I was cradled in the arms of my heavenly angel, Chance. With each word the archbishop spoke, a gentle warmth flooded my being, melting away my tears and replacing them with a radiant smile. In that sacred moment, I knew that Chance was not gone but ever-present, his love and eternal light guiding me through the shadows of grief.

As he bid me farewell, assuring me of his happiness and our eventual reunion, a wave of peace washed over me, soothing the ache in my heart. Though I remained seated throughout the service, my spirit soared with gratitude toward the divine. As the Good Friday service ended, I found myself drawn to the ancient ritual of kissing Jesus's feet, a gesture of thoughtful reverence and gratitude. But this Good Friday held a more significant significance, a loving symbol of the cherished moments I had shared with my son, Chance, and the bittersweet beauty of our final goodbye. To Chance, a Goodbye.

With a heart overflowing with gratitude, I pressed my lips to the feet of my Saviour, thanking him for granting me the gift of our goodbye and the foreshadowing of eternity with my beloved son one day. A divine message, a son's enduring love, and the assurance that in heaven, our happiest moments endure.

Chance lives on as our angel, a presence that surrounds and uplifts us. As I stepped out of the church and began my journey homeward, my mind was ablaze with the overpowering experience that had unfolded within the sacred walls of God's home. For years, this sanctuary had been my refuge, where honour and love connected, the air seemed to be at peace, and the endless depths of love knew no bounds.

As I walked, the weight of contemplation accompanied each footstep, my thoughts swirling in the wake of the divine encounter I had just experienced. Within those blessed walls, amid the flickering candlelight and the gentle murmur of prayers, I had experienced something heavenly that encouraged the very essence of my soul. In the presence of the divine, time seemed to stand still; the physical and spiritual boundaries blurred into oblivion. It was as if heaven and earth had momentarily been lifted, revealing glimpses of eternity and the infinite mysteries beyond.

In the quiet solitude of my thoughts, I found solace in the belief that love is the very structure of the universe, the essence that connects us all in a majestic partnership of existence. It is the gentle hand guiding us through the darkest of nights, the light of hope that brightens our path amid uncertainty. As I made my way home, I learned that love endures, transcending even the boundaries of life and death. In the embrace of divine love, I found peace, knowing that though our earthly journey may be fleeting, the bonds of love we share with those we hold dear are eternal, stretching across the vast span of eternity.

Then, out of the blue, came a gentle urgency tugging at my heartstrings, urging me to share a message with those who had also known the pain of loss. "Listen," the voice whispered, "listen with open hearts and keen eyes, for the departed often find ways to reach us, to remind us that they are never truly gone." Since that poignant Good Friday, Chance has visited me countless times, his presence manifesting unexpectedly through whispered words, haunting melodies, or even the marvels of modern technology, as I have previously talked about. But his visits were not reserved for me alone; they were gifts meant to be shared with all who were willing to open their hearts to the possibility of the extraordinary.

As you absorb these words and observe the signs that surround you, remember that in the quiet moments of reflection, in the subtle whispers of the wind, and in the gentle rhythms of life, our loved ones speak to us, offering comfort, guidance, and, above all, love. Welcome the possibility that even amid loss and sorrow, there lies a celestial plan, a spiritual bond that rises above the confines of mortality. Open your soul to the heavenly messages that may be waiting to guide you through life's storms.

"When tomorrow comes, and I'm not there,
Please know how much I truly care.
To my family strong, my friends, so true,
My love will always stay with you.
If the day feels cold, the skies seem gray,
Remember the laughter we shared each day.
In every story, in every song,
I'll be with you where I belong.
Though my arms can't hug you tight,
I'll send my warmth in the morning light.
In every star, in every breeze,
I'll bring you comfort and put your hearts at ease.
So, live your lives with valour and embrace,
And know I'm in a peaceful place.
Though I've departed, we're not apart,
I'll forever be with you, deep in your heart."

Habitual hero does it again

Saves family from early-morning fire

By MICHELLE MARK
Calgary Sun

Chance smiled on a northeast Calgary family yesterday as a fast-acting neighbour saved their lives.

Chance Carson, 18, raced to get the two adults and two teens out of their house at 121 Harvest Grove Pl. N.E., when he noticed their car on fire in the driveway around 3:30 a.m. as he ended a late-night phone call.

"I saw flames coming out of the car, but I was tired, so at first I thought my eyes were playing tricks on me," Carson said.

"I couldn't get the phone to work, so I threw my sister my cell phone, told her to call 911 and I ran over there and told them to get out of the house right away.

"I thought the whole house was going to go up, so my first instinct was to get them out."

This isn't the first time Carson — who said he might like to be a firefighter one day — was in the right place at the right time.

When he was just 12 years old, he heroically pulled a drowning boy from a Kelowna, B.C., area lake.

"He was underneath the water and no one else saw him but me, so I did what I had to," Carson said.

"I guess I was meant to help people — there's just something about it for me."

When fire crews arrived at the blaze, the car and double-attached garage were engulfed in flames.

"Fire crews acted quickly to remove from the garage one of the other two vehicles which were parked inside," fire department spokeswoman Deb Bergeson said, adding firefighters prevented any damage to the house.

They also were forced to cut through the roof to ventilate heat and smoke, and prevent the further spread of fire."

Homeowner Ray Hilbrecht said he is extremely thankful for neighbours such as Carson. "I can't ever thank him enough," Hilbrecht said. "I'm just so grateful he was looking out his window when he was. If it wasn't for him, who knows what could have happened?"

Fire investigators say the fire started in a faulty block heater cord in the car and made damage at about $12,000.

QUICK THINKING ... Chance Carson examines the burned-out wreck of a neighbour's car yesterday. The Calgarian alerted the family about 3:30 a.m. that their car was on fire and told them to get out of the house. Chance also saved the life of a drowning boy when he was on

— NATHAN DENETTE, Calgary Sun

michelle.mark@calgarysun.com

Chance's story, "Habitual Does It Again," is not just about a series of extraordinary acts; it's a declaration to the power of compassion and heroism that shines brightly in the ordinary. From the beginning, Chance was a remarkable young boy whose heart radiated kindness. It wasn't something he wore on his sleeve for the world to see but a quiet, steadfast force within him, guiding his every action. Whether it was helping his neighbours with simple chores or listening when someone needed a friend, Chance symbolized the spirit of a true hero in everyday life.

As a child, Chance was always eager to help, driven by an intuitive sense of purpose that few possess so naturally. His presence brought joy to those around him, whether it was raking leaves for an elderly neighbour, tidying up the yard, or simply offering a hand where it was needed. These may seem like small, trivial acts, but they were more than just chores for Chance. They were expressions of love, care, and a desire to make the world around him a little brighter. His warm and genuine smile reflected the kindness pouring out from his heart.

Of course, Chance was not perfect, no one is, but even in his imperfections, he carried a rare wisdom and empathy that opposed his youth. He had the soul of someone much older, someone who had already glimpsed the deeper truths of life. This quality made being around him comforting as if his mere presence reminded people of all the goodness that still exists in the world. Chance had a way of reassuring those around him that, despite everything, there was still beauty and light to be found.

It wasn't just his kindness that made him stand out; it was his bravery. One summer day, when Chance was just twelve, that bravery was tested in a way that would define his core. A family was enjoying a day at the beach when tragedy nearly struck. Their young child was pulled into the tumultuous waves, lost in the powerful current. A mother's scream echoed across the shore, and without a second thought, Chance sprang into action. He dashed into the water, facing the crashing waves fearlessly, and pulled the child to safety.

At that moment, Chance was not just a boy. He was a selfless, fearless hero driven by an overwhelming desire to help. There was no hesitation, no thought of personal safety, only the instinct to save a life. The image of him comforting the child and the frantic mother on the shore is forever etched in my memory. It was a moment that defined true heroism, an act born not from obligation but from a steadfast commitment to his fellow human beings.

This wasn't an isolated incident. Chance's heroism wasn't confined to moments of crisis; rather, it infiltrated every aspect of his life. Another instance that stands out is when Chance spotted smoke coming from a neighbour's house. Without a second thought, he ran to their door, banging loudly to alert them, and immediately called the fire department. His swift action prevented what could have been a tragedy, saving both lives and property that day.

But the story of Chance's life doesn't end there. His kindness extended far beyond his immediate circle of friends and family. One day, after Chance passed, I received an email from a woman who detailed how he had impacted the life of her 13-year-old son. She worked at a local bar in a small town in British Columbia that Chance frequented after his work shifts. Struggling as a single mother with a troubled son, she had confided in Chance, and he went out of his way to help.

Chance began visiting her home, mentoring her son and becoming the big brother figure the boy so desperately needed. Through Chance's guidance, this young boy found a new sense of direction, improved his grades, made new friends, and excelled in sports. This woman expressed her gratitude for Chance's intervention, saying she didn't know where her son would have ended without him. It was just one of the many lives he quietly transformed with his boundless compassion.

Chance never sought recognition for his actions, praise, or reward; he wanted to make a difference, no matter how small. That was the essence of his character: humility. He didn't need accolades or public applause to validate his worth. For him, the valid reward was knowing that he had touched someone's life, however briefly, and made it better.

At his celebration of life, amid the sea of mourners offering their condolences, a young woman I had never met approached me. With tears in her eyes and a soft voice, she shared with me a story that left me speechless. "If it weren't for Chance, I wouldn't be here today. He saved me from taking my own life," she confessed, her voice trembling with emotion. Her words echoed the sentiment of so many others whose lives had been touched by my son's kindness, bravery, and belief in the goodness of people.

In the days following his passing, I heard story after story about how Chance had impacted many lives in ways I never knew. He never shared these acts of heroism with me, and he didn't need to. He didn't perform these acts for recognition; he did them because it was who he was.

Chance was more than just my son; he was a friend, a mentor, and a guardian angel to so many. His legacy extends far beyond the few short years he spent with us, and his spirit lives on in every life he touched. His story is a powerful reminder of one compassionate soul's impact on the world and how even the smallest acts of kindness can leave ripples that last forever.

So, as I reflect on Chance's life, I realize that his story is not just a narrative of bravery and kindness. It's a call to action for all of us. Let his example inspire us to be more compassionate, to seek out opportunities to help, and to believe in the power of kindness. Let his spirit guide our actions, knowing that, like Chance, we, too, can change the world, one small act of love at a time. Let his story continue to inspire, ignite hope, and spread laughter, just as he did every day of his life.

"Financial freedom for women is not just about wealth, it's the dynamic power to shape your own destiny, seize independence and create a future with no limits."

Colleen C. Carson

And so many more....

"DAUGHTERS & SONS"

In the journey of life, they shine bright,
My daughters and my sons, a radiant light.
Each one is a treasure, a happiness to hold,
Their laughter and love, precious than gold.

With hearts of kindness, brighten my days,
Their smiles bring warmth in untold ways.
In their eyes, I see hope's endless gleam,
A witness to the beauty of their dreams.

Their footsteps echo with melodies sweet,
A masterpiece of love, within every meet.
Their innocence pure, their souls identity,
In their presence, I find my serenity.

Valleys and peaks, they stand by my side,
In every moment, their love does abide.
With tender embrace, they heal every scar,
My daughters and my sons, my guiding stars.

Their dreams soar high, their ambitions grand,
In their courage, I see a promise land.
With every triumph, my heart swells with pride,
For in their journey, I find joy as my guide.

So, here's to my daughters, here's to my sons,
In their laughter and love, our hearts become one.
For they bring me such happiness, beyond compare,
My precious ones, forever and always, I will be there.

Mama Carson

"You can't stop your life for someone to begins theirs."

Mama Carson

The Race

Sports Day rolls around, and every child receives a ribbon, even those who didn't win or maybe didn't even run the race. It seems harmless, even kind. And let's be honest, who doesn't want their child to feel like a winner? But what happens when ribbons are handed out too freely and praise flows without purpose? Overpraising children and shielding them from the sting of loss might unintentionally undermine their ability to handle life's challenges. Colleen often reflects on how important it is for children to learn from their victories and defeats. She believes that winning the race is not the true measure of success; it's the courage to run and the wisdom to accept both victory and defeat as steps toward becoming who we are meant to be.

Colleen believes that praise is a powerful tool. When used wisely, it builds confidence and encourages growth. But when overused, it can backfire. Constantly telling your child they're amazing without tying it to specific actions teaches them to rely on external validation instead of their inner drive.

For instance, if your child hears, "You're the best!" after every minor achievement, they may start associating praise with worthiness. What happens when they face a situation where the applause stops? Without the foundation of self-motivation, they might struggle to push forward or even give up altogether. Worse, over-praising for minimal effort sends the message that success requires little to no work. Instead of motivating them to improve, it can create complacency, where they settle for "good enough" instead of striving for their best.

And I mean their best, definitely not yours. Losing can feel like the end of the world to a child and sometimes to a parent, too. But every loss carries a hidden gift: the opportunity to learn and grow. I used to remind myself that when my children lost, they would learn to process disappointment, modify their efforts, and try again.

These moments teach strength, courage, and emotional intelligence. They show children that setbacks aren't failures; they're stepping stones. Losing also fosters empathy as children begin to understand the value of hard work and what it feels like to be on the other side of the finish line. Now, let's look at the other side. When children win without effort or reflection, they miss out on critical lessons about growth.

Winning isn't just about the trophy; it's about what it took to get there: the practice, the persistence, and the setbacks overcome. By focusing only on the result, we risk raising children who value the ribbon over the race. They might shy away from challenges for fear of failure or chase perfection at all costs, missing the joy of the journey.

As a parent, my goal wasn't to withhold praise but to make it meaningful. Celebrate effort, not just outcomes. I was always encouraged to say things like, "I'm proud of how hard you worked on that project," or "I saw how much focus you brought to practice." These statements reinforce the process's importance, not just the result. When your child loses, help them see it as an opportunity. Ask, "What did you learn from this?" or "What would you do differently next time?"

These questions teach them to view failure as a teacher rather than an enemy. On the flip side, when they win, encourage reflection: "What helped you succeed?" or "How will you build on this next time?" This ensures that victory isn't just a fleeting moment of glory but a stepping stone toward future growth.

As parents, it's tempting to shower our children with praise and protect them from disappointment. But life doesn't hand out ribbons just for showing up. I have learned that we risk raising children unprepared for the real world by over-praising and avoiding the tough lessons. Instead, let's raise our children by understanding that winning isn't everything and losing isn't the end.

Celebrate their effort, nurture their spirit through failure, and instill in them the understanding that true growth is born from both victories and defeats. The most enduring gift we can offer our children is not a fleeting award or moment of applause but the inner strength, courage, and wisdom to face life's ever-changing tides with grace and integrity. Consider this: Was that ribbon truly for your child's journey, or did it reflect your own desires?

"Raising children is not about protecting them from every storm but teaching them how to dance in the rain with hope in their hearts and joy in their steps."

Mama Carson

"Real power doesn't stem from dominating others,
but from empowering them."

Colleen C. Carson

"OUR LOVE"

Life moves fast, but amid the whirlwind, Colleen's daughter Belle and her have discovered something extraordinary: their unique and unflinching mother-daughter bond. It's a treasure they hold close, like finding a rare gem hidden within the chaos of everyday life. Their moments together might appear simple, even fleeting, but for them, they're magical, transforming into the most cherished memories.

In these sacred windows of time, they have evolved from being mother and daughter to becoming best friends, confidantes, and even partners in venture. Sometimes, it's as simple as curling up with warm blankets in their favourite corner of the living room, plunging into heartfelt conversations. Other times, it's grand adventures exploring new places, trying new things, and etching unforgettable memories into the composition of their lives. Wherever they are, it's the connection between them that truly matters.

We've shared everything: our dreams, fears, and even the silliest inside jokes that leave us laughing uncontrollably. We've cried together at other times, allowing tears to cleanse the pain of challenging moments. These experiences have built an unbreakable foundation for our relationship, a bond rooted in love, trust, and understanding. Belle and I have built a relationship on love, confidence, and mutual respect, and it is the foundation of everything we hold dear.

Life has a way of making time feel scarce. There are days when time feels elusive, but we treasure those moments most because we've learned that it's not about quantity but quality. Let me say it differently; it's not about how much time we share but how deeply we cherish it. Our time together is a treasure, even in the busiest seasons of our lives. These are the jewels of our journey, tucked away in life's corners, glowing with a light uniquely ours. They're simple, sacred, and beautiful.

Watching Belle grow and navigate her journey fills me with immense pride beyond words. Seeing her blossom is like witnessing the first light of dawn: delicate, wondrous, and full of promise. As her mother, I cheer her on from the sidelines, my heart swelling with joy as she walks her path in this world. Every step she takes is a witness to her courage, strength, and grace.

One memory stands out vividly in my mind. We were at a restaurant one evening, surrounded by a cozy ambiance. As we waited for our drinks, I asked her, "So, how's work treating you, Angel?" Belle's eyes lit up with enthusiasm, and the room seemed to brighten as she spoke. "It's been crazy but amazing, Mom," she shared, her voice brimming with excitement. "I'm working on some incredible projects." At that moment, my heart swelled with pride. "I'm so proud of you, Belle," I told her, my voice filled with emotion. We talked like old friends, laughter flowing freely as we reminisced, shared stories, and celebrated life's milestones. These moments, ordinary yet extraordinary, define our relationship, etching love and connection into our hearts forever.

Looking back, I remember when Belle was just a little girl. Our matching outfits on "girls' day" outings, shopping trips that turned into grand adventures, and the endless chatter about her school life and friends all brought us closer. Even when her stories weren't always easy to hear, I wanted Belle to know she could tell me anything. It was vital that she felt safe and supported, no matter what. Even as a child, Belle amazed me with her creativity. I still remember her imaginative preschool paintings, abstract yet meaningful. Later, she showed a natural flair for leadership, organizing school events and taking on challenges with an innovative spirit. Watching her grow and her talents blossom into the remarkable young woman she is today has been an incredible journey.

One dinner stands out above the rest. Amidst our laughter and the clinking of glasses, Belle leaned in with a thoughtful expression. "Mom, I've been thinking about making some changes, career-wise, maybe even moving," she said. I listened carefully, my heart swelling with admiration for her courage. "That's a big decision, Angel," I replied, my voice steady with reassurance. "No matter what, I'll be with you every step of the way." We reached across the table, our hands meeting in a silent promise of untiring support. At that moment, I saw the determination in her eyes, the same quiet strength that has always defined her. "Thank you, Mom," she said softly. "Your support means everything to me." Moments like these define our relationship: a mix of strength, trust, and unconditional love.

Belle's strength and spirit inspire me daily. She faces life's challenges with grace, her quiet determination lighting the way. As her mother, I've done my best to guide her, but now, I often find myself learning from her strength and wisdom. Our bond is a fortress built on love and trust. No matter where life takes us or how far apart we may be, it will remain unbreakable. Together, we can weather any storm, chase any dream, and celebrate every success.

To all the parents reading this: cherish every moment with your children. Make the time, no matter how busy life gets. Listen to them, encourage them, and let them know how proud you are of their unique journey. Accept them for who they are, not who you want them to be. Let's celebrate the incredible strength that comes from these relationships. Let's create spaces where our children feel empowered to dream big, take risks, and follow their hearts. To mothers and daughters, fathers and sons, mothers and sons, and fathers and daughters, your bond is your power. This bond inspires, uplifts, and shapes us to face life together with love and strength. Whether they're significant milestones or small, quiet times together, a heartfelt conversation or a shared laugh, these are the memories that will last a lifetime.

To my beautiful daughter, I want you to know that you are my greatest joy, my proudest accomplishment, and my source of inspiration. As my Belle continues to maneuver her path, I stand on the sidelines, cheering her on with a heart bursting with pride. No matter where life takes us, our bond will remain unbreakable. Together, we face every storm, chase every dream, and live fully, knowing that love is our foundation, and our journeys will be our greatest legacy.

"I love you my Precious, Angel."

"A promise is more than words; it is a pledge of trust we share."

Colleen C. Carson

"Be who you are, shamelessly and boldly; the world needs your unique light."

Mama Carson

Uncover the Mastering of Evolution...

"ME MATTERS"

Where thoughts, intuition, and life philosophy unite to expose the total power within you. This is not just a chapter; it's an invitation to master evolution by taking on the core truth: You matter. Colleen believes life's real meaning lies in the ability to influence your own evolution. "Your thoughts create your reality," she reflects. "and your intuition, when trusted, guides you through life's chaos with clarity." In this chapter, you will learn how to connect the power of your mind, the wisdom of your inner voice, and the power of your experiences to create the life you value. As you journey ME Matters, you'll discover that mastering your evolution is a deliberate choice, that blends the power of conscious thought, intuition, and a deeply personal philosophy of growth. The courage to trust yourself, the clarity to navigate challenges, and the strength to leave behind a legacy of transformation. Trust your thoughts, follow your intuition, and welcome your own evolution.

Are you ready to step into the life you were always meant to create?

Your extraordinary journey begins, welcome to...

CHAPTER THREE

"Greatness in not fame. Greatness is not fortune. Greatness is forgiveness."

Colleen C. Carson

"To save the world, we must first save the kindness in our hearts; one act of compassion, one seed of hope, and one moment of courage can ignite the change that lights up humanity."

Colleen C. Carson

"When you empower your children, you empower the world."

Mama Carson

"Wisdom is the quiet strength that whispers truths amid the noise of life."

Colleen C. Carson

"FOLLOW YOUR PASSION"

Okay, so let's talk about this whole "follow your passion" thing. It's everywhere, right? Colleen has seen it on Instagram quotes, heard it in motivational speeches, and most think the minute you find your passion, life will be sunshine and unicorns. Living your passion isn't about running off into the sunset with zero plans and expecting the world to throw money and opportunities at you. That's a great plot for a movie but in real life? Not so much. Colleen found out that living her passion means grounding her dreams in reality. She realized that it wasn't about crushing her creativity or playing it safe forever; it's about building something maintainable so that she didn't end up broke and bitter, wondering why her passion felt more like a burden.

First, Colleen's passion needed to be clear. And what she means by that is asking herself these questions: Like, what are you passionate about? "I want to help people," "I love music," or "I'm obsessed with food." Okay, great. But how? Do you want to be a nurse, a counselor, or start a nonprofit? Do you want to produce music, perform, or teach? Do you want to open a restaurant, be a food critic, or launch a cooking blog? She had to get specific. This was difficult for her because she was such a dreamer with very little patience for detail, but she learned from life experiences this was the way to go if she wanted to be successful or even more so, make an income.

Let me tell you my story. It's one of those "follow your gut" moments that stick with you. So, I planned my whole wedding, start to finish, and I loved every minute of it. It was like I had found my thing. After the big day, I couldn't stop thinking about how amazing it would be to do that as a career. It wasn't just a fleeting thought; it felt like a passion had been lit.

I'm walking down Granville Street one rainy windy afternoon, the kind of day where your umbrella flips inside out, and you're left dodging puddles. But my mind wasn't on the weather; it was buzzing with the question: *How could I turn this into a business?* Back then, wedding planning wasn't even a thing outside of venues. There were no cell phones, no social media hype, no Pinterest, and definitely no one lining up to fund a woman with a passion. It was just me, my big ideas, and a whole lot of determination. But something about that afternoon stuck with me. I told myself, *One day, I'm going to make this happen.* I don't know how yet, but I will." It wasn't about the "if," it was about the "when." I just had to figure out the "how."

Ten years later, I did it. I launched my catering and wedding planning business, and it became my world for the next eighteen years. Those years were full of incredible moments, challenges, and everything in between. I faced financial struggles, had to learn the ins and outs of the industry, marketing, and had to have an outside the box mindset, along with often feeling overwhelmed. But I persevered, and you know what? It all started with that rainy walk, and a significant passion; a dream. That's the thing about passion; it doesn't always come with a roadmap. Sometimes, it's just a rainy afternoon, a gut feeling, and the courage to say, *I'll figure it out.*

This is crucial; you need to determine if your passion is something you want to pursue as a career, a side hustle, or a hobby. And remember, one isn't superior to the other. Some passions are best kept as hobbies, and that's perfectly fine. Not every passion needs to be turned into a business. If you love painting, but the thought of turning it into a business takes away the joy, then keep it as a hobby! The key is to integrate it into your life in a way that brings you happiness, not stress. Now, let's talk about the practical side. Yes, I'm talking about money. If you're considering turning your passion into your livelihood, you need a plan. Passion alone won't pay the bills, at least not immediately. This is where many people stumble. They leap without a safety net. Instead, consider this: start small. Test the waters.

If you want to write, don't quit your job tomorrow. Start freelancing on the side. If you want to open a bakery, practice recipes at home and sell to friends before renting out a space. Build gradually to avoid a hard crash. I did this when I decided to get into sales; I started part-time and eventually transitioned into a full-time role as a sales trainer and manager. And let's not forget about the learning curve. Nobody talks about this enough. Just because you're passionate about something doesn't mean you'll immediately be good at it. Harsh, I know, but it's true. You've got to be willing to learn, fail and improve. Passion doesn't mean skipping the work; it just means you're excited to do the work. After seven years in business, I chose to take a course on starting a catering business. Had I taken that course earlier, I might have felt too intimidated to pursue my passion. Fear can be a roadblock, but the reality is that having a solid plan and taking action, despite your fears, is essential. It's that very action that empowers you to overcome your fears and succeed.

Oh, and can we please talk about sacrifice? Living your passion doesn't come without trade-offs. If you want to chase your passion, something's got to give, whether it's time, money, or comfort. You might have to work long hours, cut back on expenses, or even step out of your comfort zone to network or market yourself. Ask yourself: are you okay with that? Because passion isn't always glamorous, sometimes it's messy, challenging, and exhausting. I remember every summer and Christmas season, while my friends were enjoying their summer activities and Christmas parties, I was planning and catering. That's okay; I eventually was able to do both. I had to sacrifice a lot of personal time and comfort, but it was all worth it in the end.

And one more thing: Don't fall into the trap of thinking you must do this all alone. Why do we act like asking for help is a sign of weakness? I know I did when I first started out. It was an incorrect choice, but eventually, I started to figure it out and asked for help. Find a mentor, join a community, take a course, or do whatever you need to level up. The more people you have in your corner, the better. Remember, you're not alone in this journey.

Now, let's get real about setbacks. Because guess what? They're going to happen. You'll make mistakes. Someone will criticize you. It's all part of the process. Passion isn't a straight line; it has it's highs and lows. The trick is to not let setbacks define you. Learn from them, adjust, and keep going. Also, let's not glamorize the hustle too much. Living your passion doesn't mean burning out. Rest is part of the process, too. Take breaks. Enjoy life. Your passion should add to your life, not take it over completely. Balance, my friend. Balance.

When my daughter kicked off her passion in the super-demanding fashion industry, she made it a point to take a week or two off every three months. I remember asking her once, "Aren't you worried about taking time off from work?" Her response was gold. She said, "Who said I'm taking time off? This is my time to reflect on my progress, spark new ideas, recharge my energy, and just enjoy me for a bit. That's actually part of what makes me successful, Mom." That was her balance, and for her it work, we all have to find our balance in order to experience self-worth and self-love.

And can we take a moment to remember that passions can evolve? Maybe you start loving photography, but five years in, you realize you're more into videography. That's fine! You're not married to one passion forever. Life changes, you change, and your passions can change, too. Be flexible. My goodness, I've had a collage of passions: entrepreneur, consultant, sales trainer, business development, catering & event business, wedding planner, songwriter, writer, author, playwright, and there are probably a few more, oh yeah, there is; inspirational speaker in the forecast; what do you think?

Living your passion isn't about chasing some perfect dream. It's about integrating what you love into your life in a way that works for you. It's about taking the leap but also bringing a parachute. It's about staying grounded while reaching for the stars. And it's about enjoying the journey, not just obsessing over the destination. Passion isn't a neat, tidy path. It's messy, full of surprises, and sometimes, it's rainy afternoons that spark the biggest dreams. Here's the truth: when you balance passion with purpose and realism, you don't just live your dream; you succeed in it. And that, my dear reader, is what it's all about. If I could do it, you can too; so, what are you waiting for? Start!

"Our smile is like sunshine, our laughter is like music, together they bring joyful happiness to our journey."

Mama Carson

"SINGLISM OR COUPLEDOM"

Colleen has noticed over the years that fewer men and women are in a race to get married and that the single life is becoming an accepted choice, at least among most. Colleen believes that being single is not a problem that needs to be fixed. It's a status, like being on *"Do Not Disturb"* mode, except people keep knocking anyway. She notices that society, for all its progress, still loves to label, particularly, single women into a category somewhere between *"unfulfilled"* or *"waiting for Prince Charming."* But Colleen questions, "What if we're not waiting? What if we're flourishing?"

Colleen wants to share a little secret that she has learned along the way: being single is not just a phase; it's an art. And like any art form, it takes time, effort, and a healthy dose of humour to master. Colleen has done both and acknowledges there's empowerment in being completely independent and equal empowerment in a partnership that builds you up instead of breaking you down. Whether you're flying solo or coupled up, owning your life is where the real power lies. Relationships and being single both have their highs and lows, and anyone who tells you otherwise is just kidding themselves. Colleen's case in point is like choosing between coffee and wine. Some days, you're all about that comforting, predictable warmth; other is the want of the unpredictable and questionable.

I'll be honest: I've had my fair share of interesting relationships. I had several affairs, was engaged three times (yes, THREE times), married for 40 years, and am now in a relationship with a man I've been waiting for my whole life. And no, it's not some guy I met last week at a coffee shop; I met him online. This man? He's a dream come true, and we've been building something beautiful together for almost ten years. But here's the twist: my longest stretch of adult singlism? Came in my sixties, and let me tell you, it was empowering. It was the first time I truly understood the depth of my own power.

Now, about relationships, oh sweetheart, they are a journey. Relationships are the ultimate team sport. When you're in a relationship, you share everything good, bad, and sometimes questionable. You've got a partner for life's big moments, little moments, and everything in between. You've got someone who'll help you navigate the minefield which is your closet when you're convinced you have nothing to wear. And let's not forget the joy of having someone around to kill the occasional spider in the bathroom.

But let's keep it real for a second; relationships come with negotiation. You'll spend more time than you'd like debating the best temperature for the house (why is it always cold in the living room?) and deciding which takeout to order that becomes a drama. Want to paint the living room in a shade of "Sunset Rose?" Brace yourself for the "but what about a neutral tone?" Want to stay in bed all weekend watching Netflix? You'll probably be met with a "What's the plan for today?" suggestion. And let's talk about the sacred art of sharing a bed. Let's not. There is arguing over the "right" way to load the dishwasher (your way is correct) and negotiations over organic versus regular peanut butter. Relationships, as wonderful as they can be, require patience, effort, and the ability to laugh when things don't go as planned because they won't.

But then there's the single life, which is a beautiful thing. It's freedom in its purest form. It's a life where you don't have to check in with anyone. Your home is a space that's entirely yours, where the pillows stay where you left them. Friday nights can be an impromptu solo dance in the kitchen or a quiet evening with a book that doesn't talk back. There's a certain joy in knowing you can plan your days exactly as you please without the silent negotiations of coupledom. No compromising on what to watch, no passive-aggressive thermostat battles, just you, your preferences, and the bliss of uninterrupted self-discovery. Want to take a spontaneous trip to the beach? Done. A weekend away? Done. Live in your pyjamas for three days straight? Go for it. Remote? Yours. Want to eat an entire pizza by yourself? Do it. It's a life where every decision is yours, and every moment celebrates your freedom.

But single life isn't all rose petals and breakfast in bed (because, let's face it, you'd have to make it yourself). There's nobody to help carry in the groceries when you've made the questionable decision to buy a 24-pack of bottled water in one trip. No one to fix the leaky faucet or change the oil in your car. Nobody to rub your feet after a long day, and worst of all, nobody to cuddle up to when you hear strange noises coming from the kitchen in the middle of the night. Oh, and don't forget IKEA! Let's. Romantic holidays? Suddenly, Valentine's Day feels like an awkward third-wheel situation. And the unsolicited questions! "Why are you still single?" as if you forgot to sign up for the marriage lottery. All of them. Listen: single life teaches you to trust yourself. It teaches you the art of standing tall, making decisions, and, most importantly, realizing you are enough without anyone else. Empowerment!

Relationships should be partnerships that lift you up. When you're with someone who respects you, you've got a partner in crime. When that someone holds your hand through life's ups and downs, someone who loves you for all your quirks. Oh, that's a game-changer. But the real magic happens when you realize you don't need someone else's validation to feel worthy. You don't need a relationship to define your power. Instead of need, you want. Your power is natural; it's yours, and it's solid. Whether you're single or in a relationship, you're a powerhouse in your own right. It's about accepting yourself, quirks and all, and realizing that you are enough, just as you are.

My dear reader, the trick is owning your life stage. If you're single, you're a queen ruling your own castle. You're the CEO of your life, making decisions that support your goals and dreams. If you're in a relationship, you're still a queen; relationships offer a kind of stability and partnership that's hard to beat. There's a comfort in knowing someone's got your back, whether it's during life's big moments or just deciding which frozen pizza to buy. It's nice to have someone to laugh with, share your dreams with, and argue with because what's love without the occasional passionate disagreement over the right way to load the dishwasher? (And yes, there is a right way.)

But this is the key: whether you're single or in a relationship, the secret to happiness is owning it. I've had the best of both worlds and if there's one thing I've learned, it's that the grass always seems greener on the other side until you realize both sides need mowing. Being single isn't a waiting game, and being in a relationship isn't the finish line. It's all about loving where you are and making the most of it. If you're single, welcome the freedom, the self-discovery, and the fact that your bed is entirely yours. And if you're in a relationship, appreciate the companionship, the built-in adventure partner, and the joy of finding someone who actually understands your weirdness and loves you anyway. So, the next time someone asks, "Why are you still single?" or "Why did you settle down?" smile and say, "Because I'm living my best life."

"THE GENERATIONS OF WOMEN"

Let's take a fun stroll down the generational lane and leap into the fascinating differences between Colleen, Baby Boomer woman, Crystal and Chelsea, Millennial women, and the little firecracker known as Brynley, Generation Alpha. Each group has its quirks, strengths, and, of course, their fair share of "what the heck?" moments. If you've ever wondered how these three generations stack up, get ready for a humorous yet enlightening look at the worlds they've grown up (and are growing up) in.

Baby Boomer Women: The Original Gangsta Multitaskers (Born 1946–1964)

Ah, Colleen was part of the Baby Boomer women, the generation that brought us from poodle skirts to power suits. These ladies grew up in a time when women were supposed to be charming hostesses, cooks, and mothers who never broke a sweat. But the Boomers said, "Nah, we can do all that and have a career too." Cue the invention of multitasking.

Advantages? These women were trailblazers. They kicked down doors, entered the workforce in unison, and laid the foundation for gender equality in offices, homes, and beyond. And they did all this without the help of Google or GPS! These women figured things out the hard way by using paper maps, going to libraries for research, and, dare we say it, making phone calls.

Disadvantages? The expectations were insane. These women had to do everything, from raising kids to managing the household to climbing the career ladder, and they had to look good while doing it. The phrase "having it all" was invented to torture Baby Boomer women. Oh, and forget work-from-home flexibility. You went to the office in heels, rain or shine, even if your child had chickenpox. Also, no smartphones meant you couldn't even send a sneaky text to complain about your day!

What we love about them: These women survived it all. From bell-bottoms to the rise of feminism, Baby Boomer women have the grit of marathon runners and the determination of people who don't quit the gym in January. They're proof that you can manage 100 things at once (even if it means some serious hair-spraying along the way).

Millennial Women: The Queens of Adaptation
(Born 1981-1996)

Now we move on to Crystal and Chelsea, who are part of the Millennial women, butterflies of the modern age. These women are all about adapting, whether figuring out how to adult in a gig economy or living in a world where avocado toast is both a meal and a financial downfall. Millennials grew up with the internet, so they're the bridge between dial-up days and high-speed everything.

Advantages? Millennial women are tech-savvy, adaptable, and spirited as hell. They've navigated recessions, pandemics, and the weird transition from MySpace to Instagram without losing their minds. Millennials are the queens of side hustles. If the 9-to-5 job wasn't cutting it, you bet they were running an Etsy store, launching a blog, or moonlighting as a Lyft driver. Plus, they have the whole "self-care" thing down—therapy, meditation apps, and yoga pants all day, every day.

Disadvantages? Ah, the student loan debt. Millennials were sold the dream of "get a degree, get a job, live the dream," only to discover that degrees cost as much as houses used to and don't always come with jobs. And let's talk about the pressure to succeed. Millennial women are supposed to "lean in," break glass ceilings, and change the world: all while maintaining the perfect Instagram visual.

What we love about them: Millennial women are basically superheroes in disguise. They've learned to pivot faster than anyone, accept diversity like no generation before, and push the envelope on what it means to be a woman in today's world. Plus, they know how to order the best lattes.

Generation Alpha Women: The Future World-Changers
(Born 2010-2025)

Now let's get to the littlest ones like Brynley: Generation Alpha. These girls are still growing up, but they're already flexing their digital muscles like pros. These are the daughters and granddaughters of Millennials and Gen Xers, and they're born into a world of smartphones, smart speakers, and probably smart refrigerators that know more about what's in the fridge than they do.

Advantages? Oh, where to start? These girls are growing up in the most connected and tech-friendly world ever. Need an answer? They'll ask Alexa or Google faster than you can say "encyclopedia." Generation Alpha women will have a level of digital fluency that'll make Millennials look like tech newbies. Plus, they're being raised in a world that's (hopefully) more accepting of diversity and equality than ever before. The opportunities? Endless. These girls might grow up coding robots before they even hit high school!

Disadvantages? Social media, yikes. While previous generations only had to worry about face-to-face bullying, Generation Alpha will likely deal with digital drama from day one. The pressure to be "on" 24/7 is real. Also, there's a high chance that Generation Alpha will grow up seriously dependent on tech. They may struggle with navigating the "real" world, which can't always be solved with a quick YouTube tutorial.

What we love about them: These girls are going to be fearless. They'll have the tools and resources to push boundaries in ways we haven't even imagined yet. Generation Alpha women will grow up knowing they can be astronauts, scientists, politicians, or influencers: whatever they want. They'll have more freedom to shape their futures than any generation before them.

The Big Picture: Three Generations, One Common Connection

So, what ties these three generations of women together other than the fact that; Colleen, Crystal, Chelsea, and Brynley are related and love each other? Spirit, adaptability, and an unshakable determination to make their mark on the world. Baby Boomers started the revolution; Millennials took it to the next level, and Generation Alpha? Well, they'll finish the job and probably tweet about it, too.

While each generation of women has had its own unique set of challenges, one thing remains constant: women have always found a way to succeed, no matter what the world throws at them. Whether breaking into the workforce, juggling careers and side hustles, or navigating a digital-first world, women always find a way to keep pushing forward and laugh through the chaos with a glass of wine, scotch, or beer.

Because, at the end of the day, whether you're a Baby Boomer, Millennial, or Generation Alpha, one thing's for sure: women always find a way to rise and look fabulous doing it.

Just so you don't think I left you out:

Generation X women, born between 1965 and 1980, are the original trailblazers, earning the "latchkey generation" title for mastering independence while their parents were busy hustling. They're the cool bridge between cassette tapes and Wi-Fi, skillfully navigating personal computers while reminiscing about simpler times, like when rewinding VHS tapes was a thing! All about that work-life balance, these ladies juggle family and careers while championing diversity and inclusion like it's their superpower. With a talent for humour to tackle life's curveballs, Generation X women embody strength and adaptability, proving they can laugh through anything!

Generation Z women, born between 1997 and 2012, are the ultimate digital natives, raised by smartphones and TikTok. With confidence as bold as their favourite lip colour, they're quick to call out nonsense and tackle social issues head-on, making "OK Boomer" their unofficial battle cry. Redefining pop culture one meme at a time, they turn everything from dance challenges to DIY hacks into viral sensations while keeping it real on social media. Prioritizing mental health and armed with a sharp sense of humour, these women are like the coolest Swiss Army knives you'll ever meet ready to tackle anything and always bringing the laughs!

"SHE is HER and ME."

"HEAD HELD HIGH"

In the hustle and bustle of everyday life, Colleen often notices that people look down at their phones, the ground, or the immediate tasks before them. But she'll tell you; there's something truly uplifting about looking up, something children instinctively understand, and adults often forget. It's time for us, adults, to reconnect with that magic and rediscover the extraordinary world around us.

When children look up, they see a universe of endless possibilities. The sky becomes their playground, a vast canvas where their dreams and imaginations run wild. They gaze at the stars, believing they can reach them, and in the clouds, they find shapes and stories that ignite their curiosity. Every glance upwards is filled with wonder and joy, unburdened by the weight of everyday worries. They see beauty in the smallest things, like a butterfly dancing through the air or a leaf twirling to the ground.

Colleen realizes that as we grow into adulthood, we often lose that sense of wonder that once came so naturally. Our gaze, which was once filled with curiosity and awe, begins to decline. We become consumed by our responsibilities, problems, and routines. We need to look up and see the bigger picture, losing sight of a vast world full of beauty and potential. Colleen's perspective is crucial because she reminds us to dream, to aspire, and to believe in the opportunities that lie ahead.

Let's take a moment to reflect on what happens when we direct our gaze upwards. We are greeted by the magnificence of the sunrise, a powerful symbol of new beginnings and hope. Each dawn presents us with a fresh start, a chance to welcome the day with reviving energy and purpose. Think about it: every morning is an invitation to begin again. As the sun rises, it bathes the world in golden light, reminding us that each day offers a blank canvas on which we can paint our dreams.

When we look up, we can witness the tops of trees gracefully swaying in the wind, a beautiful reminder of their strength and growth. These trees have faced storms, droughts, and challenges, yet they stand tall, reminding us of our strength. They symbolize the strength we have within us to rise above our circumstances. The architecture of buildings around us serves as evidence of human creativity and ambition, a witness to what can be achieved when we dare to dream big. Each structure tells a story of hard work, innovation, and a vision that once only existed in someone's imagination.

Looking up connects us to the larger world and each other, reminding us that we are part of something greater. We are all unified in this beautiful montage of life, each connection adding to the richness of our experiences. So, let's celebrate that connection! Let's accept that we are not alone in our struggles or triumphs. We can lift each other up, creating a community rooted in support, encouragement, and love.

In contrast, looking down often narrows our perspective. It focuses on the immediate, sometimes to the point of missing out on opportunities and beauty around us. When we look down, we can become trapped in our worries, feeling burdened or confined. Yes, there are times we need to attend to the ground beneath us, our responsibilities, our tasks, and our daily obligations, but balancing this focus with moments of looking up is crucial. Doing so helps keep our spirits lifted and our minds open to the possibilities that await us.

Reflecting on my own childhood, I recall the simple joy of lying in the backyard with my sisters, our eyes fixed on the sky. We would share tales united from the clouds, each of us seeing something entirely unique. "Look! That cloud looks like a dragon!" one of us would exclaim, and then we'd all contribute our interpretations, merging narratives that transported us to far-off lands and adventures. It was a magical experience, a connection born from our shared imaginations that was pure gold, a treasure we can all revisit if we allow ourselves to.

And oh, the birds! Whenever a flock takes flight, I can't help but stop in my tracks. There's something deeply reflective in the way they dance across the sky, forming patterns that seem to whisper secrets if you only watch long enough. It's like nature sends a message, urging us to pause and ponder the beauty surrounding us, a rainbow appearing after a storm or the timely shift when the sun decides to sleep, and the moon begins to wake. These are all wondrous sights, and they remind us that life is full of surprises if we're willing to look for them.

Nowadays, my walks along the seawall have become my sanctuary. I step outside and soak in the world with my eyes inspirationally looking up. Sure, I notice the folks glued to their phones; I can't miss them, but me? I'm too busy absorbing the wonder above. The clouds transform into different shapes, the colours of the sunset paint the sky, and the gentle breeze carries the scent of the ocean. And let me tell you when I catch myself slipping, when my gaze starts to drift downward, I quickly lift my head and drink in that sense of boundless freedom. There's joy up there, waiting to be discovered, and I refuse to miss out.

It's funny how life's most challenging moments can lead us to the most insightful realizations. There was a time when I wasn't allowed to look up while I was caged in an abusive relationship. Every glance skyward felt like an act of defiance against the suffocating grasp of control. My spirit felt crushed, and I learned to keep my head down, focusing on survival rather than living. But then, one day, I broke free. Stepping out from that darkness, I felt the weight lift from my shoulders and lifted my eyes to the heavens. It was like breathing for the first time in months, the purest form of freedom flowing through my veins.

At that moment, I made a promise to myself, a vow carved in the depths of my soul. I swore that I would never surrender that freedom again. Every time I looked up, it would be a celebration of my strength and a tribute to my radiant spirit. Let's take a lesson from children and consciously try to look up more often. Let's lift our heads, our hearts, and our hopes.

By doing so, we can rediscover the joy of opportunities, the excitement of dreaming big, and the peace that comes from seeing the world from a higher perspective. Looking up is not just a physical action; it's a mindset, a way of accepting life with optimism and openness.

Think about it: when was the last time you allowed yourself to dream? When was the last time you looked beyond your immediate surroundings and envisioned the possibilities that lie ahead? Getting caught up in the daily grind is easy, but we owe it to ourselves to break free from that cycle. So, let's commit to seeking out those moments that inspire us. Let's surround ourselves with people who lift us up and encourage our dreams. Let's engage in activities that ignite our passion and spark our creativity.

Let's make it a point to go outside, breathe in the fresh air, and appreciate the beauty that surrounds us. Whether it's watching the sun set behind the mountains, listening to the rustle of leaves in the breeze, or simply standing in awe of the vast sky above, these moments are reminders that life is full of wonder. They invite us to reconnect with our inner child and embrace the joy of exploration.

So, the next time you find yourself caught in the grind of daily life, take a moment to look up. Whether it's gazing at the sky, admiring the treetops, or simply raising your eyes from your screen, let it be a reminder that there is always more to see, experience, and hope for. Let's reclaim that childlike wonder and allow it to guide us toward a more positive, fulfilling life.

Remember, if you keep looking down, you will never catch sight of the rainbow above. Life is a medley of experiences, and when we lift our gaze, we welcome the beauty of our surroundings and ignite the spark of inspiration within ourselves.

The journey toward a more fulfilling life begins with a single step: looking up. It's a simple action, yet it holds the power to transform our mindset and shape our reality. By appreciating this perspective, we can cultivate our spirit, foster creativity, and inspire ourselves and others to reach for the stars.

Every day is a new opportunity to uplift ourselves and those around us. So, let's take that promise to heart. Let's commit to being dreamers, explorers, and believers. Let's celebrate our strengths and acknowledge our struggles, understanding that each experience shapes us into the individuals we are meant to be. In this community of support and positivity, we can create an environment where everyone feels empowered to look up, dream big, and soar to new heights.

May we always find the courage to look up, no matter our challenges. Together, let's lift our eyes to the heavens, celebrate our journeys, and chase after the dreams that fill our hearts with joy.

The sky is not the limit; it's just the beginning. Your journey is waiting, and the universe is cheering you on. So, rise up, dream big, and let the world unfold its wonders before you. Engage your freedom, rediscover your joy, and let every glance upward remind you of the incredible possibilities that await you.

"MY CANADA"

Colleen, it's tough out there right now, isn't it? The world feels like it's in a mess. Freedom is being challenged, and those who shouldn't have power are leading the way. Bullies are in charge, and instead of standing firm, too many people are backing down, hoping for a quick fix of power or money.

Colleen feels so heartened to see governments and leaders worldwide putting courage on the back burner and choosing the comfort of cowardice instead. But she's holding onto optimism. Because there's always hope, and sometimes the quiet ones make the most noise in the end.

Colleen has always been proud of her Canadian roots, and she can't help but feel that the world knows what Canada represents. Canadians are not about flash and drama but peace, kindness, and a steady pride that quietly speaks volumes. Colleen remembers in 2010, during the Winter Olympics in Vancouver when a reporter from California, someone who had never even visited Canada, was asked what he thought of the country and its people. His response stuck with her.

He said, "Canada is one of the most beautiful countries I've ever visited, but I can honestly say I've never been anywhere where people are so respectful and kind to others." The reporter explained, "If you step on a Canadian's foot, they apologize. They're always holding doors open and saying sorry, not because they think they're wrong, but because they're just that kind of person.

They don't want you to feel uncomfortable. I'll tell you; I'll be back to this beautiful country of the most respectful people I've had the privilege to experience." I smiled when I heard those words because I do all those things, and until he spoke of them, I didn't even realize I had been doing them.

That sums it up perfectly. In a world that sometimes seems like it's losing its way, Canada stands out as a shining example of decency and respect. Canada is not perfect because I'm not perfect. Our country is about the people, and we're doing our best to live with kindness and consideration. And that's what the world needs more of right now: people who are strong enough to lead with empathy and who aren't afraid to be kind even when things seem harsh.

So yeah, I'm holding onto that optimism. There's always a silver lining behind every cloud, and Canada is a reminder of what humanity can be at its best.

But let's talk about the best country in the world, Canada, and its history since the Second World War. Since I was born, Canada has been quietly and steadily shaping the world around us. Canada's story isn't about loud declarations or power struggles; it's about diplomacy, compassion, and a commitment to making things better for all of us.

It's about seeing the bigger picture and taking small but steady steps toward peace, progress, and unity. Let me tell you how Canada went from being a quiet neighbour on the global stage to an absolute powerhouse of kindness and leadership, especially from the 1950s right up to today.

When I was growing up in the 1950s, Canada was coming out of the Second World War, and the world was trying to pick itself off the floor. Nations were being rebuilt, and new questions were rising about how to prevent all that destruction from happening again.

With all its vastness and natural beauty, Canada didn't have to shout to be noticed, but we did something that earned us a lot of respect. In the 1950s, under the leadership of Prime Minister Lester B. Pearson, Canada took a bold step onto the world stage when the Suez Crisis happened in 1956.

The world was on the brink of war, and Canada came with a peace proposal: a United Nations peacekeeping force to stop the fighting. This was a game-changer. Pearson wasn't afraid to stand up and say, "We can do this differently." And you know what? The world took notice. For his efforts, he won the Nobel Peace Prize in 1957. Imagine a Canadian winning the Nobel Prize for Peace. It wasn't a fluke; it was a sign of our direction.

Canada's reputation as a peaceful and fair-minded nation grew through the decades. In the Cold War, Canada didn't pick sides between the United States and the Soviet Union. We weren't trying to get involved in any nuclear showdown. Instead, we always called for peace talks and disarmament, encouraging everyone to take a step back, take a breath, and find another way.

Canada sent peacekeepers to places like Cyprus and Congo, where nations were in turmoil. Canadians were there to help, mediate, and keep people safe. Canada wasn't just a player on the world stage; we showed the world how peace could work.

Then came the 1980s. As a baby boomer, I remember that decade well. We were still recovering from the turbulence of the '60s and '70s, but Canada kept pushing forward, advocating for human rights and standing firm against injustice. I think of the moment in 1982, the year after my daughter, Crystal was born, when Canada spoke up for South Africa and its fight against apartheid.

The Canadian government was one of the loudest voices calling for an end to racial segregation and the recognition of the dignity and rights of every person. It didn't matter that Canada was far away from South Africa.

What mattered was that we stood on the side of what was right. I also remember how our Constitution was changed where Canada had control of it not the Queen, and one of the changes was to be a multi-cultural country, and we've never looked back. When that happened my Dad went out and got a five copies of our Constitution, brought them home and gave each of his daughters a copy, and told us we must read and even memorize it because that is about our Canadian freedom.

In the 1990s, Canada's voice for peace only became stronger. We were helping out in places like Bosnia, where a brutal war was tearing the country apart. Canadian peacekeepers risked their lives to protect civilians and keep the peace. Even in the face of violence and destruction, Canadians stayed true to the peace mission.

We learned the hard way that sometimes, peacekeeping can't fix everything, but that doesn't mean we're going to stop trying. In Rwanda, we saw firsthand how difficult it was to intervene in a genocide, and it broke our hearts. But we were there, doing what we could because that's what we believe in, helping others when they're in need.

Then came the 2000s, and things started to change again. We had September 11, 2001, and the world was never the same. Canada stood firm, joining with other countries in the fight against terrorism. But even then, Canada never lost sight of our values. We didn't just send soldiers to fight; we sent our hearts, too. We called for diplomacy, long-term peacebuilding, and humanitarian aid.

We knew that the world wasn't just about war. It was about understanding and helping people in every way possible. Canada pushed for the Paris Agreement to fight climate change because we knew the world's future was at stake. It was a reminder that Canada's commitment to global well-being didn't just come from our government; it's also came from it's citizens because that's part of who we are as Canadians.

Even today, Canada still does what it does best: helping others. Whether it's stepping up to support Ukraine in its fight for freedom or standing up for human rights in Myanmar, Canada is always on the side of justice. We're a nation that knows what it's like to struggle, and we use that knowledge to help those who are struggling today.

I'll never forget my trip to Europe as a young woman. I was told, "Make sure you sew your Canadian flag on your knapsack because people will treat you with respect. That's how Europeans felt about Canadians." Fast-forward fifty years, I returned to Europe, it was the same thing. The respect was there as it had been all those years ago.

And you know what? That's been my experience everywhere I've travelled. People all over the world, no matter where I go, have this deep admiration for Canadians. They see us as the peacemakers, the ones who keep things steady and kind.

Canada's legacy is one of steady, quiet leadership. We don't need to be the loudest voice in the room, but we ensure it's heard when it counts. We're not a perfect country, but we strive every day to be better, kinder, and more compassionate.

From the 1950s to today, Canada's journey has been one of peace, hope, and a commitment to making the world a better place. And after 74 years of life, I can say with certainty that Canada has truly earned its place as a leader in the global union. The world is better because of us, which is worth celebrating, my friends.

It's truly incredible to be part of a country that is so widely respected for its values of peace, kindness, and goodwill. The global admiration for Canadians fills me with immense pride, and I can relate to it because I, too, love our country. There's something truly special about the way we welcome others with open hearts and open minds. The most beautiful thing about Canada and its people is that we build bridges, not walls.

We choose connection over division, compassion over conflict, and unity over separation. These values are not just part of our national identity, but they are also deeply personal to me, and I wouldn't change them for anything.

"GOD BLESS, MY COUNTRY, MY OWN, CANADA."

"In a world of 'isms', rightful humanity lies not in cruelty, but in the kindness we spread, the acceptance we cultivate, and the empathy that bridges unite, and walls divide."

Colleen C. Carson

"HEAR TO LEARN"

In this world where voices define,
And thoughts undo in an infinite design,
We are awarded with gifts, simply unique,
Two ears to hear, one mouth to speak.

With ears, we hear whispers of the breeze,
And listen to tales beneath the trees.
In every murmur, a story untold,
In every secret, a treasure beholds.

Yet our mouths, wait, with patient grace,
To share our truths in the right place.
For words hold power, like seeds in soil,
They bloom in hearts, with tender toil.

Two ears, they teach us to understand,
To hear the tales of woman and man.
And when we listen, wisdom does unfold,
A gentle stream of truths untold.

We hear to learn, to grow, to find,
The hidden paths within our mind.
Each word a lesson, each silence a key,
Unlocking the doors to what we can be.

So, cherish these gifts, in life's grand art,
They guide our journey, from heart to heart.
Two ears to listen and one mouth to share,
We unite our tales with love and care.

Colleen C. Carson

"THE MALE EVOLUTION"

You know what ladies? Colleen has been around for a good while, she's seventy-four years old, to be exact, and She has seen change when it comes to what it means to be a man. And she'll tell you, many men feel like they're being backed into a corner these days. They're looking around, thinking, "Is my manhood even relevant anymore?" Some might not say it out loud, but Colleen can see it in their eyes. They feel like the world's changing so fast, and somewhere along the way, being a man started feeling like something they had to apologize for.

Colleen remembers when men took a lot of pride in being the providers, the fixers, the strong and silent types. That was their role, plain and simple. They built things with their hands, worked hard, and carried the weight of the world without much fuss. But today? Well, it's not that those things aren't valued anymore, but it sure seems they're being questioned. Colleen has heard women talk about "toxic masculinity," and suddenly, it feels like everything men thought they were supposed to be is under scrutiny. And Colleen feels, that's got to be tough.

Ladies, I've conversed with men who feel like they're walking on eggshells. They don't know if they're supposed to open doors or wait for a woman to do it herself. If they offer to pay for dinner, is it chivalry, or is it offensive? They're trying to figure out how to show up in a way that doesn't make them feel like they're losing who they are, and honestly, I don't blame them. It's confusing. And I believe it's confusing for women, as well. We got to get over this silliness that women are not powerful if they allow a man to treat them with chivalry. Absolute nonsense, only schoolgirls would think that way.

And I'll tell you something else: men were raised with a certain rulebook, and overnight, it feels like someone tore out all the pages and handed them a blank one. It used to be that being a man meant keeping your emotions in check, handling business, and not letting anything shake you. But now, they're told they need to open up, be vulnerable, and express their feelings, things they were never really taught how to do. So here they are, trying to balance being the strong, dependable man, emotionally available, and communicative. And let's be honest, that's a lot to ask, especially when you don't know where to start.

But you know, as much as men feel like they're struggling to find their place, women are watching all of this unfold, too. And it's not easy on us either. We grew up with certain expectations of what a man should be: strong, reliable, and capable. But we also wanted them to be more present, engaged, and willing to connect beyond fixing things around the house or bringing home a paycheck.

We wanted them to listen, to understand, and to be true partners, not just providers. This shared struggle is an indication to the evolving nature of gender roles and the need for mutual understanding and support.

So, while men feel like they're being asked to be more, a lot of women feel like they're finally being heard. And that's a significant shift. We've spent decades trying to break free from roles that boxed us in, and now we're seeing men face a similar challenge. But here's the deal: we don't want them to lose themselves in the process. We still admire strength, leadership, and pride. We want to see those qualities balanced with kindness, communication, and respect.

Conversations with women reveal a complex mix of emotions. On the one hand, they appreciate men's increasing emotional awareness and openness. On the other hand, they still value the traditional sense of masculinity that provides them with a sense of security, care, and even affection. It's not about men discarding their identity, but about evolving it to include more depth and dimension.

I'm not saying this transition has been smooth sailing for anyone. There are frustrations on both sides. Some women feel like they're constantly having to explain why they want men to change, and some men feel like they're being asked to fix something they didn't even know was broken. It's a learning curve, and like anything worth doing, it takes time. Acknowledging these challenges is a crucial step toward fostering understanding and empathy in the process of redefining masculinity.

The truth is men aren't being 'neutered'. They're being asked to expand, step beyond the rigid roles they were handed and welcome a version of masculinity that makes room for emotions, collaboration, and, yes, even uncertainty. And while that might feel uncomfortable, it's not the end of their manhood. It's an opportunity to redefine it in a way that works for today's world. This evolution presents a chance for men to accept a more holistic and fulfilling version of masculinity, one that allows for emotional depth and meaningful collaboration.

I think about my man, Donald. He grew up in a time when being a man meant holding it all in and handling business. But over the years, he's learned to soften in ways that have strengthened our relationship. He's still that strong, capable man I love, but now he listens more, shares more, and is not afraid to admit when he doesn't have all the answers. And you know what? That makes him even more of a man in my eyes.

Instead of seeing this evolution as a threat, men can start to see it as an opportunity to build something better, a new way of being that blends the best of the old with the new. They don't have to stop being protectors and providers, but they can add being nurturers and partners to the mix, too. Strength isn't just about muscles and money; it's also about presence and patience.

Women see the potential in this shift. We see the men we love trying to navigate a world that doesn't make it easy for them. And while we appreciate their efforts, we know it's not always fair. Society wants men to change but doesn't always give them the space or support to do it. And that's where we, as women, can step in, not by telling them they're wrong but by helping them see that there's more than one way to be a man.

At the end of the day, it's not about stripping away the spirit of manhood; it's about expanding it. It's about adding layers, giving it more depth, and offering more possibilities than ever before. Life's too short to stay stuck in old molds. And after seventy-four years of living, learning, and evolving, I can tell you this real strength isn't about standing firm against change. It's about rolling with it, growing because of it, and succeeding in ways you never thought possible.

So no, I don't buy into the idea that men are being pushed aside or erased or, as some men put it, neutered. What I see is a powerful invitation to men to step into a bigger, more enriched version of who they are, an opportunity to redefine themselves in ways that honour their uniqueness while also accepting the world around them.

If there's one thing this world still desperately needs, it's courageous men because courage is lacking. But maybe what we need is a modern version of courageous men who are less afraid of change, more open to understanding, and willing to be a part of the solution instead of holding onto outdated fears.

And here's the deal: when men and women, when all of us, decide to evolve together instead of pushing or pulling each other in opposite directions, that's when real magic happens. That's when we all get stronger. It's not about one side winning; it's about lifting each other up to be the best versions of ourselves, individually and collectively.

So, Ladies and Gentlemen: step into this evolution; don't fear it. Welcome it. We've got work to do, and trust me, it's worth every moment of growth.

"The voice of democracy empowers the people, the voice of dictatorship silences them."

Colleen C. Carson

"Our world is a vast symphony, where the environment is the orchestra, humankind is the conductor, and the animal kingdom are the players. Each tree hums as a string instrument, rivers flow like flutes, and mountains drum the rhythm of resilience. Yet, the conductor's baton wavers, sometimes lifting the melody to harmonious heights, other times silencing voices meant to sing. When humankind forgets to listen, the symphony falters; but when we unite in purpose, the orchestra plays a masterpiece, echoing a balance as ancient as the stars."

Mama Carson

"TOXIC RELATIONSHIPS"

As Colleen sat with her coffee, the steam curling into lazy swirls like her thoughts, she found herself reflecting on the people who've walked in and out of her life. Colleen thought, "It's funny how some leave a mark, like a beautiful painting, while others, they're more like graffiti scrawled in hurry, leaving behind lessons rather than beauty." But you know what? Real beauty lies in recognizing these toxic relationships, understanding their dynamics, and learning from them. It's a journey of personal growth and empowerment. Colleen has named these personalities, so let's get started.

THE RIVAL? Colleen says they have this charisma, this spark that made her think, Wow, they are special. And they were until they weren't. Colleen learned they were the kind of people who'd cheer for her as long as her success didn't outshine theirs. The moment she started to surpass them? The smiles turned into tight-lipped nods, and the support faded into backhanded compliments. They'd say, "I'm so happy for you!" but their eyes would say, "Why not me?" And Colleen would sit there, confused, wondering why her joy became a threat. She learned the hard way that their encouragement had strings attached, like a puppet show where she wasn't allowed to steal the spotlight.

It's crazy how easily a rival personality slipped into my life. I was told that to be successful, I had to outdo someone else, like make them fail so that I could win. It ended up that my biggest competition was myself. I'd set goals to prove something to myself, constantly pushing to achieve more. So, I had this boyfriend, he was super inspiring, and I admired him a lot. But after a while, it felt like everything we did together turned into a competition instead of just having fun. Whether we were bowling, golfing, dancing, it felt like a rivalry. Finally, at one of these events, I just turned to him and said, "I don't need a rival as a boyfriend." I thanked him for the life lesson, called a cab, and ended it right then and there.

The worst part? He was an incredible lover. But even that felt like a competition sometimes. Oh well, such is life! But you know what? Setting that boundary and saying, 'I don't need a rival as a boyfriend,' was liberating. It was a step towards valuing my self-worth and reclaiming my freedom.

THE TAKER? They wrap themselves in sweet words, making Colleen feel needed and valued until she was no longer beneficial to them. It was subtle at first. A favour here, a little help there. And before Colleen knew it, she was pouring from her cup into theirs, hoping they'd one day refill it. Caution: they never do. The moment Colleen stopped giving, they stopped showing up. It's like they vanished into thin air, taking her energy and leaving behind the hollow echo of her generosity.

Colleen had this girlfriend, or maybe this woman was more of an acquaintance in her life. You know the type. Once you've experienced someone like her, it becomes a lot easier to spot the same energy in others, even in a crowd. At first, she seemed complimentary and supportive and made Colleen feel like she genuinely valued her. Colleen thought, "Wow, this is someone who really has my back."

But then there was that day. She called me up in full-blown dramatic mode, asking me to do something for her, which was one of many previous requests. Honestly, it wasn't even something she couldn't have handled herself. Still, she had this way of spinning the situation, making it feel like her world was on the brink of collapse. I showed up because that's what you do for a friend, right? However, it became a laundry list of things she needed from me when I arrived. No gratitude, just more demands.

That day, though, I couldn't do it. I had another friend in the hospital who was seriously ill, and that was my priority. I told her as much, thinking she'd understand but she didn't. After that, she started ghosting me. When she did answer my calls, the vibe was off. She'd often ramble on about this new group of women she'd met while volunteering, gushing about how much they cared about her. It was clear I'd been replaced. But you know what? That was a turning point for me. I realized the importance of self-care and prioritizing my own needs. I learned that it's okay to say no, to put myself first, and to walk away from toxic relationships.

Eventually, we just drifted apart. I didn't see her anymore, which was probably for the best. But then, one day, while I was out shopping, I ran into a mutual acquaintance. We got to talking, and somehow, her name came up. That's when I found out she'd been calling me a loser behind my back. That's why she "decided" we were no longer friends.

It stung at first, but honestly? Looking back, I see it for what it was. People like that aren't friends. They're just using you to fill whatever void they have in their lives until you can't or won't anymore. And when you draw the line, they move on to the next person who will let them. It was a harsh lesson, but one I'm glad I learned.

THE MANIPULATOR? Now, that's a special kind of heartbreak that sneaks up on you when you least expect it. They have this uncanny ability to twist reality, bending things just enough to leave you second-guessing yourself. It starts innocently enough: Colleen is full of confidence, clear-headed, and sure of her choices, but by the end of it, she's questioning everything. "Am I overreacting? Was it really my fault?" They don't just gaslight you; they make you feel like the villain in a story you didn't write. This kind of manipulation can be subtle, but it's important to be aware of these tactics in your relationships.

The thing about manipulators is that it's not just about avoiding blame. No, they're far sneakier than that. Their true talent lies in planting seeds of guilt seeds so deep that you're the one watering them, watching them grow with every tear you shed. They twist your emotions so expertly that you soon blame yourself and apologize for things you didn't even do. They set bridges on fire, and somehow, you're the one left standing there, rebuilding them, trying to mend the damage they caused. And somehow, in the process, you start carrying the weight of their wrongs, as if it's your responsibility to fix the mess they've made. The injustice stings in ways you can't even put into words because no matter how hard you try; they never truly own up to what they've done.

Unfortunately, this is one of my sisters. Since I can remember, she would come out the hero, and you would come out the villain, and she would convince you that you were doing a good thing in order for her to look good in the end or that she was the victim in your plot of which you never created; she did. We had our fair share of fun, and it was like we were best friends at times.

She seemed to look up to me, and we'd plan everything together. But as we got older, things started to change in ways that were hard to ignore. I remember once being super excited about a date I had coming up. I picked out my favourite red dress, which I felt incredible in, paired it with my beautiful red shoes, and even chose some jewelry to match. Of course, I got the usual approval from my sisters, and I was feeling on top of the world.

The next morning, while my sisters were getting ready for school, I decided to treat myself. I took a relaxing bath, did my makeup, and styled my hair. Once I was all set, I headed back to my room to get dressed, only to hear my sisters shout up from downstairs, saying goodbye to me and wishing me a great date. I shouted, "I will!" and felt on cloud nine.

But when I returned to my room, everything was gone. My red dress, shoes, and even the jewelry were missing. I ran downstairs in a panic, asking my Mom if she'd moved them. Nope. My sister had decided to wear my outfit I to school. I was crushed. I couldn't believe she'd do that. I started crying, asking my Mom why my sister would wear something I had picked out for my date. My Mom said my sister told her I had given her permission to wear it.

So, the next day, I had this big confrontation with my sister in front of Mom. And, of course, she pulls the classic move; starts crying, claiming she never meant to hurt me. But here's the deal: she has this talent for playing Mom like a violin, making her buy into that innocent act. Then Mom, with all the wisdom of the ages, asks me, "Colleen, did you go on your date? Did you have a good time? Do you think you'll see this gentleman, again?"

I said yes, of course, and then she said, "So, why is this even a problem? You had a great time; everything worked out, right?" And for a second, I thought she had a point. I had a good time, and maybe I was overreacting. So, I told myself, "Alright, Colleen, just forget it. Like Mom said, you had fun, so stop making a mountain out of a molehill."

It sounded so reasonable, but deep down, I knew it was just another day in the world of letting things slide. Mom walks away, thinking everything is fine like it's all resolved. But as soon as she's gone, my sister stops crying and flashes me this sly smile. That was when I knew I'd been played, both me and my Mom. Once again, her manipulation worked. Touche!!!

THE WHINER? Colleen knows the type; they sigh heavily and repeatedly complain about the same problems yet never take a step to fix them. Their negativity is like a black hole, sucking in all the light around them. Colleen would offer advice, solutions, anything to help, but they'd swat it away with a dismissive, "Yeah, but..." They weren't looking for answers; they were looking for someone to share their misery. Colleen felt like being around them was like trying to swim while wearing weights, or hugging a cactus, or having a deep conversation with a brick wall.

Believe me, when I say whiners are a real pain in the ass and trust me, there are a lot of them out there. They come from all walks of life, no discrimination whatsoever. These are the people who pop up the minute someone else gets dismissed, like they've been waiting for their turn to shine in the misery spotlight. And let me tell you, I am not great with whiners. Don't get me wrong; I try to be patient, I really do, but it never works. Whiners absolutely thrive in misery. It's like they have a secret club whose motto is, "The more miserable, the better!" And they're all about getting their friends to join the pity party.

I could write a whole book filled with stories about these friends, but here's a summary: if you ever find yourself dealing with a whiner, don't waste your time. Unlike a real friend who needs a shoulder to cry on or someone to support them through their journey, a whiner is a whiner. They'll never change, no matter how many shoulders you offer, how much advice you dish out, or how much support you throw their way. They actually enjoy the whining. It's their happy place. So, save your energy and don't get caught in their drama. It's like feeding a bottomless pit; nothing ever fills it up. They won't change. They actually get a weird kind of joy from whining. It's like their comfort food. You can't fix that, so save yourself the trouble and let them keep whining in peace!

THE EXPLOITER? Colleen admits they were charming, even disarming. They can make you believe in their goodness and loyalty until the cracks start to show. Colleen remembers how they took her trust and treated it like a free pass to do whatever they pleased. Forgiveness? They flourished on it; they knew she would always give them another chance. They didn't just use what she gave; they exploited it and sometimes abused it, leaving her feeling foolish for believing in their potential. It's not that Colleen was naive; they were masters of deception.

Now, here's the deal. For a long time, I let the cynicism of these experiences linger. I'd replay the conversations, the betrayals, the heartbreaks, and wonder, Why me? But then, one day, it hit me. These people didn't define me; they revealed me. They showed me my capacity to trust, give, and love even when it wasn't returned. They taught me boundaries, to say no without guilt, and the power of walking away. They're dangerous, no question about it. And believe me when I say, "I've had my fair share."

But one in particular got to me; he was the worst because I thought I had gather wisdom and insight over the years. But this guy? He was a master at what he did. It started out so innocently, just a few dates, nothing serious, I figured that would be it. But looking back now, I can see he was playing me from the start.

Three months in, and I was practically dancing to his tune. He had me wrapped around his finger. I started doing everything he asked, things I would have never considered before. Hell, I even accepted another woman into our relationship, thinking it was just part of making things stronger. He had me convinced it was the way to go, actually it didn't matter to me because it wasn't about seeking a relationship with him, it was about seeking companionship.

There were signs, of course, like the fact I never knew where he lived. I know, crazy, right? But his explanation sounded reasonable at the time. He'd said, "Does knowing where I live define me? Or is your lack of confidence in my love creating distrust?" I wanted to trust him, so I stopped asking. But deep down, I told myself, who cares where he lives? It didn't change the fact that I wanted him, or I even thought I might be in love with him.

But the thing with Exploiters is that their demands keep growing. They get too much to handle, and eventually, it becomes suffocating. I'm not a woman who can be controlled, so it started falling apart. It got to the point where I had to walk away. He tried to make it a big dramatic affair, hoping I'd beg for forgiveness. But I was done, even though it left me with a broken heart.

And then there was that little bit of "insight" he expressed to me: "After a breakup, it only takes your heart nine months to be ready to love again." At the time, I just ignored it. But now, I realize that was his own little morse code to enlighten my mindset. It's easy to focus on what they took from me, but I've realized they also gave me something invaluable: clarity. Also, he was right it took me less a day of nine months to be completely over him.

I see red flags now where I used to see potential. I've learned that not everyone deserves a seat at my table, and that's okay. Some people are lessons wrapped in human form, and once you've learned the lesson, you don't need to stay in the classroom. I've made peace with the fact that I can't control how others treat me, but I can control how I respond. I can protect my peace and surround myself with people who uplift rather than undermine me and pour into my cup as much as I pour into theirs.

Here's the deal: it takes immense courage to realize that life's too short to carry the baggage of people who don't see your worth. And you know what? That's not just okay; it's empowering. I've learned to let those people fade into the background while I step boldly into the spotlight of my own story. My happiness, my peace, and my journey.

So, cheers to me, yes me, for not just enduring but surviving *The Rivals, The Takers, The Manipulators, The Whiners, and let's not forget, The Exploiters.* They may have left scars, but those scars came with lessons. They made me stronger, taught me to build boundaries, and showed me how to reclaim my peace.

And here's something you should know you're not defined by the worst people you've dealt with. Absolutely not. You're defined by how you rise above them. By the love you keep giving, the dreams you refuse to give up on, and the incredible life you're building despite everything.

Remember, it's essential to recognize the signs of toxic relationships and have the courage to walk away. It's not easy, but it is necessary for your well-being and growth. So, keep going. Keep building. Keep rising. Every step forward is a step away from the shadows they tried to trap you in. Let your light shine so bright it blinds anyone who doubts you. It's your time to grow, and nothing, absolutely nothing, can hold you back.

"A REFUGEE'S STORY"

Colleen reflects on the global refugee crisis, particularly in light of recent events in Syria. Her thoughts were sparked by watching Peace by Chocolate, the inspiring true story of a Syrian family who found refuge in Canada. The film follows Tareq Hadhad, who arrived in Canada in 2016 and rebuilt his family's chocolate business in Nova Scotia, turning it into a symbol of peace and hope. The film struck a chord with Colleen, offering her a profound perspective on how privileged Canadians are. It highlighted the freedoms and opportunities often taken for granted, especially democracy, and underscored many limited understanding of the refugee experience. Colleen admits that she, too, has been complicit in this ignorance. While she has always felt empathy for refugees, she now sees how easy it is to remain detached, cocooned in a life of comfort. The film pushed her to confront the harsh realities faced by those forced to flee their homes.

I can't imagine waking up to the sound of explosions shaking our home, with the comforting smells of breakfast replaced by the choking stench of smoke. There's no time to pack or say goodbye to the life I've spent years building. I grab what I can, maybe a cherished photo, my child's toy, or a few pieces of bread, and flee. This is the reality of a refugee, a life defined not by choice but by survival.

For over 35 million people worldwide, this unimaginable scenario is their daily reality. Refugees are forced to abandon everything familiar to escape war, persecution, and devastation. Yet their journey to safety is far from over. They face agonizing challenges, from crossing treacherous seas in overcrowded boats to navigating endless bureaucratic hurdles in search of asylum. Despite these immense trials, refugees persevere, clinging to hope for safety, stability, and dignity. I thought, what if this was my family? What if the people fleeing violence and starvation were my children, siblings, or parents? How would I want the world to respond?

Refugees are not statistics; they are human beings with stories of courage, loss, and strength. Think of a mother walking thousands of miles to shield her children from violence; she is not a burden on society; she is a hero. A young man studying by candlelight in a refugee camp is not a threat but a symbol of hope. A child learning to smile again after escaping unimaginable horrors is not an outsider; they personify the power of the human spirit. Welcoming refugees is more than a humanitarian duty; it is an opportunity. History proves that refugees enrich the societies they join. Albert Einstein, one of the greatest minds of the 20th century, was a refugee. Madeleine Albright, a trailblazer in global diplomacy, was also a refugee. Refugees contribute economically, culturally, and socially to their host countries when given the chance. They are doctors, teachers, artists, and entrepreneurs eager to rebuild their lives and give back to their communities.

Turning our backs on refugees has devastating consequences. Overcrowded camps stretch resources thin, leaving families to languish in limbo. The most significant cost, however, is moral. When we ignore the cries of the most vulnerable, we lose a part of our humanity. Compassion, though not infinite, is a renewable resource. Each act of kindness, each open door, and each supportive policy replenishes it. The global refugee crisis challenges us, you and me, to confront uncomfortable truths about privilege and empathy. Too often, people distance themselves from the plight of refugees, seeing their struggles as someone else's problem; I know I have. But the reality is that their journey is not just their story; it's our shared responsibility.

So, don't look away the next time you see images of people huddled on rafts or walking across endless deserts. See them. Hear them. Recognize their courage and strength. These individuals are not just fleeing danger but reaching for a better future. Together, we can create a world where no one is forced to flee their home and where displaced persons find refuge, hope, and the chance to thrive. It begins with awareness, empathy, and action. It requires each of us, including myself, to challenge prejudice and extend support, whether through advocacy, donations or simply educating ourselves and others.

My reflections remind me of the power of storytelling in bridging understanding. Films like Peace by Chocolate bring to life the spirit of refugees and the transformative impact of compassion. They challenge us to rise above fear and division and welcome the values that define humanity: empathy, generosity, and solidarity. I ask you, "Will you stand with those who have lost everything, shaping a world of hope, shared strength, and boundless compassion?"

"Peace is Power."

Mama Carson

"FAMILY BY DESIGN"

Colleen thinks of family like a box of chocolates. Some are sweet, some are nutty, and some are classy. But whether you were born into it or picked it out of a crowd, family is the gift that keeps on giving – and sometimes taking back – in ways only a sitcom writer could dream up. She's going to descent into the wild, wonderful world of blood relatives and chosen families and why they are both essential to keeping us sane and slightly mad... So, pay attention!

BLOOD FAMILY

Let's start with the blood family, the OGs of our life. These people have known us since we were just a huggable bundle of joy. They have seen us through every embarrassing phase, from the unfortunate bowl cut era to our brief stint as a goth in high school. Here are the eight best benefits of our blood family:

The Comfort of Unchangeable Roles: Blood family members come with pre-assigned roles. You know who the black sheep is, who the golden child is, and who will inevitably drink too much at Thanksgiving. It is like living in a sitcom that never gets canceled.

Free Therapy: Our Mom's will listen to our rant about our boss for the umpteenth time without charging a dime. She might remind us about that time we peed our pants in kindergarten, but hey, it is all part of the charm.

Unconditional Love: No matter how many times we screw up, our family will always take us back. It is like having a get-out-of-jail-free card in Monopoly, except in real life. Did you forget to call your Dad on his birthday? He will still send you socks at Christmas. That is love.

DNA Discounts: Need a kidney? A blood transfusion? Look no further than our nearest sibling. Sure, they might hold it over our head forever, but it is a small price to pay to stay alive.

Built-In Babysitters and Pet Sitters: Got kids or pets? The blood family has got our back. They are legally obligated to babysit our little ones and our furry friends. This benefit is convenient when we want to sneak off for a weekend getaway or need a few hours to binge-watch the shows our partner hates.

Food, Glorious Food: If there's one thing the blood family excels at, it is feeding us. Whether it is Grandma's secret recipe lasagna or Mom's attempt at kale smoothies, we'll never go hungry. We might need a gym membership, but our stomach will thank us.

Embarrassing Stories: Our family has a treasure trove of stories that can humble even the most ego-inflated among us. These stories are perfect for keeping us grounded and for future wedding toasts. Just remember, revenge is a dish best-served cold.

Built-in Frenemies: Siblings are the perfect combination of best friend and mortal enemy. They are always there to compete with us, challenge us, and occasionally sabotage us. It keeps life interesting if nothing else.

CHOSEN FAMILY

Now, onto the chosen family. Imagine a ragtag ensemble of characters straight out of an original sitcom, and we have got our chosen family. Together, we navigate life's absurdities, one hilarious misadventure at a time, proving that family is less about blood and more about the bonds formed over shared laughs and mutual weirdness. These are the people we meet along the way and decide to keep because we had a choice in the matter. Here are the eight best benefits of our chosen family:

Shared Interests: We can pick friends who like the same weird stuff we do. Whether it is a love for Dungeons & Dragons, an obsession with knitting cat sweaters, or a passion for karaoke, our chosen family gets us.

No Obligatory Gatherings: Friends do not make us attend awkward family reunions. Instead, we can hang out at cool places like bars, coffee shops, or that new jazz place downtown. It is much better than Auntie Audrey's house, which smells like mothballs.

Advice on Demand: Chosen family members offer advice only when we ask. Revolutionary, I know. And it is usually helpful because they have likely made the same mistakes we are about to make. Their advice often comes with wine or a Caesar, scientifically proven to improve everything.

Emotional Support: Our chosen family knows how to cheer us up with ice cream and bad movies when we're down. They also won't mention when we passed out at Auntie Ann's Christmas dinner. True friends know when to keep their mouths shut.

Flexible Roles: Our chosen family can fill in the gaps our blood family leaves. Do we need a sibling, a wise uncle, or a crazy aunt? Our friends can be whoever we need them to be, and no awkward DNA tests are required.

Dynamic Roles: In our chosen family, roles are fluid. We can be responsible for one group and the wild card in another. It is liberating and a great way to keep everyone on their toes.

Less Baggage: Friends do not come with decades of family baggage. There are no childhood rivalries, no parental expectations, and no one cares if we ate the last slice of cake. In the world of chosen families, it is a drama-free zone. Mostly.

Judgment-Free Zones: Chosen family members are like personal cheerleaders, but without the annoying pom-poms. They accept us, flaws and all, and they have got your back when you need it most. Did we wear pajamas to the grocery store? No judgment here. Confessed to eating an entire tub of ice cream after a breakup? They are bringing another tub.

THE BEST OF BOTH WORLDS

True magic happens when our blood family and chosen family blend. It is like mixing chocolate and peanut butter—unexpectedly delightful or like a perfectly mixed cocktail.

Our blood relatives get to meet the people who have become our chosen siblings, and our chosen family gets to experience the wonder of a Thanksgiving dinner with our slightly eccentric Aunt Edith. Plus, nothing bonds people faster than collectively enduring how our Dad reverses how to tell a joke, meaning the punchline is at the beginning.

When our chosen family becomes part of the fold, we have got double the support. Whether we need help moving, someone to vent to, or just a partner in crime for our next adventure, we are covered from all sides. Holiday Shenanigans, the more, the merrier! With both families in the mix, holiday gatherings are less about awkward silences and more about laughter and good times.

Introducing our blood family to our chosen family means sharing new ideas, stories, and experiences. It is like adding new flavours to a favourite recipe – things just get better and more interesting. When our families merge, friendships blossom. Our Dad might find a fishing buddy in our best friend, or our sibling might bond with our college pal over their mutual love for heavy metal. It is like watching a beautiful, chaotic symphony unfold.

In these moments, we realize the true beauty of both families. The blood family provides a sense of history and belonging, a reminder of where we come from. The chosen family offers a sense of acceptance and freedom, a tribute to who we have become. Together, they create a rich, vibrant medley of support, laughter, and occasional chaos.

They are tied to us by blood or chosen from the masses; family is the quirky, loving, sometimes annoying, but always irreplaceable foundation of our lives. They keep us grounded, lift us up, occasionally make us want to pull our hair out and give us plenty to talk about in therapy.

So, hold your families close to your heart, both the ones you are born with and the ones you choose. Laugh at the awkward moments, cherish their support, treasure the memorable moments, and enjoy the wild, wonderful ride that is life with these crazy, lovable people by your side. Because at the end of the day, family – in all its forms – is what makes our journey worthwhile.

"Failure is not meant to be your excuse, but your substance, fuel to ignite the drive within, showing you the way forward, not the way out."

Colleen C. Carson

"SENSITIVE STRENGTH OF A MAN"

In the quiet depths of every man's soul,
Resides a sensitivity, hidden yet whole.
Beneath the mask of resolute might,
Lies a heart that feels, in shadowed light.

For strength isn't just in muscles bound,
But in the tender touch, in whispers found.
In the way he holds a child's hand,
Or paints the sky with dreams unplanned.

Through trials faced and battles fought,
His sensitivity, a treasure sought.
It's in the tear that silently falls,
And in the empathy that softly calls.

The sensitive strength of a man, profound,
In his quiet actions, love is found.
With every choice, with every vow,
He shows his power in the here and now.

In moments of doubt, he stands alone,
Yet the roots of his heart are deeply sown.
For the strength he carries is built with grace,
A silent warrior, with love's embrace.

Yet strength, like thunder, roars within,
A force unyielding, beneath his skin.
In every step, in every stand,
He's the guardian of his promised land.

So let us see, in men's duality,
A harmony of strength and sensitivity.
For in the balance of these two,
Remains the spirit of what makes them true.

"I love you, Dad, forever always!" Colleen xoxo

"DEATH THE EQUALIZER"

Colleen wants to talk about something that makes many of us uncomfortable, herself included: death. It's strange, but ever since her son passed away, she lives with this constant awareness that life is fleeting, and death is part of the journey. It's almost as if his departure forced her to confront the reality that death isn't some distant concept, it's a part of our lives, always present, quietly reminding us of its inevitability.

For years, she found it difficult to plan anything beyond the next two weeks. It was as though looking too far ahead betrayed this awareness of life's fragile nature. Planning for the long term felt almost naive, like tempting fate. Yet, as time passed and she grew more accustomed to the idea of death being a silent companion, she began to loosen those restrictions.

Now, she dreams without limits. She allows herself to plan, not because she's forgotten that death is there, but because she's accepted it as part of life's package deal. There's something liberating about knowing that life will end; it makes the time we have here feel even more precious.

Since entering my seventies, it feels as if death has become more comfortable in my company. It pulls up a chair every morning, joining me for coffee as I start my day. But instead of feeling fear or dread, I greet the day with gratitude.

Each morning, when my feet hit the floor, I thank God for the gift of another day, for another chance to live, learn, and love. It's a simple ritual, but one that has become profoundly meaningful. It's a way of acknowledging both life and death, appreciating the balance between the two.

I think this is the norm for people my age. My mother, for instance, started preparing for death as soon as she hit seventy. She began giving away her collections of treasures to us kids like she was hosting her own personal giveaway show. Each gift was wrapped in love, but also in her subtle acknowledgment that her time here was ending.

She would drop little hints about wanting everything in order while she was still alive, as if sorting out her affairs would somehow make death easier to face. I remember thinking it was morbid at the time, but now that I'm in my seventies, I understand where she was coming from.

There's something about reaching this stage of life that makes death feel more real, more immediate. My mom lived into her nineties, my dad into his eighties, and yet both spent their later years with death hovering nearby, always present but never quite arriving until the very end. I suppose this is just part of the journey; the slow, steady march toward the inevitable.

Death is, after all, the great equalizer. It doesn't matter who we are, where we come from, or what we've accomplished death comes for us all. Kings and commoners, billionaires and beggars, all must eventually face the same fate.

No amount of wealth, power, or fame can shield us from it. This shared destiny unites us in a way that nothing else can. It strips away the superficial distinctions we use to separate ourselves from one another and reminds us that, at our core, we are all the same. It's humbling, yes, but also empowering. It forces us to look beyond the surface and focus on what truly matters.

In our day-to-day lives, it's easy to get caught up in the race for success, recognition, and material gain. We measure our worth by our accomplishments, our possessions, and our status, constantly comparing ourselves to others. But when we remember that death will come for us all, those pursuits start to seem less important. What really matters isn't the accolades we accumulate or the things we own: it's how we live our lives. It's the kindness we show, the love we give and receive, the connections we make along the way.

Death, in its quiet way, teaches us about the value of time. Our days are limited, and each moment is precious. Knowing that our time is predetermined can inspire us to make the most of it. It can push us to cherish our relationships, to pursue what brings us joy and fulfillment, and to live with intention.

It encourages us to be true to ourselves and our values, rather than chasing after things that ultimately hold little meaning. When we recognize that death is coming, we can begin to live more authentically, focusing on the things that truly matter.

This awareness of death also brings equality in its most reflective sense. In its presence, the distinctions between people vanish. We all return to the earth, our bodies breaking down into the same elements, becoming part of the cycle of life once more.

This natural process highlights the interconnectedness of all life, showing us that, despite our differences, we are all part of the same greater whole. It's a comforting thought, really, that we are all connected, all part of something much larger than ourselves.

Embracing this perspective can foster compassion and empathy. When we understand that everyone is on the same journey toward an inevitable end, it becomes easier to feel connected to others. We begin to see their struggles as reflections of our own, and we're more likely to offer support and kindness.

We are all walking this path together, after all, and that shared experience can bring us closer. Death, the great equalizer, reminds us of our shared humanity. It strips away the trappings of life and reveals the essence of who we are. By remembering this, we can live more meaningful, compassionate, and connected lives.

But there's one more lesson death has taught me: it doesn't reserve itself for the old. It's an equal-opportunity guest that can come knocking at any time. We often associate death with old age, as if it waits politely for us to live a full life before it intrudes. But the truth is, death can arrive unexpectedly, cutting short lives in their prime, disrupting dreams and plans.

This stark reality is one I learned the hard way when my son passed. Losing him at such a young age was a painful reminder that life is not guaranteed, and death doesn't discriminate. It taught me the importance of cherishing every moment, of valuing the people I love while they're still here. It reminded me that life's true value isn't measured in years but in the depth of our experiences and the love we share.

Recognizing that death can come at any stage has allowed me to live more fully. I no longer take time for granted. I no longer wait for the "right moment" to pursue my dreams or express my love. Death, in its inevitability, has become the guide that pushes me to live boldly, to embrace life in all its beauty and complexity. It reminds me to fill my days with purpose, to nurture my relationships, and to live in a way that honors both the living and those who have passed.

So, while death may be the great equalizer, life is our opportunity to rise above it, to live with intention, with love, and with gratitude for the time we have. And in doing so, we find a kind of empowerment that transcends the finality of death. We may not be able to escape it, but we can choose how we live in the face of it. And that, I believe, is the greatest gift of all.

"To truly sparkle, you must welcome and cherish the essence of your courageous spirit.'"

Mama Carson

"THE SILENT GUARDIANS"

In this vast, ever-changing world, there's a force that absolutely leaves Colleen in awe, a power that transforms the ordinary into something extraordinary. She has come to call them "The Silent Guardians," and honestly, she can't think of any more fitting title. They hold countless roles and names, but none carry as much weight as "Life Givers." Their transformative power is awe-inspiring, empowering us to see the extraordinary in the ordinary.

Through them, the very essence of life flows, turning us from just surviving to truly succeeding. Colleen has witnessed it, felt it in my bones; without their touch, the world as she knows it would fall apart. Love is at the center of all they do, a selfless, pure, and unshakeable love. It's the love she's seen in her own mother pour out time and time again, with no expectation of anything in return. It's the love that built Colleen's life, and she's sure countless others' lives too. Watching her Mom, she came to realize that this quiet strength, this endless giving, is what makes the world go round.

But their gifts, oh, they don't end there. These Guardians are also "Nourish Providers." They're the ones who feed us, not just with food, but with the nourishment of spirit. They give us the first taste of life's nourishment, and I think of how my Mom did this for me. Her meals weren't just about filling our tummies but building bonds and connecting generations. She was the bridge from the past to the present, and her offerings were far more than survival; they were lifelines, keeping my sisters and me secure to a legacy of love.

Then, these Silent Guardians are "Kinship Influencers" who shape communities with every breath they take. When I look back, I saw my Mom lead by example, creating a family bound by kindness, empathy, and understanding. She taught me what it means to care for others truly and how compassion is about responding with warmth and support when someone is in need. Her presence was a force, quiet and steady, but always there to guide me forward, helping me shape the values that would carry me into the future.

And when life gets chaotic, when the storms roll in, these Guardians take on the role of "Wisdom Navigators." They steer us through the roughest waters, not just with logic but with an almost supernatural intuition. I've always thought about how my Mom guided me with a steady hand through some of my toughest times. Her advice wasn't just practical; it was born from an understanding that seemed to reach far beyond what anyone else could see. She could feel where the wind was blowing, and I never felt lost with her, no matter how dark it got.

When the world gets stuck, when it feels like everything is standing still, these Guardians become the "Change Ignitors." They're the ones who spark revolutions, who wake us up to our potential and remind us that change isn't just possible; it's necessary. I remember my Mom always telling me that I wasn't meant to accept things and that I had the power to make a difference. She taught me that change starts with a single step, and she didn't just talk about it; she lived it, always pushing me to evolve and grow.

But these Silent Guardians don't just inspire; they heal. They're "Purpose Healers," mending what's broken, whether it's our bodies, hearts, or souls. I've seen it firsthand. With her quiet strength, my Mom always knew how to improve things. A warm hug, a listening ear, or just her presence was enough to heal whatever wound I was nursing. In her, I saw the kind of healing that doesn't just mend but transforms, restoring strength and purpose to whatever I'd lost. My Mom's healing touch brought comfort and security to me, even in my darkest times.

And what's even more remarkable is that their power doesn't come from what they do; it comes from who they are. These Silent Guardians are "Intuitive Energizers." They're the ones who seem to sense the unsaid, who feel what others can't. I've always thought my Mom had this gift; she knew me better than anyone and could tell when something was wrong even before I could. She didn't have to speak to communicate; her love was a language in itself, and it was enough to guide me through anything. She led with compassion and love, not force, and her energy, though gentle, was powerful enough to change the direction of my life.

They exhibit courage, too. I've seen it in my Mom, in the way she stood up for what was right, even when it was hard. The way she faced fear head-on and never backed down from doing what needed to be done. I remember her standing firm in her beliefs, even when it wasn't the popular thing to do. She was steadfast in her integrity, showing me what it meant to be true to oneself, no matter the challenge. Above all, these Guardians are the "Soul Nurturers." They breathe life not just into the body but into the spirit.

My Mom, in her quiet, steadfast way, nurtured my soul. She encouraged me to dream, to believe in myself, and to become the woman I am today. Without her, I wouldn't have the courage to be who I am. She is a "Dream Keeper," a "Promise Cultivator," and a "Justice Warrior," all of whom showed me that anything is possible if I stand up for what's right and give my all. My Mom's nurturing love made me feel cherished and deeply loved.

Without these Silent Guardians, the world would lose its rhythm, its direction, its very soul. My Mom taught me that through leadership, guiding, teaching, and inspiring others, I could leave a legacy that extends far beyond my own lifetime. And she was right. She symbolized strength, patience, and loveliness, and those are the qualities that keep my world turning. So, who are these "Silent Guardians" who shape and sustain life? Well, you probably know by now, but in the most simple, powerful terms, they are; Our Mothers. They are the heartbeat of the world, the moonlight that guides us in the dark, and the sunrise that keeps our souls moving forward. My Mom and all the Mothers like her are the ones who make the world a place of possibility. Without them, we would be lost.

"I love you, Mom, forever always, thank you!" xoxo

My God

me

From the earliest moments of Colleen's memory, her heart was deeply connected with a thoughtful love for her God. This love became her guiding light, always there to provide strength, comfort, and a sense of belonging. As she grew older, she noticed that not everyone shared this feeling. Friends would sometimes question her devotion, asking, "Why do you go to church? Why do you believe in God?" These questions often stemmed from curiosity, sometimes even skepticism, but Colleen always responded with kindness and understanding.

Her answer was simple yet reflective: "Why do I visit you?" For Colleen, visiting church wasn't a ritual or an obligation imposed by her parents or religion; it was a visit to a cherished friend, a loving presence. Just as one would visit a close companion to share moments of joy, sorrow, and everything in between, she went to church to feel her God's presence. It was about being close to the one who had always been a constant in her life. The church, to me, was not just a building. It was a sacred space where the love and light of my God felt most tangible. There, I could openly express my devotion, gratitude, and love. Every hymn sung, every prayer whispered, and every moment of silent reflection was my way of saying, "I am here because I love you." This act of worship was not about duty; it was about the deep yearning in my soul to be near my God, to feel that divine connection in every fibre of my being.

In those peaceful moments within the church walls, I found solace. The world outside could be chaotic and unpredictable, but I felt an overwhelming sense of peace there. This was where I drew the strength to face life's challenges, found the wisdom to navigate tough decisions, and felt empowered to approach each day with courage and hope. My relationship with my God was not confined to that sacred space, but the act of visiting the church was a beautiful and intentional expression of my love.

So, when my friends asked why I went to church, I hoped they could see beyond the surface of my routine. It was an intimate, personal act, like visiting someone who had always been there for me. It was about the bond I shared with my God, built on a foundation of love and trust, nurtured through every visit, every prayer, and every quiet moment of reflection. There was no need for grand explanations or debates. I knew that the presence of my God in my life could not be easily explained; it had to be felt. It was a conscious choice, one made in the stillness of my heart, to keep my God close. In moments of quiet contemplation, I would listen for the gentle whispers of my God, and in that stillness, I always found boundless love and strength.

These moments of silence became sacred. As the noise of the world faded away, I would find myself in a quiet peace. My soul opened to the mysteries of life, and in the quiet, I could hear the whispers of my God: soft, tender, and ever-present. This whisper wasn't a loud, commanding voice but a gentle reminder of the love, compassion, and strength that had always been with me.

In the sacred stillness, I could feel the boundless love of my powerful God. It was a love that knew no limits, welcomed my imperfections, and lifted me. This divine love was like a mighty river, flowing endlessly, nurturing my spirit and guiding me toward understanding and mercifulness. It was a love that forgave, that healed, and that always offered a way forward. The strength I felt in those moments wasn't ordinary. My God's power carried me through the most difficult times in my life. When I felt weak, God's strength was there to carry me. When I felt vulnerable, my God was my refuge. In the darkest corners of my soul, His light shone brightly, reminding me that I was never alone, no matter what.

My relationship with my God was personal and unshakable. My God wasn't distant or detached from my life; He was ever-present, a constant source of courage, peace, and love. I could see a light that never faded when I listened to my God's whispers. This light symbolized hope, enlightening my journey forward. It reminded me that no matter how difficult life became, my God's light would always guiding me back to a place of love and safety.

Through this sacred communion, I gained wisdom and insight into my life. My God's whispers helped me see the beauty in everyday moments and the divine presence in all things. Whether it was the smile of a stranger, the gentle quiet of a sunrise, or children's laughter, I saw my God's hand at work. These moments reminded me that life was purposeful and that my God always guided me.

One relationship that held a special place in my heart was with Mother Mary, who I affectionately call, "My Spiritual Mom." It all began when I was a fourth-grade girl, sitting in class with Sister Mary Daniel, who shared a story that would leave a lasting impression.

The story was about a little boy named Joe wanting a Christmas train. Joe prayed to God for the train but didn't receive it. The next Christmas, his grandfather told him that while praying to God was good, he should have also prayed to Mother Mary "because what son says no to his Mother's request?" That story stuck with me. It made perfect sense to me. From that day forward, I started praying to My Mother Mary, and over the years, I've experienced how powerful that relationship has become. I know that praying to Mother Mary does work. Mother Mary became my divine go-between, always there to help guide me along life's journey.

As much as I cherished my Catholic upbringing where I served as a reader and religious teacher, I found myself grappling with the injustices, oppression, and inequality within the church. These struggles led me to leave, seeking a more accessible, happier life through my relationship with my God and my Mother Mary. I've often reflected on what my life would be like without that connection to my God. I know, without a doubt, that without His presence, my heart would feel broken, and my soul would feel lost.

The world could be overwhelming with all its challenges and difficulties, but I found peace knowing that I didn't need a formal religion to feel my God's love and presence. All I needed was my faith, my heart full of love, and the understanding that my God's love was unconditional, always there, guiding me through every step of my journey. And wherever my God was present, that was sacred ground.

Ultimately, Colleen's love for her God wasn't about rules or rituals. It was about a deep, personal connection that brought peace, strength, and joy into her life. It was about listening to the gentle whispers of her God's love and knowing, without a doubt, that she was never alone. *"God Bless You!"*

"Accept life's imperfections; for within lies the power to achieve greatness."

Colleen C. Carson

"BLINK OF AN EYE"

In the blink of an eye, life slips away,
A fleeting dance beneath the sun's warm rays.
Like whispers carried on the wind's soft sigh,
Our time on Earth, a breath, then passes by.

Each dawn awakens with a promise bright,
Yet dusk descends, and fades into the night.
In the vast duration of the cosmic sea,
Our journeys but a speck, a mystery.

Life is short, a fragile, precious bloom,
A collection of joy, of grief, of gloom.
We chase our dreams, we stumble, we rise,
With tears of laughter, and with mournful sighs.

So let us savour every fleeting hour,
Embrace the rain, and glory in the flower.
For in the collage of time's design,
Each moment lived becomes a charm divine.

Though fleeting be our time beneath the sun,
Let's fill our days with love, with laughter spun.
For in the end, when shadows softly fall,
'Tis love and legacy echoes through it all.

Colleen C. Carson

"Vision fuels the dream, and passion lights the way."

Mama Carson

"KEYS PLEASE"

Alright, let's cut the fluff and get real. Colleen believes men have had the reins for centuries, steering the ship, sometimes into an iceberg. And now? It's time for a change. No, this isn't about bashing men; it's a nudge, a gentle one if we're feeling kind, to rethink leadership for the world we live in now. Look around, especially here in Canada. We're at a crossroads, mostly thanks to decisions made by you guessed it, the guys in charge.

And let's be brutally honest: some of these guys seem more interested in clinging to power than actually doing something useful with it. Meanwhile, Colleen says, "Enough with waiting in the wings, ladies. Take the damn lead already." Remember Elizabeth Warren's words? "If you're not at the table, you're on the menu." That's not just a soundbite; it's the reality check we all need.

Here's the deal: sometimes, it's not even the men holding us back; it's women. We're our own worst critics, letting petty jealousy or self-doubt do the job society started. So, what's it going to be? Sit at the table or keep letting someone else decide what's for dinner (spoiler: it's not you)?

Colleen's got a point when she says, "We've handed the keys to our kingdom to men for way too long, hoping they'd fix the mess they mostly created." And sure, they've made some progress, but let's not pretend they're not thrilled about real change. You can feel the unease around women taking charge; it's practically a national sport. But screw that. It's time to rewrite the playbook.

Look, fear and envy aren't just buzzwords; they're legitimate roadblocks. And they're not exclusive to one gender. But if we want a future that looks different, we've got to push through them. Here's the truth: nothing changes if we don't challenge ourselves to be bold enough to blow past the status quo. Back in the day, society tried to shove me into a box labeled "know your place." And guess what?

Plenty of women still get handed that same box. But those old rules? They're only as real as we let them be. Progress means breaking down every barrier, visible or not and refusing to hand those keys back.

Now, let's talk stats. The first woman to lead a Fortune 500 company didn't show up until 1972. Fast-forward to 2024, and only 52 women hold those roles. That's one per year for over half a century. Bravo, patriarchy. And Canada? Out of 533 top jobs, just 52 belong to women. Yeah, let that sink in. And don't get me started on politics. Sure, motherhood is powerful, but running a country?

Equally badass. Other nations have elected women leaders, but Canada gave Kim Campbell a blink-and-you'll-miss-it moment and the U.S.? Still stuck in its "women aren't strong enough" rut. Even in 2024, a qualified woman runs for President and loses, not because she isn't capable, but because sexism, plain and simple, is alive and well on both sides. American Dream? More like American Excuse.

Let's not pretend the resistance to women in power is anything but an outdated boys' club clinging to relevance. And the cost? Everyone pays. Look at some of the guys running the show; it's uninspiring, to say the least. When women can't see themselves in those positions, the message is clear: "This isn't for you." But you know what? Screw that noise. Leadership isn't some exclusive men's club. It's for anyone with the guts to step up.

The fight for equality isn't a sprint; it's a hike. We've made strides, but the hurdles still stand tall. It's not just about snagging a seat today; it's about clearing the path for tomorrow's leaders, so they don't have to jump through the same hoops. Mentorship, networking, and lifting each other up aren't optional; they're part of the game plan. And if the old boys don't like it? Cool. We'll outlast them. Let's be clear: this isn't about being polite or waiting for an invitation. It's about flipping the script, breaking the barriers, and proving that leadership isn't about gender; it's about grit, skill, and vision.

Here's the deal: we've been conditioned to believe leadership looks a certain way: stoic, authoritative, masculine. But guess what? That's a load of crap. Leadership isn't about barking orders or flexing power for the sake of it. It's about making decisions that matter to people, to communities, to the planet. And frankly, a lot of men in charge have been treating leadership like their personal clubhouse. Newsflash: the world is on fire, and their sprinklers aren't cutting it.

Women bring a different energy to the table, one that's collaborative, empathetic, and solution focused. Not because we're saints but because we've had to juggle a million things while constantly proving our worth. Do you think balancing a budget is tough? Try managing a career, kids, society's expectations, and a relentless inner critic without dropping the ball. And yet, the resistance persists. Why?

Because empowering women means shaking up a system that's been stacked against us from day one. That kind of change scares people, men and women alike. It challenges norms, and humans hate discomfort. But you know what's scarier? Staying stuck.

Oh, and a quick story. One night, I'm at my Mom's house, sipping wine while my sister and ex-boyfriend debate voting. He goes, "Why bother? Politicians are all corrupt." My mom and sister snap back with, "No vote, no right to complain." Then they look at me. I took a sip, locked eyes with his, and dropped this gem: "If it wasn't for the women at this table, you wouldn't have your freedom of speech." So yes, always vote. Men and women fought for that right. Some died for it. The least we can do is honour their fight by showing up.

So, here's my call to action: women, stop dimming your light to make others comfortable. Speak louder. Take up more space. Be unapologetically ambitious. The world doesn't just need you; it depends on you. And for anyone still clutching their pearls over the idea of women running the show, let me leave you with this: get comfortable because we're not asking anymore.

"War may shape history's chapters, but peace engraves its legacy into the hearts of generations."

Mama Carson

"PROTESTING"

In the streets where voices rise,
Protesting under changing skies,
Two sides of a fervent call,
Echo loud, where hearts enthrall.

Pro: Bold banners shout truth unbound,
Injustice faced, in sight and sound,
Courage blooms where rights ignite,
Protest fuels the fight for rights.
With every step, a stand is made,
For freedoms lost, or never paid,
Unity in voices strong,
Changes are made, still the road is long.

Con: Yet amid this noble fray,
Chaos lurks, in disarray,
Violence stains the noble cause,
Tainted by unruly claws.
Order tense, amidst the storm,
Lost in turmoil, values torn,
Lost in anger's bitter gale,
Unity starts to frail.

Conclusion: So, protest, with purpose pure,
But guard against the riot's lure,
Conversion is in a peaceful march,
Change is born from a dignified arch.
In dialogue and rationalized plea,
The path to justice, clear to see,
Pro and con, in balance weighed,
In protest's image, the world remade.
Colleen C. Carson

"MALE EGO"

Alright, ladies, let's have some real talk about the male ego because, honestly, it's one of the greatest unsolved mysteries of our time. Grab a cocktail, settle in, and let Colleen express the male ego as she sees it, a transformation worthy of its own Netflix docuseries.

Colleen swears that if someone could map it out like Google Earth, she'd be better off, and so would you. Back in her day, the male ego was simpler and smaller. Society had this idea of men that were as rigid as those hairdos from the '50s, where men had their shit together. It was all about being the provider, protector, and occasional furniture assembler. You know, the guy who kept his feelings locked up tighter than a diary and never let you see him sweat. Emotions? Ha! Those were for women and poorly written soap operas.

Yep, male ego emotions? Forget about it. Colleen confirms that men showing vulnerability back then was like admitting they didn't know how to barbecue a steak; it just wasn't done. And he sure as heck never cried, if he did? Well, he better be chopping onions.

And don't get me started on that ridiculous excuse for bad behaviour, "Boys will be boys." I could feel my blood pressure spike every time I heard that phrase. Seen it as the ultimate hall passes for immaturity, recklessness, or just plain bad manners. I called it out for what it was: nonsense wrapped in a tired cliché. It's not cute. It's not funny. And as far as I'm concerned, it's just straight-up Bull Shit!

These days, things have definitely shifted. Men are no longer expected to be emotionless robots and thank goodness for that. The old rules? Out the window. Men have traded their castles for co-ops, and now it's her palace, complete with throw pillows he pretends to hate but secretly fluffs when no one's watching.

And as for "bringing home the bacon"? He's also expected to cook it, figure out how to use the air fryer, sauté and serve a side of kale, and clean the dishes afterward. Equality, Ladies, equal opportunity. And "he who wears the pants in the family"? Please, really? She's wearing the pants, the blazer, and the stilettos. Thank you very much. She's looking outrageously confident at the same time. And, if a guy's not folding laundry while discussing his feelings about last week's couple's therapy session, he's outdated.

Oh, lets talk about bringing home the bacon. Brian once had the nerve to suggest I should "get a job to help with the bills." Keep in mind that I was already running a home business, wrangling kids, and multitasking like I was auditioning for Cirque du Soleil, but apparently, that didn't count in his little world.

The kicker? Our food bill had been a miraculous $60 a week for the last ten years because, apparently, I'm some kind of budget wizard and the rest of our bills hadn't budged either; so who was actually bringing home the bacon? But sure, honey, I'll add a whole new job to the mix while keeping everything else running like a well-oiled machine. Seems totally fair, right?

Fine, I thought, let's play fair. So, as a team player, I wrote up a list of responsibilities we'd split right down the middle: kids' doctor appointments, school drop-offs, housework, meal prep, you name it. I handed him the list, and the man looked at me like I'd just handed him a calculus exam.

"What is this?" he asked, his voice dripping with confusion with that oh-so-aggravating tone. I smiled sweetly and explained, "Teamwork!" You know what he did? He flat-out refused. Suddenly, my getting a job wasn't so important after all. Funny how that works, right? It was like the idea of actually sharing the load short-circuited his brain. Meanwhile, I was already working my tail off, but because it didn't fit his little narrative, it didn't count. Ignorance truly is bliss, isn't it?

You might be wondering why I shared my story. Well, it's because his male ego got in the way of finding a positive solution. Imagine if he had just come to me and said, "Hey, I'm feeling really stressed about our bills. Do you have any ideas on how we could adjust the budget to make things easier?" That would have been a whole different conversation. Instead, he made me feel like I wasn't contributing anything to our finances, completely overlooking everything I was already juggling and without a shred of appreciation.

Don't get me wrong; I think a healthy dose of egoism can be a good thing. It can push you to stand tall and go after what you want. But the male ego? That's a different beast. Too often, it seems to block personal growth and holds back the kind of open communication and self-awareness that make life better, not just for you but for everyone around you. And from time to time, it's more of a roadblock than a bridge to growth, a better, more balanced life, and a more giving human being.

But let's give credit where it's due; guys today are making an effort. They're showing up for school pickups, learning the difference between a duvet and a comforter, and even getting comfortable with the idea of sharing their feelings. I mean, they've still got a ways to go. Let's not pretend we're living in a Utopia, but the progress is undeniable. There's freedom in letting go of that nonsense. Men don't have to fit into those old, rigid molds anymore. They can be stay-at-home dads, pursue creative careers, or, heaven forbid, take up yoga and actually enjoy it. They can cry during The Notebook and still know how to grill a steak. It's not about losing their masculinity; it's about redefining it. I love it; sign me up.

Hey, there are still challenges. Toxic masculinity hasn't vanished into thin air. It's still whispering nonsense like "real men don't talk about their feelings" or "you're weak if you ask for help." And that harms everyone: men, women, kids, the dog, and even the goldfish. We all feel the fallout when men are stuck trying to live up to outdated ideals. It's heartbreaking, and it has to change.

And here's why it has to change: we're saving lives, literally. Did you know male suicide rates are nearly double those of women? That's a crisis, not a coincidence. Much of the problem lies in how society has conditioned men to bottle everything up. But when they feel safe to open up, seek help, and let go of the "tough guy" act, we see those statistics start to shift. It's not weakness; it's survival.

There's another incredible benefit: it could bring less domestic violence. The old ideals of dominance and control have caused untold harm in relationships. When men accept emotional awareness and equality, the cycle of violence, I believe, will begin to break. It's about preventing harm and creating homes filled with respect, safety, and genuine partnership. Everyone wins women, children, and, yes, men, too.

And ladies, let me tell you, it's refreshing. The best part? Seeing men step up, share the load, and be emotionally present is like watching a real miracle unfold. Sure, they're not perfect, but none of us are. What about the effort? That's what counts. It's about breaking free from outdated ideas and creating relationships built on mutual respect, trust, and a whole lot of teamwork. Men supporting these changes frees women from doing all the emotional heavy lifting.

The male ego has come a long way, and while there's still work to do, the progress is worth celebrating. So, here's to the new male ego, which is still a little messy but a whole lot better. And as we keep encouraging the men in our lives to grow, let's not forget to cheer for ourselves, too. Because in this partnership thing? We're the real MVPs (most valuable players).

And if they can laugh at themselves along the way, even better. Watching men accept their humanity, flaws, and feelings is magical. Here's to more of that. And if they can finally master folding that fitted sheet? Well, that's just the cherry on top.

"SHE LOVES HER ME"

A promise of new beginnings, drawing ever near.
In dawn's first light, a whisper, soft and clear,
The past, a shadow fading, the future yet untold,
An image fresh and waiting, stories to unfold.

Each step a declaration, each breath a hopeful sigh,
The world in tinges of sunrise below a boundless sky.
With strength of being salutes the morn,
In the heart, a seed of courage, ready to be born.

Take a step, no rush, no race, follow where you're led,
Mistakes will happen, but they're lessons, not to dread.
Keep your heart open, let your joy pave the way,
Each sunrise whispers, "You've got this, own today."

Welcome new pathways, where dreams dare to roam,
Where the soul finds its melody, the heart feels at home.
Cast off the chains of yesterday, let worries drift away,
For today is but a prelude to a brighter, braver day.

The echoes of old chapters blend with new refrain,
The memories of moments, in joy and even pain.
In the cradle of beginnings, power is to be found,
Each dawn, a new chance, to rise from ordinary ground.

In life's sun rise, let her possibilities spiral,
In her journey of realizing the spirit of a girl.
With courage a compass, her dream a guiding star,
Her journey told of extraordinary tales in her memoir.
For she lives in her journey of self-discovery.
Certain in the wisdom that she loves her me.

Colleen C. Carson

"MIRROR ME PLEASE"

Ah, vanity, thy name is woman! Or it's just Colleen after her third cup of coffee and a smoothie. But let's be honest: vanity is an equal opportunity employer, yet somehow, it's decided to give the job offer to us ladies first. Colleen's vanity struts around like a lioness in stilettos, demanding attention while simultaneously battling with that little voice in her head saying, "Are those wrinkles or just new highlights?" Honestly, her mirror is her mistress, who deserves a medal for service as best friend, therapist, and the occasional frenemy, mirror me, please!

When we stand in front of our mirrors, it's not just a quick peek; it's a scientific expedition. We lean in so close that we may be searching for that lost pore or rogue eyebrow hair on an archaeological dig. And that mirror? Poor thing never gets a break. It's like, "Ugh, I look so tired!" or "Is that a wrinkle, or am I just overly hydrated?" Meanwhile, our mirror doesn't talk back, unlike some people we know, right ladies?

Now, let's talk about morning rituals. For men, the bathroom is a no-frills zone: splash, scrub, and boom, they're done! But for women? Oh honey, we transform that place into a beauty bazaar! It's a symphony of lotions, potions, and what might be a small army of products. Cleansers, toners, serums, and by the time we finish our "base layer," we're practically glowing like we just found the Holy Grail of skincare. Seriously, the radiance could light up a stadium!

Then comes the makeup application, an intricate process that should be an Olympic sport! It's an art form; we're not just putting on makeup but creating a masterpiece! Witnessing a woman transform from a sleep-deprived zombie to a radiant goddess is like watching a caterpillar become a butterfly, only with more eyeliner and glitter.

There is the foundation to even out the complexion, concealer to hide any trace of human imperfection, blush to add that "I-just-ran-through-a-meadow" flush, and highlighter to ensure our cheekbones can be seen from space. And the eyes! There are eyeshadows, eyeliner, mascara, brow pencils, and probably a tiny comb for eyelashes; why not? By the end, our face is a masterpiece that could stop traffic. Literally, if we see our reflection in a car window that is not up to our standard, we will halt and fix it right there on the sidewalk.

But perhaps the pièce de résistance of female vanity is our hair. Oh, the hair! Men have it easy: wash, rinse, maybe some gel, and out the door. Women, on the other hand, treat their hair like a prized poodle at a dog show. There is washing, conditioning, deep conditioning, leave-in conditioning, heat protection, blow drying, straightening, curling, and sometimes all in one morning, which could power a small country.

Bad hair days can ruin an entire week, while good hair days are celebrated like national holidays. And heaven forbid a man dares suggest our hair looks anything less than perfect; you might as well insult her entire ancestry while you are at it.

And let us remember our wardrobe, that bottomless pit of fashion delights. A man's wardrobe is straightforward: a few shirts, pants, and suits for those special occasions. Women's closets resemble the magical kingdom of Narnia, except there are designer labels and stilettos instead of a lion and a witch.

There is an endless array of options for every possible scenario: work clothes, gym clothes, casual clothes, date night clothes, clothes for brunch with our girls, clothes for staying in but still looking cute, just in case. And yet, men know we will stand there amid this avalanche of fabric and lament, "I have nothing to wear!"

A declaration that rivals the absurdity of claiming the Earth is flat. Shoes, ah yes, the Achilles' heel of many a woman's vanity. Men typically need a few pairs of sneakers, dress shoes, and boots. We women, however, have shoes for every occasion, mood, and weather condition.

Heels in various heights could double as lethal weapons; flats could rival the comfort of walking on clouds; boots could withstand an arctic expedition; and sandals and wedges, each pair more essential than the last; the options are endless. And yet, despite the agony inflicted upon our poor feet, we women will endure the torture in the name of fashion. The sacrifices we make for you men are commendable, if not slightly masochistic. Once again, men have socks, ties, cufflinks, and puffs; that's about it. Oh, but for us women, the accessories are like an array of jewelry, scarves, hats, belts, and let's not forget, the handbags.

A woman's handbag should always be like Mary Poppins' carpet bag, a seemingly bottomless pit containing everything from makeup and mints to a small pharmacy and a full-course meal. The weight of some of our bags could rival a dumbbell at the gym, yet we carry it all with such grace because we never know when we might need a travel-size hairspray or a spare pair of earrings. From a man's point of view, this obsession with appearance can be bewildering.

Men wonder why women need five shades of red lipstick or nail polish that change colour in the sun. How silly of them! But here's the deal: while men might scratch their heads at the sheer complexity of it all, men can't help but admire our dedication and skill. In our quest for beauty, we, women, turn the ordinary into the extraordinary. We transform getting ready into an art form, a daily celebration of self-expression.

Once again, gentlemen, when you find yourself confused by a woman's elaborate beauty routine or bewildered by her overflowing wardrobe, remember: behind every perfectly styled mane, every swipe of mascara, every spritz of perfume, and meticulously applied lipstick is a declaration of independence, a small yet fierce rebellion against the ordinary, and really, who can argue with that?

Because, in the end, our vanity is a marvel to behold, a symphony of extravagance and abnormality. It may baffle you, men, at times and frustrate you occasionally, but don't forget to appreciate its sheer audacity. In a world filled with chaos and uncertainty, our vanity inspires unapologetic self-expression, a reminder that indulging in a little bit of fabulousness is always worth it. And let's be honest, who doesn't need a sprinkle of fabulousness in their lives?

Think of it this way: when you see us standing there, contorted like a yoga instructor in front of the mirror, it's not just vanity; it's an epic quest for perfection! A quest we take on with the courage of a lioness (in stilettos, of course). And trust me, our mirrors may never get a day off, but they are witnesses to our bravery and creativity.

So, the next time you hear us sigh in front of our overflowing closet, know that we are battling the formidable beast known as "the fashion crisis," armed with the valiant determination to conquer whatever wardrobe mishap the universe throws us. We'll face it head-on, even if it means trying on 17 outfits before settling on the one that makes us feel like the queens we are!

And as for the never-ending collection of shoes? Well, let's say that each pair tells a story. The stilettos that scream "confidence," the comfy flats that whisper "let's take on the world," and the boots that say, "I am ready for whatever adventure awaits me." Yes, it might look like chaos, but it's our beautiful chaos, each item a tool in our quest to conquer the day with style and flair.

Remember, men, our obsession with appearance isn't about vanity; it's about empowerment! It's about striding into a room and owning our presence, leaving a trail of admiration (and maybe a little bewilderment) in our wake. The truth is, when we feel good, we do good. We conquer our to-do lists with the vigour of a superhero, and let's face it, we look fabulous doing it!

So, as you try to decipher our beauty rituals and the mysteries of our handbags, know that every ounce of effort is fueled by the desire to shine. We are the glow in a dim room, the laughter in a quiet space, the sparkle that makes life a little brighter. Vanity? Perhaps. But also, strength, creativity, and a hearty dose of humour.

So, here's to us, the regal Lionesses of the vanity jungle! May we continue to strut, preen, and paint the world with our dazzling brilliance. And remember, the next time you find yourself questioning our choices, accept the chaos, grab a front-row seat, and enjoy the show! Because when it comes to a woman's vanity, it's not just an act; it's an extravagant performance, and you're lucky to be part of the audience!

"In the calmness of silence, we discover the formation of our thoughts, the whispers of our souls, and the wisdom of our life."

Colleen C. Carson

"MY WHISPERS MY LEGACY"

I've walked this road, through joy and pain,
Leaving pieces of me in the rain.
Some things fade, some things stay,
But my legacy will find its way.

The words I spoke, the love I gave,
Are echoes of the life I've brave.
Like seeds I planted, deep and true,
My legacy lives on in you.

I wasn't perfect, but I cared,
Tried to love, tried to be there.
In every smile, in every tear,
I hope my whispers still appear.

The years may change, but still I know,
The heart I gave will always grow.
Even when I'm not around,
My legacy's there, in every sound.

So, when I'm gone, don't cry too long,
Just know my legacy will stay strong.
With every hug, with every kiss,
My whispers will live on in this.

And in your dreams, you'll feel my touch,
A quiet love that means so much.
For though I'm gone, I'm never far,
My legacy shines like a guiding star.

So, as you walk, remember me,
In the silent moments, woe or glee.
For I am with you, in every breath,
My legacy lives on, beyond my death.

Mama Carson

"PLACE AT THE TABLE"

There were many times Colleen was the only woman in the room. And she'll tell you, it wasn't always a glamorous, empowering experience. In fact, most of the time, she felt like she was stepping onto a stage without knowing her lines while the audience, mostly men, watched, silently judging whether Colleen belonged there at all.

Let's be honest. It's hard not to feel like an outsider when you're the only woman in a room full of men. But over time, Colleen discovered that true power lies not in blending in but in standing out with purpose. Her realization didn't come overnight. But when it did, it was a moment of empowerment, a realization that her uniqueness was not a hindrance, but a source of strength and confidence.

Back then, fitting in was the key to success. You know, playing the game. Dress the part, speak their language, laugh at their jokes, even the ones that weren't funny (even the tasteless ones). I'd walk into those boardrooms, conferences, and meetings trying to make myself as inconspicuous as possible and believe me when I say that was a very difficult feat for a woman of my character. I would try to keep my head down and work hard enough; I'd eventually be accepted and eventually earn a place at the table. Brace yourself: it doesn't work that way.

Instead, I found myself shrinking, becoming a version of me that didn't feel quite right. I'd sit there, nodding along, hesitant to voice my ideas in case they sounded too different, too radical, or heaven forbid, too *"feminine."* But here's the deal: the more I tried to blend in, the more invisible I became. And let me tell you, invisibility is not a superpower in the professional world.

The turning point came during one particularly grueling meeting in my early career. I was surrounded by men in suits, all throwing around jargon like it was some secret code I hadn't been given. They were debating a major decision, and I knew they were missing a critical perspective. I sat there, heart pounding, telling myself to stay quiet and let them figure it out. But something snapped in me that day. I thought, *"What's the worst that could happen? They ignore me? Been there. Done that."*

So, I spoke up. And guess what? They listened. Not all of them, of course; some barely glanced up from their notes, but a few actually paused, considered my point, and acknowledged it. That was when I realized that my unique female perspective wasn't just valid but essential. From then on, I made a conscious decision: I wouldn't blend in anymore. I was going to stand out, and I was going to do it with purpose.

Now, don't get me wrong. Standing out isn't always easy, and it certainly doesn't mean walking in with a megaphone and demanding attention. It's more about being confident and owning your place at the table. It means speaking up when you have something valuable to contribute, even if your voice shakes. It means challenging the status quo not just for the sake of it but because you genuinely believe there's a better way.

I remember this one-morning meeting as if it were yesterday. This guy, my so-called rival, couldn't handle the fact that I was outselling and out-recruiting him. So, naturally, he took every chance to try and get under my skin, hoping I'd slip up or, worse, fall into that old stereotype of the *"emotional woman"* who couldn't handle the pressure. Classic, right? He'd throw little digs my way, like pointing out that I didn't smile enough or, even better, that I didn't greet everyone like some social butterfly before the meeting started.

At first, I let it slide. What did it matter? But after a while, it started to eat at me. And then, one morning, something clicked. I realized Me matters. My energy, my presence, my worth, they all matter. And I was done playing small. So, there I was, sitting at the table, jotting down some notes, when he strutted in like he owned the place.

As usual, he made his little comment about my 'morning behaviour' in front of the whole room, like clockwork. But that day? Oh, that day was different. I looked up at him with no smile, and in my best 'mom' voice, you know, the one, the tone that stops you in your tracks, I said, *"Victor, my smile is my currency. I spend it on people who actually bring value into my life, not on those who have nothing to offer but their ignorance. And as for greeting my colleagues before the meeting? If you weren't late every morning, maybe you'd actually experience it."* I swear, you could've heard a pin drop. Then I asked, *"Anything else, Victor?"*

He never brought it up again. And that morning? That morning, I walked away with my head held a little higher, knowing I didn't just stand my ground I owned it. Because when you realize your worth, you stop letting people rent space in your mind for free. But let's not forget, it's also important to take care of your mental well-being in these situations. I made sure to take some time for self-care after that encounter, to remind myself of my worth and recharge for the next challenge.

Let me tell you something I've learned after decades of experience: confidence isn't something you're always born with. You build brick by brick through experience, failures, and those little victories that remind you of your worth. And sometimes, you have to fake it till you make it. Trust me, I've done my fair share of power poses in bathroom mirrors before big meetings. But it's not just about faking it. It's about preparation, about knowing your worth and the value you bring to the table. It's about reminding yourself that you are not just a token diversity hire but a competent professional who deserves to be there.

Of course, not everyone will appreciate you standing out. Some will see you as a threat. Others will brush you off, assuming you're only there to tick a diversity box. And sure, that stings. But here's the deal: being underestimated can be your greatest advantage. There's something incredibly satisfying about proving people wrong, about showing them that you're not just in the room to observe but to make a real impact.

When I decided to jump into the auto industry, Ford Motors was among the first to hire women in sales. I landed the job and never sold a car in my life, but hey, minor details. They stuck me at a desk in the back with a pile of training manuals and left me to "learn." I knew cars needed oil changes but had no clue why. Transmission? Engine? They were both important, but why two? Yeah, I was in deep.

So, I did what any intelligent woman would do: I played the *"helpless little lady"* card. The guys underestimated me, and that was my golden ticket. They spilled all their top sales secrets, and I soaked it up like a sponge. Lesson learned: being underestimated is a superpower. The real VIP of the dealership wasn't the General Manager. It was the receptionist. She was the one answering calls from future customers while the boys were busy outside smoking and complaining. So, I got to know her, listened to her gripes, and boom, she sent all the hot leads my way. First month? Zero sales. The GM started sweating, but I told him, *"Relax, when I'm ready, you'll see."* And when I was ready? Ten cars in one week. That was practically unheard of back then.

I played the *"helpless little lady"* card when selling cars in Calgary. Dressed to impress in my chiffon ruffled blouse and sky-high stilettos, I'd stroll out with my male customers, asking them all about the trucks, ones I already knew inside and out. But hey, they loved showing off their knowledge.

When they were done, I'd flash a smile and say, *"Well, you clearly know everything about this beauty, so let's head inside and make it official."* And just like that, bam! Another truck sold. This experience taught me the power of understanding customer psychology in sales. It's not about what you know but about making the customer feel knowledgeable and in control.

Moral of the story? Success isn't just about what you know; it's about who you know, working smarter (not harder), and finding people who've got your back. Trust me, you don't have to do it alone: mentors, allies, and a good receptionist can make all the difference.

Looking back on seven decades of life, I realize that standing out with purpose isn't about being loud or aggressive; it's about being authentic and intentional. It's about recognizing your strengths and using them to bring something valuable to the table. I remember what Senator Elizabeth Warren said, "If you don't have a seat at the table, you're probably on the menu." I love this quote! It's about understanding that your perspective, shaped by your experiences, challenges, and triumphs, is precisely what the world needs.

So, if you ever find yourself as the only woman in the room, remember this: You are not there by accident. You belong. And blending in? That's overrated. Stand out, not just for the sake of standing out, but with a clear sense of who you are and what you bring to the table. The truth is that real power doesn't come from conformity; it comes from authenticity, purpose, and the courage to own your space. At 74, I didn't just learn how to navigate those rooms full of men; I learned how to own them. And if I can do it, trust me, so can you.

"Human connection structures humanity."

Colleen C. Carson

"IN LOVE WITH LOVE"

You know, when it comes to feelings, love takes the cake. It's this crazy, beautiful whirlwind that merges its way through every part of our lives. It's tough to pin down, yet it knows how to sneak into the most unexpected moments. Love doesn't care about time, culture, or situations; it just walks in and makes itself at home, filling our days with a sense of wonder and endless possibilities. It's the glue that holds us together, the spark for creativity, and the push we need to really discover who we are.

For Colleen love is so much more than just the butterflies and the crazy excitement that comes with having a crush. It's all about being totally captivated by the spirit of another person. Think about that magnetic pull that draws you to someone or that thrill you feel just being near them. Colleen does know those stolen glances and butterflies in your stomach? That's love casting its spell.

But here's the deal: love isn't all fireworks and romantic gestures. It runs way deeper than that. It's found in the quiet moments, those easy smiles, and the comforting silence where you know someone just gets you without saying a single word. I've shared a cup of coffee on a random Tuesday; it's not flashy at all, but with the right person, it has turned into an extraordinary memory that has stuck with me. It's all about finding magic in the ordinary.

And let's talk about the thrill of it all because love is an adventure for me! It's like jumping onto a train without knowing where the ride will take you next. When I've open up to someone, letting them see the real me, it's both exhilarating and terrifying. Trusting someone enough to let them in means removing my walls and being vulnerable. It's a risk, but isn't that the best kind?

When I truly love someone, it compels me to confront parts of myself I might prefer to ignore. It test of patience, challenges my beliefs, and forces me to face those insecurities I'd rather keep buried. Yes, love can get messy, and not every moment will be smooth sailing. But the growth that comes from navigating those ups and downs together? It's transformative. Love makes me better; it helps me be a better person, mom, and partner. It's a journey of self-discovery and personal growth that is both challenging and immensely rewarding.

Love has a remarkable ability to cut through the noise of our modern world. In this era where division seems to be everywhere-race, religion, politics-love remains indifferent to all of that. It's a beautiful reminder that, at our core, we are all just people seeking connection. Love is a precious reminder that binds us together, revealing that kindness, empathy, and hope can shine even in the darkest of times. It's a universal language that we all understand and yearn for.

Love is not something to be taken for granted. It's not a passive feeling; for it's an active choice, a commitment that requires time, effort, and a lot of faith. Whether it's the small acts of kindness that say, 'I care,' or the grand gestures that echo the words, 'I love you,' love always leaves its mark. It's a journey that I'm fully invested in, and I'm ready to put in the work because I know that the rewards of love are worth every ounce of effort.

Love is the fire that fuels my passions and the soothing balm that calms my heart when life throws curveballs at me. Love can be stormy and unpredictable, but I wouldn't change anything about it. Through love, I've found meaning and connection in a world that can often feel overwhelming.

I've learned to welcome those little moments: the tiny, sparkly bits of love that I hold close. Think about it: Watching the sunrise and feeling that surge of hope bubbling inside, knowing each new day is another chance to grow and explore the beauty life has to offer. It's in the everyday stuff, the fun laughter with my precious Crystal, who has a knack for curling up right next to me or remembering the reassuring pats from Chance whispering that everything would be okay.

It's in sending a thoughtful message to a friend who's having a tough time or melting into Donald's gaze when he looks at me like I'm the only person that matters. Those are the moments that make love feel so real and alive.

Love appears in many forms: through words, small gestures, and even those comfortable moments of silence. Whether it's quietly whispering, "I miss you," bursting into laughter over a shared meal or just relishing the calmness of being together, love has this ability to show up and make its presence felt. I love to think of love as this ongoing conversation that's been going on forever.

From handwritten letters that were the most precious form of communication to the emojis zipping back and forth late at night, love has always been our way of saying, "I see you, I feel you, I love you, I care." Isn't that what we all really want? To be seen, valued, and loved in a world full of distractions?

Deep down, love reminds me that I'm never really alone. We're all part of something more significant, beautiful, and interconnected. So, here's my advice: Don't wait another moment! Speak up, send that message, make that call. Let them know they matter, whether it's to someone in the same room or across the globe. Life's too short to bottle up love!

Because, at the end of the day, love isn't just a feeling; it's action, a choice, and how we choose to live. When we nail it, love has the power to change everything. So, let's welcome this ordinary, extraordinary journey called love and make the most of every moment. After all, it's the greatest journey we'll ever have. Are you ready to soak it all in?

"Life is what you accomplish, love is where you flourish, and legacy is who you nourish."

Colleen C. Carson

All

"A FRIEND'S BRUNCH"

Here's a little tale of serendipity and heartfelt moments that led to something beautiful. Colleen's dear friend Tatiana, who used to be her neighbour here in Vancouver, is returning to her roots in Madrid, Spain. Tatiana reached out to Colleen, asking if they could share a final brunch while saying their goodbyes before Tatiana departure. While goodbyes aren't exactly Colleen's favourite, but she agreed, and they met up without a hint of farewell.

As they enjoyed their meal, their conversations flowed effortlessly, as they always do. One story led to another, and soon, Colleen shared a deeply personal experience that she had with her Guardian Angel. As she recounted the story, Colleen noticed tears in Tatiana's eyes. When Colleen finished, Tatiana wrapped herself in a hug and confided that as Colleen was narrating her Angel story, she felt the wings of an angel wrapping around her, bringing her a sense of comfort and peace.

The past few months have been particularly challenging for Tatiana. Though eager to return home, she harbours a deep-seated fear of flying. When Tatiana shared her experience with Colleen, she reassured her, "Tatiana, you no longer need to worry or fear the flight. Your Guardian Angel has made their presence known and will keep you safe on your journey." They both laughed, and Tatiana called for the check.

As they walked back to Colleen's place, Tatiana asked if Colleen's Angel story was part of her book. Colleen told her it wasn't, and with a thoughtful tone, Tatiana insisted, "You must include this in your book." And so, Colleen did. As you read this story, may it open the door for your Guardian Angel to visit and bring you peace.

My heartwarming story will hopefully fill your day with positivity and wonder. I have always believed that there are Angels among us, entities of light and love, often called Guardian Angels. My spirituality in these celestial guardians is connected with my belief in God, Mother Mary, and the eternal kingdom of heaven. This belief has been a steadfast comfort in my life. Still, it took on a reflective and personal significance when I realized that my son Chance personifies this divine protection for me, his sister, and Dad. The realization fills my heart with reflective joy and my soul with a sense of peace. Allow me to share a story that transformed my belief into an unquestionable reality, reinforcing my spiritual convictions in a way that has only grown stronger since that moment.

It was an ordinary day, with one exception: Brian was leaving on a business trip. I drove him to the airport and took Crystal and Chance on an adventurous outing, ending in a special dinner at McDonald's, an exciting treat for them, given how seldom they visited the restaurant. Upon returning home, I prepared Crystal and Chance for bed, allowing them to enjoy their favourite show and a plate of sliced fruit as their nightly treat. After tucking them in and ensuring their comfort, I set about organizing the kitchen for breakfast in the morning and then took a soothing bath before finally crawling into bed.

As I lay there, facing the window, my back facing the entryway to my bedroom. An unexpected wave of fear washed over me. It was as though an invisible suspect of danger had settled around us. I strained my senses, listening intently for any indication that my subconscious might have picked up on something unsettling.

The fear grew in intensity, enclosing me in a paralyzing dread. I felt as though I were frozen, unable to move or act to protect my children. Then, an unsettling sensation occurred I felt someone crawl into my bed and press against my body. My mind raced with both panic and anger, fueled by the terror that this intruder might bring harm to my loving children. I mentally prepared myself to leap out of bed, grab a lamp, and defend my children.

Amid this turmoil, the intruder wrapped its arms around me. The grip was firm and obstinate, and my instinct was to cry out for help.

However, I knew such a cry could jeopardize my children's safety. Instead, I offered a silent prayer to God, pleading for divine intervention.

In those moments of desperation, what followed was nothing short of miraculous. The arms locked around me that had been perceived as a threat began transforming. The tension in my body gave way to a sense of comfort as the fear dissolved and was replaced by tranquility. At that moment, I understood; it was not an intruder, but my Guardian Angel protective wings wrapped around me. The angelic presence brought me an overwhelming sense of peace, and as the wings began to fade, I knew without a doubt that I was under divine protection. I felt a serene assurance that all was well.

With fear replaced by serene assurance, I hurriedly got out of bed to check on Crystal and Chance. They were sound asleep, their innocence untouched by the night's disturbance. I methodically turned-on lights around the house and checked all the locks on doors and windows, finding everything secure. After ensuring my children were safe once more. Returning to my bedroom, I offered a heartfelt prayer of gratitude to my Guardian Angel, my God, and my Mother Mary.

From that night onward, I have never doubted the presence of my Guardian Angels. The only change has been that Chance, my beloved son, has become my most attentive and cherished Guardian Angel, a guiding light of protection and love for our entire family and friends. We each have Guardian Angels who are ever-present and vigilant, gently guiding and protecting us.

Their celestial presence unites into the foundation of our lives, offering an untiring reassurance and a thoughtful reminder of the divine love that encloses us. In their quiet vigilance, we find the strength to face our fears, the courage to welcome new beginnings, and the comfort of knowing we are never alone. Accept their gentle whispers and let their loving support enlighten your path, and every so often send them a prayer of gratitude.

"ACTIVIST AND COMMUNITY"

Hey, can I tell you a little secret? Colleen's been trying to make a difference in her community for as long as she can remember. It's something that's always been part of her, like an itch she couldn't ignore. And honestly, it all started when Colleen was just a child, running around with a big heart and probably too much curiosity for her own good.

Back then, Colleen's version of "community service" looked a lot like her bringing home stray dogs and cats that she thought were homeless. She'd show up at the door, proud as could be, with a scruffy little mutt in tow, convinced she was saving the world one furry friend at a time. But Colleen's Mom? Oh, she had other ideas. She'd take one look at Colleen, sigh, and march her right back to wherever she found the poor animal. "They have a home," she'd say, shaking her head, and Colleen would reluctantly return them to their actual owners. Looking back, Colleen laughs; she was too eager to be a hero.

But hey, that eagerness didn't fade with age. By the time I was sixteen, I had graduated from rescuing pets to knocking on doors with a clipboard in hand, fighting to make a real change. I was on a mission to get people to sign my petition to ban leg-hold traps, you know, those cruel things that trap animals in the most painful ways imaginable. I didn't have experience, I didn't have connections, but I had passion. And I'll tell you something: standing on porches, explaining my cause, and convincing people to put their names down made me realize something: people actually listen when you care enough to speak up. Sure, some slammed the door in my face (okay, more than a few), but others listened, signed, and encouraged me to keep going. That's when it really hit me: change starts with showing up. Activism counts!

By the time I hit twenty, I was submerging even deeper into community work, and somehow, I found myself as the youngest campaign manager for a famous councillor for Vancouver City

Council. I'll admit, at first, I was in way over my head. Managing a political campaign at that age? It was equal parts thrilling and terrifying. But I threw myself into it, learning everything I could, shaking hands, making calls, and getting people excited about something bigger than themselves. It was intense, exhausting, and sometimes frustrating, but I loved every minute of it. I was part of something important that could change lives... HE WON!!!

And then came the experience that truly changed me. The one that left a mark on my heart forever. I became one of twelve women involved in the early days of Rape Relief, a movement that provided support to women who had been sexually abused or assaulted. Rape Relief wasn't some fancy organization with a big budget and resources; we were a group of women sitting on the floor of an old building on Broadway, because, well, chairs were a luxury we couldn't afford. But we made up for what we lacked in funds with determination and heart.

We worked in shifts, answering calls in the middle of the night from women who needed anyone to talk to. These calls weren't just about venting; they were desperate cries for help. And we weren't just voices on the other end of the line; we were there for them, walking alongside them every step of the way, from the rape kit at the hospital to the police station and, eventually, to the courtroom. It was heartbreaking, raw, and often overwhelming but also powerful. Being able to stand beside someone during one of the worst times of their life and show them they weren't alone? That's a feeling you don't forget.

Life, of course, has a way of shifting priorities. When I became a Mom, my focus naturally turned toward my children, but that didn't mean my passion for community work faded; it just evolved. Instead of petitioning or managing campaigns, I found myself in their schools, raising funds to improve their learning environment. Whether it was organizing and planning events like walkathons, fashion shows, or volunteering in the classroom, I threw myself into it with the same energy I always had. I also spent a lot of time mentoring students, helping them build confidence and believe in themselves. Let's be honest: school can be tough, and sometimes, a child needs someone to remind them they're capable of amazing things.

And here's what I've learned over the years: helping others isn't just about making a difference in their lives; it also changes you. It makes you a better person, a better neighbour, and a better citizen. When you step outside your little world and lend a hand, you realize how connected we all are. And the best part? You don't have to do something huge to make an impact. Small acts; listening, showing up, lending support can create moves that go further than you'd ever expect.

It's easy to feel like the world is too big, too messy, and too complicated to fix. But when we come together and focus on what we can do, even if it's just in our neighbourhoods, we create something powerful. You can't solve global issues overnight but can make a difference in your local community. Whether it's volunteering at a shelter, mentoring a student, or simply checking in on an elderly neighbour, every little bit adds up. And don't think for a second that you need to have it all figured out. Trust me, I sure didn't when I started. I just had a desire to help and a willingness to try. That's all it takes. One step, one act of kindness, one moment of saying, *"Hey, I can do something here."* And you know what? That energy is contagious. When people see you care, they start to care, too.

So, if you're sitting there thinking about how you can get involved, start small. Look around and see what needs attention. Is it your child's school? A local charity? An issue you're passionate about? Jump in. It doesn't have to be perfect, and you don't need all the answers. Just start. Community work has been a lifelong journey for me. It started with me dragging stray dogs home and evolved into something I could never have imagined. And if there's one thing I know for sure, it's this: giving back isn't just about helping others; it's about growing, learning, and becoming the kind of person who leaves the world a little better than they found it. So, what do you say? Want to make a difference in your community?

"There were many times, I was the only woman in the room. I discovered that true power lies not in blending in, but in standing out with purpose."

Colleen C. Carson

"Bullying amputates the spirit, severs self-worth, and silences potential; yet the heart can shape new pathways, reclaiming power and renewing the soul."

Mama Carson

"Being tolerant is the silent force that allows us to grow and learn."

Colleen C. Carson

"LIFE"

There are many definitions when it comes to the word "life." Some people view life through the lens of time, the period between the birth and death of a living thing, especially a human being. The dictionary might tell you that life is a noun, a word that names something, such as a person, place, thing, or idea.

All of this is informative, sure, but when Colleen thinks about life, what resonates most with her is not the technical definition. Life, to her, is about living. And that's where real magic happens, where the essence of it all begins. And if we're going to talk about living with Colleen, well, she couldn't help but reflect on her own journey and what it's meant to live her life.

Colleen's life hasn't been a flawless fairytale, but it's also been far from a series of unfortunate events. It's been like a home, not a house, a real, lived-in, cozy space. Let me explain. You know how some houses you walk into just feel right? They're welcoming and warm, and even if the décor isn't Pinterest-perfect, you'd rather spend your time there because it feels good. It's got character, heart, and stories whispered from room to room.

Then, there are those other places; they're just houses. There's nothing particularly wrong with them, but they're more of a pit stop than a resting place. They are lovely to look at but lack soul. A spot to hang your hat, but not necessarily one where you'd want to sit down for a cup of tea and a conversation. A home is something you feel deep in your soul. And that's how Colleen has tried to live her life, like a home full of warmth, love, and, yes, imperfections. But those imperfections are the very things that give her life.

Well, if I were to describe my life, it would fall squarely into that first category: a home. It hasn't always been the most glamorous place. Sure, it's seen some wear and tear, but it's lived in, comfortable, and full of warmth. It's where love lives and memories bloom. Someone asked me the other day, "What do you think is most important in life?" Without hesitation, I said, "Life, love, and my legacy." I know some people might think that's too simple of an answer, but I stand by it. Simple, those three words is what makes our lives truly rich.

There's a certain beauty in the ordinary that we often overlook. We get so caught up in trying to do something extraordinary that we forget to appreciate the simple things. But simple doesn't mean small, and ordinary doesn't mean boring. In fact, some of the most extraordinary things in life are wrapped in ordinary moments.

Take a morning cup of coffee, for example. It's a routine for many, an ordinary part of the day. But when you stop and really appreciate it, the warmth of the cup in your hands, the smell of freshly brewed coffee, and the quiet before the day begins, it becomes something more than just a drink. It becomes a moment of peace, a small slice of joy. That's what I mean by ordinary being extraordinary. It's not always about grand gestures or big events; it's about finding beauty and meaning in the little things, too.

This mindset has helped me get through tough times. I try to find comfort in the small, ordinary moments when life feels overwhelming. There have been days when everything seemed to be going wrong, but then I'd step outside and feel the sun on my face, and suddenly things didn't feel quite so bad. Sometimes, the simplest things remind us that life is still beautiful, even when it's hard.

Love is my foundation. It's the beams and bricks that hold everything together, the warmth that fills every corner. Without love, life feels hollow, like walking into an empty house where the echoes of your footsteps are the only sounds. Love is what makes us feel connected; whether it's the love between partners, parents, and children or even the love, we share with friends and acquaintances who cross our paths in unexpected ways.

I think back to the love I've experienced in my life, and it's not just the grand romantic gestures that come to mind but the small, everyday moments that constructed themselves into the structure of who I am. It's the way a smile from an acquaintance or even a stranger can lift your mood or how a kind word can make the heaviest day feel a little lighter.

And let's not forget the love we give ourselves because how we treat ourselves sets the tone for how we live. Loving yourself enough to chase your dreams, forgive your mistakes, and welcome the journey, a life well-lived. Love is the pulse that keeps life moving; in my experience, it's the foundation of everything.

You might think love is shared and that everyone experiences it. But let me tell you, not everyone knows how to recognize love in its most subtle forms. Sometimes, love is simply letting go of what no longer serves you or learning to trust yourself enough to stand up for what you deserve. Other times, it's about being there for someone without needing to fix anything, just being present.

That's love, too. Just last week, a lovely woman stepped out of the elevator, and I could see the weight of loss in her eyes: she had lost her son just a few months ago. I smiled, gently took her hand, and asked how she'd been. Her face softened, and she began to smile. "You have the most beautiful smile," she told me, "It makes my heart feel better, and you're always so kind." Then she hugged me warmly and said, "Don't ever change. You are someone extraordinary; you're an angel!"

Why am I sharing this? Because the love we exchanged in that moment was unforgettable. She made me feel special, and for those few moments, I helped her forget her sorrow and feel a little joy. It was a simple, beautiful reminder of how powerful kindness can be and how a smile or gesture can lift someone's heart. Moments like these remind me that even in the face of loss, there's always room for hope and connection, but most importantly, love.

Do you ever notice how even the hardest tasks don't feel as heavy when you love something or someone? Love has this magical way of lightening the load, of transforming ordinary moments into something extraordinary. Looking back on my life, I see that it's not the big events that stand out the most. Sure, there were grand celebrations and significant milestones, but the little moments of love shine brightest. Those times when someone showed up for me when I needed it or when I made someone laugh, on a day they really needed it. Those moments, they stick. They make life feel like a home instead of just a house.

I believe love is like the soft, worn-in armchair in the corner of your favourite room. It's the comfort you return to again and again, the place where you feel most at peace. And much like that chair, love becomes more valuable with time. It doesn't lose its strength or significance; if anything, it deepens. Love is at the core of every cherished memory I carry with me, and it's what makes the hard times bearable. Without it, what are we really living for?

What about life? We don't live in isolation. No matter how brief their stay, the people who cross our paths all add something to our story. Some people leave permanent imprints, like etchings in stone, while others are more like footprints in the sand: there for a moment, then washed away. But each one matters. Every person I've met has brought a little something into my life. Sometimes it's laughter, lessons, or sometimes it's heartbreak. And I wouldn't trade any of it because those lives have shaped mine.

There's a saying that people come into your life for a reason, a season, or a lifetime. I've found that to be true. Some people show up in our lives like a summer breeze, light and fleeting. Others are more like an old oak tree's roots: steady, strong, and dependable. Both types of people are necessary. The trick is recognizing the value of everyone who enters your life, even when they don't stay forever.

I've always believed that the beauty of life lies in the connections we make and the stories we share. One of the greatest gifts we can give ourselves is the courage to open our hearts to others. Yes, it means you risk pain. Yes, it means you will be vulnerable. But what's the alternative? Closing yourself off? Building walls so high that no one can reach you? I've seen people live that way, and believe me, they are living in those houses where no one comes to visit and if they do, they don't stay long.

That brings me to legacy, the memories, the stories we carry with us. If love is the foundation and life are the people who fill our home, then legacy are the memories: the furniture, the photographs on the mantel, and the shelf of trinkets. Memories are what make life rich. They are the moments we hang onto when time passes too quickly or when people are no longer with us.

But here's the thing about memories, they're not all good, and that's okay. Life isn't perfect, and neither are the memories we create. Some are bittersweet, filled with what-ifs and might-have-beens. Some are painful reminders of lessons learned the hard way. But even those memories are valuable because they remind us of where we've been and how far we've come.

When I reflect on my memories, the big, flashy moments don't always stand out. I hold onto the little things, conversations at the kitchen table, the way the sunlight dances through the trees on a perfect summer morning, and the sounds of laughter, the echoing of "I love you" through the house because they fill my life with meaning and moments cherished.

In every celebration, whether grand or simple, cameras flash to capture moments and create memories. I recall a time when, during one of those gatherings, a dear friend noticed me standing alone in a corner of the room. She came over, concern in her eyes, and asked, "Are you okay?" I smiled and replied, "Yes, why do you ask?" She said, "Well, you're just standing here alone, and I was worried something was wrong."

With a gentle smile, I reassured her, "Oh no, nothing is wrong at all. You see, while I'm often the one taking photos and making sure everything is wonderful, I always take a quiet moment for myself. It's my way of capturing the beauty of love and happiness being shared, I store that memory in the album of my heart, where it can never be lost or misplaced." We hugged, and then we went our separate ways, both carrying the warmth of that moment we shared.

There's something to be said for the quiet beauty of an ordinary day, when you look back on your life: they define you. It's the accumulation of little moments, small acts of kindness, shared laughs, and even the hard times that you survived. Those are the things that give life its texture, its depth.

At the heart of it all is the act of living. Life, as I've come to see it, isn't just something that happens to us. It's something we actively participate in. We don't just exist; we live. We wake up every day and make choices, some big and some small, but each one contributes to our lives.

It's about noticing the details, savouring the sweetness of a quiet morning, or finding joy in the way your favourite song makes you feel, or that early evening stroll around the seawall with your thoughts as your dear companion. It's about accepting the highs and the lows, the triumphs and the struggles because they're all part of your story.

Living isn't about waiting for the perfect moment or the perfect version of yourself. It's about welcoming the now, flaws and all. There's been times I've caught myself waiting for the right opportunity, waiting for things to be easier, waiting to feel ready. But here's the deal: life doesn't wait for you. It keeps moving, whether you're ready or not. So, I decided long ago to stop waiting and start living. I made a promise to myself to be present, to savour the little things, and not to take any of them for granted.

Living is messy, unpredictable, and sometimes downright depressing, but it's also beautiful, joyous, and full of possibility. It's a journey with no set map, and that's what makes it so exciting. You never know what's around the next corner, and that's part of the magic. I've learned to trust the process, even when I don't understand it, and to appreciate the detours as much as the main road.

As I've gotten older, I've come to realize that living well isn't about having everything figured out. It's not about having all the answers or achieving all your dreams. It's about finding peace within yourself and a sense of home within your heart. Just like the difference between a house and a home, life isn't just about existing; it's about creating a space where you feel grounded, connected, and at peace with who you are.

Also, in those ordinary moments where laughter is shared over coffee, those quiet conversations beneath the stars, and the unexpected adventures, the extraordinary reveals itself.

These experiences ignite a thoughtful sense of gratitude and fill me with awe at the sheer beauty of life. To me, this is the essence of life: vibrant, purposeful eras, each an invaluable opportunity to reflect, gain wisdom, and welcome the fleeting magic of existence. With the love and presence of my children and dear ones, I am reminded of the power and grace that infuse every moment, making this journey extraordinary beyond measure.

Once again, home isn't a place. It's a feeling. The sense of belonging comes from knowing that no matter what happens, you have a foundation of love, life, and legacy to fall back on. It's about feeling safe in your own skin and comfortable with the life you've built, even when it's far from perfect.

And that's what I mean when I say that life is like a home, not just a house. It's about creating a life that feels lived in, filled with warmth and love, memories and laughter, struggles and growth. It's about building something you can look back on at the end of the day and say, "This is my life. This is my love This is my legacy."

"Forever Always!"

"Fear is wise when it cautions, but unwise when it paralyzes our dreams."

Colleen C. Carson

"This is *your* page; where you hold the power to define who you are! Write a bold definition of yourself and tape a photo that captures your incredible energy beneath it."

"Say yes to life's imperfections; in them lies the power to achieve success."

Colleen C. Carson

"Each wrinkle tells a story of laughter, wisdom gained, battles fought, and the spirit that defines the nobility of aging."

Mama Carson

"Love is the heart's melody, life's symphony, and the soul's dance."

Colleen C. Carson

"Don't give top billing to those who treat you like a backup act. Life's too short for roles that don't value your star power."

Mama Carson

To My Dear Reader,

Life is such an extraordinary journey wrapped in the most ordinary of days, isn't it? One moment, you're going through the motions, and the next, you're uncovering pieces of yourself you never knew existed. This power of self-discovery is like finding treasure in the places you walk by everyday, empowering you to realize your full potential.

Like sipping coffee or staring out the window, these seemingly ordinary things often lead you to the extraordinary. It doesn't always come with fireworks or neon signs; sometimes, it's a quiet thought that whispers, "You can do this," or the courage to rise when life dares to knock you down. It's this courage that makes our self-discovery journey so brave and inspiring.

As we take steps to understand ourselves better, accept our flaws, and celebrate our wins, no matter how tiny they may seem, we are on a journey of self-discovery. It's about realizing that even on the most ordinary days, we have the power to spark extraordinary change within ourselves and the world around us.

You are the hero of your own story, a story that only you can tell with courage, love, and a little bit of sass (because why not?). And in case you need a reminder, it's okay to stumble, to pause, to wonder. The best journeys don't come with maps; they come with discovery.

*So, here's to you, your spirit, your dreams, your beautifully messy, ever-evolving self. Let's keep turning the ordinary into the extraordinary, one moment at a time, and never stop believing in the masterpiece that is **YOU**; unique and stunning.*

The magic is already within you, just waiting to shine. Keep exploring, keep growing, and never forget: the greatest discovery is the one you make when you see just how extraordinary you truly are.

With gratitude,

Colleen

Life
Love
Legacy

"Life is your story to create, a legacy written with courage, purpose, joy, and, above all, love."

Colleen C. Carson